FEMINIST
INTERPRETATIONS
OF
AUGUSTINE

RE-READING THE CANON

NANCY TUANA, GENERAL EDITOR

This series consists of edited collections of essays, some original and some previously published, offering feminist re-interpretations of the writings of major figures in the Western philosophical tradition. Devoted to the work of a single philosopher, each volume contains essays covering the full range of the philosopher's thought and representing the diversity of approaches now being used by feminist critics.

Already published:

FEMINIST INTERPRETATIONS OF AUGUSTINE

EDITED BY
JUDITH CHELIUS STARK

THE PENNSYLVANIA STATE UNIVERSITY PRESS
UNIVERSITY PARK, PENNSYLVANIA

Library of Congress Cataloging-in-Publication Data

Stark, Judith Chelius.
Feminist interpretations of Augustine / edited by Judith Chelius Stark.
p.   cm.—(Re-reading the canon)
Includes bibliographical references and index.
ISBN-13: 978–0-271–03257–3 (cloth : alk. paper)
ISBN-13: 978–0-271–03258–0 (pbk. : alk. paper)
1. Augustine, Saint, Bishop of Hippo.
2. Feminist criticism.
I. Stark, Judith Chelius.
II. Title.

BR65.A9S68   2007
270.2092—dc22
2007013662

The Pennsylvania State University Press is a member of the Association of American
University Presses.

It is the policy of The Pennsylvania State University Press to use acid-free paper. This
book is printed on Natures Natural, containing 50% post-consumer waste, and meets the
minimum requirements of American National Standard for Information
Sciences—Permanence of Paper for Printed Library Material, ANSI Z39.48–1992.

Contents

Preface

Nancy Tuana

Take into your hands any history of philosophy text. You will find compiled therein the "classics" of modern philosophy. Since these texts are often designed for use in undergraduate classes, the editor is likely to offer an introduction in which the reader is informed that these selections represent the perennial questions of philosophy. The student is to assume that she or he is about to explore the timeless wisdom of the greatest minds of Western philosophy. No one calls attention to the fact that the philosophers are all men.

Though women are omitted from the canons of philosophy, these texts inscribe the nature of woman. Sometimes the philosopher speaks directly about woman, delineating her proper role, her abilities and inabilities, her desires. Other times the message is indirect—a passing remark hinting at women's emotionality, irrationality, unreliability.

This process of definition occurs in far more subtle ways when the central concepts of philosophy—reason and justice, those characteristics that are taken to define us as human—are associated with traits historically identified with masculinity. If the "man" of reason must learn to control or overcome traits identified as feminine—the body, the emotions, the passions—then the realm of rationality will be one reserved primarily for men,[1] with grudging entrance to those few women who are capable of transcending their femininity.

Feminist philosophers have begun to look critically at the canonized texts of philosophy and have concluded that the discourses of philosophy are not gender-neutral. Philosophical narratives do not offer a universal perspective, but rather privilege some experiences and beliefs over others. These experiences and beliefs permeate all philosophical theories whether they be aesthetic or epistemological, moral or metaphysical. Yet this fact has often been neglected by those studying the traditions of philosophy. Given the history of canon formation in Western philosophy, the perspective most likely to be privileged is that of upper-class white males. Thus, to be fully aware of the impact of gender biases, it is imperative that we re-read the canon with attention to the ways in which philosophers' assumptions concerning gender are embedded within their theories.

This new series, Re-Reading the Canon, is designed to foster this process of reevaluation. Each volume will offer feminist analyses of the theories of a selected philosopher. Since feminist philosophy is not monolithic in method or content, the essays are also selected to illustrate the variety of perspectives within feminist criticism and highlight some of the controversies within feminist scholarship.

In this series, feminist lenses will be focused on the canonical texts of Western philosophy, both those authors who have been part of the traditional canon, and those philosophers whose writings have more recently gained attention within the philosophical community. A glance at the list of volumes in the series will reveal an immediate gender bias of the canon: Arendt, Aristotle, Beauvoir, Derrida, Descartes, Foucault, Hegel, Hume, Kant, Locke, Marx, Mill, Nietzsche, Plato, Rousseau, Wittgenstein, Wollstonecraft. There are all too few women included, and those few who do appear have been added only recently. In creating this series, it is not my intention to rectify the current canon of philosophical thought. What is and is not included within the canon during a particular historical period is a result of many factors. Although no canonization of texts will include all philosophers, no canonization of texts that excludes all but a few women can offer an accurate representation of the history of the discipline, as women have been philosophers since the ancient period.[2]

I share with many feminist philosophers and other philosophers writing from the margins of philosophy the concern that the current canonization of philosophy be transformed. Although I do not accept the position that the current canon has been formed exclusively by power relations, I do believe that this canon represents only a selective history of the tradition. I share the view of Michael Bérubé that "canons are at once the location, the index, and the record of the struggle for cultural representation; like any other hegemonic formation, they must be continually reproduced anew and are continually contested."[3]

The process of canon transformation will require the recovery of "lost" texts and a careful examination of the reasons such voices have been silenced. Along with the process of uncovering women's philosophical history, we must also begin to analyze the impact of gender ideologies upon the process of canonization. This process of recovery and examination must occur in conjunction with careful attention to the concept of a canon of authorized texts. Are we to dispense with the notion of a tradition of excellence embodied in a canon of authorized texts? Or, rather than abandon the whole idea of a canon, do we instead encourage a reconstruction of a canon of those texts that inform a common culture?

This series is designed to contribute to this process of canon transformation by offering a re-reading of the current philosophical canon. Such a re-reading shifts our attention to the ways in which woman and the role of the feminine are constructed within the texts of philosophy. A question we must keep in front of us during this process of re-reading is whether a philosopher's socially inherited prejudices concerning woman's nature and role are independent of her or his larger philosophical framework. In asking this question attention must be paid to the ways in which the definitions of central philosophical concepts implicitly include or exclude gendered traits.

This type of reading strategy is not limited to the canon, but can be applied to all texts. It is my desire that this series reveal the importance of this type of critical reading. Paying attention to the workings of gender within the texts of philosophy will make visible the complexities of the inscription of gender ideologies.

Notes

1. More properly, it is a realm reserved for a group of privileged males, since the texts also inscribe race and class biases that thereby omit certain males from participation.

2. Mary Ellen Waithe's multivolume series, *A History of Women Philosophers* (Boston: M. Nijoff, 1987), attests to this presence of women.

3. Michael Bérubé, *Marginal Forces/Cultural Centers: Tolson, Pynchon, and the Politics of the Canon* (Ithaca: Cornell University Press, 1992), 4–5.

For Donez,
with love and gratitude

Introduction

Judith Chelius Stark

Augustine is one of the first writers to speak directly to us across the centuries from the far reaches of the late Roman Empire. We hear his voice especially through his great work the *Confessions*, a text unique in the literature of the ancient world. Ostensibly, Augustine addressed this work to God, but as an accomplished public speaker, he had many audiences in mind when he composed the *Confessions* (most likely between the years 397 and 401 c.e.).[1] When he returned to North Africa after his baptism, he planned to start a small Christian community away from the intrigues and distractions of the emperor's court in Milan, where he had been an official rhetor and teacher of rhetoric since 384. Although safely back home in North Africa, he was not safe from the needs and aspirations of the North African church, whose bishops quickly pursued him, first for ordination and then to become co-bishop with the aging Bishop Valerius of Hippo. He himself was reluctant to pursue these appointments, but he did not refuse them when they were offered to him. By this time in his life (391 c.e.), he saw the hand of God working in and through human agency in all its manifestations.

Even though Augustine speaks to us with such vibrancy (especially in the *Confessions*), contemporary readers should not be misled by what appears to be an easy access to his mind and heart. The contours and constraints of the Mediterranean world of the fifth century were such that few of the presuppositions of our time and place suit Augustine's world. In the past half century, however, scholars have worked hard to render that world much less remote and alien. The starting point for all discussions of Augustine's life remains Peter Brown's classic biography, *Augustine of Hippo*. Another of Brown's works, *The World of Late Antiquity*, does a great deal to make that world more accessible than ever before.[2] The studies of James J. O'Donnell also deserve particular mention: his early biography of Augustine (1985); his three-volume edition and commentary on the *Confessions*; and his most recent in-depth, contemporary study, *Augustine: A New Biography*.[3]

What sort of work is the *Confessions*? There is no one category into which this book can be placed, since it encompasses elements of Augustine's life story (to age thirty-three and his return to North Africa); extended philosophical explorations on evildoing, the human will, God's nature, memory, and time; and detailed scriptural interpretation of the opening verses of Genesis. And he wrote all this in the form of an extended prayer to God. If it can be called autobiography in any real sense, it is at the same time considerably more and less than what is typically thought to fit into that genre. Scholarly debates abound on the structure, contents, composition, and interpretations of the *Confessions*—a text that is only one of Augustine's many contributions to Western thought.[4] If he had written only the *Confessions*, Augustine's place in Western letters would have been secured. In fact, the *Confessions* joins a cast of more than ninety books, almost three hundred letters, and more than four hundred surviving sermons (of the approximately eight thousand it is estimated that he preached).

Along with the *Confessions*, his other masterpieces, *The City of God* and *On the Trinity*, deserve mention. Either one of these two texts would have given Augustine an important place in Western thought, the former a work on Christian philosophy of history and the latter a study of the triune nature of God along with complex iterations of the inner workings of the human mind as the image of the triune God. The fact that his literary output was so vast and far reaching is astonishing in itself. Moreover, Augustine accomplished these feats while fulfilling his duties as bishop in a busy urban center in North Africa, duties that included spiritual, ecclesiastical, and civic obligations.

Augustine's story is a classic case of a brilliant young man moving from the margins of society through talent and cultivated connections to the centers of power and privilege. As a young teacher of rhetoric in Carthage, he had his sights set on nothing less than a prestigious appointment at the imperial court in Italy. By 384, Augustine had secured just such an appointment and was engaged to marry a young heiress, probably from an old Roman family. On the surface and in his professional ambition, everything was going according to his plan. But as he himself acknowledged when he wrote the *Confessions* a dozen or so years later, God had other plans for him. In the opening lines Augustine sounds the leitmotif that persists throughout his long life—the counterpoint of the restless heart searching for rest: "You, O God made us for yourself, and our hearts are restless until they rest in you" (*Confessions* 1.1.1). As tortuous as his hero Aeneas's wanderings had been, finally bringing him to rest on the shores of Italy, the wanderings of Augustine's mind and heart finally bring him to his conversion in a garden in Milan in 386 C.E. His professional life had been moving precisely along his intended path, but in his inner life he felt deep confusion and distress. As a young man of nineteen in Carthage, he began the arduous searching that eventually culminated in his dramatic conversion thirteen years later. For years he struggled to come to a true understanding of evil, the nature of God, the powers and limits of his soul. He pursued these questions not merely as topics of philosophical import, but as issues that required of him deep, personal engagement. This searching led him to a ten-year association with the Manichees, a brief foray into skepticism with the final intellectual breakthrough coming as he read the works of the Neoplatonists. The culmination of his conversion to Christianity occurred in Milan in 386 when the deep divisions of his will were healed after he read a text from Paul's Epistle to the Romans. There the apostle enjoined him to "clothe himself in the Lord Jesus Christ and make no provision for the flesh and its desires" (Rom. 13:13–14). The singing voice of a child that urged him to "take and read; take and read" brought him to the text that spoke to the heart of his dilemma—from his youth onward the trajectory of his ambition had focused on making provision for pleasure and success in the world. Reading Paul's text in the garden in Milan released him at once from this ambition and he now set his life on an entirely new course.[5]

Soon after his conversion to Christianity, Augustine resigned his imperial appointment as professor of rhetoric, using a persistent chest ailment as the reason for his resignation. Then along with an assortment of family members, friends, and a few pupils, he retired to a villa near Milan for an extended time of leisure devoted to philosophical conversations, thinking, and writing. Although he had been on the verge of exhaustion from his intense spiritual crisis and the demands of his career, these months of cultivated leisure (*otium*) resulted in a set of books that reflect both the lively conversations Augustine conducted with his associates and the particular issues that he was thinking through at this time. These included sets of arguments against the skeptics (including a precursor to Descartes's later project), views on order and God's providence, and his newly emerging understanding of human happiness. Augustine and his entourage stayed at the villa from September until March, when they returned to Milan so that he, his son, and his friend Alypius could prepare for their baptism at the cathedral in Milan.

At the stirring and dramatic Easter vigil service (April 24–25, 387), Augustine entered the deep water of the baptismal pool and was thrice immersed by Bishop Ambrose. Along with the rest of the newly baptized, Augustine would have come from the austerity and darkness of the baptismal pool into the cathedral, ablaze with lighted candles. There he participated for the first time in the full celebration of the Eucharist with the assembled community of fellow believers (Confessions 9.6.14).

Some time later that year (387) Augustine made his way to Ostia (the port city of Rome) accompanied by his mother, his son, other family, and friends. The group intended to set sail for North Africa before the onset of winter. While in Ostia, he and his mother shared a powerful awareness of God's immediate presence (Confessions 9.10.23–26). Only days after this event, his mother died and in the Confessions Augustine speaks with great power and eloquence of his son's and his own grief over Monica's death. Shortly before her death, Monica had released Augustine and his brother from the family obligation to bury her body with her husband's in the family plot across the sea in North Africa. Augustine was astounded by this conversation and saw this as another sign of his mother's spiritual advancement—she who had been so attached during her life to family rituals concerning the dead no longer needed her sons to fulfill that traditional obligation about her body's final resting place. After his mother's death, Augustine returned to Rome and continued to write, finally making his way to North Africa by 388.

Augustine intended to establish a small celibate Christian community dedicated to prayer and to study, supported by the modest income from his family property. However, as a well-educated, prominent, and newly converted Christian, Augustine could not have hoped to live in quiet obscurity for long. As evidence of his own intention, for three years Augustine carefully avoided visiting any cities in his area that were lacking bishops in order to prevent being recruited by the local congregation to accept an appointment. His close friend Alypius had already been drafted to become bishop of Thagaste (their hometown) and Augustine hoped to avoid a similar fate. When he traveled to the ancient port city of Hippo to look for a new location for his community, he did so feeling confident that Hippo already had in place a resident bishop. Augustine, however, did not appreciate the lengths to which Bishop Valerius would go to capture this rising young star whose Latin rhetorical skills far exceeded his own. While Augustine was attending services in the church, Bishop Valerius preached a sermon detailing the predicaments facing their congregation. All eyes turned to rest on Augustine. By the clamor of the congregation, he was prevailed upon to accept ordination and within four years (395), he was made co-bishop with the aging Bishop Valerius. Upon Valerius's death in 396, Augustine became sole bishop and over the following thirty-four years gained enormous prominence in the North African church. Because of the range and reach of his writings that amazingly survived the partial destruction of Hippo by the Vandals soon after Augustine's death in 430, his influence soon spread far beyond the narrow range of Roman North Africa and the limits of his own life. In fact, Augustine became one of the major architects of medieval Christian culture in the West.

There is hardly a theme, question, or topic of philosophical or theological import that Augustine did not address in the vast corpus of his books, lectures, letters, and sermons. Many of these views he forged in the heated controversies of his day either in his searching as a young man or through his leadership as a major figure in North African Christianity. His route to Christianity took him through philosophy, the Manichees, Neoplatonism, and Paul's Epistles. Even though he explicitly rejected the Manichees and his association with them, Augustine never rejected the philosophy or principles of the Neoplatonists that he considered compatible with Christianity. In fact, Augustine was the major architect of the grand synthesis of Christianity and Platonism that was to hold sway until Thomas Aquinas's appropriation of Aristotle for Christian purposes in the thirteenth century. In a compelling rejoinder to the query "What has Athens to do with Jerusalem?" posed by the earlier Christian writer Tertullian, a fellow North African, Augustine answered with a resounding affirmation of the value of Neoplatonism to Christianity and of his lifelong project of "believing in order to understand."[6] Soon after he was ordained in Hippo, he began a series of public debates against the teachings of the Manichees—the group to which he had belonged for almost ten years. His public trouncing of the Manichean leader Fortunatus was so thorough and decisive that Fortunatus was forced to retire from the lists and leave Hippo. In matters of church organization and political strength (but not intellectually), the Donatists, however, proved to be far more enduring opponents, since they considered their church to be the true North African Christian Church. Under the direction of their bishop, Donatus of Carthage, their leaders claimed that they had remained faithful to the Scriptures and had not handed them over to the imperial authorities during the last great persecution under the emperor Diocletian (303–5 c.e.). When Augustine returned to North Africa in 388, the two sides had hardened through successive appointments of bishops and were entrenched in two opposing views of the nature of the church. Despite the fact of his own North African heritage, he came to this controversy very much as an outsider. Augustine brought with him to his office as priest and then bishop of Hippo a view of the value of reason and philosophy to Christianity, forged in his own spiritual crises and conversions. This habit of mind hardly prepared him for the fierce and local sectarianism that was threatening the unity of Christianity in the struggles between the Catholics and the Donatists in North Africa.

This controversy preoccupied Augustine for almost twenty years and involved not only highly contested views of the nature of the church—namely, was the church only for the pure (Donatist view) or was the church a comingled affair of sinners and the saved (Catholic/Augustine's view)?—but also questions of the uses of the force and authority of the state to resolve religious controversies. These matters are not simply the remote battles of a time long past, but figure as eerie harbingers of later conflicts that erupted during the Reformation and still persist today. Eventually Augustine came to sanction the power and force of the state, as Luther did later, when he judged that religious strife threatened the security of society. Still, with Augustine's injunction to "compel them [the Donatists] to come in," he articulated a theory of suppression that becomes much more chilling when effected by men less sensitive and careful than he.[7]

Again, these issues of force, the violent tactics of the repressed, and questions about which religious group holds the correct understanding of the Scriptures or the tradition not only are the stuff of history, but also find contemporary expression in various forms of current religious fundamentalisms. As the upholders of "purity" and correct practice, the Donatists were the fundamentalists of their day, staking their claim not only on a "true" understanding of texts, but also on the right actions of their leaders. The Donatists believed that these views and practices put them in a position of purity in relation to a threatening and contaminating world. Augustine articulated a view of the church and the course of human history under divine guidance that held out the promise of the world's salvation and transformation even in the midst of war, repression, and violence of all sorts. As the strife with the Donatists was coming to a head, culminating in a conference at Carthage under the direction of Marcellinus, the emperor's representative (in 411), news arrived that Rome had been sacked by the Goths (August 410). This event sent shock waves through the Western empire. Summing up the feelings of the time, Jerome cried from his cell in Bethlehem, "If Rome can be attacked, who is safe?"[8]

Within two years of the state-sanctioned suppression of the Donatists, Augustine began to write *The City of God*. He initially intended it as a response to charges that Rome was being punished for rejecting the worship of the traditional Roman gods and replacing them with that new, upstart god from the eastern Mediterranean. Taking up this challenge with more than his usual verve, Augustine paints a sweeping canvas of God's providential history in which not even the Roman Empire, in all its might and majesty, is essential to God's plans. Augustine's text is the counterweight to the epic poem he had loved and wept over as a student—the *Aeneid*—in which the embattled hero struggles to fulfill Jupiter's (and the emperor Augustus's) vision of Rome's destiny in the world. In Augustine's view, there was no such easy reckoning. All human societies are equally called to task and the intermingling of both good and bad in this world makes it impossible to identify the church with the city of God or to equate the Roman state (or any other city or state, for that matter) with the earthly city. The distinctions that play out on the social and political stages are in reality a matter of love as the direction of the will. The earthly city (as much as it can be discerned) is inhabited by those who are driven by selfish love, while those inhabiting the city of God ground their lives in love of God and love of neighbor. Augustine thereby subjects all governments and societies to a radical critique and so undermines any claims to ultimate or self-sufficient authority. It is fascinating to see Augustine, the Roman citizen, going to the heart of Roman authority and power and finding not justice or fulfillment of a divine destiny but the corrupt and violent *libido dominandi* (lust for power) that holds within it the seeds of its own destruction.

Pelagius and His Views

For the last two decades of his life, Augustine was embroiled in one, final controversy, this time with a British monk named Pelagius and his supporters. It is very difficult, if not impossible, to do justice to the complexity of these drawn-out and acrimonious debates here, so it should suffice to indicate some of the issues that Augustine and his opponents wrangled about during this long controversy. These included the moral state of human beings after the first sin of Adam and Eve; the effects of this "original sin" on their descendents; sin and death in the human condition; the ability (or lack thereof) of humans in this fallen state both to will and effect good deeds; the importance of baptism (especially for infants); the nature of God's grace and its mysterious workings; interpretations of Paul's Epistles (especially Romans) on these points; and the role of concupiscence, the body, and sexual intercourse in the fallen state of humans. To complicate matters further, it is safe to say that Augustine and Pelagius, each in his own way, defended *both* the workings of the human will *and* the effects of God's grace.[9] Since each of these issues listed above is too complex to consider in any comprehensive way here, readers will do well to consult Augustine's many works written during this controversy, as well as the extensive secondary literature on Pelagianism.[10]

Positions became even more fraught after condemnations were leveled against Pelagius and his followers by the church councils (Carthage and Milevis in 417) and imperial decrees (418). As a result of these polemics, Augustine's views evolved over time as he emphasized the penal character of the present human condition more explicitly and stridently than ever before. One of Augustine's major foes in the later phases of this controversy was a young Italian of noble birth named Julian, whose father was a bishop. Julian himself was a married priest who was to become bishop later in life. He was a formidable intellectual opponent to Augustine and their dueling tracts form a treasure trove of this complicated controversy. In an ironic twist of document citation, Julian used some of Augustine's earlier works in effective attacks on the bishop of Hippo. In the midst of this debate, Augustine developed a more thoroughgoing theory of original sin than he had ever done before. The problems with this doctrine continue to haunt certain segments of Christianity, while the debates continue about human agency and God's assistance in human efforts to make morally good choices.

The final years of Augustine's life coincided with the collapse of Roman North Africa under pressure from the invasion of the Vandals. As refugees flooded into Hippo, Augustine was not inclined to apocalyptic visions of the end of days (even the sack of Rome in 410 had not led him to such views), but to clear and calm assessments of the relative value of this life as compared to the next.[11] Augustine died in August 430 as Hippo was besieged by the Vandals. Soon Hippo was captured and partially destroyed, but, amazingly, Augustine's writings survived. Positioned at the end of the Roman Empire in the West (the last Roman emperor died in 476), Augustine's works capture the brilliance, form, and shape of the crises and concerns of his times. At the same time, he unknowingly helped lay the foundations of a medieval Europe that was to rise from the ashes of Roman culture, transformed by the doctrines of Christian thought and the accumulation of ecclesiastical power held by the church of Rome.

Augustine and Women

Monica, His Mother

Any discussion of Augustine's relationship to women can start only in one way—with his relationship to Monica, his mother. While it is the most obvious place to start, it is also the most problematic. The temptation to indulge in popular psychologizing about this famous mother-son duo is great, but also greatly to be resisted. Three excellent chapters in this collection address many facets of their complex relationship and will be considered later in this Introduction, but some comments are in order to bring Augustine and his relationships to and writings on women into sharper focus.

Augustine's enormously complex relationship to Monica must be set in the context of the highly stratified and hierarchical world of late Roman society. Even in a world undergoing rapid social and cultural changes (for example, the last great persecution of the Christians under the emperor Diocletian ended just a few years before Constantine, the emperor, newly converted to Christianity, issued the Edict of Toleration in 313), there were certain fixed points in attitude and custom that essentially were not up for debate. One of these was the status and role of

women in society. Over the course of Roman history there were important changes in Roman law regarding children, women, and marriage.
Nevertheless, the fundamental presuppositions and attitudes about girls
and women and the importance of regulating their marriages, dowries,
and inheritance by law remained constant. Some examples of these
changes include those regulating the tutors (guardians) who directed
property decisions for women, changes in laws about the legal status of
betrothal (whether a breach was actionable or not), and the new laws in
374 c.e. prohibiting child exposure.[12] For reproductive reasons, girls and
young women married young. In general, the legal age for girls in Roman
law was twelve years old, although there were some variations depending
on social class. We can also surmise that there were fairly high rates of
maternal and infant deaths (including the common practice of abandonment and exposure of infants, especially girl babies, until it was prohib-
ited in the late fourth century). Although there were different types of
marriages, in general a young woman moved from the legal protection
and authority of her father to that of her husband, and if she were widowed, her oldest adult son exercised authority over her. Still, one should
not underestimate the influence of the Roman matron both within the
family and beyond. But her influence, all the same, was largely indirect,
mediated, and highly circumscribed by networks of family and professional relationships and by social class. In that world and depending on
social class, marriages were arranged, with dowries and property very
much on the table. These arrangements were considered connections
between families for economic and social well-being and advancement,
not as choices based on something so fleeting and unstable as *eros* or
amor. This is not to say that real, enduring affection was lacking in marriages in the Roman world; one need only read the poignant inscriptions
on the gravestones that husbands often erected for their beloved wives.

Augustine's parents, Patricius and Monica, belonged to the small,
property-owning classes that filled the fertile North African plains surrounding Carthage in the Roman province of Numidia. For hundreds of
years North Africa figured prominently in the economics of the Roman
Empire as an important source of agricultural products, especially grain.
Patricius was a Roman citizen, which, after the economic reforms of Diocletian, meant rigid and burdensome taxes and civic duties. Monica was
a Christian but, as was the custom of the day, did not have her three
children baptized as infants. With the onset of a childhood illness, Mon-

ica came close to having Augustine baptized, and it is instructive to read in the *Confessions* the reasons she hesitated to do so:

> I then begged for the baptism of your Christ, my God and Lord, urging it on the devotion of my mother and of the mother of us all, your Church. My physical mother was distraught. . . . She hastily made arrangements for me to be initiated and washed in the sacraments of salvation, confessing you, Lord Jesus, for the remission of sins. But suddenly I recovered. My cleansing was deferred on the assumption that, if I lived, I would be sure to soil myself; and after that sudden washing the guilt would be greater and more dangerous if I then defiled myself with sins. (*Confessions* 1.11.17)

Since the early years of Christianity, adult baptism was the norm for full membership into the church. Many people considering baptism would delay the ritual, since they thought life as a Christian was such a radical and demanding departure from their previous lives. Also, before "original sin" became an accepted doctrine in Christianity (largely as a result of Augustine's later writings), infants were not considered sinful and so did not need baptism as much as those who were able to sin; nor were infants able to participate in the catechumenate—the rigorous program of instruction and preparation preceding baptism.

Just as Augustine comes alive to his readers over a millennium and a half after his time, Monica emerges from his pages as a much deeper and more complex figure than the ambitious, interfering mother she is often depicted as being. Clearly there are elements of the domineering mother, but there is far more to Monica than such depictions can accommodate. In contrast to the vibrant portrayals Augustine paints of his mother, his father, Patricius, remains a shadowy figure. There is one exception to this in the *Confessions* where Augustine recounts his father's appreciation of his son's sexual coming-of-age. This is the famous scene in the baths in Thagaste where Patricius realizes that his son is becoming sexually mature and that he could hope for grandchildren in the not too distant future (*Confessions* 2.3.6). Both Patricius and Monica had high ambitions for their brilliant younger son and they made considerable sacrifices to have him educated, first in nearby Madouros and then later in Carthage, the leading Roman city in North Africa. When Augustine was sixteen, Patricius could not afford to continue sending him to school. During that year of idleness at home, Augustine perpetrated his famous theft of pears, which years later in the *Confessions* provided him the occasion to meditate on the complex features of human evildoing (*Confessions* 2.4.9–10, 18).[13] His father's meager resources were augmented by financial help from a local man of wealth and prominence, Romanianus. Not only did Romanianus contribute to Augustine's education, he came to share Augustine's enthusiasms for the Manichees and also for starting a small philosophical community when he, Augustine, Alypius, and other friends were in living in Milan (*Confessions* 9.8.17).[14] Despite the social stratification of the time, Roman society was increasingly open to new blood (the *novus homo*, or new man) from the provinces. With the right combination of luck, talent, patrons, and connections a young man from the provinces, like Augustine, could scale the heights of the imperial administration. By the time of his conversion at age thirty-two, Augustine was well on his way to achieving all that he and his parents had hoped for. After Patricius's death, Monica had become a permanent member of her son's household. When Augustine left Carthage to teach rhetoric in Rome in 383, he, like his hero Aeneas, left a woman he loved weeping on the shores. Monica was no Dido, however, and she did not let her precious son escape—either from her or from his obligation to take her into his household and care for her. Soon after his departure, Monica joined him in Rome and stayed with him until her death in 387.

And what a woman she was! When she beseeched a local North African church leader for advice in guiding her son, the bishop demurred. Refusing to take no for an answer, Monica persisted. He still declined to take on the new Manichaean enthusiast, but he also took the measure of her motherly resolve—even God himself will not be able to reject her prayers: "Go away from me: as you live, it cannot be that the son of such tears shall perish" (*Confessions* 3.12.21).

Monica was a person to be reckoned with both in the household and in the advancement of her son's career plans. She had set ideas about how her brilliant younger son should conduct his life. When he returned home as a young man who had become a Manichaean, Monica had no hesitation in refusing him entry to her home (*Confessions* 3.11.19). She was far more distressed by his Manichaean affiliation than she was about his concubine and their young son. Augustine depicts Monica as critical and demanding, especially of him, but he has the last word about her in the moving and not uncritical portrait he paints of Monica's early life and her marriage to Patricius (*Confessions* 9.8.17–9, 22). While he is full of praise for her unswerving devotion to God and the church, that does not blind him to her real faults and failings. Just as with his own sins, Augustine seizes his mother's faults as the opportunity to praise God for his saving action in his mother's life. Monica becomes a major character in Augustine's *Confessions*, one whose life is also a vibrant testimony to the reach and power of God's grace. At the villa outside Milan, she also appears as a participant in the dialogues held during the months of quiet retreat and conversation that followed Augustine's conversion. With his spiritual crisis resolved, his own life has taken a new direction. He also comes to a new understanding of his mother's talent for philosophical discourse, untrained and uneducated though she was (*Confessions* 9.4.8).[15] Monica was to die only a year and a half after Augustine's baptism but she did not depart this life without having gained a deeper appreciation in the eyes of her son.

Augustine's conversion was also about women; that is, it led him to repudiate the married life. He opens *Confessions* 8 in very revelatory ways: the Neoplatonists have helped him resolve some of his long-standing philosophical questions, but in his personal and professional life he was still deeply troubled. He knew what he wanted to do—become a celibate Christian—but, as he writes, he "was still tightly bound by love of women" (8.1.2). He realized that marriage was certainly acceptable within the church, although he was drawn to what Paul enjoined—to choose the "better" way of celibacy (1 Cor. 7:8), by becoming a "eunuch for the sake of the kingdom" (Matt. 19:12). Part of his dilemma about marriage and its obligations was also bound up with his earlier attraction to a life devoted to philosophical pursuits lived among a community of fellow thinkers, all of whom, of course, were men. The ideal of such philosophical communities included shared property, sexual celibacy, and removal from the storms and demands of civic engagement. When Augustine and his friends had considered establishing such a community years earlier, the plans foundered when they failed to take their fiancés and mistresses into account (*Confessions* 6.14.24). Nonetheless, it is clear from the opening of *Confessions* 8 that Augustine was drawn to such a community. His rejection of marriage was also entangled in his own powerful sexual desires. In a later section his "loves of old" appear to him and taunt him: "'Are you getting rid of us?' And 'from this moment we shall never be with you again, not for ever and ever.' And 'from this moment this and that are forbidden to you for ever and ever'" (8.11.26).

The prospect of living without an active sexual life fills Augustine with dread, but at the same time his strong sexual needs provoke feelings of shame and guilt. His deep conflicts demonstrate the private and personal part of his struggles with his sexuality and his efforts to contain sexual activity within legitimate marriage. However, he also wants to reject marriage because of the civil and social obligations that it entailed: professional advancement, maintenance of property, care and education of children (especially as his heirs), and the demands of a wife and a household. His sexual desires are certainly part of the picture, but Augustine was feeling increasingly hemmed in by the public obligations of such an arrangement. It is interesting to see how Augustine constructs his dilemma at the opening of book 8: should he continue with the career path he had pursued since age eighteen and on which he had already traveled far (success, marriage to an heiress of an old senatorial family, establishment of a large and powerful household from which he could advance his career and provide patronage to others); or should he accept conversion to *celibate* Christianity and reject ambition, success, marriage, and further career advancement in the imperial court?[16] Not only was it significant for Augustine himself that he set up the alternatives in this way, but his personal conversion provided tremendous justification for the emergence of celibacy as the privileged state in Western Christianity as it grew in strength and popularity in the late Roman Empire. Augustine was familiar with the celibacy of the Desert Fathers; in fact, the story of Antony of Egypt's sudden conversion plays a crucial role in the narration of conversions that immediately preceded his own. Furthermore, there were small Christian communities of celibates in the western Mediterranean as well, but they were not so numerous or well established as they were in the east. So Augustine's conversion to celibate Christianity not only marked a decisive watershed in his own life, it also provided powerful arguments for later theological developments and practices of celibacy and sexual asceticism in Western Christianity. His own struggles with sexuality and his later texts on marriage, virginity, and celibacy come to be writ large on the whole course of Western Christianity for centuries to come. When Augustine returned to North Africa and settled in Hippo, he established a protomonastery/seminary for the care and training of young men to serve North African churches during a crucial time for Christianity in those provinces.

Augustine's Companion

The other woman in Augustine's life was his companion (concubine). They began living together soon after Augustine arrived in Carthage

(371) and continued to do so for more than a decade. Early on they had a son whom they named Adeodatus. A living arrangement such as they shared was not all that unusual in the late ancient world, especially for a young man of Augustine's talent and ambition.[17] He would have expected to remain in a kind of common-law marriage until his professional life was well established. At that time, he would have then arranged a marriage to a young woman whose family wealth and status would have matched his ambition. In fact, these were precisely the plans Monica began to put in place for him soon after their arrival in Milan in 384. After Augustine become engaged to a girl from a Catholic family, keeping his concubine with him in his household was not considered socially acceptable. In the few places in the *Confessions* where Augustine writes about his companion and their relationship, there is unmistakable evidence of his attachment to her, although he never gives her name or any other biographical details by which to identify her. The language he used later in the *Confessions*, written fifteen years or more after she left the household to return to North Africa, shows the depths of his feelings for her: "The woman with whom I habitually slept was torn from my side because she was a hindrance to my marriage. My heart which was deeply attached was cut and wounded, and left a trail of blood. She had returned to Africa vowing that she would never go with another man. She left with me the natural son I had by her. But I was unhappy" (*Confessions* 6.15.25).

It is also clear that in retrospect Augustine condemned his own behavior when he contrasted his actions to hers: she returned to Africa vowing to remain chaste. In contrast, he cannot wait the two years until the heiress to whom he is engaged attains the legal age to marry, so he takes another woman. Presumably, his fiancée is about ten years old, since she is two years shy of the legal age to marry, which was twelve. We know even less about this second woman than we do about his companion of many years and virtually nothing about the young heiress to whom he was briefly engaged. We do know the deep feelings Augustine had for his companion and how painfully he felt the separation from her. The language he used fifteen years later to describe it is vivid and revealing. He writes about her dismissal in passive way: "She was torn from my side" as a hindrance to his marriage and his heart was "cut and wounded, and left a trail of blood" (6.15.25). He wrote nothing about how she felt about this dismissal. Augustine only recounted her deeds, not her feelings. This account is all about him. Even when he contrasted her vow of celibacy with his urgency to find another woman prior to his marriage, his focus was on his behavior—and he does not come off very well in the contrast. Even after he found another woman "to share his bed," he deeply felt the pain of losing her. Again, Augustine focused on his pain even when it was contrasted to her noble deeds.

The paragraphs directly following this section hold an important key to understanding Augustine's actions at the time. There he described his friendship with Alypius and Nebridius and the deep philosophical conversations they shared. The serenity, reciprocity, and sharing of minds they experienced stand in sharp juxtaposition to what he called the "flood of indulgence in physical pleasures," that is, his sexual activity with his concubine. Augustine's sexual desires reduced his concubine to the means for him to achieve pleasure, whereas he loved his friends "for their own sake; and I felt that in return they loved me for my sake" (*Confessions* 6.16.26). It is important to see that Augustine did not castigate his sexual activity with women because it reduced them to a means to an end, namely, satisfying his sexual desires (which in fact it did and of which he seemed to be somewhat aware). No, the problem that he had was that in his submitting to this "erotic indulgence," sexual activity further immersed him in the material world and blinded him to the prospect of rising to see the "light of moral goodness and of beauty to be embraced for its own sake—beauty not seen by the eye of the flesh, but only by inward discernment" (*Confessions* 6.16.26). He could arrive at such a vision through philosophical conversation with his (male) friends and on a rare occasion even with his mother some weeks before her death. Not only is sexual activity with his concubine (or even with a lawful wife) not a way to achieve this vision, it is a tremendous obstacle to achieving it. The soul is tortured in this state: "turned this way and that, on its back, on its side, on its stomach, all positions are uncomfortable" (6.16.26). In a reprise of the opening lines of book 1, Augustine writes, "Our heart is restless until it rests in you [God]" (1.1.1). Philosophical conversations, peer friendships with men may help prepare us for this repose, but in Augustine's view, sexual activity will never do so. As we will see below, in the following section, Augustine considers the only acceptable sexual activity to be held within the bounds of lawful marriage and only for the sake of reproduction. The past and current doctrines of the Roman Catholic Church owe a great deal to Augustine's views on this subject.

Two other women of a metaphysical but auspicious sort figure in Augustine's life—one makes a brief appearance as he is on the verge of his moral conversion in *Confessions* 8, and the other opens her arms to receive him soon after his conversion to celibate Christianity. The first is a figure whom he called "Lady Continence." She appeared to him in the midst of his fierce struggle with himself and just prior to the denouement of his conversion. In the complex of factors in his conversion, we saw that Augustine aspired to a specific way of life within Christianity—as a celibate Christian. And it was precisely this way of life that he found so difficult to imagine and attain on his own. No wonder, then, that this section of *Confessions* 8 is peopled with a host of models, exemplars, stories, visions, and voices that prompted his conversion. His conversion is no "flight of the alone to the alone" as in Plotinus but more along the lines of a competition in the arena with the spectators taking sides and shouting encouragement to the contestants. Augustine was doing battle to the death with his "old loves," who continued to tug and pull at him, persistently reminding him that he could not live without them: "'from this moment this and that are forbidden to you forever and ever' . . . and what filth, what disgraceful things they were suggesting!" (8.11.26). The "this and that" of his old loves was nothing less than sexual activity, and, as he wrote a few sentences later, "the overwhelming force of habit was saying to me: 'Do you think you can live without them?'" (8.11.26). His divided will was paralyzed by the force of his old habits struggling against the will that wanted to commit him to this new way of life.

Suddenly the vision of "Lady Continence" appeared before him, and the language he used to describe her was in direct contrast to what he considered his shameful and disgraceful sexual habits. Continence was "serene and cheerful without being dissolute, enticing" him in an "honorable way," holding out her arms "to receive and embrace" him (*Confessions* 8.11.27). Even as continent, she was not a solitary or barren figure, but was accompanied by throngs of people who lived lives of continence and chastity: young people, men and women both, and widows and elderly virgins. She spoke to the heart of Augustine's painful inner struggle: the problem lay with his efforts to achieve what he wanted to do entirely on his own power. Her injunction to him was a reminder that none of those living chastely has done so exclusively by his or her own power: "Why are you relying on yourself, only to find yourself unreliable? Cast yourself upon the Lord, do not be afraid. He will not withdraw himself and let you fall" (8.11.27).

This personification of continence as a woman stands in stark contrast to Augustine's love of women, to which he felt "tightly bound," as he put it in the opening paragraphs of book 8. Here at the culmination of his spiritual crisis, a woman appeared to him, enticing him, but not seductively, and embracing him, but not sexually. She was chaste but was still the "fruitful mother of children." Lady Continence drew Augustine away from his "old loves" of sexual pleasures and opened him to the prospect of a life committed to the last important "woman" in his life—holy Mother Church.

Augustine needed one more visitation to resolve his crisis and it came with the voice of the singing child: "Take and read; take and read." In picking up the text from Romans 13, Augustine was drawn from his illusion of arrogant self-sufficiency by which he thought to achieve his ambitions in the Roman world. He had finally come to realize the limits of his own power by experiencing the division and paralysis of his will. The vision of a woman, the voice of a child, and the words of Paul's Epistle all conspired in God's plan to do for him what he never could have done on his own.

Holy Mother Church

While mourning the mother who gave him birth and rejecting the woman who gave him a son (and the prospect of marriage entirely), Augustine returned to North Africa ready to embrace the one "woman" who would occupy his mind and enthrall his heart for the rest of his life— Holy Mother Church.

It is tempting to view Augustine's conversion from success, marriage, and ambition in the Roman world of public affairs to celibate Christianity as a repudiation of the "father principle" and a full and final embrace of the "mother"—that is, Holy Mother Church. Augustine's own writings, especially in the *Confessions*, provide a great deal of material for this view, especially in the period leading up to his conversion. Moreover, in the very few instances in which Augustine mentioned his father, Patricius, he did so in denigrating and other negative ways. And this is the father who had scrimped and saved in order to send Augustine to the best center for education available in North Africa. Without doubt Carthage did not have the status of Rome, but it certainly vied with Alexandria (Egypt) as a center of culture, learning, and sophistication and it was to Carthage that Patricius sent his talented son. This move began the course of study that was to culminate in Augustine's appointment as professor of rhetoric in Milan thirteen years later. It is not all that unusual for sons not to be grateful to their fathers, but given Augustine's typical emotional honesty in many other matters, his virtual indifference to his father is striking indeed. It is even more remarkable when set against how much he wrote about his mother, both in depth and in detail, and about his relationship to her. When he does write about Patricius, Augustine often does so with disdain, presenting his father in a very unfavorable light. Even at his death, Patricius did not even merit a paragraph on his own in the *Confessions*. Augustine mentioned his father's death tangentially as having happened two years earlier and in the context of funds his mother gave him to buy books after the death (*Confessions* 3.4.7). Moreover, this casual aside stands in marked contrast to Augustine's extended lament at the death of a good friend while Augustine was teaching in his home-town. Years later, as Augustine recalled the impact of his friend's death, the memory of this loss gives rise to one of the most beautiful descriptions of friendship in ancient literature (*Confessions* 4.4.7–9, 14). The contrast with Augustine's casual remark about his father's death could not be more pointed.

The question remains: does Augustine's conversion entail the rejection of the father and the affiliation or identification with the mother? Re-becca West was one of the first twentieth-century authors to construe the event in such psychoanalytic terms and she thought this was precisely what happened. West describes Monica's struggle to hold on to her un-ruly son and its effects on Augustine: "It was fortunate that in her religion she had a perfect and, indeed, noble instrument for obtaining her desire that her son should not become a man. Very evidently Christianity need not mean emasculation, but the long struggles of Augustine and Monica imply that in his case it did. Monica could have put him into the Church as into a cradle. He would then take vows of continence and annul the puberty she detested."[18] West then argues that the Roman Empire repre-sented the world of men, where Augustine could have succeeded and surpassed the lowly position and modest achievements of his father, whereas to accept the church presented him with a standard that rejected worldly power and might altogether. According to West, this realm of the church represented his mother's values over the worldly values of his father.

By the end of the fourth century and the beginning of the fifth, how-ever, the situation in fact was far more complex. A sense of the decline and decay of the empire pervaded the air even before Alaric's disastrous sack of "eternal Rome" in 410. With the triumph of Christianity, energy and momentum shifted to the church. Witness Ambrose's amazing situation—he entered the basilica of Milan as an official representing the emperor and emerged as the leading candidate to become bishop of Milan. Acclaimed by the congregation, Ambrose accepted the vox populi and went on to lead the Catholics of Milan during their struggle with the Arians at the court of the emperor.[19] Men of action, purpose, and resolve were coming into the church in droves. Their motives for so doing undoubtedly were very mixed, since membership in the church was the grease that lubricated much political and social advancement at the imperial court. So Rebecca West's dichotomy is too facile, but even if she overstates the case between the competing claims of the "father" and the "mother" in Augustine's case, there is no doubt that along with many Africans of his day, Augustine personified the church as the Holy Mother. As Peter Brown writes, "This Church was the *strong woman*. . . . In a land which, to judge from Monica, had a fair share of formidable mothers, the *Catholica* the Catholic Church, was The Mother."[20] Brown cites the early architect of North African Christianity, Bishop Cyprian of Carthage, a martyr in 258 C.E., a hundred years before Augustine's birth and before the Donatist controversy threatened to destroy the fabric of the North African church. Cyprian evokes the mother to personify the church: "One Mother, prolific with offspring: of her we are born, by her milk we are nourished, by her spirit we are made alive."[21] It is impossible to exaggerate the richness of Augustine's language about God as Father and the Christian Church as Mother, informed with biblical images, allusions, and resonances. Not only is the church the nurturing and protective mother, Augustine described the church using homespun images of life in the countryside of North Africa. For example, the church is the protective nest for the newly hatched young birds. Perhaps Augustine saw himself as one of the fledglings seeking solace and protection. Some years later he used the image of the nest to describe the church: "In the nest of the Church, they could grow like fledglings in safety and nourish the wings of charity with the food of sound faith" (*Confessions* 4.16.31).

Augustine's culminating conversion experience in 386 contains many layers of meaning. Clearly, one aspect entailed his rejection of the claims, responsibilities, and public obligations that an imperial appointment and marriage into an established Roman family would have required of him. He understood his conversion as a complete turning away from that course of life for which he had single-mindedly prepared himself since his youth in Carthage. But if he had thought that his conversion and return to North Africa as a newly baptized Christian could have insulated him from the local struggles and controversies of the North African church, he was to find out otherwise very quickly. At his conversion, Augustine chose God's claims over the urges of his sexuality and entanglements with real women of flesh and blood. While Augustine was planning to live in a kind of protomonastic Christian community, local leaders of the North African church had other things in mind with the return of this highly educated and well-connected native son to the land of his birth. It may not have been the imperial administration that claimed him, but the travails and controversies in North African life were no less demanding and acrimonious than what he had left behind in Milan. As priest and then bishop, Augustine produced many letters and sermons that reveal his struggles to balance his obligations as church leader with his deep interests in the writing projects that occupied him virtually until his death.

Feminist Appraisals of Key Augustinian Themes

Apart from Aristotle (whose writings on women are fairly limited), it is difficult to find a figure in Western thought whose legacy is more contentious and problematic in the views of many feminists than Augustine's. In the past three decades many studies have appeared that engage Augustine's thinking on women and other related key issues that are of interest to feminist scholars and to other researchers as well.[22] Far more than most other thinkers in the tradition, Augustine is the man whom feminists love to hate. He has been portrayed (and in many cases, rightly so) as the single most important thinker whose highly negative and problematic views of human sexuality continue to haunt Western Christianity to this day. In some other studies, his contributions to issues of sexuality and the role of women are seen as great improvements on the highly circumscribed and instrumental attitudes and sexual practices of the late Roman world, especially as these affected women. This volume contains a range of views on Augustine. That fact, in and of itself, indicates that there is not one feminist view on Augustine and his legacy, and also that feminist

analyses of Augustine are constantly undergoing revisions and reapprais-
als in light of new scholarship.

Beyond the most obvious topic of the role of women (which is dealt
with in a number of the essays in this volume), a number of other topics—embodiment, human sexuality and virginity, marriage and widowhood—that are related to Augustine's views on women are now presented
to provide some context for the essays that follow. Even though these
topics also bear on Augustine's view of the human predicament in general, they have particular implications for the situation of women both in
theory and in practice. They also provide a general framework for the
essays in this volume in which the contributors present their specific
assessments of his writings and their influences.

Embodiment

Not a man to shrink from challenges, Augustine set himself a daunting
task in his intellectual program. Augustine is one of the major architects
who forged the synthesis of Platonism and Western Christianity in late
antiquity. This synthesis was to become the predominant model for understanding and explaining Christian doctrine until the eleventh century, when Aristotle's works became more widely available through the
Arabic texts that had been used by Muslim thinkers for many years. To
forge this synthesis Augustine took from the Scriptures the principle that
all creation is good, having been created good by a good God. From the
Platonists, he inherited the tendency to view the material world with a
great deal of suspicion, at times moving perilously close to downright
rejection. He also wrestled to extirpate from his thinking the Manichaean position that claimed the material world and the human body were
the sites of the evil force in the cosmos, attempting to overcome the
good by entrapping it in matter. Augustine struggled mightily with these
contradictory perspectives. Although he insisted in many texts that the
material world is good in the metaphysical sense (that is, on the level of
its ultimate being), he did not entirely escape the Platonic suspicion of
matter, including, indeed especially, a suspicion of the human body.

In appropriating Platonism, Augustine believed that human beings are
composed of two entities, the soul and the body, and there is no question
which one is to be preferred. Just as he accepted this dualistic view of
human beings, he also accepted the ordering and hierarchy that gave

prominence to the soul over the body and, in general, the superiority of the spiritual over the material. Augustine viewed the human being as a "soul using a body" and it is evident that the soul doing the using is clearly superior to the body being used.[23] Elsewhere he describes the soul as "a rational substance designed to rule the body."[24] As he developed his mature thought, Augustine was not so interested in figuring out the role and functioning of the human body (except insofar as it is the site of temptation for the soul), nor in specifying the ways that soul and body interact in the production of knowledge. In fact, toward the end of his great work *The City of God* in a section in which he was wondering how the damned will be tortured and with what kind of fire (spiritual or material), he was still perplexed by how soul was joined to the body: "That conjunction is utterly amazing and beyond our powers of comprehension."[25] Also in his later works, especially in *The Trinity*, Augustine was much more interested in explaining the spiritual and intellectual powers of the soul as reason, memory, and will than in giving an account of the ways in which the body provided data for the mind's operations. Whether he was articulating his theory of knowledge as "divine illumination" or as "the eternal and seminal reasons," Augustine was convinced that the senses should be under the direction of reason.

Still, Augustine did not hesitate to state that the soul was to love and take care of the body, just so long as one does so "reasonably and wisely."[26] And for that to happen, one needs instruction about doing this well because of the fallen state of human beings. This fall was the moral lapse that occurred in the Garden of Eden and not a "fall" that preceded one's birth, as in the view that human souls have "fallen" into bodies. Augustine seems to have rejected this account of the origins of human souls and their bodies.[27] However, the first sin of Adam and Eve leads to the tendency of their descendents to sin, which Augustine understood to be an isolated and absorbed love of self that refuses to practice love of God and love of neighbor as one's self. Love of neighbor, for Augustine, did not exclude care for the neighbor's bodily needs: "If you consider yourself in your entirety, your soul and your body, and your neighbor in his entirety, his soul and body (for man is composed of soul and body), no class of objects to be loved has been omitted in these two commands."[28]

Since Augustine was such a complex thinker who produced a large body of works over a long period of time, works that he himself reviewed painstakingly a few years before his death, it is a challenge to reflect the depth and intricacies of his thinking without oversimplifying his ideas.

This challenge is made even more daunting when one takes into account the many layers of meaning in his texts and the diverse rhetorical devices that he was so fond of deploying, as he worked through an enormous range of philosophical, theological, and historic/cultural issues during his life. The topic of embodiment in Augustine's thought benefits from this reminder, as George Lawless informs readers in a number of essays on Augustine. In "Augustine and Human Embodiment," Lawless remarks that when considering the dualities that Augustine delights in displaying, "he oscillates by coming down on both sides of the binomial [for example, soul and body] at the same time, or at different times depending upon the particular context."[29] Lawless notes that the "antinomies" of Greek-Roman thinking that Augustine held need to be understood so that contemporary readers may avoid the "impression that Augustine's reasoning is partial, biased and one-sided."[30] Nonetheless, when reading Augustine's views on body and soul, it is clear that he is not simply using rhetorical contrasts and juxtapositions for emphasis and effect. Rather, he is developing metaphysical positions with important implications. Augustine very well may have been coming down on both sides of the "binomial," but he landed on each one very differently.

In the midst of the culminating crisis of his conversion in *Confessions* 8, Augustine is tormented by his past habits (mostly sexual in nature), of which he desperately wanted to rid himself in order to accept Christianity. His language reveals the ways in which he identified his true self as the soul that is trying to be released from the entangling habits of his body. He experienced the body as a weight, a chain, and a harsh bondage for the soul. Augustine's soul and body are locked in combat, and he used the language of Paul's Epistles to describe the struggle—"The flesh lusts against the spirit and the spirit against the flesh" (Gal. 5:17): "I was split between them, but more of me was in that which I approved in myself [the soul or spirit] than in that which I disapproved [the body or flesh]. In the latter case, it was no more I, since in large part I was passive and unwilling rather than active and willing" (8.5.11). Further on, Augustine identified himself with the "I" that took delight in the "inward man, but another law in my members fought against the law of my mind and led me captive in the law of sin which was in my members" (citing Rom. 7:22 in 8.5.12). In referring to this text, Susan Bordo notes that the language Augustine used here casts the body as alien, a confinement, a limitation, and the enemy.[31] What Bordo does not show is that this was only the beginning of the culmination of Augustine's struggle and that the deeper struggle involved the division of the mind or soul itself. Not only were soul and body in conflict, but the soul is divided against itself. Augustine experienced this state as a paralysis of the will. He had created this division and paralysis by forming habits that implicated the body but that, on his own, he could not repair. The body was the incidental field on which part of this struggle took place, but the most debilitating and, in fact, more important struggle for Augustine took place within the will itself, far beyond the reaches of the body. In fact, Augustine was amazed that in the heat of this struggle the body obeyed the will, but the will did not obey itself (8.8.20). The body, then, is bypassed for the real struggle that took place deep within his soul or mind. When the struggle was finally resolved, his body followed his soul, particularly by rejecting ambition, marriage, and sexual relations. Here we see the triumph of the true self over the body that is directed and used by the self, according to the "law of the inner man" (Rom. 7:22). Through his conversion Augustine has discovered and claimed his true inner self and so he will no longer "make provision for the flesh and its desires" (Rom. 13:14).

Clearly Augustine had both practical and theoretical difficulties with the human body, but what are his views specifically on women's bodies? The ways in which men are embodied are very different for Augustine from women's embodiment. The body was certainly an encumbrance for both men and women, but the weight women are required to bear and the price they must pay for embodiment are far more onerous than those visited upon men. One example suffices: women's embodiment (as women) prevented Augustine from considering them to be as fully made in God's image as men. Some scholars argue that the fact that Augustine saw fit even to raise the question about whether women are to be considered as made in God's image at all and that he gives a qualified (indeed, even tortured) answer in the affirmative modulates the criticism against him on this point.[32] Giving Augustine his due, it is remarkable that he took the question of women's imago status this far, but it is also important to see that the qualified affirmation he gave founders precisely on the fact of women's bodies. In contrast to some other early Christian writers such as Tertullian, Augustine does appear to be more measured and nuanced in his views, but he cannot move fully beyond the deep suspicions he harbored about the human body with its urges and needs, especially when it comes to human sexuality. We now turn to this problematic and vexed topic.

Human Sexuality

"But I was an unhappy young man, wretched as at the beginning of my adolescence when I prayed to you [God] for chastity and said, 'Grant me chastity and continence, but not yet.' I was afraid that you might hear my prayer quickly, and might too rapidly heal me of the disease of lust which I preferred to satisfy rather than suppress" (*Confessions* 8.7.17). If Augustine showed deep suspicion and ambivalence about the body, the decibel level moves to another register entirely in his discussions of human sexuality. The famous quotation above appears in the *Confessions* just at the beginning of the culminating struggle that finally leads to his conversion to Christianity, and in it Augustine harks back to his adolescent drive for sexual adventure and pleasure. But instead of taking delight in his escapades, he recalls the wretchedness he felt at that time and that he still felt at age thirty-two. What accounts for his wretchedness and misery as he recalls these in the narrative? He has moved into the highest circles of the imperial administration; he is engaged to marry an heiress of an aristocratic family; he is surrounded by friends and associates who value him; and he is living in a household of family members, including his mother, Monica, and his son, Adeodatus, who was born to him and the woman he loved from his youth. He has dismissed his woman companion, since he had become engaged to the young girl, but because he cannot live without having a woman with him, he takes another mistress. And he is miserable and unhappy. At the opening of book 8, it is clear that a big part of the problem for Augustine was sex. He wanted to continue this pleasure in his life and yet he felt ashamed and guilty about his urgent need for sexual gratification. He himself sets up the dichotomy that constitutes the framework of his conversion at the end of book 8: he no longer wanted honor and success in the world of the emperor's court, but he was "still firmly tied by woman" (8.1.2). He knew that marriage was acceptable within the Christian Church, but he was moved by Paul's exhortation to "something better" that would imitate Paul's example of celibate service within the church. Augustine ended the paragraph in this section of the text with a reference to Jesus's saying that there are "eunuchs who have castrated themselves for the sake of the kingdom of heaven. He who is able to receive this, let him receive this" (Matt. 19:12 cited in 8.1.2). Augustine very much wanted to abide by this teaching, but was also terrified at the prospect of living a celibate life. As the narrative unfolds, his struggle with sexuality constitutes a recurring theme in the final battle to accept Christianity. It is not all about sex, since there were many complex layers that went into the final conversion. His difficulties, however, in renouncing his sexual habits and his ambivalence about his arranged marriage continued to plague him throughout the account. It bears repeating that Augustine himself set up his conversion on the horns of this dilemma: either he continues with his plan for ambition in the world, including marriage, that entailed duties of public life and the household or he converts to celibate Christianity and rejects all his former ambitions, including sexual relations. There was no requirement that he renounce sexual practice. He required this of himself. Even priests within the church continued to marry well after his time. In an ironic twist of history, Augustine's own personal struggles formed the foundational experiences that continued to influence his many and extraordinarily important teachings on sexuality. In his case, the personal became the philosophical and the theological, particularly with regard to his attitudes toward human sexuality and practice and their impact on the West.

As with many other philosophical and theological theories that he developed in his lifetime, Augustine's views on human sexuality were forged in the fires of controversy in which he became embroiled soon after his ordination to the priesthood. His first great opponents on these matters were his old friends and associates, the Manichaeans. During the early 390s as he became more active as a priest in the community, reading and appropriating ideas from the Bible, he argued against the Manichaean identification of the material world with the force of evil. In that context, he also criticized the sexual abstinence of the Manichaean "elect" who refrained from sexual intercourse because of their belief in the evil nature of matter. Against that view, Augustine began to develop his view that sexual intercourse is acceptable in its place and for the correct purpose: only within marriage and for the sake of reproduction. This, in essence, is the view that he maintained throughout his many treatises on sexuality, marriage, and family life and is the view that still holds sway in the Catholic Church of today.

During the 390s Augustine immersed himself in studying Paul's Epistles, also becoming aware of the many debates that were occurring in Christian circles about the nature and practices of asceticism. He began to be less optimistic about the person's abilities to effect good actions and moral reform and, with regard to sexuality, to engage in sexual behavior unaffected by inordinate desire (concupiscence). He puzzled over Paul's teachings and wrote commentaries on them during the 390s. One text in particular loomed large in his thinking: "For I do not do the good I want, but the evil I do not want is what I do. Now if I do not do what I want, it is no longer I that do it, but sin which dwells within me" (Rom. 7:19). He began to adopt a less optimistic (or he might have said, more realistic) view of the power of the human will not only to choose, but actually to accomplish good deeds. Moreover, he revised his clear landscape of marriage to include unresolved and unruly dimensions of desire that are not in the control of either reason or will. Perhaps the many family and marriage problems brought to him by the members of his congregation were the spurs that prompted him to revise his thinking about the human condition and its prospects for self-improvement.

As Elizabeth Clark writes in her introduction to a collection of Augustine's texts on sexuality and marriage, Augustine "tried to stake a middle ground between the claims of resolutely ascetic writers who hinted that marriage and reproduction were unworthy experiences for Christians, and those, in contrast, who made out that no preference was to be given to ascetic living."[33] In attempting to stake out this middle ground, Augustine made clear that, although marriage was an acceptable state within Christianity, the preference was unmistakably on the side of celibacy and consecrated virginity. Not only were these latter states good in and of themselves, but they were of a higher order than the married state. Clearly, this "better way" was for those few who were able to "accept such a teaching" (Matt. 19:12). Clark's introduction also serves to outline the important controversy with the Pelagians that occupied Augustine during the last years of his life. During this controversy, Augustine was prompted to articulate his ideas on original sin, the enduring power of lust (even after baptism), and the position that "marriage and reproduction *were* goods, despite the view he simultaneously expressed concerning the Original Sin's transmission and the wickedness of lust."[34] The Pelagians cleverly used some of Augustine's more optimistic texts against him and accused him in his later thinking of readopting the Manichaean positions about the evil of the material world and its powers over the body, especially with regard to sexual behavior. In his arguments against them, Augustine worked out more fully than he had ever done before his views on the positive aspects of marriage, even though marriage, he claims, still falls short of celibacy or consecrated virginity.

Finally, it is clear that in dealing with this complex issue of human sexuality, Augustine relied heavily on the language of hierarchy, control, and subordination of women to men. In that effort, he did not depart from the typical Platonic strategy of attempting to override the unruly passions by the superior workings of reason. What he did add to the discourse was a forceful rationale for such control set within the Adam and Eve story, within which he developed the doctrine of original sin with its enormous implications for the moral lives of their descendents. As the notion of sexual control became more elusive and fraught, Augustine even considered sexual intercourse within legitimate marriage to be tainted by lust and to be somewhat sinful when it is not directed toward reproduction.[35] In Augustine's mature view, it was far better to attempt sexual renunciation altogether than to live in such a way that allowed sexual pleasure to gain the upper hand. In his masterful analysis of the twists and turns of the ancient world's view of the human body, Peter Brown emphasizes the enormous impact of Augustine's thinking about the body and sexuality on the West: "An ancient Roman's harsh distrust of sensual delight and a fear that the body's pleasures might weaken the resolve of the public man added a peculiarly rigid note to Augustine's evocation of human beings forever exposed to merciless concupiscence. He created a darkened humanism that linked the pre-Christian past to the Christian present in a common distrust of sexual pleasure. It was a heavy legacy to bequeath to later ages."[36]

The Essays

With a thinker as influential and contested as Augustine is in the West, it should come as no surprise that the contributors to this collection use a variety of approaches and methodologies in analyzing his works. They assess his impact on the tradition in a variety of ways, often coming to very different, if not contradictory, conclusions. This is as it should be with a thinker of the stature of Augustine. Clearly the writers in this volume take seriously their scholarly obligations to text, context, and methodology while making clear the distinctions that are required to understand a figure so distant from our own time and culture. If Augustine should be understood in the context of his times, does that stance exonerate him from the charge that he provided powerful legitimation for the subordination of women in Western culture? Complicating matters even further, scholars make the appropriate distinctions between Augustine's impact on his own times and his relevance for today. These issues are well represented and argued about in this volume of essays.

We are fortunate to begin this collection with an essay by Rosemary Radford Ruether, whose influence on feminism and scholarship about Christianity over the past thirty years can hardly be overstated. The range of her contributions is enormous: studies of individual Christian thinkers, the theological roots of anti-Semitism, the intersections of religion and sexism, women's leadership in the churches, the impacts of sexism on theology and theological language, feminist liturgical practices, the governance of the American Catholic Church, Christianity's impact on the construction of the modern family, and the role of religious nationalism in the Israeli-Palestinian conflict, as well as ecofeminism, world religions, and globalization. In all these areas, Ruether displays rigor, insight, and creativity, which express her deep and broad understanding of the role of religion in historical contexts and present-day dilemmas. In her contribution here, "Augustine: Sexuality, Gender, and Women," Ruether provides a valuable overview of Augustine's thinking on gender, sexuality, and the status of women before the Fall, after the introduction of sin into the world and in the world to come. In all these states, women are at a disadvantage despite the declaration in Genesis 1:27 that both male and female were created in God's image and likeness. A number of contributors to this volume return to this text and this dilemma for Augustine: in what senses are women made in God's image? Ruether argues that in Augustine's view women can never be considered as "image of God" in the full sense in which men are directly from creation. Not only is this distinction central to social relations on earth, but a hierarchy prevails in heaven as well. Women and men are both resurrected bodily, but women's bodies will be "transformed" so that the parts of their bodies that have to do with sexual practice and childbirth will become, in Augustine's words, "fitted to glory rather than to shame." Since Augustine's thinking on these matters has been considered "normative" for centuries, feminists and others must engage in analyses and critiques of Augustine to "salvage what is helpful in Augustine's views, freed from the biases that have distorted the humanity of both women and men."

The "salvage operation" continues with the following four essays, which consider Augustine's relationship with his mother, Monica, as well as his views of women. The first essay in this section on Monica, written by Anne-Marie Bowery, is titled "Monica: The Feminine Face of Christ." Bowery uncovers and recovers the more feminist-friendly ideas and approaches that can be detected in Augustine's works, by focusing on his treatment of Monica in the *Confessions*. Bowery conducts a review of some of the current literature on Augustine, especially with reference to his views on women. By foregrounding the negative assessments of women that were common in his time and culture, Bowery does not exonerate Augustine, but clearly shows that his own misogynistic views cannot be fully separated from the powerful assumptions of his time. Bowery notes that few contemporary scholars have used Augustine's portrait of Monica to challenge and reframe the masculine character of the divinity. She proceeds to do so in her essay and argues that Augustine's depiction of Monica can be used to "feminize the view of Christ." Bowery's strategy provides leverage for new ways of thinking about Christ, who is the divine person most fully gendered as masculine. As the Christ figure, Monica functions in Augustine's text symbolically and rhetorically as the model Christian and as mediator to the divine. By mediating Augustine's spiritual journey, Monica represents the mediating nature of Christ. Bowery is largely optimistic about the implications of these strategies for the development of more feminist and woman-friendly approaches to the Western canon and to Augustine's enormous influences in the tradition. Along with other contributors to this volume, Bowery underscores the relational dimensions of spiritual experience that she finds in Augustine's journey and in his depictions of Monica. She also emphasizes his focus on the personal as a powerful principle for developing new ways of thinking in philosophy and theology. From this perspective, Augustine's own insights provide ways to counteract the tremendous damage his texts have caused in Western views of women, thereby reframing how both men and women regard women in society and their relation to the divine.

In the following essay, "Augustine's Rhetoric of the Feminine in the *Confessions*: Woman as Mother, Woman as Other," Felecia McDuffie argues that the intersecting lines of Augustine's thinking plot his positive views of woman as mother along with the "shadow figure of woman as other," displaying a much more "ambiguous" significance of woman. Grounded in Augustine's experiences with Monica, McDuffie shows how Augustine appropriates the language of the feminine and then masculinizes it in order to attribute certain characteristics to God. In so doing, she demonstrates a strategy that allows Augustine to "separate the positive attributes of the feminine" from the more problematic nature of women as embodied and gendered. Monica was the starting point and then union with God (the divine father with nurturing features) is the culmination of Augustine's and every Christian's journey to an "eternal bliss" that recapitulates the baby at the mother's breast. McDuffie also shows that Augustine's "powerful rhetoric of the feminine" fails to make significant differences for real women, who still occupy an inferior position and who are left with "only half their being—the dangerous other."

The third essay in this section on Augustine's mother, "Confessing Monica," was jointly written by Virginia Burrus and Catherine Keller. The authors take up the vexed question of the structure and coherence of Augustine's narrative in the *Confessions* and show that his descriptions of Monica serve polyvalent purposes: biographical, hermeneutical, meta-physical, and biblical. In Augustine's iteration of these dimensions, the authors indicate how he conflates the discourse on Monica with Wisdom, Scripture, the new Jerusalem, and his exegetical projects in books 11–13 of the *Confessions* about the creation of the world. Far beyond any hagio-graphical intentions, Augustine's narrative about his mother, with aspects of Eve and Dido very close to the surface, is transformed into the search for the "incorporeal" or "spiritual matter" (the "heaven of heavens" of book 13), as the creature that clings to the eternal God. The authors' textured analysis holds out the prospect of recovering and thawing out the "frozen embryos" that may still lodge deep within the fixed Platonic foundation of Augustine's thinking. A "constructive theology of becom-ing" may still be a dream or "fantasy," but the "theological potentialities of the *Augustinian Wisdom Mother*" can still be seen, if only in bare out-line. Burrus and Keller end their essay by evoking Hannah Arendt's early work on Augustine and her insistence on the value of Augustine's notion of "natality." This fact of having been born leads to acts of human free-dom; and it is the source and wellspring of the capacity to bring some-thing new into the shared world of the human condition. Natality brings us to a more replete display and play of the mother (not the grieving mother à la Mary and Monica) or the immutable (frigid) Sapientia, but the joyful mother (Kristeva's *jouissance*), who may very well supersede the Mary/Eve binary of Western Christianity's master narrative.

Rebecca Moore's contribution, "O Mother, Where Art Thou? In Search of Saint Monnica," conducts the search for the real Monica within the "women-of-worth" genre of the early Christian hagiographical tradition. Moore uses the North African spelling—Monnica—to reflect the name's pre-Roman origins, while other contributors use the spelling (Monica) that is more common in the literature. Moore contrasts the normal expectations of the genre with Augustine's narrative, in which

Monica remains "maternal and female" while not always emerging in the most positive light. Even with his critical portraits of his mother, Moore argues that we may come to glimpse Monica's countenance by paying closer attention to Augustine's offhand details and negative remarks. Neither motherhood nor femaleness need be sacrificed in displaying the woman-of-worth, although Augustine himself remains ambivalent about these features in Monica. Each carries both powerful negative and positive charges, with Augustine neither resolving nor overcoming the tensions between them. In fact, Moore argues that Monica's presence and participation in the Cassiciacum dialogues confronts Augustine with two models of spirituality—the experiential (as found in the female Monica) and the philosophical (represented by Augustine and the other men). Safely on the other side of his conversion, before which Augustine considered women a hindrance to his full embrace of the celibate Christian, Augustine can now see Monica as representing women's contributions to the philosophical life. Unsophisticated though she is, Monica is full of faith and, in fact, is much more wholehearted in her traditional piety than her son is (or perhaps can ever hope to be). At least, she remains both woman and mother in Augustine's account. Those features may have impeded her own spiritual development, but she may have been redeemed in her son's eyes by being an important vehicle of his conversion.

We now move to the other woman in Augustine's life—his companion of many years and the mother of their son, Adeodatus. Margaret Miles's contribution is titled "Not Nameless but Unnamed: The Woman Torn from Augustine's Side." Miles poses the question about whether it is possible to reconstruct his companion's historical presence, to which she answers, yes and no. Her essay traces the trajectories of these contrary, but not contradictory, responses. Miles resists the temptation (to which Garry Wills falls prey) to name Augustine's partner, and in so doing she underscores the lack of subjectivity that Augustine imposed on her in the *Confessions*. Miles will not redeem her from this denial of subjectivity and that strategy leads her to reexamine some assumptions of current feminist historiography. When Augustine dismissed his companion as an obstacle to his marriage, she vowed to live the rest of her life as a celibate. Miles argues that by examining her choice "within her social and cultural situation, we will know all that we can know about her." Miles goes on to show that that turns out to be more than might be expected in one's first reading the *Confessions*. After all, and to Augustine's embarrassment, she converted to celibacy before he did, but as Miles notes, "at greater cost." Even though the partner is sent away, "she went on her own terms." Is this the way to overcome seeing her simply as the victim or vehicle in Augustine's own story about his journey? Miles displays a number of lenses so that the unnamed companion can be seen in less dismissive ways. She made her choice—the choice for celibacy—but it was a choice, in a sense, foisted upon her. In the world of late antiquity, women's lives continued to be dictated by their relationships to men, which rendered "women's social positions terrifyingly unstable." Miles does not seek a way around that historical reality, but surmises that the companion's choice for celibacy would have placed her in the center of the ascetic movement that was gaining tremendous momentum in the newly Christianized empire (380s c.e.). Still, by the end of her essay, Miles returns to the "tantalizingly inaccessibility" of Augustine's companion in a text that seems largely uninterested in her and "was presenting her in a way that supported his own celibacy." In the end, it turns out to be all about Augustine. But Miles also shows that Augustine's failure to integrate the intimate, sexual part of his life is connected "to his inability to understand concern and care for the world as a forum for spiritual growth and concern."

We may not know the name of Augustine's companion, but we do know the names of the women with whom he corresponded in his collection of letters. The following two essays focus on these letters and show how Augustine addressed the many problems brought to him by a number of prominent women of his day. As the bishop of Hippo, Augustine was very careful in his day-to-day interactions with women. He spoke to a woman only in the presence of one or two other persons and never in his personal residence. He did not even make an exception for his elder sister (also unnamed) or his three nieces, all of whom were religious women living in a convent in Hippo. Despite maintaining his distance in face-to-face dealings with women, he is not hesitant to speak his mind directly when he is asked his views on family and church matters or when he becomes embroiled in controversies in which some prominent women also played a role.

Joanne McWilliam's essay, "Augustine's Letters to Women," reveals the wide range of issues occupying him in these letters. As McWilliam notes, Augustine addressed matters that are very similar to those he handles in letters to men, with one very important exception—public affairs. Despite that deficiency, the small number of letters written to women is remarkably diverse in contents and tone. What emerges is very much the pastoral side of the work Augustine engaged in as the leading church official in Hippo. He is comforting in his letters of condolence, direct in his letters of advice (by turns conciliatory or admonitory in letters dealing with controversies), and profuse in letters that have implications for women in the religious life and in others that function like minitreatises on prayer. Larger issues of the day are also reflected in these letters: dispositions of property disputes; church rituals and administration; the growing ascetical movement; and increasing anxieties about the security of Rome, especially as experienced by a number of wealthy women who had fled with their families to the safety of North Africa.

As small in number as these letters may be, they show how much Augustine was entangled in the daily tasks of church leadership for a large and contentious congregation living in the midst of profound and anxious changes. Although these women do not loom large in the public world of these events, McWilliam conveys the tone and texture of Augustine's leadership, constantly on call for advice and adjudication. At least in written form, Augustine responds to women's requests for advice, assistance, and consolation, and as McWilliam notes, "Whatever Augustine might have thought of women's bodies, he did not discount their intellectual powers," a point that is evidenced in this fascinating collection of letters.

The second essay on Augustine's letters to women comes from E. Ann Matter and is titled "De cura feminarum: Augustine the Bishop, North African Women, and the Development of a Theology of Female Nature." Matter takes Augustine's letters to women as a group and investigates what his position as a bishop (in a particular setting) led to in formulating "Augustine on women" and in creating "a Christian theology of 'women's nature.'" In dealing with individual letters, she shows (as does McWilliam) the range of Augustine's issues in his letters to women, especially adding to the discussion an awareness of his concerns about the fractious nature of church discipline and the theological disputes in which he was embroiled at the time, particularly with the Donatists and the Pelagians. Matter proposes going beyond the usual lenses of "sex and his mother" to see how his letters to women and works written at around the same time express his thoughts on women "in the context of his other theological preoccupations." McWilliam gives the view from within the letters themselves, whereas Matter provides the broader theological and cultural settings to illuminate the larger issues surrounding this correspondence.

The following three chapters in this collection address a range of topics bearing on Augustine's views of women, sexuality, the nature of the human person, love, desire, and language about gender and sex. All these raise significant questions for feminist writers, and Augustine's role in articulating the Western Christian views on these matters cannot be overstated. In my own essay, "Augustine on Women: In God's Image, but Less So," I review the vexed question of whether Augustine considered women to be made in God's image, just as men are. The literature on this topic in the past thirty years is considerable. That fact comes as no surprise, since this question stands at the heart of Augustine's discourse on women and has both theoretical and practical implications. In the first part of the essay I review that literature and show how a number of authors use at least two strategies to understand Augustine's position: first, placing him within the context of his time and culture, which entertained no serious questions or doubts about the subordinate role of women; or second, showing that, given the misogyny of many other early Christian writers, Augustine's view is in fact no worse than, but even represents an improvement over these other views on women. At least, the argument goes, he admits women to some sort of spiritual equality with men, thereby according them some imago status. As other studies have done, I begin with an analysis of Augustine's convoluted text on women in *The Trinity* book 12, but then I situate his discourse on women within his larger project in books 12 and 15. I also show that in order to be accorded imago status, women must pay a price that is never required of men, namely, to become disembodied and degendered as women. Finally, I infer from Augustine's highly developed paradigm of interrelationship based on equality, mutuality, and reciprocity that he discovers as the inner life of God and the inner life of humans that he had the conceptual tools at hand to bring this same paradigm to human relationships and to women. The fact that he did not do so is one of the great failures of Western Christianity and one that scholars and activists are still striving to overcome.

The following essay in this section, "To Remember Self, to Remember God: Augustine on Sexuality, Rationality, and the Trinity" is by Julie Miller. Miller begins by wondering about joining together the experience of sexuality and the doctrine of the Trinity. Once again, Augustine's life, works, and impact on Western Christianity are the wellsprings of the analysis, and she sees these sources as more of the problem than the solution. Miller argues that neither Neoplatonism nor patriarchal principles can provide the framework to develop a "full-bodied love of God, let alone love for another human being, particularly a person of the opposite sex." She is not surprised to discover that the results of both Augustine's experiences and his doctrine of the Trinity lead to "a self-contained trinity and an abject fear of intimate human relationships." Miller shows how Augustine's experiences of intimate and sexual relationships involved pain and a deep sense of loss of self. This is not just his particular experience, however, but one that finds its root and cause in the Fall. Since Adam and Eve loved each other too much, they lost knowledge of God and so lost themselves as well. No wonder Augustine finds it much safer to refrain from sexual involvements entirely. In its place, Miller argues, Augustine develops a theory of the Trinity and of human beings as its image in which the drive to love and rest in God does not result in pain and loss of self. This is a "fail-safe" and distant God who draws human beings to act out a "mindful love of God."

Miller critiques traditional psychoanalytic theory, with its emphasis on separation and autonomy as the hallmarks of maturity. In its place Miller draws on feminist versions of attachment theory that challenge these hallmarks and replace them with achieving intersubjectivity as the mark of maturity and human integration. In such a model of human development, a person need not fear pain and loss of self, but can accommodate, even embrace, them. Augustine's understanding of God as the self-contained Trinity will yield to a transformed view of God more attuned to the full subjectivity of women and men. Intersubjectivity can replace domination and subordination, and human relationships will also benefit from a "full-bodied and full-souled theology of sexuality" that does not extirpate sexual desire from longing for God.

The essay that follows, "The Evanescence of Masculinity: Deferral in Saint Augustine's *Confessions* and Some Thoughts on Its Bearing on the Sex/Gender Debate," by Penelope Deutscher, was first published in 1992 at the height of the sex/gender debates. Her essay is a fine example of the ways Augustine's work continues to inspire debate on highly charged contemporary issues. Deutscher unpacks the linguistic distinctions between the coupled terms *woman* and *feminine* or *man* and *masculine* to see if there are real terminological or usage distinctions between each term in the set. Using Augustine's *Confessions* as the prime exhibit in her argument, Deutscher sees the opposition between man and woman as "theologically grounded." Then "God" as the third term/being is introduced; to this, man is both imaged and contrasted. "Man" and "woman" then become stand-ins for the underlying mind/body opposition. Deut-scher argues that as the body, even the masculine body, is displaced onto the feminine, what is essential to man recedes and "moves toward a di-vine point." Yet because man cannot coincide with God, "all that is progressively isolated from man and devalued as 'not man' is displaced onto the feminine." The result is a structural confusion that should not surprise theorists, but could, in fact, lead to some clarity about the reasons for the confusion between and among these terms.

And "now for something completely different," we come to the last entry in the collection—a poem titled "To Aurelius Augustine from the Mother of His Son," by Ann Conrad Lammers. In this contribution, we see that Augustine's legacy continues to inspire and provoke many responses—in this case, poetry about Augustine's dismissal of his com-panion and mother of their son. Lammers gives creative and imaginative "voice" to the woman who, as Miles noted in her essay, was "not name-less, but unnamed." We see informed imagination and literature giving "voice" to those whose voices and words were not considered sufficiently important to be preserved in the tradition.

Concluding Comments

Augustine's influence continues to be felt—for both good and ill—throughout the reaches of Christianity in the West, as well as wherever his texts are read and debated in global settings. Clearly his impact is enormous and his works continue to challenge and engage feminists to this day. Nonetheless, some feminist authors, among them Mary Daly, have moved far beyond any engagement with his ideas.[37] They conduct their philosophical and theological investigations in new territories and attempt to purge their thinking about God, women, men, and the social order of any vestiges of what they consider to be his deleterious influ-ences. Since, as they see it, the effects of his views have been so pervasive and pernicious, Daly and others reject the prospects of engaging August-ine's writings in any meaningful or productive ways. Two consequences, at least, follow from this strategy: first, there is an isolation and marginali-zation of contemporary feminist thinking from the mainstream of philos-ophy and Christian theology; second, by virtue of such marginalization, the articulation of feminist theories precisely on the margins becomes creative, challenging, and a leading edge of thinking, thereby moving contemporary discourses in new directions. The first is a "separation strategy" that a number of feminists have adopted in other areas, one that seeks to avoid the conceptual traps that have given powerful legitimation to women's subordination in Western patriarchy.

The contributors to this volume take a variety of standpoints with regard to Augustine's views on women, as well as to the ways his writings supported and justified women's subordination in the West. However, they share at least one common perspective—that it is worth the effort and dedication to engage, challenge, and critique both Augustine's texts (in their own time and place) and the ways his writings have been understood and applied in the past sixteen hundred years. Earlier in this Introduction, I called this strategy a kind of "salvage operation" in which a number of contributors uncover and recover the elements in Augustine's thinking that are more compatible with feminist approaches than one might think at first glance. Another approach considers that since Augustine's texts and their influence are so enormous in the West, feminist authors cannot afford to ignore them. To do so runs the risk of giving over theology and philosophy to those who champion simplistic, distorted, and misogynistic readings of his texts. If nothing else, this rich collection of essays gives ample proof that while there is much in Augustine to challenge and critique, the nuanced essays in this collection open the doors to rereading and reorienting his writings in ways that provide fruitful spaces for feminist discourses.

Two interrelated areas that stand in urgent need of feminist thinking and reorienting are gendered embodiment and sexuality. Recently a highly revelatory entry appeared in the encyclopedia on Augustine, *Augustine Through the Ages* (an otherwise excellent collection), in which the citations for gender and sexuality are set down as "Gender, Sex → Asceticism; Women."[38] This one citation calls for an examination of the very way the entry is constructed. Unpacking this citation would lead to an analysis, among other points, of how women are considered to be the "gendered" other, while men stand for the universal human person. Furthermore, one could examine the embedded claim that sexuality is best understood and should be subsumed under the disciplinary practices of asceticism.[39] This very thin and distorted view of human sexuality fails to address how Christian ideas and practices have contributed to sexual repression for many centuries. It also shows serious neglect of the thinkers and clinicians who, for the past one hundred years, have made invaluable contributions to richer, more authentic views of gendered embodiment and human sexuality than had ever been available in the past. In contrast, engaging the writings of Augustine, as the authors have done in this collection, reveals the depths as well as many of the sources of the problems associated with gendered embodiment and sexuality in Western discourses and practices. Their approaches also provide important resources for rethinking ways to address these problems in Christianity. Feminist authors are engaged in difficult tasks in the West, especially in dealing with questions about human sexuality. In brief, they are thinking through the ways sexuality and sexual practices are constructed and validated beyond the fear and repression so often associated with Christianity. In so doing, they are challenging the exploitation and commercialization of sexuality in contemporary societies, where the deep human and spiritual dimensions of human sexuality are often ignored or obliterated. The pioneering efforts of feminist authors have enormous implications for conceptualizing and practicing our personal and social lives as gendered, embodied, and sexual women and men.

A compelling question arises here: does Christianity have anything to contribute to these discourses about integrated and genuinely human sexuality? Given the fact that institutional Christian churches have often championed sexual repression and control and that the recent sexual-abuse scandals by clergy and others within the churches have eroded the moral leadership of the churches, it may seem naively optimistic that new conceptual frameworks and new understandings of human sexuality could emerge from these quarters. Given their problematic history, can Christianity or Augustine contribute to finding new and radically different solutions? Perhaps not from these quarters as they have been understood and practiced for many years, since, as Audre Lorde emphasized, "we cannot dismantle the master's house with the master's tools."

We feminists, however, are embarked on projects of forging new tools to construct paradigms that are more genuinely expressive of the creative, gendered standpoints that we both occupy and transform. In this process, we might even find some useful foundation stones and support beams from the ur-habitat of the early Christian communities and their powerful witness to the Gospel. If we are serious about being pilgrim communities, on the move to a destination that is both longed for and lived out in the here and now, we had better not become too settled or comfortable. Moreover, we should guard against what Augustine considered to be the fundamental error/sin of living here and now as though it were ultimate and that we had no other destination. The radical ambivalence of living in the world, but not of it, need not lead to rejecting the world's claims on us nor to neglecting pressing issues of social justice. Neither need this ambivalence lead to triumphalism or absolutizing any one dogmatic answer to the pressing issues of the day. In these tasks, Augustine's works have much to offer and can be read, reread and reframed in new and exciting ways, as these essays show so well.

In the ongoing work of thinking through gendered embodiment and human sexuality, feminist authors are going to the heart of these matters. In so doing, they challenge the conceptual frameworks that support casting gender, embodiment, and sexuality in terms of domination and violence. As Elizabeth Johnson notes:

> Feminist thinking prizes dialectical connectedness that flourishes in a circle of mutuality. . . . If the self is defined by a dialectic of friendly, constitutive relation, then it becomes possible to reconcile previously dichotomous elements: self and other, most basically, and consequently matter and spirit, body and soul, passions and mind, embodiment and self-transcendence, women and men, humanity and earth. . . . Oppositional, either-or thinking which is essential to the hierarchical dualistic pattern of reality is transformed by a paradigm of both-and. Regarding humanity's connection to the earth, women's wisdom suggests that the relation is not one of "over against" and "superior to" but "together with" moving in an interactive circle of mutual kinship.[40]

Thinking through the new frameworks can help create new policies and practices that radically challenge the continuum of domination and subordination in which women's bodies and the sexual practices visited upon women have become the very texts upon which these power relations have been inscribed and enforced. At stake is the fundamental and biblical charge to be "stewards" of God's good earth, acknowledging the reality of the basic goodness of the earth (Gen. 1). Many feminist authors bring together an analysis of the interlocking patterns of domination that have been used against women, non-elite men, and the earth itself in patriarchal cultures, especially in the West. As Rosemary Radford Ruether wrote in her introduction to *Gaia and God: An Ecofeminist Theology of Earth Healing*:

Ecology and feminism, brought together in the unified perspective of ecofeminism, provide the critical perspective from which I seek to evaluate the heritage of Western Christian culture. The goal of this quest is earth healing, a healed relationship between men and women, between classes and nations, and between humans and earth. Such healing is possible only through recognition and transformation of the way in which Western culture, enshrined in part in Christianity, has justified such domination.[41]

Where we may go with this latest incarnation of the "great work" that feminists have been engaged in for almost two hundred years has yet to be discovered. Wherever that turns out to be, the voices and works of feminist authors and activists will have made invaluable contributions along the way.

Notes

1. For a discussion of the dating of the Confessions, see James J. O'Donnell, Augustine: Confessions, 3 vols. (New York: Clarendon Press, 1992) (vol. 1, Introduction and Commentary; vol. 2, Commentary on Books 1–7; vol. 3, Commentary on Books 1–8), 1:xli–xlii. There O'Donnell argues for reading the Confessions "as a work written entirely in 397 (vol. 1, xli).

2. The work of Peter Brown deserves particular mention for both the depth of his scholarship and the elegance and vitality of his writing. The starting point for all discussions of Augustine's life remains Brown's unsurpassed biography, Augustine of Hippo (Berkeley and Los Angeles: University of California Press, 1969; 2d ed. with supplementary essay, 2000). See also Peter Brown, The World of Late Antiquity (New York: Harcourt Brace Jovanovich, 1980).

3. James J. O'Donnell, Augustine (Boston: Twayne, 1985); Augustine: Confessions, vols. 1–3; Augustine: A New Biography (New York: HarperCollins, 2005).

4. For a sampler of the scholarly discussions about the style, contents, and import of the Confessions, readers may consult Brown, Augustine of Hippo, chap. 16, "The 'Confessions,'" 158–81. Brown notes: "The Confessions are a masterpiece of strictly intellectual autobiography. Augustine communicates such a sense of intense personal involvement in the ideas that he is handling, that we are made to forget that is an exceptionally difficult book. Augustine paid his audience of spiritales the great (perhaps unmerited) compliment of talking to them, as if they were as steeped in Neo-Platonic philosophy as himself" (167). For an incisive discussion of the various views concerning the historicity of the Confessions, see O'Donnell, Augustine (1985), 66–69. O'Donnell give some pertinent advice to the reader of the Confessions: "With Book 10, the reader must give up all hope of concluding that the Confessions is autobiography in any conventional sense. What narrative line there had been is lost altogether and a more complex literary strategy obtrudes its presence upon the reader. . . . The place to begin to seek an authentic reading of this work is still with the fact of prayer" (76). See also O'Donnell, Augustine: Confessions, vol. 1, on recent debates about the Confessions, especially the relationship of books 1–9 to the last four, books 10–13 (xxii–xxxii); on the structure of Confessions; and for O'Donnell's comments that not only is the work about Augustine, more impor-

tant, it is about God and the grand orchestration of God calling all humanity back to himself: "In this way the work is both itself an act of confession, and at the same time a model and pattern for other acts of confession, by Augustine and by his readers, at other times and places. There is no paradox in suggesting that this intricate interplay of images and patterns is both the culmination of Augustine's theological mediations and at the same time a feat possible in the fourth century only for someone who had read Plotinus, and read him very well" (xli). For the biographical elements in the *Confessions*, see O'Donnell, *Augustine: A New Biography*, 37–41; for the overall composition, tone, method, and what Augustine said and chose not to say in his work, see 63–70. As O'Donnell writes, "The *Confessions* aren't about Augustine, they're about his god. Everything he wrote comes back to that obsession, even (or rather especially) this triumph of self-absorption. . . . One book, two readings, theological and autobiographical. To sketch this duality will be one way of trying to do justice to the many-sidedness of the book, making it harder to forget that books are often a good deal more complicated than their authors imagine" (63). For other readings of *Confessions* as narrative plus some sort of "autobiography" and for the enormous influence of his text, see, for example, Elizabeth de Mijolla, *Autobiographical Quests: Augustine, Montaigne, Rousseau, and Wordsworth* (Charlottesville: University of Virginia Press, 1994), esp. chap. 1, "Augustine: *Confessions*," 13–45. De Mijolla writes, "Truth assured—and the scriptural phrases, figures, and forms found for them—Augustine achieves what few autobiographers attempt: the complete explanation of a life. In the *Confessions* nothing is fortuitous, nothing gratuitous, and what is mysterious is only so to Augustine, God having reasons for the least to the greatest event in his life. . . . Making what is known of God's omnipotence stand in place of what is unknown to man's limited cognizance, Augustine's explanation of his life is valid for every Christian life. The Scriptures grant the truths, at once theological and autobiographical, that are to suffice for the faithful" (45). See also Franciose Lionnet, *Autobiographical Voices: Race, Gender, Self-Portraiture* (Ithaca: Cornell University Press, 1989), in which the author reads Augustine (and Nietzsche) "not to use them as male paradigms or antimodels to be criticized and refuted: I want to examine how dimensions of their work that might be called feminine tend to be either ignored or coded in reference to a more "masculine" and hierarchical framework. . . . My reading of Augustine will thus lead to the deconstruction of gender as we commonly understand it in contemporary terms" (19). Lionnet's work is but one example of the multiple readings and uses to which Augustine's text has been put by either appropriating or deconstructing its status as, what Lionnet calls, an *archtexte* (37).

5. Augustine, *Confessions*, trans. Henry Chadwick (New York: Oxford University Press, 1992), 9.2.4 (all subsequent citations are from this translation unless otherwise noted).

6. Augustine, *On Free Choice of the Will*, trans. Anna S. Benjamin and L. H. Hackstaff (New York: Bobbs-Merrill, 1964), 2.2.39.

7. For an analysis of Augustine's role in the controversies with the Donatists, see Brown, *Augustine of Hippo*, 212–80 and W. H. C. Frend, *The Donatist Church: A Movement of Protest in Roman North Africa* (Oxford: Oxford University Press, 1952); see also Garry Wills, *Saint Augustine*, Penguin Lives Series (New York: Viking Penguin, 1999), 101–13.

8. Jerome, *Letter 123,16*, in *Jerome's Letters*, trans. Jerome Labourt (Paris: Société d'Edition Les Belles Lettres, 1961), 93.

9. Eugene TeSelle, "Pelagius and Pelagianism," in *Augustine Through the Ages*, ed. Allan D. Fitzgerald (Grand Rapids, Mich.: Eerdmans, 1999), 633–40.

10. Augustine, *The Spirit and the Letter* (412); *Against Julian* (423, six books); *Against Julian* (429–30, unfinished at the time of Augustine's death in 430); *Nature and Grace* (413); and a collection of at least twelve other shorter works, for example, *Guilt and Remission of Sins* (411), *Proceedings Against Pelagius* (417), *Marriage and Concupiscence* (419–21), *Grace of Christ and Original Sin* (418), *Grace and Free Will* (426), and *The Predestination of the Saints* (429). For a representative sample of Augustine's writings against the Pelagians, see also Elizabeth Clark, ed., *St. Augustine on Marriage and Sexuality* (Washington, D.C.: Catholic University of America Press, 1996), 71–105. As with so many

of Augustine's works, the secondary literature is extensive. Here are a few good starting points: TeSelle, "Pelagius and Pelagianism," 633–40, including an excellent bibliography, and Jaroslav Pelikan, *The Christian Tradition I: The Emergence of the Catholic Tradition* (Chicago: University of Chicago Press, 1970), esp. chap. 6, "Nature and Grace," with particular references to the Pelagian controversies, 297–307, 312–22. James J. O'Donnell covers substantive points in the controversy; see *Augustine: A New Biography*, 261–78, 281–86.

11. Augustine, *Letter* 228, in Saint Augustine, *Letters*, trans. Wilfrid Parsons (New York: Fathers of the Church, 1956), 144.

12. For an excellent discussion and analysis of the legal aspects of the lives of girls and women, see Jane F. Gardner, *Women in Roman Law and Society* (London: Croom Helm, 1986), esp. chaps. 2–4 on the guardianship of women and on marriage; for the examples of the changes in Roman law, see 6, 20–22, 45–47.

13. Augustine writes a lengthy analysis of his youthful prank, which he uses as the occasion to meditate on larger questions of the pride, envy, and emptiness that often accompany sinning. The fact of having companions in the deed leads him to observe, "Had I been alone I would not have done it—I remember my state of mind to be thus at the time—alone I would have never done it. Therefore my love in the act was to be associated with the gang in whose company I did it" (2.8.16). An early and insightful example of what I call (to my students' chagrin) "pear pressure."

14. See also Brown, *Augustine of Hippo*, 21, 54, 90, on Augustine's patron Romanianus and their ongoing association and O'Donnell *Augustine: A New Biography*, 10, 17, 44, 89.

15. See also Monica's participation in Augustine's early dialogues at Cassiciacum, esp. *The Happy Life*.

16. For an analysis of precisely this dilemma of Augustine's own making, see O'Donnell, *Augustine: A New Biography*, 74–78.

17. For a more complete discussion of how a man of Augustine's class and ambition would have considered the relationship he had with his concubine, see Brown, *Augustine of Hippo*, 61–63, 88–90. See also O'Donnell, *Augustine: Confessions*, 2:383–85 and O'Donnell, *Augustine: A New Biography*, 38, 49.

18. Rebecca West, *St. Augustine* (Edinburgh: Peter Davies, 1933), 34.

19. For an account of Ambrose's selection as bishop of Milan in 347 C.E. by the congregation in the cathedral, see Henri Daniel-Rops, *The Church of Apostles and Martyrs*, vol. 2 (Garden City, N.Y.: Image Doubleday, 1962), 346–47.

20. Brown, *Augustine of Hippo*, 212.

21. Cyprian, *On Unity*, 5, as cited in Brown, *Augustine of Hippo*, 212.

22. For an excellent review of the literature on these topics over the past three decades, see E. Ann Matter's article "Women," in *Augustine Through the Ages: An Encyclopedia*, ed. Allan D. Fitzgerald (Grand Rapids, Mich.: Eerdmans, 1999), 890–92.

23. Augustine *On the Morals of the Catholic Church* 1.27.52.

24. Augustine *On the Magnitude of the Soul* 13.22.

25. Augustine *The City of God* 21.10.

26. Augustine *Christian Doctrine* 1.25.26.

27. For the purposes of this Introduction, I have not entered into the debates about Augustine's views of the origin of the soul that have been generated by Robert J. O'Connell's excellent and provocative studies *Augustine's Early Theory of Man A.D. 386–391* (Cambridge, Mass.: Belknap Press of Harvard University Press, 1968) and *St. Augustine's Confessions: The Odyssey of Soul* (Cambridge, Mass.: Belknap Press of Harvard University Press, 1969).

28. Augustine *Christian Doctrine* 1.26.27.

29. George Lawless, "Augustine and Human Embodiment," in *Collectanea Augustiniana*, ed. B. Bruning, M. Lamberigts, and J. Van Houtem (Louvain: Leuven University Press, 1990), 175.

30. Ibid.

31. Susan Bordo, *Unbearable Weight: Feminism, Western Culture, and the Body* (Berkeley and Los Angeles: University of California Press, 1993), 145.

32. Kari Elisabeth Børresen, "In Defence of Augustine: How *Femina* is *Homo*," in *Collectanea Augustiniana*, ed. B. Bruning, M. Lamberigts, and J. Van Houtem (Louvain: Leuven University Press, 1990), 411–28 provides one of the more prominent examples of this strategy.

33. Clark, *St. Augustine on Marriage and Sexuality*, 8.

34. Ibid., 10.

35. Augustine *The Good of Marriage* 6.6.

36. Peter Brown, *The Body and Society: Men, Women, and Sexual Renunciation in Early Christianity* (New York: Columbia University Press, 1988), 426.

37. Mary Daly, *Beyond God the Father: Toward a Philosophy of Women's Liberation* (Boston: Beacon Press, 1973); see also *Gyn/Ecology: The Metaethics of Radical Feminism* (Boston: Beacon Press, 1978); *Pure Lust: Elemental Feminist Philosophy* (Boston: Beacon Press, 1984). For an excellent overview of the trajectory of Daly's thinking and her relationships both to Western Christianity and philosophy, see Wanda Warren Berry, "Feminist Theology: The 'Verbing' of Ultimate/Intimate Reality in Mary Daly," in *Feminist Interpretations of Mary Daly*, ed. Sarah Lucia Hoagland and Marilyn Frye (University Park: Pennsylvania State University Press, 2000), 27–54.

38. Allan D. Fitzgerald, ed., *Augustine Through the Ages: An Encyclopedia* (Grand Rapids, Mich.: Eerdmans, 1999), 376.

39. The term *asceticism* is derived from the Greek *ascesis*, which originally referred to the training the athlete undergoes for performance and competition.

40. Elizabeth Johnson, *Women, Earth, and Creator Spirit* (New York: Paulist Press, 1993), 27–28, quoted in Mary Ann Hinsdale and Phyllis H. Kaminski, eds., *Women and Theology: Annual Publication of the College Theology Society*, vol. 40 (Maryknoll, N.Y.: Orbis Press, 1994), 267–68.

41. Rosemary Radford Ruether, *Gaia and God: An Ecofeminist Theology of Earth Healing* (San Francisco: Harper and Row, 1992), 1, quoted in Hinsdale and Kaminski, *Women and Theology*, 268.

1

Augustine: Sexuality, Gender, and Women

Rosemary Radford Ruether

There are few lives of any historical person that have been so often re-counted, analyzed, and psychoanalyzed as that of Augustine. This is largely the result of his work the *Confessions*, as well as of the accurate perception that much of his teaching on sexuality, sin, grace, and predes-tination is heavily conditioned by his personal experience. Any discus-sion, therefore, of Augustine's views on sexuality, gender, and women must include some discussion of his personal journey.

Augustine was born in 354 C.E. in the North African town of Tagaste of a pious Catholic mother and a pagan father. Augustine seems to have disliked his father, whose harsh, prideful, and libidinous nature reflected characteristics he wished to shun in himself. Although he would finally embrace his mother's Catholic Christianity, and even make his mother the symbol of the church and the mothering nature of God, in his youth her church represented to him a naive religiosity unworthy of his intellectual acumen. Yet Augustine was loved deeply by both parents and seen by them as the family's rising star. His father dug deeply into his pockets to invest in the education of his bright son, who was to rise through his wits from their hometown to the provincial capital of Carthage and finally the imperial cities of Rome and Milan.[1]

This educational and career trajectory meant that Augustine did not consider containing his youthful sexual urges through legal marriage to a hometown girl. Only at the end of his rise into the company of the imperial elite could he hope for a suitable marriage into a family of high rank. Thus sometime soon after he arrived in Carthage (371), Augustine settled for monogamous concubinage to a woman whom he loved, very likely herself a Catholic catechumen, but whose social origins precluded the advantageous marriage that he sought.[2] This relationship would last for about twelve years. Although Augustine would later portray it as solely a bondage to sinful lust, it was an accepted convention in his society and one his parents understood.

In the first year of their relationship, Augustine's common-law wife bore him a son, lovingly named Adeodatus, or "gift of God." In the same year that his first and only child was born, while he pursued his higher education in Carthage, he also became an auditor with the Manicheans, a Persian sect that he believed offered deeper insights into the nature of good and evil than those he found in his mother's simple faith. The Manicheans promoted birth control as a way of preventing souls from being born into bodies, and it is likely that Augustine began to practice birth control at that time to prevent further children. It is notable that his concubine bore him no more children in their subsequent years of sexual congress together.[3]

After completing his studies at Carthage, Augustine became a teacher of rhetoric. His mother was distraught at his Manicheanism and refused to let him into the family home. Augustine planned his escape from her motherly demands by moving to Rome, leaving her weeping like Dido on the shores of Carthage.[4] But unlike Dido in Virgil's epic, Augustine's mother did not commit suicide but pursued her errant son to Milan, where, a few years later, she would receive the satisfaction of seeing him baptized into the Catholic faith. In Rome Augustine became the tutor of the sons of the nobility. The Roman pagan aristocracy appreciated Augustine both for his brilliance and for his heterodoxy, which put him outside the realm of their rivals, the bishops of the Catholic Church.[5]

Augustine would soon move on to the city of the most powerful of such Catholic bishops, Ambrose of Milan. By 384, at the age of thirty, Augustine was on the brink of accomplishing the goals of his upwardly mobile career. He was acclaimed as a teacher by the highest circles of society and was engaged to marry the daughter of a high-ranking Milanese Catholic family, but she was not yet twelve years old—the legal age for girls to marry under Roman law. In such a marriage there was no question of intellectual companionship; it was only another stepping-stone in this "brilliant career." His concubine was sent packing back to North Africa, vowing her fidelity to the relationship by entering continent life. Augustine, unable to contain his sexual needs while he waited for his bride-to-be to come of age, took a short-term mistress.[6]

By this time, however, Augustine had also begun to listen to the sermons of Ambrose, bishop of Milan, who combined the most sophisticated philosophical education with membership in a senatorial family. Ambrose introduced Augustine to an allegorical interpretation of Scripture, which allowed the young rhetor to see that his intellectual knowledge and rhetorical training need not be offended by what he considered the barbarous language of the Christian Bible. Ambrose also promoted a stern asceticism and demanded celibacy of his clergy. In this view, sexual continence was closely linked with full commitment as a Christian.

Augustine began to struggle to commit himself to the Catholic faith and to be baptized, a decision that for him was virtually identical with the renunciation of sexual relations, including the jettisoning of his advantageous marriage and resignation from his imperial appointment in Milan. His feelings of deep impotence as he sought to use his intellect to master his unruly will and feelings, "bent on these lower things," would come to define his theology of the fallen self. He would vehemently defend his views, in conflict with theological rivals, such as Pelagius, who maintained the freedom of the will. Augustine believed that it was only through a direct intervention of God in divine grace, which broke his self-will and gave him the power of obedience to the will of God, that he was able to make the leap of conversion to Christ and renounce sexual relations.

Augustine describes in detail his frantic efforts to make a decision against all his "old attachments. They plucked at my garment of flesh and whispered, 'Are you going to dismiss us?'" He imaged Continence as a chaste, beautiful woman standing at the other side of the barrier and beckoning him to cross over:

> She stretched out loving hands to embrace me. . . . With her were countless boys and girls, great numbers of the young and people of all ages, staid widows and women still virgins in old age. And in their midst was Continence herself, not barren but a fruitful mother of children, of joys born to you, O Lord, her Spouse. She smiled at me to give me courage, as though she were saying, "Can you not do what these men and these women do? Do you think they find the strength to do it in themselves and not in the Lord their God? It was the Lord their God who gave me to them. Why do you try to stand in your own strength and fail? Cast yourself upon God and have no fear . . . for he will welcome you and cure you of your ills."[7]

Augustine felt himself filled with shame, flinging himself down in a garden and weeping. Then hearing the voice of a child singing, "Take it and read," he took up the Scriptures to read the first passage that came to his eyes, lighting upon the passage from Romans 13:14: "Arm yourself with the Lord Jesus Christ and spend no more thought on nature or nature's appetites." At reading these words he felt transformed by "the light of confidence that flooded into my heart and all darkness of doubt was dispelled."[8]

The theological implications of this conversion experience would only gradually reshape Augustine's still-Platonic theology and philosophy. In the first stage of his appropriation of his new Catholic identity, he retired with like-minded friends, as well as his teenaged son and his mother, to a country estate, where they engaged in philosophical discourse. He had now gained a new respect for his mother, whose "simple piety" was able to hold its own in such educated dialogue. His first Platonizing writings, such as the *Soliloquies*, *On the Happy Life*, and *On the Immortality of the Soul*, stem from this period of "Christian leisure" at Cassiciacum.

He soon made plans, however, to return to his hometown in Tagaste, there to found some kind of monastic community. While staying in the port city of Ostia in preparation for the journey home, he and his mother, Monica, experienced a moment of joint transcendence in which they soared mentally into the heavens and touched divine Wisdom:

As the flame of love burned stronger in us and raised us higher toward the eternal God, our thoughts ranged over the whole compass of material things in their various degrees up to the heavens themselves from which the sun and the moon and the stars shine down on earth. Higher still we climbed, thinking and speaking all the while in wonder at all you have made. At length we came to our own souls and passed beyond them to that place of everlasting plenty. There life is that Wisdom by which all these things that we know are made. . . . And while we spoke of eternal Wisdom, longing for it and straining for it with all the strength of our hearts, for one fleeing instant we reached out and touched it.[9]

Monica took ill and died a few days later. Augustine's son, Adeodatus, died a few years later, perhaps in 390.[10] Although Augustine intended to live in a monastic community, he soon found himself asked to preach and then to be ordained by the local bishop. By 395 he had been raised to the episcopacy along with several of his learned friends, who had returned with him from their studies to join his ascetic, philosophical circle. Augustine quickly assumed the role of a leading bishop in North Africa, and this role would shape the second half of his life until his death in 430.[11]

Unlike other ascetic leaders of his day, such as Jerome and Rufinus, Augustine had no women friends.[12] His only female mentor had been his mother, acknowledged only at the end of her life. While his relations with his male colleagues were warm and heartfelt, his few letters to women show him as reserved and authoritarian with the female sex.[13] Like many men of his day, he assumed that true *amicitia* (friendship) was possible only between equals, that is, between men. Augustine considered that God's only purpose in creating women was for reproduction, since for any other task a man would have made a more fit companion than a woman.[14] He seemed unable to imagine a relation to a woman that would not involve sexual attraction, and he strictly forbade his priests from ever speaking to a woman alone, even a relative, a practice he himself followed as well.

Augustine's mature theological anthropology would be hammered out in a series of controversies with enemies: First, there were his old confreres, the Manicheans, with whom he sparred over the nature of evil. Then there were the Donatists, who represented the popular North African church that for more than a hundred years had claimed to be the

true church of the martyrs against the Catholic Church as the church of
the empire. Augustine would argue with them about the true nature of
the church, universal and mixed, rather than pure and local, and about
the validity of the sacraments apart from the worthiness of the minister.
Finally, he would resort to coercion with the help of the state to "compel
them to come in" to what he regarded as the one true church.[15] Then
there were the Pelagians, who challenged Augustine's construction of
original sin, the bondage of the will, grace and predestination, and his
peculiar interpretation of sexual lust.

In an effort to clarify his own understanding of human nature in relation to gender, sex, and sin, Augustine would return again and again to
Genesis 1–3. Augustine had dealt with these passages in his *Two Books of
Genesis Against the Manichees* in 388–89, and then again in 393 in an
attempted commentary on Genesis, which was never completed; he
broke off his exegesis right before Genesis 1:27, on the image of God,
male and female.[16] He returned to these biblical texts in the final three
books of the *Confessions* and then in a monumental work in twelve books,
On Genesis Literally Interpreted, which he worked at from 404 to 420.[17]
He also dealt with the first three chapters of Genesis in books 11–14 of
The City of God, written by 417–18. He attempted final clarifications of
his teaching on sex and sin in the writings of his old age against the
Pelagian-leaning bishop, Julian of Eclanum, who claimed that Augustine,
in making sexual pleasure evil made creation itself evil, thereby showing
that he was still a Manichean.[18] Augustine's reflections on these themes
are also scattered in his treatises on marriage, on virginity, on adulterous
marriage, and on marriage and concupiscence.

In his early writings on Genesis against the Manicheans Augustine
followed the Origenist tradition, itself rooted in the Platonic biblical exegesis of the Hellenistic Jew Philo.[19] The human being was seen as first
created as a spiritual unity without division into male and female. The
image of God refers, not to the physical body, but to the "interior man"
or intellect through which humans rule over the lower creation and con-
template eternal things. Male and female originally meant the union of
mind and soul, *sapientia* and *scientia*, the mind or wisdom being masculine, and the soul, which mediates sense knowledge, feminine. In their
original harmonious union the male part would have ruled over the female part of the inner self. Together this unitary human being would
have reproduced mentally, creating "spiritual offspring of intelligible and

immortal joys." Only after the Fall did sexual differentiation appear and "carnal fecundity" linked to sin and death arise.[20]

In his later writings Augustine moved away from this Platonic approach, insisting that Adam and Eve were created from the beginning with real physical and sexually differentiated bodies. Gender differentiation, sexual intercourse, and physical offspring were part of God's original design for creation, not just characteristics that appeared only after sin and as a remedy for mortality.[21] But he still claimed that God first created, before the physical creation, a nongendered Idea of Humanity, the intellectual "image of God" found in all humans, male and female.[22]

But in the actual production of the human being, God created the male first and then made the female from the man's side to indicate the relationship of superiority and subordination by which the genders are to relate to each other in the social order.[23] Although women too have the intellect soul, socially they represent sense knowledge (scientia), which is activated only under the command of the male ruling mind. For Augustine gender hierarchy is a part of the original design of creation, not something that happened only after the Fall.

In paradise Adam and Eve would not have died, not because their bodies were not physical, because their bodies would have been so united with the intellectual part of their souls in union with God that the body would have been prevented from dying. Adam and Eve were intended by God to have sexual intercourse and to reproduce physical offspring through whom the full number of the human community, intended for eternal life, would have been born over time. Adam would have sown his seed in Eve without any experience of lust or concupiscence as a rational act fully under the control of his mind, as a farmer sows his seed in a field.[24] Moreover Eve would have remained virginal in both intercourse and childbirth, never losing her hymen or "bodily integrity," a notion that suggests something less than a fully corporeal process of sex and birth. Augustine would explain how unfallen Eve and Mary could give birth without losing their virginity (hymen) by suggesting a similarity to the way the risen Christ could pass through doors without opening them, again suggesting a ghostly rather than physical body.[25]

But this lust-free generation never happened, because the creation of Eve was followed straightaway by the Fall. Although Adam and Eve were created with the ability to obey God and hence not sin, they used their free will to disobey God. The serpent, which represents the enticement to disobedience to God and the preference for selfish desires, first approached Eve, because as a woman she had less rationality and self-control and was closer to the "lower" or female part of the soul; hence she was more easily deceived. Following I Timothy 2:14 Augustine claims that Adam was not deceived. He knew better, but he consented to go along with Eve as an act of kindly companionship, lest she be left alone outside paradise.[26]

Although Eve's deception initiated the fall of humanity, it could not have happened without Adam's consent, since Adam represents the intellect and commanding part of the soul. For Augustine, the sensuous part of the soul may be tempted by desire, but this desire cannot be carried into action without the consent of the intellect. Thus Adam and Eve are both culpable, but in different ways. Adam's particular sin lay in losing male rank by obeying his wife (his lower self), rather than making his wife obey him as her "head."[27] Thus we see that, despite Augustine's theoretical position that both Adam and Eve have intellects, when referred to as a couple, men and women are continually treated as representing hierarchically graded "parts" of the self: mind and body, intellect and passions, superior and inferior, the one commanded to rule and other to obey. Or to put it another way, the male is a whole human being with both intellect and desires, but commanded to control the desires through the intellect. But the female is treated as though she were predominately the lower part of the self, commanded to be under male control and rebellious if they desire to be in charge of themselves and to make their own decisions.

The question of whether women were made in the image of God was debated in Augustine's time, and several prominent church fathers, such as Ambrosiaster, had decided that they were not.[28] Part of the problem was how to interpret an apparent contradiction between two key texts: Genesis 1:27, which seemed to give women the image of God with men, and I Corinthians 11:7, where Paul declared that men should not cover their heads because they are the image of God, whereas women should cover their heads because they are only a secondary reflection of the image of God in the male.

This debate was aggravated by two meanings given to the concept of "image of God," one having to do with the human as representative of God's sovereignty over the created world and the second with the idea that the soul reflects the nature of the divine essence. This second aspect was linked to the intellect, seen as a reflection of the divine Mind. Moreover, if women were not in the image of God, there was the question of whether she was redeemable at all. But the church had always assumed that women were redeemable. From the first days of the church's existence, it had baptized women equally with men.

Augustine "solved" this problem by splitting women into two perspectives. As *homo* women too were human, had a share in the intellect, hence were made in the image of God and had a redeemable soul. But this intellect remained somehow latent for Augustine, a possession that women could not use autonomously as an agent in their own right. As Calvin was to make clear in his exegesis of this same text, that aspect of the "image" that has to do with rule over others was not given to women.[29] In her bodily, sexual, and social nature woman is not *homo*, but *femina*, and as such represents the lower, sense perception part of the self and its temptations to sensual pleasure. Presumably woman as *homo* should keep her own lower self under control through her intellect. But socially she is *femina* and thus both symbolizes that lower part of the self that the male should keep under control in his own body and also is that lower self separated out from the man and standing under his necessary control.[30]

Thus, as *femina*, women are not the image of God, but represent the sense world that should be dominated by male headship. Augustine would express this notion of woman in his treatise *On the Trinity*, as he struggled to resolve the contradiction between the Genesis text that gave women the image of God and that of I Corinthians 11, which denied it:

> In what sense, therefore, are we to understand the Apostle that the man is the image of God and consequently is forbidden to cover his head but the woman is not and on this account is commanded to do so? The solution lies, I think, in what I have already said when discussing the nature of the human mind; namely, that the woman together with her husband is the image of God, so that whole substance is one image. But when she is assigned as a help-mate, a function that pertains to her alone, then she is not the image of God; but as far as the man is concerned he is by himself alone the image of God, just as fully and completely as when he and the woman are joined together in one.[31]

Thus, although women are also acknowledged to "have" an intellect in themselves, they never can represent the image of God by themselves, but represent the lower self that makes up one whole only under the male, while the male stands for the image of God both autonomously and as ruling husband over the woman. The total androcentrism of this anthropology is stunning.

Augustine believed that, because of the Fall, the human race had lost both its original immortality and its freedom of the will. It was plunged into sin and death, manifest in a profound disorientation of the mind's control over its will and desires.[32] No longer do the sexual parts of "man" (that is, the male genitalia; he never explains the counterpart in women) move in calm obedience to the mind, but, rather, the fallen body experiences a war "between the law in the members that wars against the law of the mind."[33] In sexual attraction and intercourse, the male experiences the erection of his penis, which is not (as it would have been in paradise) under the control of his mind.[34] The act of intercourse itself only takes place together with concupiscence or a "filthy rush" of pleasure.

The erection of the penis that happens spontaneously, outside mental control, expresses the subjugation of the mind to its lower urges. This is, for Augustine, the very picture and prime manifestation of that penalty of the Fall by which the masculine is subjugated to the inferior feminine. In sexual activity the male mind falls under the control of its inferior self, the desires. Since no sexual act can be carried out without concupiscence, for Augustine this meant that every sexual act is both sinful in itself and is the means by which original sin of Adam is transmitted to his descendents.[35] One has the contradiction that this sinful disorientation of mind to body is manifest only in the male body, but it is women who are seen as "stimulating" and hence causing this sinful concupiscence in the male.

Thus the woman, but not the man, should veil herself to prevent her from causing this sinful response in the male. Augustine assumes but never asks if women feel any pleasure in this sexual act, and what it would mean for their sinfulness if they did not! Indeed, basic to Augustine's treatment of women and the "feminine" is that he is never able to really think about women as persons in their own right, but only in their relation to the male, either as rightly subjugated and submissive to the male or as wrongly tempting the male to descend to his lower self, which she represents.

Augustine sees this relation of male ruling intellect to feminine desire as intrinsic to the order of the cosmos as God intended. Thus it belongs to the original order of things. But in paradise woman would have willingly submitted to male control in a harmonious union, just as the soul

in its male and female parts were united as one. Thus the Fall is fundamentally a "disordering" of right relations of male over female, mind over
body, with the desires subverting the mind. The libidinous woman out of
the control of male authority and acting on her own is the prime social
expression of this disordered state, mirroring the dominion of desire over
reason within the male.

Thus the good Christian woman must coercively subject her own desires, as well as guard herself from the eyes of men.[36] She must always be
aware that in herself she represents the temptation of desire and hence of
sin. Moreover men have the obligation to restore right order by coercively
subjugating women when necessary; that is, if women behave independently. Augustine even suggests that a husband is occasionally justified in
giving an unruly wife a beating. Moreover, a wife at marriage should hand
over her financial assets to her husband and never seek to make any
decisions on her own, without his consent.[37] Like the "good feminine" of
the lower part of the soul, she is there to execute the orders of her husband, not to initiate anything on her own.

Augustine prefers the image of the relation of husband to wife as master to slave, *dominus* to *ancilla*, a marked departure from the growing
cultural view of his time, which thought of husband and wife more as
senior and junior partners. He also flies in the face of legal changes in the
Roman practice of marriage, which did not hand over the government of
the father over his daughter (*pater potestas*) to the husband in marriage
(marriage *sine manu*) but allowed the wife to remain a member of her
own lineage. This type of marriage both allowed the woman to retain
control of financial assets she brought into the marriage and also forbade
the treatment of a citizen wife as a slave; namely, in beating her. Thus
Augustine's view of the husband-wife relation sharply worsened the condition of woman as wife in Christian marriage, in comparison with legal
and social patterns of his time.[38]

The good Christian wife distinguished herself by her total abnegation
of her will to that of her husband, even if he be violent and ill tempered.
Here Augustine's picture of his own mother, Monica, in relation to his
father is seen as exemplary of the ideal.[39] However, Augustine did not
believe that women should passively acquiesce to the sexual affairs of
their husbands, but he hints that the wife herself may be responsible for
such affairs. Marriage should channel and control the male libido by
keeping it tied to one "vessel," and if this does not happen, the wife has
failed.[40] A wife is never allowed to withdraw from sexual relations with

the husband on her own, without his consent, even if she wishes to adopt a life of continence.[41] This anticipates the medieval view that a wife must put her duties to be sexually available to her husband over her own health or moral aspirations. She should submit to the sexual demands even of a leprous husband.[42]

Augustine had particular problems with the ascetic woman who claimed independence through her choice of continence. On the one hand, he greatly extolled continence and believed that the best marriage was one that had sex only for procreation or in which the partners even vowed permanent continence to live as "brother and sister." But this is allowable only if both agree. This is the only place where the relation of man and wife is mutual, for the man also cannot make this decision without the consent of his wife. But a woman who makes such a decision without the consent of her husband is doubly wrong, denying her husband both the "marriage debt" and hence potentially driving him into fornication, and also refusing the due submission of a wife to her "head."

Here Augustine departs from a long-standing but contested pattern in Christianity, in which the woman who chooses virginity was seen as gaining a certain autonomy from male and family control, able to dispose of her life and assets independently. Popular Christian lore was filled with tales of women, such as Thecla in the *Acts of Paul and Thecla*, who rejected marriage for virginity and thereby gained the right to travel and even preach and baptize.[43] Male church leaders had long been ambivalent about such independence in female ascetics, both affirming their choice as one of higher holiness and yet trying to rein in their independence. In Augustine's day many such female ascetics came from rich and noble families, and so the bishop had to be circumspect in his treatment of them, since he was often dependent on them for patronage and gifts to the church.

Augustine manifests some of this ambivalence in his letters to such rich and highborn ascetic women as Albina, mother of the ascetic pair Melania Junior and Pinianus (Melania's husband), who had fled to North Africa after the sacking of Rome and whom some of his congregants sought to waylay as patrons of the local church.[44] But his general principles are clear. Virginity is a higher good than marriage, and marital continence is superior to sex in marriage, but such decisions are allowable to women only if authorized by their husband or the bishop, the new *pater familias* of the Christian community. Moreover, the Christian ascetic manifests her continence of heart, not only in her outward dress, which veiled her body from male gaze, but also in her total humility and submission to those in authority over her. She should not appear in public but maintain strict segregation in the private world of home or monastery. An ascetic woman who claims independence, who travels about on her own and makes decisions about her own money, manifests thereby that she is no true virgin at heart. Her monastic robes only conceal a libidinous whore at heart, if not in fact.[45]

In the late fourth century a sharp debate broke out in the Latin Church over the relative status of virginity and marriage. There were sharp attacks against the popular new asceticism that was drawing the flower of the youth of the Roman elite to choose virginity over marriage and hence to fail to reproduce the male lineage on which Roman administration and imperial rule depended. About 382 a Latin cleric named Helvidius wrote a tract in which he claimed that both marriage and celibacy were of equal status. This equality was exemplified in Mary, Jesus's mother, who conceived Jesus virginally, but after his birth had normal marital relations with her husband, Joseph, and bore him those children whom the gospels refer as the brothers and sisters of Jesus.[46] This view conflicted with popular church tradition, which made these brothers and sisters half-siblings of Jesus, children of Joseph but not of Mary. Mary was believed to have remained virginal, not only in the conception of Jesus, but also in his birth and thereafter (*in partu* and *post partum*), having taken a vow of virginity in childhood.[47]

Jerome took up the cudgels against Helvidius, using strained exegesis to insist that the brothers and sister of Jesus were cousins, children of a sister of Mary (improbably also named Mary). Thus Joseph also remained a lifelong virgin, acting only as guardian of Mary, Jesus's ever virgin mother. Jerome was particularly indignant that marriage and virginity could be seen as equally holy. He painted a repellent view of married life for women, filled with the "prattling of infants, noisy clamoring of the whole household, the clinging of children to [the wife's] neck, the computing of expenses," and the flagrant lust of the husband's parties.[48] Jerome insisted that holiness was possible only when marital sex was given up and women withdrew into a life of prayer and mortification. This did not imply leaving the home, but converting the home into a quasi-monastery, as many of Jerome's noble ascetic women friends, such as Marcella, had done. Such married women "imitate the chastity of virgins within the very intimacy of marriage."[49]

Another challenge to the superiority of celibacy over marriage came from one Jovinian, himself a monk, who objected to the teaching shared by Jerome, Ambrose, and Augustine that the sexually continent would have a higher place in heaven than faithful baptized married people. Jovinian insisted on the equality of the community of the saved. Virgins, widows, and married people would all receive the same reward in heaven if they had been equally faithful.[50] A common proof text for the thesis of ascetic leaders that there would be a higher reward in heaven for the sexually continent was Mark 4:20. Here it is said that the "good soil" on which seed of the gospel falls are those who "hear the word and accept it and bear fruit, thirty, sixty and a hundred fold." Jerome, Ambrose and Augustine all interpreted this text to mean that virgins are the ones who bear fruit a hundredfold and continent widows sixtyfold, while faithful husbands and wives could expect at best only thirtyfold.[51] As David Hunter has recently shown, as united as Ambrose, Jerome, and Augustine were in defending the doctrine of Mary's perpetual virginity (as the exemplar of the value of virginity over the married state), these writers' tone, emphases, and uses of Scripture in their arguments differed to some extent. For example, in Hunter's study of their uses of Psalm 45 in these debates with Helvidius and Jovinian, he shows that Ambrose and Jerome weigh in by emphasizing the analogies among the asceticism of the virgin bride, the church as the bride of Christ and consecrated virgins as brides of Christ. Augustine uses the same texts to strike an ecclesiastical tone that includes all the baptized as members (or brides) of Christ under the authority of the bishops.[52]

Jovinian's tract was a frontal attack on this hierarchy of holiness. His views were roundly rebuked by all three church leaders and condemned at synods in Rome and Milan. Jerome wrote a rebuttal of Jovinian's views that became an embarrassment to his colleagues because of its satiric denigration of marriage. Jerome conceded that marriage was still permitted in the Christian era, but insisted that it had been superceded by the higher glory of virginity, which anticipates the heavenly state. Thus he left the impression that it was impossible to live a genuinely Christian life and not abstain from marital sex.[53]

Augustine sought to repair the negative impression created by Jerome's intemperate defense of the superiority of virginity and continent widowhood over marriage. He was also attempting to establish a middle ground between Jovinian's views on the equality of celibacy and marriage and the Manichaean and other Christian ascetical views that rejected marriage.[54] In his treatise On the Good of Marriage, he tried a more measured approach, defending marriage as still allowable, although no longer necessary, within the Christian era. Marriage is good by reason of three "goods" that it brings. These are progeny, constraint of concupiscence, and sacrament. Marriage's highest good is the producing of children, but it also channels the sexual urge into faithful wedlock, thus avoiding the worse evil of fornication. Marriage also symbolizes the union of Christ and the church and thus expresses the sacramental bond of the Christian community with Christ.[55]

However, Augustine viewed the sexual act as corrupted by concupiscence even in marriage and thus innately sinful, although forgiven or allowed if undertaken within marriage and for the sake of progeny.[56] Original sin was transmitted through the sexual act because of its innate sinfulness.[57] Sex in marriage was also allowable for those unable to reproduce, since it had, as a secondary good, the channeling of concupiscence, thus avoiding the greater evil of fornication.[58] But marital sex was never allowed for pleasure for its own sake, when conception was intentionally avoided; that is, through contraception, a matter on which Augustine probably had some considerable experience, as suggested earlier. Such marital sex purely for pleasure was "pure lust" and equivalent to fornication.

Augustine never allows that sex itself could be an expression of love. He can only think of sex in marriage as the lowering of the male to his inferior self, "dragging the manly mind down from its heavenly heights to wallow in the flesh." In a startling exegesis of the command in the Sermon on the Mount to love one's enemies, Augustine compared this to the love a husband has for his wife. Husbands are told "in one and the same woman to love the creature of God whom he desires to be renewed, but to hate the corruptible and mortal conjugal connection and sexual intercourse; to love in her what is characteristic of a human being, but to hate what belongs to her as a wife."[59] Thus the wife is an enemy of the man's true self. Augustine imagines that husband and wives might eventually become friends when they grow older and give up sex, but the sexual act itself is always thought of by Augustine as an expression of enmity between the couple, not of love.

Like Jerome, Augustine believes that marriage, although allowed for these modest "goods," is no longer commanded or given divine blessing in the Christian era. When God created humanity at the beginning, he blessed reproduction to allow the full number of human beings from which Christ is to be born.[60] Indeed, the patriarchs of the Old Testament were even allowed multiple wives, to hurry up this process. Augustine solemnly declares that the patriarchs derived no pleasure from this multiple sex with several wives, for they were just doing their duty as commanded by God. Moreover, polygamy is allowable, although polyandry is not, because there can be multiplicity in those who are subjugated but must be unity in the master who commands.[61] The analogy of husband to wife is that of master to slave. A master can have many slaves; a slave cannot have many masters.

But with the birth of Christ the new era of the virginal has dawned in the last era of world history, anticipating the culmination of this temporal world and the dawn of the eternal age, "when there will be no more marriage or giving in marriage." Thus reproduction was no longer necessary, since the work of the church was to convert those who were presently living. The state of life that is truly Christian, anticipating salvation in the world to come, is virginity.[62] Thus Augustine too, although in more sober language than Jerome, suggests that virginity is not only better than marriage, but also that, in some sense, marriage is sub-Christian, while virginity or sexual continence represents those spiritual offspring reborn in the fertile womb of Mother Church.

This view that virginity is the ideal Christian state of life leaves no room for doubt in Augustine's mind that Mary must have remained a virgin her whole life. She could not have "regressed" to the lower state of marriage. For Augustine, Mary alone is the one unambiguously good woman. In her the feminine lower soul is totally at the service of God.[63] She recapitulates Eve by turning around the sin of Eve. As Eve would have been able to do if she had not become a sinner, Mary conceives and gives birth virginally. Although conceived in sin, she was cleansed in the womb of actual sin, so she led a sinless life.[64] Augustine would not have accepted the idea of the Immaculate Conception. Since Mary was the product of her parent's sexual act, she, like all humans except Jesus, inherited sin from her parents. Mary is the way that Augustine brings women into salvation, since Jesus's maleness means that he represents males, and women cannot represent him. Mary is the mother only of Jesus's humanity, and Augustine avoids the title "Mother of God," which might suggest that her motherhood includes his divinity.

But Mary is also spiritually Christ's spouse and thus represents the church as spouse of Christ and mother of spiritual offspring. For Augustine, praise for the fruitfulness of motherhood has been transferred entirely to the church. Actual mothers bear children in sin, transmitting sin to their offspring, and so only in the church is there true motherhood where those born in sin are reborn spiritually. Yet Mary, for Augustine, represents *scientia*, not *sapientia*.[65] *Sapientia*, or Wisdom, for Augustine is the masculine part of the soul, despite its feminine gender in Latin and the long tradition in Judaism and other Mediterranean religions of representing Wisdom as female. Mary as the feminine cannot represent Wisdom, but only the lower realm of sense knowledge and bodiliness, although totally subservient to the divine will.

This also means, for Augustine, that it is inconceivable to think of God as in any way feminine. God is wholly masculine-spiritual. God is pure reason and has sovereignty over lower things, containing in himself no change, emotions, or corruptibility. He creates humans out of gratuitous love, but in no way has need of them. In relation to God we are all women, needy and dependent on God, but God has no needs in himself.[66] In the *Confessions* Augustine appears to make God motherlike. Like a mothering parent God chose him from conception, sought him out, pursuing him until he was converted and came into his true home, the church, as did his own mother. But in his later writings Augustine will strictly purge his imagery of God of any mothering traits. His imagery for God became that of the strict *pater familias*, the stern father who must chastise his son for the son's own good and punishes sinners. God's love becomes punitive rather than gentle or nurturing.

Redemption, for Augustine, is finally an eschatological state in which all rebelliousness of creature against creator has been overcome. Redemption is not simply the restoration of the original state of creation but goes beyond it. The first humans were able not to sin and not to die, but the redeemed humans of the resurrection will be raised beyond the mortal body and free will. In their union with God, they will no longer be able to choose to sin. This union with God is defined, not as our choice of God, but God's sovereign choice of us (the elect few).

Since women represent and incarnate the lower realm of sense knowledge, some Christian thinkers debated whether women would be resurrected in a male body, thus losing that which linked them to sin. Augustine insists that women will be resurrected in a female body, since male and female is part of the original creation of humans, but those parts of the female body that have to do with sex and childbirth will be transformed, so they become "fitted to glory rather than to shame."[67] What Augustine had in mind is not clear. Are woman's womb, vagina, and breasts incompatible with bodily resurrection? In what way are they "transformed?" There is no comparable talk of transforming the male genitalia in the resurrected body.

Women will be in no way inferior to men in the heavenly state of life. The subjugation of women in the first creation that had to do with their sexual and maternal nature will disappear. Women who have lived the spiritual life will shine as gloriously as men, based on the inward image of God, which they were given at the original creation, but which remained hidden in postlapsarian society. Only eschatologically is gender hierarchy overcome, but at the price of the excising in women of all that has to do with their specific female functions, sex and childbearing.

But heaven is not egalitarian for Augustine. There is a new hierarchy, the hierarchy of holiness. Here perpetual virgins will receive the highest reward, continent widows next, and married people last, while sinners are condemned to eternal woe. Thus while the superiority of male over female is abolished in heaven, the hierarchy of virginity over marriage remains eternally in the ranks of the saints.

Augustine remains the classical theologian for the Western Christian tradition. His was a brilliant mind, and his voluminous writings grew from a lifetime of grappling with the relation of the Christian tradition to his own spiritual journey. His views cannot be easily dismissed. One has to come to terms with the profundity of his thought. Yet he was also deeply shaped by views of gender and social hierarchy of his times that molded the way he experienced his own body, sexuality, and social relations with men and women. Women and men in the Western Christian tradition have suffered for a millennium and a half from the ways Augustine's views on these matters have been treated as normative. We need to critique these views, not superficially, but through a deep evaluation of their underlying assumptions, to salvage what is helpful in Augustine's views, freed from the biases that have distorted the humanity of both women and men.

Notes

1. Augustine Confessions 2.3; Peter Brown, Augustine of Hippo (Berkeley and Los Angeles: University of California Press, 1967), 29–31.

2. See Kim Power, Veiled Desire: Augustine on Women (New York: Continuum, 1996), 94–104.

3. Peter Brown, The Body and Society: Men, Women, and Sexual Renunciation in Early Christianity (New York: Columbia University Press, 1988), 390. See also Power, Veiled Desire, 100. See Elizabeth

A. Clark, "Adam's Only Companion: Augustine and the Early Christian Debate on Marriage," *Recherches Augustiniennes* 21 (1986), 147.

4. See *Confessions* 5.5. Power suggests that Augustine is intentionally making a literary illusion to Dido in Vergil's *Aeneid*; see *Veiled Desire*, 84–85.

5. Brown, *Augustine of Hippo*, 69–70.

6. *Confessions* 6.13–15. Brown, *Augustine of Hippo*, 88–89.

7. *Confessions* 8.11.

8. Ibid., 8.12.

9. Ibid., 9.10.

10. Peter Brown puts Adeodatus's death in 390 (*Augustine of Hippo*, "Chronological Table," 74, 135).

11. Ibid., 138–45.

12. For these ascetic "couples" (Jerome and Paula, and Rufinus and Melania the Elder), see Rosemary R. Ruether, "Mothers of the Church: Ascetic Women in the Late Patristic Age," in *Women of Spirit: Female Leadership in the Jewish and Christian Traditions*, ed. Rosemary R. Ruether and Eleanor McLaughlin (New York: Simon and Schuster, 1979), 71–98 and Rosemary Rader, *Breaking Boundaries: Male/Female Friendship in Early Christian Communities* (New York: Paulist Press, 1983).

13. On Augustine's letters to women, see Power, *Veiled Desire*, 108–13.

14. Augustine *On the Literal Meaning of Genesis* 9.5.

15. See W. H. C. Frend, *The Donatist Church: A Movement of Protest in North Africa* (Oxford: Clarendon Press, 1952) and Brown, *Augustine of Hippo*, 212–32.

16. Augustine, *Two Books of Genesis Against the Manichees* and *On the Literal Meaning of Genesis: An Unfinished Book*, ed. Roland J. Teske, in *The Fathers of the Church*, vol. 84 (Washington, D.C.: Catholic University of America Press, 1991).

17. Augustine, *The Literal Meaning of Genesis*, in *Ancient Christian Writers*, vol. 41–42, ed. J. H. Taylor (New York: Newman Press, 1982).

18. Augustine, *Against Julian*, in *The Fathers of the Church*, vol. 35, ed. Matthew A. Schumacher (New York: Fathers of the Church, 1957).

19. See Philo, "On the Creation of the World," in *The Essential Philo*, ed. Nathan Glatzer (New York: Schocken, 1971), 28–34.

20. *Genesis Against the Manichees* 1.19.30.

21. *City of God* 12.24–25 and *On the Literal Meaning of Genesis* 6.19.

22. *City of God* 12.21.

23. *Literal Meaning of Genesis* 9.5.

24. *City of God* 14.22–24.

25. Augustine *Letter* 137, in Saint Augustine, *Letters*, vol. 3, trans. Wilfrid Parsons (New York: Fathers of the Church, 1953), 24; see also Power, *Veiled Desire*, 179.

26. *Literal Meaning of Genesis* 11.42; *City of God* 14.11.

27. *City of God* 14.11–12.

28. Ambrosiaster, *Questions on the Old and New Testaments*, Question 45, secs. 21–26. See also Power, *Veiled Desire*, 55–56.

29. See Rosemary Ruether, *Women and Redemption: A Theological History* (Minneapolis: Fortress Press, 1998), 122; also John L. Thompson, "Creata Ad Imaginem Dei, Licet Secundo Grado: Women as the Image of God According to John Calvin," *Harvard Theological Review* 81, no. 2 (1988): 137–38.

30. For discussion of this anthropology, see Power, *Veiled Desire*, 131–57.

31. *On the Trinity* 12.7.10.

32. *City of God* 14.15, 16, 21. *The Literal Meaning of Genesis* 11.37; see also Power, *Veiled Desire*, 133–34.

33. Paul's Epistle to the Romans 7:23.

34. *City of God* 14.16; *Against Julian* 4.5.35.

35. *Against Julian* 5.15–16.

36. *The Literal Meaning of Genesis* 11.37; see also Power, *Veiled Desire*, 133–34.

37. Power, *Veiled Desire*, 159–60.

38. Ibid., 121–23.

39. *Confessions* 9.9.

40. Power, *Veiled Desire*, 125–27.

41. See particularly Augustine's letter to Ecdicia, *Letter* 262, in Saint Augustine, *Letters*, vol. 5, trans. Wilfrid Parsons, 262–63; see also Power, *Veiled Desire*, 111–13.

42. See Eleanor McLaughlin, "Equality of Souls, Inequality of Sexes: Women in Medieval Theology," in *Religion and Sexism: Images of Women in the Jewish and Christian Traditions*, ed. Rosemary R. Ruether (New York: Simon and Schuster, 1974), 225–26.

43. See Ruether, *Women and Redemption*, 41–43.

44. Augustine, *Letters* 124, 125; see also Power, *Veiled Desire*, 117–18. On the history of this ascetic family, see Ruether, "Mothers of the Church," 88–92.

45. Power, *Veiled Desire*, 192–94.

46. Jerome, "On the Perpetual Virginity of the Blessed Mary Against Helvidius," in *Dogmatic and Polemical Works*, trans. John N. Hritzu, *The Fathers of the Church*, vol. 53 (Washington, D.C.: Catholic University Press of America, 1965), 30–36.

47. The doctrine of the virginity of Mary *in partu* is defended in the apocryphal gospel, The Evangelium of James.

48. Jerome, "On the Perpetual Virginity," 20; pp. 40–41 of Hritzu's translation.

49. Ibid., 21; pp. 42–43 of Hritzu's translation.

50. Jovinian's four propositions were as follows (1) virgins, widows, and married women, if they do not differ in other works, are of the same merit; (2) those who have been born again in baptism with full faith cannot be overthrown by the Devil; (3) there is no difference between abstinence from food and receiving it with thanksgiving; and (4) there is one reward in the kingdom of heaven for all who have preserved their baptism. See Jerome, *Adversus Jovinianum*, J.-P. Migne, ed., *Patrologiae Cursus Completus: Series Latina* (Paris, 1878–90), vol. 23, col. 224. See also Jerome, *Against Jovinianus*, in *Jerome: Letters and Select Works*, ed. Philip Schaff and Henry Wace, *Nicene and Post-Nicene Fathers of the Church*, vol. 6 (Peabody, Mass.: Hendrickson, 1995), book 1, 3, pp. 347–48.

51. For fourth-century church fathers' uses of Mark 4:20 to mean differentiated rewards of virgins, widows, and married people, see Jerome *Epistles* 22.15, 48.3, 66.2, 120.1, 9; *Adversus Jovinianum* 1.3; for Augustine, see *Holy Virginity* 45; on Ambrose, *On Virginity* 1.60.

52. David G. Hunter, "The Virgin, the Bride, and the Church: Reading Psalm 45 in Ambrose, Jerome, and Augustine," *Church History* 69, no. 2 (2000): 281–303. Hunter writes toward the end of his article: "Profoundly influenced by his struggle against Donatism, Augustine's reading of Psalm 45 emphasized the authority of the (male) bishop in establishing the universal character of the (female) church. Rather than serving as a warrant for sexual asceticism, Augustine's discussion of the bridal imagery of Psalm 45 created an image of the church whose universal character, embodied in the universal episcopate, vastly overshadowed any individual's ascetical effort" (302). See also his articles "Resistance to the Virginal Ideal in Late-Fourth-Century Rome: The Case of Jovinian," *Theological Studies* 48 (1987): 45–64 and "Helvidius, Jovinian, and the Virginity of Mary in Late-Fourth-Century Rome," *Journal of Early Christian Studies* 1 (1993): 47–71. As Hunter writes in concluding this last article: "It was difficult to articulate coherently the idea of the 'superiority' of virginity over marriage without either deprecating marriage and sexuality or introducing odious distinctions within the church. This was essentially the point being made by Helvidius and Jovinian. The appearance of Augustine's *De bono conjugali* and *De sancta virginitate* early in the fifth century reveals how much dissatisfaction there was with the solutions of Ambrose and Jerome. And the reappearance of the issue of sexuality and original sin in the later phases of the Pelagian controversy is an indication of how deeply troubling this linkage between sexuality and sin was to Western Christians" (70).

53. Jerome, "On the Perpetual Virginity," 20–22; pp. 40–43 of Hritzu's translation; see also Jerome *Against Jovinianus*, book 1, 39–40, pp. 376–79; book 2, 37, p. 415.

54. See David G. Hunter, "Augustinian Pessimism? A New Look at Augustine's Teachings on Sex, Marriage, and Celibacy," *Augustinian Studies* 25 (1994): 153–77. Although Hunter acknowledges that "Augustine's teaching does not exclude the possibility that there are certain remnants of Manichean ideas in particular aspects of his teaching" (176n90), he attempts to emphasize Augustine's more positive assessments of sexuality that Hunter states may be found in some of Augustine's earlier writings; see esp. 154–63.

55. Augustine, *On the Good of Marriage*, English translation in *Treatises on Marriage and Other Subjects* (New York: Fathers of the Church, 1955).

56. Augustine writes: "In marriage, intercourse for the purpose of generation has no fault attached to it, but for the purpose of satisfying concupiscence, provided with a spouse, because of the marriage fidelity, it is a venial sin; adultery or fornication, however, is a mortal sin. And so, continence from all intercourse is certainly better than marital intercourse itself which takes place for the sake of begetting children. While continence is of greater merit, it is no sin to render the conjugal debt, but to exact it beyond the need for generation is a venial sin" (*On the Good of Marriage* 6, 7).

57. For Augustine's views on the transmission of original sin through sexual intercourse, conception, and the birth of infants, see *City of God* 16.27 and *Against Julian* 5.15.54.

58. *On the Good of Marriage* 3.3.

59. Augustine *Commentary on the Lord's Sermon on the Mount* 1.5, 41; see also Power, *Veiled Desire*, 160.

60. *On the Good of Marriage* 17–20; *On Marriage and Concupiscence* 1.9–10.

61. *On the Good of Marriage* 17.

62. Augustine *Holy Virginity* 9,16.

63. Power, *Veiled Desire*, 171–97.

64. *On Nature and Grace* 42.36; *Sermon* 290.6; see also Power, *Veiled Desire*, 178.

65. Power, *Veiled Desire*, 176.

66. Ibid., 215–27.

67. *City of God* 22.17.

2

Monica: The Feminine Face of Christ

Anne-Marie Bowery

To Augustine's theological man, woman as a theological datum is the visible incarnation of sexual desire and lust, the carrier of evil and guilt, the occasion of man's original Fall and subsequent transmission of sin.

In "Beyond Mary and Eve," Margaret Maxey provocatively suggests, "The theological task of 'liberating' women would get underway primarily by

This essay is dedicated to the memory of Carl Vaught. His intensely personal engagement with the *Confessions* inspired so many students, myself included, to take up the words of Augustine and interweave them into their own lives. I would like to thank the Baylor University Research Committee and the College of Arts and Sciences Summer Sabbatical Committee for the financial support I received during this project. Randall Colton, now of Eastern University, was an immensely helpful research assistant during the stages of this project. The members of my various Augustine seminars deserve special thanks for their constant enthusiasm for learning and their willingness to listen to various formulations of this project. Judith Stark provided helpful suggestions throughout the final stages of revision.

rejecting and counteracting an Augustinian inheritance."[1] Many dimensions of Augustine's thought suggest that feminists would do well to follow Maxey's advice.[2] However, we should not prematurely divorce Augustine from feminist concerns.[3] Over the past thirty years, scholars have explored the social, political, and historical context in which Augustine wrote.[4] Given an increased awareness of Augustine's intellectual milieu, some aspects of Augustine's theology support a positive comparison to both his predecessors and his contemporaries with respect to his views about women.[5] For example, Augustine's reading of the Garden of Eden story treats women more sympathetically than either Philo or Origen.[6] Furthermore, Augustine acknowledges that women are the spiritual equals of men and he insists upon the salvation of both sexes.[7] Augustine's *Confessions*, particularly its detailed portrait of Monica, offers another fruitful avenue for reassessing Augustine's relevance for contemporary feminist philosophy and theology. In this essay, I argue that Augustine presents Monica as a feminized image of Christ. Augustine's portrait of Monica allows us to reframe the masculine image of divinity that lies at the heart of the Christian doctrine. Indeed, as Elisabeth Kari Børresen remarks, "Atypical use of female metaphors describing God or Christ in the Christian tradition can be used as a starting point for a new theology."[8]

In this essay, I survey the range of scholarly interpretations of Monica. First, I address those scholars who regard Monica negatively, either by condemning her for meddling in Augustine's life or by dismissing her spiritual insights as primitive and emotionally driven rather than intellectual. I also briefly discuss some Freudian analyses that explain Augustine's preoccupation with Monica as the manifestation of an unresolved oedipal struggle. I then turn toward more positive treatments of Monica. Some scholars see her as an image of the Virgin Mary. Others view her as a symbol of the church. Still others treat her as emblematic of Augustine's belief in the sexless universality of spiritual experience.

In the second section of the essay, I draw upon the work of several scholars who emphasize the mediating role of Monica. I then argue that Augustine uses the figure of Monica to feminize the image of Christ. He does so by presenting her as a model Christian; by describing her ability to ascertain the will of God through her dreams, visions, and spiritual experience; and by describing her mediating presence at each discernable stage in his movement toward Christian conversion. As the *Confessions* progresses, Augustine portrays their relationship as a microcosm of Christian community. The communal nature of their relationship symbolizes the inexorably communal nature of Christian spiritual experience. Finally, I suggest that Augustine's presentation of Monica provides a useful paradigm for contemporary feminist reevaluations of canonical Christian theology.

Looking at Monica in the Secondary Literature

Negative Views

Eric Ziolkowski perceptively observes that "in our own century Monica has seemed to intimidate psychologists and church historians (a mostly male bunch), not all of whom view her positively as a mother and wife." A brief survey of the literature bears out his point. Robert Ottley remarks, "Monica was by no means faultlessly virtuous and wise; she had a touch of African fanaticism." Muriel Spark calls her "deeply primitive." Carl Levenson refers to her as the "all-absorbing Monica."[9] Negative views of Monica tend to emphasize her misunderstanding of Christian doctrine and subsequent miseducation of Augustine, her lack of intellectualism, and her overinvolvement in Augustine's life. Concerning the first point, some scholars accuse Monica of failing to raise Augustine according to sound Christian values, citing her lax discipline and improper moral guidance. Ottley charges, "She cherished some worldly ambitions, and in her upbringing of Augustine made some grave mistakes which the providence of God overruled for good."[10] Concerning her failure to transmit appropriate Christian values, many scholars are harsh in their judgment. For example, Gerald Bonner claims, "There is no evidence to show that, in his childhood, Augustine received any thorough or satisfying instruction in the Christian faith."[11] These views emerge out of a sense that Monica's Christian commitment lacked intellectual depth. Bonner typifies this view: "Monica, though a saint, was not an educated woman. . . . She was certainly unqualified to deal with the problems which were in his youth to perplex her brilliant son."[12] Scholars are also suspicious of Monica's extreme maternal devotion. On this point, Carl Levenson writes, "Monica gives, wants only to give, and suffocates her son with her gifts." John O'Meara imagines that Augustine "felt impelled to fly from her and Africa." Robert O'Connell even alleges, "Her devotion to Augustine had much of the 'daughter of Eve' about it."[13]

Indeed, aspects of the early books of the *Confessions* support these negative views. Augustine mentions several limitations of Monica's character: she and her husband, Patricius, laugh at Augustine's corporal punishment (1.9.14), and "she took no care" to see him married at an early age (2.2.4). Augustine also recounts Monica's passionately excessive involvement in the unfolding course of his life. For example, early in Augustine's life, she asks a bishop to intercede: "She pressed him with more begging and with floods of tears. . . . He was now irritated and a little vexed and said: 'Go away from me; as you live, it cannot be that the son of these tears should perish'" (3.11.21).[14] Later, Monica follows Augustine to the seaport of Carthage and begs him to take her to Rome. He escapes without her, but she eventually follows him to Italy and rejoins him in Milan (5.8.15, 6.1.1). Augustine recounts Monica's attempts to find him a suitable marriage partner and her role in sending his mistress away (6.13.23).[15] At this point in the narrative, Augustine believes that Monica's devotion to him and her machinations on his behalf exceed the bounds of normality. He remarks, "She loved to have me with her, but she much more than most mothers" (5.8.16).[16] It is important to realize that Augustine's treatment of Monica changes as the *Confessions* progresses. Indeed, the *Confessions* can be read as an account of Monica's own spiritual development. Augustine's portrait of her becomes increasingly positive because Monica's character becomes increasingly admirable.[17]

As one might expect, Augustine's emotional preoccupation with his mother has occasioned several Freudian analyses of the *Confessions*.[18] These interpretations regard the *Confessions* as Augustine's attempt to resolve his oedipal complex. Paul Rigby asks, "Does Augustine seek from God simply the satisfaction of his infantile desires? Does he abandon self-consciousness, free will and personhood in God? Is the spirit of the ethical community of the Catholic Church for Augustine just the working out of the Oedipus conflict: omnipotent desire, instinctual murder, remorse and guilt?"[19] Some of Augustine's remarks about Monica support a Freudian interpretation. He acknowledges that Monica's love exceeds the bounds of a normal maternal bond. For example, Augustine admits, "She loved me with a love that was too much of the flesh" (5.8.15). He believes that "the longing she felt for her own flesh and blood was justly chastised by the whip of sorrow" (5.8.15). However, such a reading does not fully explain Monica's prominent role in the *Confessions*.[20] Furthermore, Elizabeth Clark makes an important point about the limitations of Freudian analysis: "Our notions of normalcy and deviance cannot be readily applied to a society in which, for example, slaves who were subject to the violence and sexual whims of their owners were the primary caretakers of the owners' children or in which a thirty-year-old man's engagement to a ten-year-old girl—Augustine's case—raised no eyebrows."[21]

Positive Views of Monica

Despite the prevalence of these negative views about Monica's relationship with Augustine, scholars rightly observe that much of the *Confessions* presents a compelling picture of Monica.[22] For example, Colin Starnes nicely underscores Augustine's use of Monica as a model for faithfulness and Atkinson points to her lasting influences as a model of Christian motherhood.[23] However, Augustine's purpose in presenting Monica was not simply to extol her many Christian virtues. He does not merely chronicle the praiseworthy role she played in his conversion any more than he writes the *Confessions* as an exact reenactment of his spiritual development.[24] By his own admission, Augustine writes for a community of believers. He envisions "the ears of believing sons of men, sharers in my joy, conjoined with me in mortality, my fellow citizens and pilgrims" (10.4.6). He writes so that he might serve others (10.4.6) and glorify God by bringing others to the Christian life. As a highly trained rhetorician, Augustine was well aware of the persuasive impact of his prose. To further his rhetorical and evangelical end, Augustine carefully presents his journey from sin to salvation. To enhance the persuasive impact of his story, Augustine interlaces classical imagery and Christian symbolism into the account of his life.[25] Similarly, he weaves several layers of imagery and symbol into his portrayal of Monica. In the remainder of this section, I will discuss three interpretations of Monica's function in the *Confessions*: as a symbol of the Virgin Mary, as a representative of the church, and as an example of the universality of spiritual experience.

Monica as Mary

The field of Mariology is immense and varied.[26] Mary's symbolic meaning varies according to specific historical and social circumstances. In 431

C.E., one year after Augustine's death, the Council of Ephesus established the Theotokos doctrine, which affirms that since Mary's child, Jesus, is God, Mary should be referred to as Theotokos, or "bearer of God." Augustine's emphasis on Monica as the womb of his both spiritual and physical births prefigures this theological understanding of Mary as the bearer of God. In fact, Augustine describes Monica as if she were Mary: "She anxiously labored to convince me that you, my God, were my father rather than he" (1.11.17). If we follow Augustine's descriptive analogy here, Monica functions as Mary, Theotokos. Extending the analogy even further, Augustine himself becomes Christ, the offspring of Theotokos. In book 4, Augustine points to the Theotokos doctrine again: "He came into the Virgin's womb where the human creation was married to him, so that mortal flesh should not for ever be mortal. Coming forth from thence 'as a bridegroom from his marriage bed'" (Ps. 18.6) (4.12.19). In book 5, Augustine employs the bridal imagery to explain their relationship. When talking about the remnants of their sin, he refers to himself as Adam and calls Monica Eve (5.8.15–9.16). Monica, like Mary, becomes the new Eve.

This symbolic understanding of Monica as Mary, as the new Eve, significantly elevates her status in Augustine's narrative because she becomes an active agent in Augustine's conversion process. According to Rosemary Radford Ruether, Mary receives a similar elevated status in the Gospel of Luke: "She serves as "co-offerer of the sacrifice at Golgotha with him." Ruether explains further, "The idea of Mary's co-redemptive role in part goes back to the early analogy between Christ as the new Adam and Mary (or the Church) as the new Eve."[27] If we view Monica as a symbolic representative of Mary, then she cooperates in Augustine's conversion along with Christ.[28] Although the similarities between Monica and Mary are striking, there are many other layers of symbol at work in the figure of Monica.[29]

Symbol of the Church

Monica also represents the church. This second level of symbolism dovetails with her function as the Virgin Mary. In Augustine's epoch, Mary was regularly associated with the church and the church was associated with the Holy Mother. Ester Dotson affirms that "Augustine repeatedly treats Mary as a symbol and personification of the Church."[30] Throughout the *Confessions*, Augustine alludes to the symbolic relationship between the church and Monica. For example, he remarks, "I then begged for the baptism of your Christ, my God and Lord, urging it on the devotion of my mother and of the mother of us all, your Church" (1.11.17). In book 7, he refers to "our spiritual mother, the Catholic Church" (7.1.1). If, as Dotson suggests, "the Church is the new Eve, born from the Sacraments of the water and the blood that flowed from the side of Christ, the second Adam," Augustine's portrayal of himself as Adam and Monica as Eve strengthens the association between Monica and the church (5.7.15–9.16).[31] Some scholars have associated Monica's tears with the sacraments, the water of baptism and wine of the Eucharist.[32] Normally, the church is the body that administers the rites associated with these items. Here, as the symbolic bearer of these sacred rites, Monica bears the redemptive power of the church: "This water was to wash me clean, and to dry the rivers flowing from my mother's eyes which daily before you irrigated the soil beneath her face" (5.8.15).

The church plays many functions in the spiritual life of individual believers. The church is often regarded as the spirit of the Lord manifested in a communal form. Not only is the church the community of believers, but it also provides a visible and physical home for them. The fact that Augustine and Alypius go into the house where Monica is right after their conversion also bears out this comparison between Monica and the church. Monica is the only person mentioned as being present in the house that they enter immediately following the conversion (8.12.30). Quite literally, they enter into the house of Monica. They enter into the house of the Lord.[33]

The comparison between Monica and the church is compelling on many levels. However, Augustine's ambiguous description of Monica's relationship to Christian doctrine makes it difficult to read her as a symbol of the church. For example, he remembers her failure to baptize him after he had recovered from a life-threatening illness: "My cleansing was deferred on the assumption that, if I lived, I would be sure to soil myself" (1.11.17). Although Monica's decision was in keeping with standard practice in the Western churches at this time, Augustine faults Monica for her failure to baptize him. He contrasts his own active "begging" for baptism, with a passive decision on her part to defer it (1.11.17). Another example occurs when Augustine recounts how, "in accordance with my mother's custom in Africa, she had taken to the memorial shrines of the saints cakes and bread and wine, and was forbidden by the janitor"

(6.2.2). Augustine's assessment of her does not seem entirely fair. For example, when Monica knew that the bishop ordered the prohibition, "she accepted it in so devout and docile a manner that I myself was amazed how easy it was for her to find fault with her own custom rather than to dispute his ban" (6.2.2). He also ignores her attempts to regulate his sexual escapades. He speaks of her "womanish advice which I would have blushed to take the least notice of" (2.3.7). Augustine also describes Monica's lax attitude about his sexual conduct: "Although she had warned me to guard my virginity . . . she did not seek to restrain my sexual drive within the limit of the marriage bond" (2.3.8). On some level, Augustine holds Monica responsible for his descent into the "steaming cauldron of illicit love" (3.1.1). However, if one takes the entire *Confessions* into account, his presentation of Monica's Christian practice is largely positive. As Augustine's faith matures, he recognizes the profound depths of Monica's spiritual commitment.

The Equality of Spiritual Experience

Although remarks about the inferiority of women pervade the Augustinian corpus, Augustine's treatment of Monica suggest that a woman can attain the same intellectual and spiritual insights about divinity as men.[34] In *Confessions* 9, Augustine offers a detailed account of a mystical vision that he and Monica experience simultaneously. The joint nature of their vision stands in stark contrast to Augustine's solitary intellectual ascent to the One. In book 7, Augustine's only company is the Neoplatonic books that "admonished [him] to return into [himself]" (7.10.16). In book 9, Monica accompanies Augustine on every step of the spiritual ascent. Here, they are "alone together" (9.10.23). They "talk intimately" together; they look out over the garden together; they search together; they ask questions together (9.10.23). The ascent continues and they are "lifted up together" and "enter into their own minds" (9.10.24). In book 7, Augustine sees the God who is, but he cannot sustain the vision. He falls back into himself and retains only a "memory of that which is" (7.10.17). In book 9, both he and Monica see Eternal Truth and Perfect Wisdom, if only in some "small degree" (9.10.24). They do not fall away from this experience of perfect wisdom but they do return to the temporal constraints of human speech (9.10.24). Furthermore, Augustine presents this shared experience as a spiritually perfect one. In contrast, he characterizes the Neoplatonic vision in book 7 as lacking the crucial element of Incarnation. There, Augustine finds fault with the Neoplatonic texts because they did not reveal the truth of Incarnation: "That the 'Word was made flesh and dwelt among us' I did not read there" (John 1:13–14), (7.9.13). Even though the Incarnation is not specifically mentioned at the height of the mystical moment, Augustine does not qualify the experience that he and his mother share as deficient in any way.[35] This passage of joint ascent in book 9 attests to Augustine's belief that women and men have the same access to and experience of divine revelation. Differently put, their shared mystical experience represents the sexless universality of spiritual experience. It is available to all humanity, regardless of gender.[36]

To emphasize this universality, Augustine regularly employs feminine imagery to describe God and God's actions.[37] Early in the *Confessions*, he remarks, "I was welcomed by the consolations of human milk; but it was not my mother or my nurses who made any decision to fill their breasts, but you who through them gave me infant food" (1.6.7). Here, God replaces the maternal function of feeding. This imagery appears in Augustine's *Second Discourse on the Psalms* as well: "He who has promised us heavenly food has nourished us on milk, having recourse to a mother's tenderness. For just as a mother, suckling her infant, transfers from her flesh the very same food which otherwise would be unsuited to the babe . . . so our Lord, in order to convert His wisdom into milk for our benefit, came to us clothed in flesh. It is the Body of Christ, then, which here says: And thou shalt nourish me" (30.9).[38] When Augustine explains that "God does not work under the limits of time," he employs maternal imagery. God's love resembles "a bird that broods over its eggs, the mother somehow helping in the development of her young by the warmth from her body through an affection similar to that of love."[39] Augustine's use of maternal images for God reflects a larger intellectual tradition. Kenneth Leech catalogs numerous "references to God as mother in the patristic period. Clement of Alexandria, Origen, Irenaeus, John Chrysostom, Ambrose and Augustine all use this image." Leech concludes, "It is therefore wrong to see the symbolism of divine motherhood as something very marginal to orthodox spirituality, or as something found only in heretical and Gnostic writings."[40] Augustine's description of God as having feminine attributes aligns him with these aspects of the Christian tradition. His description of Christ, the Son of God, as somehow partaking in these attributes is shared by other patristic writers as well. For example, "John Chrysostom speaks of Christ as sister and mother. He relates the maternal symbolism to the nourishing work of Christ in the Eucharist."[41] Sally Cunneen remarks that Augustine himself "did not hesitate to use the feminine image of Sophia for Jesus." Rita Bradley lists numerous examples in Augustine's theological writings and sermons that employ divine maternal imagery for both God and Christ.[42] Curiously, she does not consider the *Confessions* where Augustine provides a sustained feminine image of Christ: his mother, Monica.

Monica as Mediator: The Feminine Face of Christ

Several scholars have emphasized the mediating role that Monica plays throughout the *Confessions*. For example, in his discussion of Monica's dreams, Leo Ferrari calls her a "mediatrix." In a similar vein, Clarissa Atkinson asserts "Monica mediated his conversion by her prayers and tears." When considering the importance of the Ostia experience, Kevin Coyle notes that Augustine "prais[es] his mother as the chief instrument whereby he has learned to seek only truth." Paul Rigby calls her "God's representative for Augustine." Although there are numerous references to Monica's mediating function, scholars, as a general rule, do not link her mediating function with the possibility of her serving as a Christ-symbol. One exception is Silvia Benso, who describes Monica's dramatic role in the *Confessions* and suggests, "Monica rises to a *figura Christi*."[43]

Even in our contemporary world of unprecedented sexual equality, there are great internal and external strictures against rethinking Christ as inhabiting a female form. According to the Christian story, Christ does not simply take human form; he assumes masculine form. Since the masculinity of Christ is so firmly entrenched in the Christian story, even when a woman functions as a Christ figure, we have difficulty naming it as such. Unfortunately, our difficulty with thinking about Christ beyond a masculine form limits our understanding of Christ. The Incarnation is made manifest as gendered humanity, as a man, a man who was relational, spiritually attuned and compassionate to all and concerned with enhancing the humanity of all women and men, but a man nonetheless. Tragically, given a variety of cultural biases that favor the masculine over the feminine, the masculinity of Christ can eclipse the primary function of Christ: to be the means by which humans (all humans regardless of sex) come to know God's love.

In what follows I show how Augustine's portrait of Monica helps us to expand our understanding of Christ. To this end, I explore two aspects of Augustine's portrayal of Monica that demonstrate how she functions as a Christ figure. First, she is the model Christian. As such she represents the path that Augustine must accept. Second, she mediates Augustine's spiritual journey in a number of important ways. In doing so, she embodies the mediating nature of Christ.

Monica: The Model Christian

Most Christians strive to be like Christ, to live as Christ lived, to act as Christ acted, to be as Christ is. Christians often turn to other Christians to find models of Christian action. Augustine is no exception. Monica functions as Augustine's model Christian. For the most part, Augustine lauds Monica's Christian virtues. He testifies to Monica's faithfulness. Augustine writes, "For my mother, your faithful servant, wept for me before you more than mothers weep when lamenting their dead children" (3.11.19).[44] In book 5, he lifts her virtues up to God: "Would you despise the contrite and humble heart of a chaste and sober widow, liberal in almsgiving, obedient and helpful in serving your saints, letting no day pass without making an oblation at your altar, twice a day at morning and at evening?" (5.9.17). Monica is humble, sober, generous, and obedient to the Lord. Augustine continues his description of Monica's ideal Christian virtue. He describes her as someone "coming to your Church with unfailing regularity, taking no part in vain gossip and old wives' chatter, but wanting to hear you in your words and to speak to you in her prayers?" (5.9.17). In book 9 of the Confessions, Augustine offers his final account of Monica's Christian virtue in that she overcomes the limitations of her female form and attains "a virile faith" (9.4.8). He also mentions her taking a leading part in defending Ambrose when he encountered political problems with Justina (9.7.15). Before recounting their shared spiritual experience overlooking the garden in Ostia, Augustine narrates an account of her human life that portrays her as a model Christian. Except for the "wine tasting" episode, Augustine generally describes her in idyllic terms. She was "brought up in modesty and sobriety. . . . She was made by you obedient to her parents . . . and served her husband as her lord" (9.9.19). She ceaselessly attempts to convert Patricius to Christianity and "at the end when her husband had reached the end of his life in time, she succeeded in gaining him for you" (9.9.22). He continues lauding her Christian virtues: she offers good counsel to others, she is a peacemaker, she wins the love of her in-laws, and she serves the servants of God (9.9.19–20). Given this portrayal of Monica as an ideal Christian, it is not surprising that Augustine portrays his journey to Christianity as a journey in which he becomes more and more like Monica. Augustine emphasizes this association between Monica and Christ when he narrates the crucial moment when he "puts on the Lord Jesus Christ" (8.12.29). There, we see that Augustine becomes like Monica in terms of both her religious commitment and her emotional response. For example, when Augustine finally weeps at the conversion scene, he imitates Monica's faithful actions. Ziolkowski perceptively observes, "The tears which Augustine finally could not restrain recall those of Monica."[45] Augustine's final comment about this important moment also illustrates Monica's role in his conversion. He stands "firm upon that rule of faith on which many years before you had revealed me to her" (8.12.30).

Monica as Christ the Mediator

Monica functions as a Christ figure in three ways. First, she motivates Augustine's spiritual rebirth in Christ. Second, she has dreams, which reveal to him the word of God. Third, Augustine's use of metaphors of closeness and distance show how Augustine's movement toward the Christian life and his movement toward Monica parallel each other. This parallel movement suggests her mediating influence on his conversion.[46]

First, Monica mediates Augustine's Christian conversion by motivating his spiritual rebirth in Christ. This aspect of Monica's mediation might be confused with her symbolic function as the Virgin Mary. Certainly, Monica physically gives birth to Augustine just as Mary physically gives birth to Christ. However, according to the Theotokos doctrine, Mary is the physical bearer of God. She is not the conduit of his spiritual rebirth. Augustine characterizes Monica as a physical and spiritual mechanism by which he is born anew in Christ. Clearly, Monica is Augustine's physical mother, but Augustine again and again emphasizes that Monica is a spiritual mother as well: "With a pure heart and faith in you she even more lovingly travailed in labour for my eternal salvation" (1.11.17). Later he remarks, "She suffered greater pains in my spiritual pregnancy than when she bore me in the flesh" (5.9.16). Colin Starnes affirms this assessment of Augustine's rhetorical use of Monica: "Augustine always speaks of his baptism as a rebirth and, both here and elsewhere, refers to Ambrose and Monica, respectively, as the father and mother of his second birth."[47] In her role as spiritual mother, Monica functions as more than a symbol for Mary. She becomes a Christ-like mediator between Augustine and God.[48]

Second, Monica's dream reveals the will of God.[49] In this sense, Monica functions as a Christ-figure because she mediates between God's will and Augustine's will. Her dream about the ruler makes God's will apparent to Augustine: "Her vision was one of herself standing on a rule made of wood. A young man came to her, handsome, cheerful, and smiling to her at a time when she was sad and 'crushed with grief' (Lam. 13). He asked her the reasons why she was downcast. . . . She had replied that she mourned my perdition. He then told her to have no anxiety and exhorted her to direct her attention and to see that where she was, there was I also. When she looked, she saw me standing beside her on the same rule" (Ps. 9B:38/10A:17) (3.11.19).

At the time the dream occurs, Augustine argues with Monica's interpretation of it; he does not readily accept her mediation. Despite his argument, Monica remains firm in her interpretation. Her insistence on her understanding of God's will influences Augustine even more than the content of the dream itself. He writes, "I was more moved by your answer through my vigilant mother than by the dream itself. My misinterpretation seemed very plausible. She was not disturbed and quickly saw what was there to be seen, and what I certainly had not seen before she spoke" (3.11.20).[50] In retrospect, Augustine believes that Monica's dream foretells his eventual conversion. In fact, he explicitly recalls this dream when he narrates his conversion. After recounting the conversion in book 8, he describes himself as standing on "the rule of faith" (8.12.30).[51] Monica's dream brings Augustine to a greater understanding of the divine source of his salvation. Like Christ, Monica holds God and his works within her.[52]

Augustine portrays Monica as having direct insight into the will of God and as a receptacle of divinity.[53] She is a living space in which God works. This treatment of Monica recalls Jesus "making a place in his father's house" for us.[54] Elsewhere in the Confessions, Augustine uses this same imagery to describe Monica's mediating function. In book 2, when Augustine narrates the events of his early life, he remarks that "in my mother's heart you had already begun your temple and the beginning of your holy habitation (Ecclus. 24:14)" (2.3.6), and later at the end of the autobiographical chapters, Augustine explains that "she was the kind of person she was because she was taught by you as her inward teacher in the school of her heart" (9.9.21).

Third, the metaphors of closeness and distance that Augustine uses throughout the *Confessions* illustrate how Monica mediates Augustine's spiritual journey. Carl Levenson notes that Augustine consistently talks about being far from God and drawing closer to accepting Christ.[55] Throughout the *Confessions*, Augustine also moves away from and comes closer to Monica. His physical distance from Monica directly parallels his spiritual distance from God. When Augustine moves away from Monica, he moves away from Christ. Whenever he tells about some change in his faith journey, he also mentions Monica. Let us see how these metaphors of closeness and distance illustrate Monica's role in Augustine's conversion.

In book 1, Augustine discusses his infancy and laments his separation from God. Most references to Monica are fleeting and she is not mentioned by name. He mostly refers to the specific physical aspects of motherhood, being in the womb (1.6.9) and receiving nourishment (1.8.2). Augustine acknowledges that he first heard about Christ from Monica and that she insisted that God was his real father (1.11.17). Monica's faith provides the first mechanism through which Augustine moves closer to God. Augustine also remarks that Monica knew of the temptations that would confront him (1.7.18). As Augustine describes his early education, he does not mention his mother. His education overshadows her influence. Not surprisingly, he sees this early education as detrimental to his growth as a Christian (1.8.21, 1.16.26). In book 2, Augustine narrates how his lustful desires led him away from God. Augustine notes that Monica "feared the twisted paths along which walk those who turn their backs and not their face toward you" (Jer. 2:27) (2.3.6). Nonetheless, Monica remains silent and does not intervene or arrange a marriage for him. Similarly, Augustine notes that God "was silent when in reality I was traveling farther from [Him]" (2.3.7). Augustine does not mention Monica during the famous pear-stealing episode, after which he perceives his distance from God as extreme. Augustine describes his state as "a region of destitution," a wasteland (2.10.18). Neither God nor Monica has a place in Augustine's inner landscape at this point.

The next reference to Monica occurs in conjunction with a work of Cicero, the first book that put him on fire for the truth (3.4.7). Monica believed that his study of rhetoric would lead him to God; "she thought it would do no harm and would be a help to set me on the way towards you, if I studied the traditional pattern of a literary education" (2.3.8). When Augustine again begins to catalog his sins (taking a mistress, laughing at his friend's deathbed conversion), his references to Monica are sparse. We do learn that "during this time this chaste, devout, and sober widow, one of the kind you love, already cheered by hope but no less constant in prayer and weeping, never ceased her hours of prayer to lament about me to you" (3.11.20). At this point in Augustine's life, Monica's presence, like his awareness of God's presence, remains largely unnoticed. Even so, Augustine does mention the mediating power of Monica but notes that her mediation failed to bring him to God: "Her 'prayer entered into your presence' (Ps. 87:3), nevertheless you still let me go on turning over and over again in that darkness" (3.11.20).

These parallels between distance from Monica and distance from the path toward the Christian life continue as he discusses his involvement with the Manichees. This involvement marks the point of his greatest distance from God. Not surprisingly, we learn that Monica has banished Augustine from her home during this time (3.11.19). When Augustine describes his disillusionment with Faustus, the Manichaean bishop, he attributes this change in attitude to both God and Monica: "I decided to be content for the time being unless perhaps something preferable should come to light." He then refers to God's hidden providence, and "by my mother's tears night and day sacrifice was being offered to you from the blood of her heart, and you dealt with me in wonderful ways" (5.7.13). By mentioning the "blood of her heart," Augustine explicitly links Monica to the blood of Christ.

The spatial interplay of closeness and distance occurs throughout books 5 and 6. Augustine intends to sail to Rome. In retrospect, he views this movement as one that "pursued a false felicity" (5.8.14). To do so, Augustine abandons Monica at the seaport and, after his arrival in Rome, he falls desperately ill (5.8.15). At this point Augustine realizes he was better in youth because he was closer to what Monica wanted for him (5.9.16). Even though she is physically separated from her son, Monica prays for him, and her intercessory prayers bring him closer to God.

When Augustine speaks of his next movement toward Catholicism, he acknowledges Monica's influence. In fact, he mentions the influence of both parents: "I therefore decided for the time being to be a catechumen in the Catholic church, which the precedent of my parents recommended to me, until some clear light should come by which I could direct my course" (5.14.25).

As Augustine speaks of failing to find God, although he was "drawing closer" (5.13.23), he also moves closer to Monica: "My mother, strong in inner devotion, had already come to join me, following me by land and sea, and in all dangers serenely confident in you" (6.1.1). Monica then begins to arrange a marriage for Augustine with the hopes that "once married [he] would be washed in the saving water of baptism" (6.13.23). However, she realizes that this action may not have brought Augustine closer to God. Since, as Augustine notes, "by a certain smell indescribable in words, she could tell the difference between your revelation and her own soul dreaming" (6.13.23). As a result, she changes her own course and in doing so helps bring about Augustine's eventual conversion.

The distance and closeness metaphors continue in the last three autobiographical books of the *Confessions*. We continue to see how Augustine's movement toward Christ parallels a movement toward Monica. Book 7 relates Augustine's Neoplatonic vision of the One. He begins by lamenting that "my heart had become gross (Matt. 13:15) and I had no clear vision even of my own self" (7.1.2). Since Augustine's reading of the books of the Platonists (7.9.13) is an important stage of his spiritual journey, one would expect him to mention Monica. However, she does not appear at all in this portion of the text.[56] What are we to make of her sudden disappearance? One possible way to make sense of her absence involves acknowledging that Augustine describes a Neoplatonic vision.[57] While there are certainly similarities between Neoplatonism and Christianity, there is a crucial dissimilarity as well. Neoplatonism does not incorporate the Incarnation; "That the 'Word was made flesh and dwelt among us' I did not read there" (John 1:13–14), (7.9.13). Given that Augustine understands this vision in non-Christian terms, it is less surprising that Monica, a symbol of Christ the mediator, does not appear here.

The next mention of Monica occurs at the end of book 8. After Augustine and Alypius read the text of Paul's Epistle to the Romans (13:13–14) and resolve their respective struggles about embracing the Christian life, they immediately go in to tell Augustine's mother (8.12.30). As one might expect, "she was filled with joy. . . . She saw that you had granted her far more than she had long been praying for in her unhappy and tearful groans" (8.12.30). Since Monica is not present with Augustine at this crucial moment, one could argue that her mediating function has diminished. Such a judgment would be premature, however. A careful examination of these crucial moments reveals Monica's abiding presence. First, she is in the house that overlooks the garden the entire time this conversion experience occurs. In this sense, she symbolically oversees the experience. One could even imagine that it is Monica herself who chants those fateful words, "Tolle, lege," that cause Augustine to pick up the writings of Paul. Second, recall Augustine's startling vision of Lady Continence (8.11.27).[58] Augustine's description of the vision of Lady Continence bears striking similarity to his descriptions of Monica. Like Monica, Lady Continence is "serene and cheerful without coquetry, enticing me in an honorable manner to come and not to hesitate" (8.11.27). Augustine sees her as the mother of many children who has the Lord as her spouse. In this stressful situation, in his "unprecedented state of agitation" (8.11.27), it is possible that Augustine conjures up an image very similar to that of his mother, beckoning him, making the final steps safe for him. Augustine envisions a warm welcoming mother exhorting him toward the Christian life. The maternal aspects of this image are even more pronounced when one remembers that Augustine also sees numerous young men and women who have taken up this virtue and are embraced in the arms of Lady Continence. Finally, Augustine ends his narration of his conversion by reminding his audience of the dream that Monica had in book 3. He remarks, "I stood firm upon that rule of faith on which many years before you had revealed me to her" (8.12.30).

The shared mystical vision at Ostia marks the culmination of the autobiographical chapters. It provides a foundation for the intellectual reflections on memory, time, eternity, and creation. It is worth noting that Augustine's experience in the garden in Milan, as profound as it was, does not lead to his immediate renunciation of the secular life. Augustine remains a "salesman of words" (9.5.13). He waits until after his vintage vacation and after experiencing lung disease and toothache, two afflictions that make his teaching difficult, before renouncing his career ambitions. Several months later, at the Easter service, Augustine finally receives the sacrament of baptism.

At this point, Augustine chooses a life wholly dedicated to Christian service. Along with his son, Adeodatus, and his friends Alypius and Evodius, Augustine searches for a new way of living. They make this decision jointly: together, they decide how to best live their lives according to Christ. Augustine reflects, "We were together and by a holy decision resolved to live together. We looked for a place where we could be of most use in your service; all of us agreed on a move back to Africa" (9.8.17). Once again, Monica plays an important role. Before Augustine moves back to Africa and embarks upon the life that will lead him to become bishop of Hippo, his mother dies. Before her death at "Ostia by the mouth of the Tiber" (9.8.17), Augustine and Monica share an experience that cements Augustine's faith and enables him to "forget the past and reach forward to what lies ahead" (Phil 3:13) (9.10.23).

Monica and Augustine stand alone together "leaning out of a window overlooking a garden" (9.10.23).[59] They "talked very intimately about the quality of the eternal life of the saints" and they "drank in the waters flowing from your spring on high" (9.10.23). Augustine continues describing how they experience eternal Truth together: "Our minds were lifted up by an ardent affection towards eternal being itself. . . . We ascended even further." At every stage, Monica is with him. Together they "entered into our own minds. We moved up beyond them so as to attain to the region of inexhaustible abundance where you feed Israel eternally with truth for food" (9.10.24). He uses starkly erotic language to describe their experience: "They talk intimately"; "the mouth of the heart [was] wide open" (9.10.23). They are lifted up with "ardent affection." He recalls that they "talked and panted after it" (9.10.24). Finally, "in a flash of mental energy [they] attained the eternal wisdom which abides beyond all things" (9.10.24). Although the experience is momentary, a fleeting instant, Augustine insists that "my mother and I reached out in thought and touched the eternal Wisdom which abides over all things" (9.10.24). He experiences every aspect of this mystical experience with Monica. What she sees, he sees. What he sees, she sees. What he hears, she hears.[60] A number of scholars have pointed out the communal nature of the experience shared by mother and son as a kind of prelude to the social life of the saints in heaven.[61] In particular, John Quinn stresses the crucial role that Monica played in this extraordinary event: "It was Monica who played the collaborator role or, more precisely, as a necessary condition of Augustine's elevation, a quasi-magisterial office in the school of Christ, the supreme teacher. . . . On this occasion Monica was the teacher and Augustine the student, she the master and he the apprentice."[62] Once again, Monica functions as the feminine face of Christ, in this case, Christ the teacher. Moreover, just as "hearing" played a key role in Augustine's moral conversion in *Confessions* 8, hearing, in addition to seeing, is one of the significant features of the Ostia experience. Whatever happened that day, Monica and Augustine shared an "audition" as well as a "vision" together.[63] Although James O'Donnell warns against trying to figure out exactly what happened at Ostia, when Augustine wrote about it later, he himself had no doubt that "all such experiences come from the Christian God."[64] Whatever the event was and how and if it might be distinguished from what Augustine described in *Confessions* 7 (10.16), O'Donnell emphasizes that the experience is more accurately described as an "audition" than as a "vision." It is the silencing of all human language and of the tumult of all earthly things that creates the space in which "we would hear in person without mediation him in whom we love those things" (9.10.25). The "chattering boy" (1.8.13) who loves words and language would have to come to silence and stillness for such an experience to occur. Monica and other adult figures first taught Augustine the power of words (1.8.13) and so it is fitting that Augustine shares with her the quieting of human language and out of the silence of their minds and hearts, "he alone would speak not through them [material things] but through himself" (9.10.25). This intense experience, however, cannot last, and they return to the realm of human conversation that "has a beginning and an end" (9.10.24). After this final vision, Monica remarks that her role on earth has reached its end. She explains the entire purpose of her life in terms of bringing Augustine to Christianity and to a point where he dedicates his life to the service of God (9.10.26). Only at this point does Augustine genuinely stand together with Monica on "the rule of faith" (8.12.30). At last, Monica's mediation is complete. The fact that her death follows almost immediately reinforces the Christ-like dimension of her role in Augustine's life. Her death stands at the crossroad between Augustine's pre- and postconversion life. As Augustine goes through her death, he enters into Christian life. Silvia Benso notes, "Surely by chance, when Monica dies Augustine is 33 years old. But it is not by chance that Augustine lets the reader know it (9.11). As Christ is thirty-three when he dies and resurrects to the new and eternal life with his Father, so is Augustine when, through the death of his mother, he comes to new life in the imitation of her own way of living in tension."[65]

By way of conclusion, I suggest that this reading of Augustine's treatment of Monica can provide a model for feminist attempts to interpret canonical figures sympathetically rather than combatively.[66] While feminist scholars should directly confront the troublesome aspects of Augustine's theology, we should not be tempted to dismiss the whole of Augustine as a result. Unfortunately, serious engagement with Augustine's thought can lead one to this stance. For example, in her excellent article "Augustine on Rape," Mary Pellauer provides a devastating critique of Augustine's position on rape. Pellauer's serious intellectual involvement with Augustine's insensitivity leads her to a "crisis of faith." She turns to a male pastor, a masculine face of Christ, for solace. For various reasons, he does not listen. Pellauer laments, "He had done to me precisely what Augustine had done to the consecrated virgins: he hadn't listened." As a result, Pellauer seeks solace elsewhere; "I turned to a woman pastor." This time, Pellauer chooses a feminine face to represent Christ to her; "she represented the Gospel to me."[67] Through this feminine face, Pellauer finds grace and reconciliation. Pellauer's intellectually compelling and emotionally moving article reveals a need for strong feminine images of Christ, like the one that Augustine's treatment of Monica provides.

In her book *Memories of God,* Roberta Bondi poignantly expresses the existential dangers that can arise from a limited patriarchal conception of Christ. In this confessional narrative, Bondi relates a lifelong, painful struggle to find a space of spiritual comfort and specifically feminine mode of expression in her chosen patriarchal Baptist religion. For Bondi, the problems with religion started early, with the belief that "my heavenly father's standards for females had to be stricter than my earthly father's." She confesses, "My inadequacies filled me with guilt, and my femaleness overwhelmed me with shame." She describes the overall effect of this shame: "As for God, I found that in public prayer, the very use of the name Father would regularly fill me with a sense of inadequacy, helplessness, and depression." Bondi eventually finds a space for the feminine within a Christian framework. In addition, she reconciles with the patriarchal conception of religion. Although she develops a concept of God the mother, she finds a way to pray to God the father: "To invoke God's fatherhood as a mighty corrective against all the murderous images of fallen fatherhood that hold our hearts and person, our churches and our world captive."[68] Careful attention to Augustine's portrayal of Monica provides us with the occasion to rethink the strict association with Christ and the masculine form. Recognizing a Christ-symbol in feminine form can enhance our understanding of the nature and workings of Christ and provide spiritual solace for seekers such as Bondi, who strive to understand Christ as a person of the Trinity with love and relationality at the heart of the dynamic life of God.

Augustine's rhetorical presentation of Monica, particularly her role in his experience at Ostia, provides an example of the relational dimension of spiritual experience. Christ is not simply the Son of God. He brings about an instantiation of the triune nature of the divine. For a Christian, the divine is not simply God, but Father, Son, and Holy Spirit. The Trinity gives expression to the relational nature of spiritual experience, which, as an experience of the presence of God, should bring about a changed heart in the individual. Nonetheless, a "saved" individual is not the end of the story. A spiritually changed individual relates to others in the world in a new way.

The dramatic context of book 9 makes the relational nature of Augustine's Christian commitment apparent. He opens this section of the text by explaining his existential dilemma. He has made a decision to "put on the Lord Jesus Christ" (8.12.29), but he decides not to make any radical departure from his secular career. Unfortunately, he remains "a salesman of words in the markets of rhetoric" (9.2.2) until the time comes that he "could resign with due formality" (9.2.2). As Augustine makes the decision to live his life in a way that will fully reflect his Christian faith, he describes this decision as one that occurs within a communal context. It is not simply that God has converted Augustine's soul, but his language makes clear that God had worked on all of them jointly. He writes, "Our plan was formed with your knowledge but was not publicly known, except to our intimate circle. It was agreed among us that it was not to be published generally" (9.2.2). Within this communal context, Augustine renounces his public position as a teacher of rhetoric.

Other examples of the relational dimension of Augustine's understanding of Christianity occur in this last autobiographical book as well. For example, he mentions Verecundus's situation, which keeps Verecundus from making the full Christian commitment with them. Despite this limitation of married life, Verecundus is still an important part of Augustine's community and even provides "hospitality at his expense for as long as we were there" (9.5).[69] Augustine also mentions Nebridius's joining of the community of believers: "Soon after my conversion and regeneration by your baptism, he too became a baptized Catholic believer" (9.3.6). Finally, Augustine's vacation begins. He and Alypius live together with

Monica in a country villa (9.4.8). After two months of communal study, Augustine resigns his post and Alypius decides to be baptized at the same time as Augustine (9.6.14). Their joint baptism, along with that of Augustine's son, Adeodatus, symbolizes the relational context of all Christian commitment. All these examples of the relational nature of Augustine's early Christian experience set the stage for his description of the shared mystical vision with Monica.

Their shared mystical vision is the final expression of the relational nature of Christian experience. The fact that Monica is a woman may, in and of itself, symbolize the relational dimension of this experience. A significant body of contemporary feminist scholarship discusses how women come to ethical decisions differently from men.[70] According to Carol Gilligan, men tend to work in terms of general rules and apply them to specific cases. Women tend to look at any particular situation more relationally, in terms of specific people involved with the situation and how each person will be affected by an ethical decision. Christ as depicted in numerous gospel stories seems to use this feminine form of decision making. For example, he rejects the Pharisees and their numerous rules and regulations.[71] He frequently shocks people with his compassion for others and his ability to take into account the specific needs of a specific person in a specific situation.[72] Marianne Ferguson explains that women, like Christ, identify themselves in terms of relations with others. According to Ferguson, women view themselves "as the nexus of multiple relationships." She argues that many women see prayer as furthering this function: "Women often see the connecting patterns of prayer that help strengthen their own web of relationships. Praying seems to connect the various threads of their own lives."[73] The *Confessions*, as a long extended prayer, portrays Augustine's struggle for unification. Through this prayerful act of writing, he unites the disparate parts of his life. In this sense, Augustine's *Confessions* provides a model of prayer in keeping with the model Ferguson articulates.

Finally, in terms of philosophy and theology more broadly, this reading of Augustine may lead to an increased awareness of how much personal experience influences the expression of philosophical and theological truth. Although the poignant expression of personal experience in feminist writing has a long history, the expression of personal experience within the philosophical and theological canon is often suppressed.[74] Augustine's *Confessions* is an important exception to this tendency. Augustine does not simply offer theological arguments that explain his conversion to Christianity. Rather, he tells the story of his life, the personal journey that leads him to that garden in Milan. Since this highly personal example occurs in such a canonical text, it can help traditional scholarship become more receptive to the personal dimensions of philosophical and theological discourse.

Notes

1. Margaret Maxey, "Beyond Eve and Mary: A Theological Alternative for Women's Liberation," *Dialog* 10 (1971): 116–17; the quotation in the preceding epigraph is at 115.

2. First, Augustine regards women as the primary bearer of sin. Augustine associates the female womb, the origin of incarnate existence, with sin, sexuality, and separation from God (*Confessions* 1.7.12). Given this view, Augustine claims that women, even Christian women, create obstacles for a man's spiritual life (*Confessions* 9.3.5). Second, Augustine claims that women are naturally subservient to men. See *On the Literal Meaning of Genesis* 11.37.171, 8.23.44, 11.37.50. Third, at times, Augustine maintains that woman qua woman is not created in the image of God. See *On the Trinity* 12.7.9–13.21. (In contrast, see *Confessions* 13.33.47). For a sustained consideration of the effects of this sort of misogyny on the philosophical tradition, see Genevieve Lloyd, *Man of Reason: "Male" and "Female" in Western Philosophy* (Minneapolis: University of Minnesota Press, 1984).

3. Indeed, the essays in this collection illustrate how much would be lost by a refusal to engage with Augustine.

4. William Alexander, "Sex and Philosophy in Augustine," *Augustinian Studies* 15 (1974): 197–208; Jean La Porte and Ellen Weaver, "Augustine and Women: Relationships and Teachings," *Augustinian Studies* 12 (1981): 115–31; Eugene TeSelle, "Serpent, Eve, and Adam: Augustine and the Exegetical Tradition," in *Collectanea Augustiniana: Augustine Presbyter Factus Sum*, ed. Joseph T. Lienhard, Earl C. Muller, and Roland J. Teske (New York: Peter Lang, 1993), 341–61; Graham Gould, "Women in the Writings of the Fathers: Language, Belief, and Reality," in *Women in the Church: Studies in Church History* 27, ed. W. J. Shields and Diana Wood (New York: Basil Blackwell, 1990), 1–13.

5. Elisabeth Kari Børresen is a good example. On the whole, her mammoth study, *Subordination and Equivalence*, originally published in 1968, paints a negative portrait of Augustine; see *Subordination and Equivalence: The Nature and Role of Woman in Augustine and Thomas Aquinas*, trans. Charles Talbert (Washington D.C.: University Press of America, 1981). However, she modifies this position in her more recent work. She explains, "My present, more positive assessment of Augustine results from a more negative judgment of his doctrinal framework, namely the male-centered conformity of both scriptural texts and their subsequent interpretation." See "In Defence of Augustine: How *Femina* is *Homo*?" in *Collectanea Augustiniana*, ed. Bernard Bruning and Mathijs Lamberigts (Louvain: Leuven University Press, 1990), 411.

6. Lloyd, *Man of Reason*, 1984; TeSelle, "Serpent, Eve, and Adam," 1993.

7. *On Faith and Creed* 4.9. Based on considerations such as these, Hilary Armstrong notes that Augustine "is often more balanced and positive—and not, as sometimes seems to be assumed, more unbalanced and negative—in his attitude to the body, sex and marriage than most of his Christian contemporaries" (*St. Augustine and Christian Platonism* [Villanova: Villanova University Press, 1967], 11).

8. Børresen, "In Defence of Augustine," 425.

9. Eric Ziolkowski, "St. Augustine: Aeneas' Antitype, Monica's Boy," *Literature and Theology* 9

(1995): 3; Robert Ottley, *Studies in the Confessions of St. Augustine* (London: R. Scott, 1919), 5; Muriel Spark, "St. Monica," *Month* 17 (1957): 310; Carl Levenson, "Distance and Presence in Augustine's *Confessions,*" *Journal of Religion* 65 (1985): 505.

10. Levenson, "Distance and Presence in Augustine's *Confessions,*" 5.

11. Gerard Bonner, *St. Augustine of Hippo: Life and Controversies* (Norwich: Canterbury Press, 1986), 39. For a good discussion of this issue, see Joanne McWilliam, "The Study of Augustine's Christology in the Twentieth Century" in *Augustine: From Rhetor to Theologian,* ed. Joanne McWilliam (Waterloo: Wilfred Laurier University Press: 1992), 183–205.

12. Bonner, *St. Augustine of Hippo,* 39. See John O'Meara, *The Young Augustine* (London: Longmans Green, 1954), 38 and Spark, "St. Monica."

13. Levenson, "Distance and Presence in Augustine's *Confessions,* 505; O'Meara, *The Young Augustine,* 109; Robert O'Connell, "Sexuality in Saint Augustine," in *Augustine Today,* ed. Richard John Neuhaus (Grand Rapids: Eerdmans, 1993), 68.

14. Unless otherwise noted, all references are taken from Augustine, *Confessions,* trans. Henry Chadwick (Oxford: Oxford University Press, 1992).

15. For an excellent reading of the importance of the abandoned mistress, see F. B. A. Asiedu, "Following the Example of a Woman: Augustine's Conversion to Christianity in 386," *Vigiliae Christianae* 57 (2003): 276–306.

16. See also *Confessions* 3.12.21.

17. My thanks to Michael Foley of Baylor University for mentioning this point to me.

18. For a good overview of this literature, see Paul Rigby, "Paul Ricoeur, Freudianism, and Augustine's *Confessions,*" *Journal of the American Academy of Religion* 53 (1985): 93–114.

19. Ibid., 106.

20. See Donald Capps, "Augustine as Narcissist: Comments on Paul Rigby's "Paul Ricoeur, Freudianism, and Augustine's *Confessions,*" *Journal of the American Academy of Religion* 53 (1985): 115–28.

21. Elizabeth Clark, "Theory and Practice in Late Ancient Asceticism: Jerome, Chrysostom, and Augustine," *Journal of Feminist Studies in Religion* 5 (1989): 29.

22. Ottley mentions her "tenacity of purpose" (*Studies in the Confessions of St. Augustine,* 5); Cahill lauds "Monica's devotion to her son, her incessant prayers for his conversion away from Manicheanism, his long resistance and spiritual return to Catholicism, and his suffering upon her death)" Lisa Sowle Cahill, *Sex, Gender, and Christian Ethics.* (Cambridge, U.K.: Cambridge University Press, 1996), 176.

23. Colin Starnes, *Augustine's Conversion: A Guide to the Argument of Confessions I–IX* (Waterloo: Wilfred Laurier University Press, 1990), 62; Clarissa W. Atkinson, "Your Servant, My Mother": The Figure of Saint Monica in the Theology of Christian Motherhood," in *The Female in Sacred Image and Social Reality,* ed. Clarissa W. Atkinson, Constance H. Buchanon, and Margaret R. Miles (Boston: Beacon Press, 1985), 139.

24. See Carl Vaught, *Encounters with God in Augustine's Confessions Books VII–IX* (Albany: State University of New York Press, 2004), 19–21.

25. Ziolkowski, "St. Augustine," 1–23.

26. See Jaroslav Pelikan, *Mary Through the Centuries: Her Place in the History of Culture* (New Haven: Yale University Press, 1996) and Hilda Graef, *Mary: A History of Doctrine and Devotion,* vol. 1, *From the Beginning to the Eve of the Reformation* (New York: Sheed and Ward, 1963).

27. Rosemary Ruether, *Mary: The Feminine Face of the Church* (Philadelphia: Westminster Press, 1977), 33, 65–66.

28. Maureen Tilley traces Augustine's various uses of Mary in his Sermons. See "Mary in Roman Africa: Evidence for Her Cultus," Oxford Patristic Conference, August 2003.

29. For several other aspects of the various "Monica functions" in the *Confessions,* see Elizabeth Clark, "Rewriting Early Christian History," in *Theology and the New Histories,* ed. Gary Macy (New York: Maryknoll, 1998), 89–111.

30. Ester Dotson, "An Augustinian Interpretation of Michelangelo's Sistine Ceiling: Part II," *Art Bulletin* 61 (1979): 226.

31. Ibid.

32. See Leo Ferrari, "Monica on the Wooden Ruler (*Conf.* 3.11.19)," *Augustinian Studies* 6 (1975): 193–205.

33. Lenore Wright, "Trading Spaces: The Construction of Sacred Dwellings in Augustine's *Confessions*," Pruit Memorial Symposium, October 2001.

34. See Joanne McWilliam, "The Cassiacum Dialogues," in *Augustine Through the Ages: An Encyclopedia*, ed. Allan D. Fitzgerald (Grand Rapids, Mich.: Eerdmans, 1999), 135–43.

35. It is true that this entire conversation is about "'forgetting the past and reaching forward to what lies ahead' (Phil. 3:13)" and that Augustine makes clear that "we were searching together in the presence of the truth which is you yourself" (9.10.23); nonetheless, with respect to what they actually see and hear, the Incarnation is not mentioned. Instead, the experience is starkly Neoplatonic in nature.

36. Some feminists argue that the assumption of the model of generic humanity ultimately affirms the primacy of male experience in the guise of generic humanity. See Lloyd, *Man of Reason* and Iris Marion Young, "Polity and Group Difference: A Critique of the Ideal of Universal Citizenship," *Ethics* 99 (1989): 250–274; Hilary Davis, "The Tyranny of Resistance, or The Compulsion to Be a Good Feminist," *Proceedings of the Annual Meeting of the Philosophy of Education Society* 47 (1991): 76–86.

37. O'Connell, "Sexuality in Saint Augustine," affirms "the sensitivity with which he depicts God's feminine side" and "the boldness of the frankly sexual imagery he brings to that depiction" (65).

38. *St. Augustine on the Psalms*, trans. Dame Scholastica Hebgin and Dame Felicitas Corrigan, vol. 2 (Westminster, Md.: Newman Press, 1961).

39. *On the Literal Meaning of Genesis* 1.18.36.

40. Kenneth Leech, *Experiencing God: Theology as Spirituality* (San Francisco: Harper and Row. 1985), 355–56. Leech notes that "the Catholic liturgical and spiritual tradition preserved the feminine and maternal symbolism, but much of it became dissociated from God" (358).

41. Ibid., 356.

42. Sally Cunneen, *In Search of Mary: The Woman and the Symbol* (New York: Ballantine Books, 1996), 113; Rita Bradley, "Patristic Background of the Motherhood Similitude in Julian of Norwich," *Christian Scholar's Review* 8 (1978): 101–13.

43. See Leo Ferrari, "The Dreams of Monica in Augustine's *Confessions*," *Augustinian Studies* 8 (1979): 17; Atkinson, "Your Servant, My Mother" 142; Kevin Coyle, "In Praise of Monica: A Note on the Ostia Experience," *Augustinian Studies* 13 (1982): 94; Rigby, "Paul Ricoeur, Freudianism, and Augustine's *Confessions*," 98; Silvia Benso, "Monica's Grin of Tension," *Contemporary Philosophy* 15 (1993): 8.

44. Later, he specifically links her "motherly love" with her Christian devotion (9.4.8).

45. Ziolkowski, "St. Augustine," 13.

46. Levenson notes this parallel. However, he does not fully draw out the implications about Monica's mediating role.

47. Starnes, *Augustine's Conversion*, 129.

48. In this way, Augustine's use of Monica prefigures a late medieval tradition, which culminates in the writings of Julian of Norwich. See Bradley, "Patristic Background."

49. See Ferrari, "The Dreams of Monica in Augustine's *Confessions*," 3–17. He establishes that in Augustine's historical context, "the dream is a revelation of God to the dreamer" (6). He also notes that "the *Confessions* contains no accounts of Augustine's own dreams, [and] the same applies to all other characters in the work, with the exception of his mother, Monica" (6).

50. See Ferrari, "Monica on the Wooden Ruler."

51. See Ferrari, "Monica on the Wooden Ruler" and Ziolkowski, "St. Augustine."

52. Note Jesus's explanation to Phillip that "the words that I say to you I do not speak on my own; but the father who dwells in me does his works" (John 14:10).

53. See *Confessions* 6.1.1 where Monica is not surprised that Augustine no longer associates with the Manichees.

54. When recounting Monica's dream in book 3, "He then told her to have no anxiety and exhorted her to direct her attention and to see that where she was, there was I also" (*Confessions* 3.11.19), Augustine draws upon John 14.2ff.

55. Levenson, "Distance and Presence in Augustine's *Confessions*."

56. See Jennifer Hockenberry, "The He, She, and It of God: Translating St. Augustine's Gendered Latin God-Talk into English," paper presented at the International Congress for Medieval Studies, May 1999.

57. For a discussion of the interpretive issues regarding this point, see Vaught, *Encounters with God*, 9–10.

58. Asiedu, "Following the Example of a Woman," offers a very different reading of the Lady Continence image. Asiedu asks, "If Lady Continence is presenting herself as a woman and showing Augustine examples of those who have chosen her way, examples for Augustine to follow, what more likely candidate for such fare than the woman who had made a vow of sexual renunciation after years of living with Augustine?" (295).

59. Janice Stabb, "Standing Alone Together: Silence, Solitude, and Radical Conversion," *Contemporary Philosophy* 15 (1993): 16–20.

60. On the auditory dimensions of this experience and in the *Confessions* more generally, see Vaught, *Encounters with God*.

61. Andrew Louth, *The Origins of Christian Mysticism: From Plato to Denys* (New York: Clarendon Press, 1981), 136. John M. Quinn, "Mysticism in the *Confessiones*: Four Passages Reconsidered," in *Collectanea Augustiniana, Augustine: Mystic and Mystagogue*, ed. Frederick Van Fleteren, Joseph C. Schnaubelt, and Joseph Reino (New York: Peter Lang, 1994), 268–71.

62. Quinn, "Mysticism in the *Confessiones*, 270.

63. Gerald Bonner, "Augustine and Mysticism," in *Collectanea Augustiniana, Augustine: Mystic and Mystagogue*, ed. Frederick Van Fleteren, Joseph C. Schnaubelt, and Joseph Reino (New York: Peter Lang, 1994), 133–34.

64. Augustine, *Confessions*, vol. 3, commentary by James J. O'Donnell (New York: Clarendon Press, 1992), 127.

65. Silvia Benso, "Monica's Grin of Tension," *Contemporary Philosophy* 15 (1993): 8.

66. For an excellent example of how feminist approaches can revivify traditional philosophy of religion, see Grace Jantzen, *Becoming Divine: Towards a Feminist Philosophy of Religion* (Bloomington: Indiana University Press, 1999).

67. "Augustine on Rape: One Chapter in the Theological Tradition," in *Violence Against Women and Children: A Christian Theological Sourcebook*, ed. Carol J. Adams and Marie M. Fortune (New York: Continuum, 1995), 233, 234, 235.

68. Bondi, *Memories of God*, 25, 26, 27, 41.

69. Verecundus does "depart this life a baptized Christian," *Confessions* 9.3.5.

70. See Marianne Ferguson, *Women and Religion* (Englewood Cliffs, N.J.: Prentice Hall, 1995), 215. See also Carol Gilligan, *In a Different Voice: Psychological Theory and Women's Development* (Cambridge, Mass.: Harvard University Press, 1982). Some recent literature has suggested that there are significant flaws in Gilligan's research and methodological assumptions. See Iris Marion Young, "Asymmetrical Reciprocity: On Moral Respect, Wonder, and Enlarged Thought," *Constellations* 3 (1997): 340–63.

71. See Mark 7:1–8; Mark 10:2–12; Luke 6:1–5; Luke 12:27–54.

72. See Mark 7:24; Luke 7:11–17; Luke 8:40–56; Luke 12:41–48.

73. Ferguson, *Women and Religion*, 218, 235.

74. Susan Bernstein, "Confessing Feminist Theory: What's 'I' Got to Do with It?" *Hypatia* 7 (1992): 120–47, and Susan Babbitt, "Political Philosophy and the Challenge of the Personal: From Narcissism to Radical Critique," *Philosophical Studies* 77 (1995): 293–318.

3

Augustine's Rhetoric of the Feminine in the *Confessions:* Woman as Mother, Woman as Other

Felecia McDuffie

In his *Confessions,* Saint Augustine refers to the unremembered begin-ning of his life and its unknown ending in images that parallel each other suggestively. In describing his beginning he says, "I was given the comfort of woman's milk. But neither my mother nor my nurses filled their breasts of their own accord, for it was you who used them, as your law proscribes, to give me infant's food. . . . I did not wish for more than you gave, and . . . my nurses gladly passed on to me what you gave to them" (1.6).[1] In a much later evocation of his final, anticipated union with God after death, he looks forward to a similar state of dependence and satisfaction: "When at last I cling to you with all my being, for me there will be no more sorrow, no more toil. Then at last I shall be alive with true life, for my life will be wholly filled by you. You raise up and sustain all whose lives you fill" (10.28).

Augustine moves in these two passages from describing an Edenic state before desire to a beatific state in which desire is subsumed in fullness. In the first, the mother and mother surrogates function as passive conduits uniting God and the child. In the second, God becomes Mother to the childlike soul. In the Confessions, however, Augustine speaks mainly of fallen life between these two realms of the Mother, a life of separation, emptiness, and desire. In the second passage above he goes on to say, "But my life is not yet filled by you and I am a burden to myself" (10.28). In this realm of separation, Augustine encounters woman not only as mother, but also as "other," an object of his own unsatisfied desire—the desire that turns him away from God.

I will use the passages above as reference points from which to explore Augustine's representations of woman and the feminine in the Confessions. This examination reveals that while the figure of woman as mother plays a significant and positive role in the work, the shadow figure of woman as "other" plays an equally significant but more ambiguous part. The Confessions is the product of considerable skill in the arts of language. Augustine employs representations of women and the feminine as powerful rhetorical tools to evoke the fallen territory that he believes all humanity inhabits as well as the eschatological paradise in which he, and all faithful Christians, will find union with God. Figures of women function as synecdoches in the work for each of the magnetic poles between which humanity vacillates: the temporal pleasures that draw them away from God and the promise of eternal bliss that pulls them toward union with God as the fountain of being (8.10).

Augustine's rhetoric of the feminine is, of course, inextricably bound up with his theology of gender and his portrayal of the women in his own life story. Both the narrative and the theology of the Confessions subordinate women, while also reluctantly admitting their power over masculine reason. This uneasy combination subverts what Augustine saw as the proper and necessary hierarchies of God's creation. In order to overcome the problems of this reversal of hierarchies, the Confessions finally separates woman from the feminine in ways that have had lasting repercussions for the understanding and status of women in the history of Christianity. Whether or not Augustine consciously intended this separation or its consequences, his rhetoric accomplishes it in three ways: it renders the women closest to him less dangerous by masculinizing or idealizing them; it appropriates the qualities of the feminine-as-love-object for Augustine as the paradigmatic male seeker; and, finally, it assigns the territory of the mother to a masculine God. Although Augustine uses the rhetoric of the feminine to great effect, the core metaphors of the eschatological union with God subsume the feminine into the masculine, thereby losing the value of the feminine precisely as feminine.

While the mention of mothers and love objects may suggest a psychological study, my intent here is different. My aim is not to enter Augustine's psyche but, rather, to enter into the text of the *Confessions*. Peter Brown has astutely warned anyone attempting a psychological study of Augustine that "it is as difficult as it is desirable to combine competence as an historian with sensitivity as a psychologist."[2] Since my competencies are in literary and historical analysis, I intend to examine Augustine's rhetoric of the feminine from those perspectives: as a literary artifact in a historical context.

Woman as Mother

Augustine first refers to women in the *Confessions* when he uses the phrase "the comfort of woman's milk" as a synecdoche for all of God's providential mercy and care that formed him, brought him to birth, and provided for all of his needs (1.6). He describes his mother and nurses as passive conduits through which God provides the food that gives him life. As he sees it, they gladly subject themselves to the will and law of God, passing on unselfishly and naturally the abundance that God has given to them. They live as passive, obedient, and (apparently) unfallen servants of a paradisal order outside actual human experience, except perhaps in the most fleeting of moments. He imagines one such moment in the unity between a mother and the child at her breast. Even though Augustine believes that a child is actually bound by original sin from the moment of conception, his description of the loving mother and the passive child *metaphorically* evokes the childhood of the human race and the Edenic state of a humanity at peace with God. He describes another of these paradisal moments in the vision he and his mother, Monica, shared at Ostia. They are speculating on what eternal life, the eschatological union with God, will be like. Augustine says that they "laid the lips of our hearts to the heavenly stream that flows from your fountain, the source of all life" and "for one fleeting instance we reached out and touched" the eternal Wisdom of God (9.10). Falling away from this instant of union, "we returned to the sound of our own speech, in which each word has a beginning and an ending—far, far different from your word, our Lord, who abides in himself for ever, yet never grows old and gives new life to all things" (9.10). In both these paradisiacal moments, Augustine points to the past and future of humanity, domains free from separation and enclosure of the individual person from the greater whole. The actual state of humanity, and the state in which Augustine lives his life, is one of separation from God, of exile from paradise. This state of separation gives rise to desire, to distinctions, and to language—all characteristics of fallen existence.

Augustine's paradoxical depiction of the feminine in the *Confessions* reflects a more basic tension to which he turns again and again, explicitly and implicitly, in his meditations: the tension between the eternal present of union with God and the world of time, the "havoc of change" (11.29) in which all created things are mutable and contingent (12.6, 7). The created world, although good because God created it, does not partake in the fullness of God's being. Created from nothing, even its being is "little more than nothing" (12.7), and all the individual things of that creation, no matter how beautiful, are continually passing away (4.10). If the believer tries to find fulfillment in any created thing, the soul will be "torn by desires that can destroy it." Since created things are contingent, they cannot last (4.10). Only union with God can finally satisfy human desire, because only God is eternal. Augustine uses images of the feminine to depict both these states: the torment of desire for created things and the bliss of union with the Uncreated God.

In the glimpses of union with God that Augustine depicts in his description of his nurses and the vision at Ostia, his relationships with women are unmarred by desire. As a newborn, he did not wish for more than God provided (1.6). In the vision at Ostia, he and Monica are as brother and sister, drinking from the fountain of life and passing beyond their own souls "to that place of everlasting plenty, where you feed Israel forever with the food of truth" (9.10). But neither of these blissful states can last. Augustine and Monica fall away from their brief contact with Eternal Wisdom into the divided realm of language, leaving their "spiritual harvest" behind (9.10). Even his newborn self soon fell from its state of grace. Based on his observations of other babies, he describes the move from contentment with God's gifts to one of dissatisfaction. He says he "began to realize where I was and to want to make my wishes known to others, who might satisfy them." He describes his frustration and rage at his discovery that he was separate from other people and could not communicate his desires to them. This transition mirrors the devastating results of humanity's Fall. Because of their disobedience, all humankind is separated from God and all are divided within themselves (for instance, 8.10). Their wills can no longer turn naturally, in love, to the good. Rather, provided with all they need by their creator, they perversely look away from him to outer objects in the world to fulfill their never-satisfied desires. Augustine's baby self is cast out of the Eden of undifferentiated satisfaction to a fallen world of pain, separation, and hunger. After further describing his supposed state as a baby, Augustine says that "since no trace of it remains in my memory, it need no longer concern me" (1.7). To the contrary, the power of this lost unity affects his narrative and his theology profoundly. In fact, this throwaway line is an ironic harbinger of the extensive exploration of memory that Augustine conducts later in *Confessions* 10. It is precisely because the traces do remain that all these matters of his life at every stage come to concern him.

Most of the positive representations of women in the *Confessions* are of mothers, whom Augustine tends to place in a realm different from the other women who are the objects of his mature desires. His depicts his own mother, Monica (despite some negative associations to be explored later), as a model Christian woman. Obedient to her God, she also dutifully submits to her philandering husband and devotes herself to her son. Augustine believes that she nurtured his spiritual as well as his physical life. As milk came through her to the baby Augustine, she also "suckled" him on the name of Christ (3.4). She was also a channel for God's words counseling him against lust in his later life (2.3). She offered up her tears to God for his salvation from spiritual death (3.11). The framing scenes of Augustine's account of his life and conversion (books 1–9) center on Monica. The heart of his story begins with her nurturing milk and ends with his tears at her death.

The other actual mother in the *Confessions* is the woman Augustine lived with for many years, the mother of his son. Even though he experiences some degree of happiness and union with her, he never reveals her name. He describes his forced separation from her as a rending that "crushed my heart to bleeding because I loved her dearly" (6.15). Although their union was outside the law of God, this woman is "redeemed" into the realm of the pure mother by the vow of chastity she takes as she returns to Africa, leaving their son with Augustine.

There are also five symbolic "mothers" in Augustine's work: continence, Scripture, charity, church, and Jerusalem. Continence, the direct opposite of woman as a provocation to lust, is "not barren but a fruitful mother of children, of joys born of you, O Lord, her Spouse" (8.11). Scripture sustains the weak "as a mother cradles an infant in her lap" (12.27). Charity as a mother shows indulgence "when a man first enters the cradle of the faith . . . until the new man reaches perfect manhood" (5.5). Mother Church nurtures the faithful, who grow up "like fledglings" in her safe nest, "nourishing the wings of charity on the food of the faith that would save them" (4.16).

The most significant of these symbolic mothers is Jerusalem, the mother of Augustine's promised end, with God as her "Father, her Guardian, and her Spouse. . . . Jerusalem my beloved mother, where *my spiritual harvest is* laid, the fountainhead of all that I know for certain on this earth" (12.16). Augustine's depiction of Jerusalem lies at the heart of his exploration of the tension between eternity and time. In *Confessions* 12, he identifies the eschatological Jerusalem with the "Heaven of Heavens" that God created in the beginning, "before days began" (12.9). He says that this "heaven" is an intellectual creature, "created Wisdom . . . that intellectual nature which is light because it contemplates the Light" (12.15). This Wisdom is "our mother, the Heavenly Jerusalem, which lasts eternally in heaven" (12.15). He depicts this mother as a child, who clings to God with "all the strength of its love," drawing warmth and light from God, just as the child Augustine longs to draw the milk of union from the breasts of God in the passages with which I began this essay. Augustine depicts the Mother Jerusalem as the model for the soul's union with God in eternity. Although she is created, and it was possible that she would fall into the world of change, because of her pure love of God she never turned about from contemplation of Him to herself or to any lower creature (12.15). Through the rapture and joy she found in this union with God, she escaped the world of mutability and change, transcending "every vicissitude of the whirl of time" (12.9).

The real mothers in Augustine's narrative only *point to* a territory of fulfillment and security outside the realm of desire. The metaphorical mothers *inhabit* this eschatological realm. They encompass the love and nurture Augustine associates with human mothers, but are free from the ambiguities and frailties of mortal women. Augustine places these metaphorical mothers in the proper hierarchical relationship: subject to the rule and purposes of God and unstintingly giving to the child-Christian. The believer need not fear, with them as representatives of feminine good, the agonies of loss Augustine describes at the departure of the woman he loved or at Monica's death.

Woman as Other

Apart from these mothers and, possibly, women who have dedicated themselves to continence (and are thus effectively removed as possible sexual objects; see 8.11), Augustine portrays women as obstacles along the path to God. Although he firmly asserts the original goodness of all God's creation (including women and the material world), in the fallen world, the love of the material becomes a danger. He admonishes believers to look within their own souls for God, and to turn their love and desire from any created thing to the Creator. For Augustine, as the paradigmatic aspirant to salvation within the narrative, woman as other hinders both these tasks. In the story of his conversion, Augustine clearly indicates that sexual desire was the decisive obstacle that blocked his path to God. In book 7 of the *Confessions* he vividly describes the anxiety and even "agony" (7.7) that attended his struggle through the intellectual barriers that had prevented him from fully embracing the Christian faith. Those struggles, however, pale in comparison to the final battle he describes in book 8. Even as he studied philosophy, he notes, he postponed "renunciation of this world's joys." He conveys the epitome of those joys, and of his struggle, in his well-known plea to God, "Give me chastity and continence, but not yet" (8.7). The last barrier on his journey is the "disease of lust," the desire to find satisfaction in women's bodies instead of the "chaste beauty of Continence," who beckons to him from the other side of the barrier (8.11).

Unlike some early Christian authors, Augustine takes care not to blame women for his own lust. He grants them spiritual equality with men by virtue of their rational natures. He carefully stresses that although God created male and female, in his "spiritual grace they are as one," with "no more discrimination between them according to their sex than . . . between Jew and Greek or slave and freeman" (13.23). He credits Monica and the mother of his son with virtue and strength beyond his own at times (for instance, 6.15, 9.9). In the *Confessions*, he does not blame women themselves for being the objects of male desire, nor does he hold Eve primarily responsible for all the subsequent ills of humankind. According to Augustine, Adam is the actual transmitter of original sin to the human race (8.10, 10.20, 13.20). Since all the human race was "in" him, original sin descends from Adam to his children and from father to child. Augustine says that the "seed that flowed from [Adam]" gave birth to "this bitter sea, the human race" (13.20; see also *City of God* 14.11).[3]

Equality on a spiritual level, however, does not imply that women stand on an equal footing in the order of creation. Augustine portrays women generally as inferior to men: weaker, less subject to reason, and more associated with the material and things of the body. He explicitly accounts for this inferiority only at the end of the *Confessions*. While he says that men and women are equal insofar as they have "rational intelligence," he makes it clear that this equality is only an abstraction. In reality, as an embodied creature, woman is "physically subject" to man, just as the natural impulses should be subject to reason (13.32). The scriptural interpretation that undergirds the assumption of women's lower status in Augustine's worldview appears more clearly in the extensive account of creation and fall in *The City of God*, books 13 and 14. There Augustine states succinctly that woman was created inferior to man (*City* 14.13). God made Eve secondarily, out of Adam's body (*City* 12.24, 13.14). Augustine's assignment of responsibility for original sin to Adam lies not in any desire to exonerate Eve, but, rather, in his belief in her inferior position. As stated above, Augustine believes that the whole human race derives from Adam and inherited original sin from him. This may relate, at least in part, to the common notion in the ancient world that women supplied only passive matter in the generation of a child, while the father supplied the "form." Further, in Augustine's account, the wily serpent goes to Eve first, "no doubt starting with the inferior of the human pair so as to arrive at the whole by stages, supposing that the man would not be so easily gullible" (*City* 14.11). Since God intended Adam to rule over Eve as reason should rule the passions, Augustine may also have considered him more morally culpable for his failure to exercise his superior rational capacities over her.

Since the Fall disrupted the natural order in which man was subject to God, woman to man, and passion to reason, women (and men's passion for them) are impediments to any man seeking salvation and a holy life. The only "safe" women are those who are securely back in their hierar-

chical places: the mothers subject to the law of God through proper relationship to the male (to God, to husband, to God-as-husband, and to the
male child). These positive representations of the feminine, however,
tend to be two dimensional: personifications (such as Church and Scripture), nameless figures who represent the purity of Mother Continence
(such as the unsullied virgins and "staid widows" of 8.11), the nameless
wet nurses who are stand-ins both for Monica and for the nurturing care
of God, or women made doubly harmless by their absence and vows of
chastity (like the mother of his son). Even Monica, the only three-di-
mensional woman in the *Confessions*—indeed the only woman who has
a name—is idealized as the work progresses into an almost perfect veneer
of submission and purity.

Augustine characterizes actual women outside this imaginary realm of
the mother in two ways: he identifies them by analogy with the lower
faculties of the human person and he depicts them as the objects of his
own lust. Both these identifications lie in uneasy territory for Augustine.
In his version of the creation story, he analogically associates man with
reason and woman with the appetites, and he states:

> Just as in man's soul there are two forces, one of which is domi-
> nant because it deliberates and one which obeys because it is sub-
> ject to such guidance, in the same way, in the physical sense,
> woman has been made for man. In her mind and her rational
> intelligence she has a nature the equal of man's, but in sex she is
> physically subject to him in the same way as our natural impulses
> need to be subjected to the reasoning power of the mind, in order
> that the actions to which they lead may be inspired by the princi-
> ples of good conduct (13.32).

Woman's *nature* may be equal to that of man in the area rational intelligence, but this does not imply any sense of equality between men and
women in the world. As a gendered being, woman is physically subject to
man, made for him and subject to his control. One might push the analogy and infer that her own will might not lead to "good conduct," without the arbitration of (male) reason.

Male reason, unfortunately, is fallen. Instead of ruling over the "natural impulses" (all the appetites, including sexual desire) that reside in his
"lower" parts, man's higher reason and will become slaves to the "futile
muttering of [the] lower self" and "the unclean whispers of the body"

(8.11). In *The City of God*, Augustine points to the refusal of the penis to obey the dictates of reason and its tendency to react to uncontrolled desire as a particularly humiliating and disconcerting mark of the Fall (*City* 14.17, 18). Woman becomes in the *Confessions* an analogy for the lower faculties (and the body) over which humanity has no control and a synecdoche for the complex of disordered desire that draws people away from God and disrupts all natural hierarchies. This metaphorical woman exists outside the law of God and the control of male reason—she is a dangerous "other." Augustine evidences a keen awareness of this danger in his attitude toward flesh-and-blood women after his conversion. Augustine once wrote in a letter to a young man, "What is the difference whether it is in a wife or a mother, it is still Eve (the temptress) that we must be aware of in any woman."[4] In this instance, even the figure of the mother does not escape condemnation. This attitude toward women led Augustine to increasingly distance himself from women in his own life and to advocate the same practice to other men. Peter Brown has pointed to the fact that as bishop, Augustine—even more than Jerome or Ambrose—"moved in a monochrome, all-male world. He imposed strict codes of sexual avoidance on himself and his own clergy. He would never visit a woman unchaperoned, and did not allow even his own female relatives to enter the bishop's palace."[5]

Even Monica, Augustine's example of Christian motherhood, becomes a problematic "other" when her lower faculties overcome her reason. She weeps "floods of tears" and is "wild with grief" when Augustine leaves her to go to Rome. He associates her grief with the legacy of Eve (*Confessions* 5.8), "seeking in sorrow what with sorrow she had brought into the world." Although on one level Monica has Augustine's spiritual interests at heart, on another she seems aligned on the side of the "flesh," ambition, and worldly interests. She tries to arrange an advantageous marriage for him, and she delays his baptism and instead lets the "tides of temptation" beat on him (1.11). She tries selfishly to keep him from God's will in his providential journey to Rome. Although Monica night and day "poured out her tears" and "offered her heart-blood in sacrifice" to God for Augustine (5.7), the positive connotations of these images are undercut by their suggestive metaphorical relationship to the "bitter sea," an image Augustine uses to represent uncontrolled emotion, sin, and the flesh (see for instance, 13.17, 20, 24). As mentioned above, Monica's imperfections are smoothed over as the narrative of the *Confessions* progresses. In Augustine's approving portrait of her in later life, he tellingly says that although she had the "weak body of a woman," she had the "strong faith of a man, the composure of her years, and a mother's love for her son" (9.4). He distances her as far as possible from the weakness, emotion, and erotic taint of woman as "other."

Augustine also identifies women as the objects of a desire he describes as uncontrollable and deeply disturbing. Although he does not overtly blame women themselves for men's lust, he uses "woman's love" as a synecdoche for the whole complex of fallen desire, fallen nature, and loss of control that he says tormented him personally and that he identifies as the barrier between humanity and God. Augustine absorbed the Platonic notion that to find God one must turn away from the "other" of the created world and instead enter "the depths of [the] soul" (see, for instance *Confessions* 7.10, 10.7).[6] In Augustine and Monica's vision at Ostia, their thoughts ascend through a hierarchy of material things to their souls and then to heaven (9.10). In spite of his orthodox assertion of the goodness of God's creation, Augustine's fear that humanity will be overcome and drawn down by the material far outweighs any positive view of the contemplation of creation as a way to God in the *Confessions*. In Augustine's view, the soul can know God as creator through looking at the world, but it gets trapped at the level of the material because its love of material things is too great (10.6; also 2.5). Although he also absorbed to some extent the Platonic idea that the ascent to God can begin from outward creation, Plato's path that begins with the body of the beloved and the power of erotic desire would have been anathema to him precisely because the body of the beloved was so alluring and because he feared he would not be able to free himself from its thrall.[7] In this way, it would not have functioned as the starting point of his desire, but as the end point where he would have been further mired in the physical and unable to rise above it. In the narrative of his own life, August emphasizes that his love for beauty of the "lower order," most especially the love of women, did not lead him up to God but down into sensuality, vice, and despair (4.13).

In Augustine's theology, any love of the material is by definition partial and tends to lead humanity away from the unity of God, who is the fountain of life (*Confessions* 3.8). In general, Augustine saw love of God and love of the material world as "either/or." The soul tends "toward things of the lowest order" and it becomes "inflated with desire for things outside itself" (7.16). Those who seek goodness in external things "nibble at empty shadows" (9.4; see also 4.10, 10.27, 13.21). The created order, including other people, can only be loved only "in" God and not for itself. Only by continence, the withdrawing of desire and its fulfillment from the things of the outer world, can the believer be "made as one and regain that unity of self which we lost by falling apart in the search for a variety of pleasures" (10.29). Augustine's discussion of "things to be enjoyed (*frui*)" and "things to be used (*uti*)" in *On Christian Doctrine* illuminates this point. As in the *Confessions*, Augustine is careful not to blame material things themselves as barriers to God, but, rather, humanity's misuse of them. Things that are to be used, including material things, can aid believers and sustain them as they move toward blessedness. However, if the Christian clings to them, they become obstacles that impede and even deflect the believer away from the path to God (*Doctrine* 1.4). All mutable things must lead us to the Trinity itself, the only thing to be enjoyed for its own sake (*Doctrine* 1.10).

Augustine draws this notion of unity of self in part from the Platonist philosophers he read prior to his conversion. For instance, while Plotinus believed that on a cosmic level matter is good, on an individual level the body is a problem for the soul and weighs it down. For Plotinus, happiness was "bliss self-contained," and such self-contained unity was essential to happiness (Plotinus, *Ennead* 1.4.5). The *Confessions* promises this bliss in the eschatological union with God represented through the figure of the mother. It requires a turn away from woman as an objective other, an "other" Augustine associates with the passions, the body, the lower faculties, and, especially, the sexual desire he wishes to disown. Through this maneuver, Augustine can begin to dissociate his "true self" from those aspects of himself that he finds disturbing and problematic. Real women are disavowed/rejected, while the qualities he wants to retain of the idealized feminine are transferred onto God.

When every other desire, including those for wealth and worldly success, no longer held any attraction for Augustine, he says that he still found himself "held firm in the bonds of woman's love" (*Confessions* 8.1). Although in his extended discussions he clearly accepts moral responsibility for the concupiscence and divided will that hold him back from the highest form of life dedicated to God, it is instructive to note that at this crucial juncture in the narrative he displaces his own lust onto the object of that lust—a classic case of projecting his own unwanted desires onto the object he desires. For Augustine, woman as "other" is the ultimate *external* object, the most desired and thus the epitome of all the dangers of desire. Augustine depicts his own experience of sexual activity as something almost unbearably attractive, yet so ultimately unsatisfying, tormenting, and fragmenting that he must contain it and cut it off from his "true self." He characterizes sexual desire and activity as loss of self, loss of control, and loss of reason. Sexuality is wildness and frenzy (2.2), a chain that holds him earthbound (6.12). However, he equates the control of bodily desire with regaining the lost "unity of self" (10.29). As a young man he says that he "cared for nothing but to love and be loved," but that bodily desire obscured his heart (2.2). This "love," according to Augustine, was only desire, since "material things which have no soul could not be true objects for my love" and his real need was for God. Even the body of the beloved serves the fallen person only as an object for lust and depravity (3.1). True love relates only to God, or to the souls of other people "in" God. The love that leads to blessedness is an undivided love (*Doctrine* 1.4), and the Trinity alone is the only proper object of the soul's "enjoyment" (*frui*). Other things and people can be "used" (*uti*) to turn the soul to God, but only if they present no danger of deflecting the pilgrim soul from its journey to heaven. Women can be proper objects of love only as to their souls and only to the extent that the differences of their gender have been erased through holiness, old age, or sexual renunciation.

Augustine also portrays women as practical obstacles to a life of withdrawal from the world. When he and his friends were planning to leave public life and take up a communal existence of cultivated leisure and study, women stood in the way.[8] Augustine was planning to marry, and some of the others already had wives. As Augustine recalls, "When we began to ask ourselves whether the women would agree to the plan, all our carefully made arrangements collapsed and broke to pieces in our hands and were discarded. Once more we turned to our sighs and groans" (*Confessions* 6.14). Here again women are the occasion of fragmentation and grief, binding men to the material world of the senses and the social world of obligations and ambition.

Two particularly significant vignettes in the *Confessions* relate to Augustine's rejection of the material (and the feminine). The first occurred just before his conversion in book 8, when a visitor tells him the story of Antony, the Egyptian monk. Augustine comments on the monks' ability to savor the sweetness of God and "of the fruitful wastes of the desert" (8.6) through their lives of celibacy, sacrifice, and rejection of the world. The desert as a metaphor for the spiritual life appealed to Augustine because it was obviously "wiped clean" of anything that could appeal to the lower appetites. Only in such a "de-natured" nature could the spirit become fruitful. This fruitful desert contrasts with the "barren waste" that Augustine says he had made of his own spirit by his attachment to the material and his separation from God (2.10). In this way Augustine sets up the paradoxical juxtaposition of the spiritual fruitfulness of the desert against the barrenness of the world with its enticements, especially to the physical desires and appetites. The second story is of Monica's "basket full of the fruits of the earth," which it was her custom to take to the shrines of saints on their memorial days. In Milan, under the influence of Ambrose, she "learned to bring to the shrines of the martyrs a heart full of prayers far purer than any of these gifts" (6.2). This privileging of prayers over the fruits of creation as a way to God is part of Monica's adoption of more "masculine" virtues as the narrative progresses, as well as a foreshadowing of her son's turning from the material to the spiritual, from the outer to the inner, from woman as other to God as mother.

As I will explore in the rest of this essay, however, the "masculine" virtues of reason, control, ambition, and even philosophical contemplation finally fail Augustine in his quest for redemption. He turns instead to the "feminine" virtues of selfless love, nurturance, receptivity, humility, and passivity. Since these virtues are "higher" in the inverted hierarchy of the Kingdom, in which the last shall be first, Augustine separates them from their problematic association with actual women and appropriates them for the masculine through his identification of them with himself and his God. This rhetorical appropriation takes two forms: first, all the other mother figures in the work become secondary to God as the Mother of Augustine's child-self; second, Augustine takes the role of receptive beloved to God as Lover.

God as Mother, Augustine as Child

While the *Confessions* uses figures of the mother to point to the eschatological union with God, Augustine's images of God as Mother form a powerful and more direct way to speak of God's care and love. God is a safer and a more reliable source of spiritual nurture and the actual guarantor of the heavenly union to come. He is also the only truly worthy object of human love—the only one to be truly and fully enjoyed (*frui*). In relation to this Mother God, Augustine can separate himself altogether from the problems attendant on association with the feminine in the person of real women (as well the difficulties of fallen masculinity) and resume the asexual role of the child. In this twofold strategy Augustine is able to overcome the dichotomy of "woman as mother/woman as other" and to avoid the pitfalls of his sexual desires for women that he found so problematic. In this strategy Augustine, as the infant self with the God-mother, is able to imagine a blissful union without the messy complications of adult sexual relationships. In Augustine's theology, desire for a half-remembered blessedness and happiness motivates the search for God and can only find its true fulfillment in him. However, Augustine confesses that he has a problem accounting for the human idea of happiness and puzzles over whether happiness is actually somewhere in our memory (*Confessions* 10.20). He asks, "Where and when . . . did I experience a state of blessed happiness, so that I am enabled to remember it and love it and long for it?" (10.21). This state of blessed happiness that Augustine "remembers," yet does not remember, is the state of union with God that he chooses to depict in terms of the primal union between mother and child in the passage from book 1 of the *Confessions* that opens this essay.

In the second passage referred to at the beginning of the essay, Augustine speaks of union with God after death in terms that could suggest the same union of mother and baby. He depicts himself as a child, dependent and clinging to a God who sustains and fills him (10.28). He uses the same feminine imagery for God at many points in the *Confessions*. He pictures God as the Mother to whom the faithful soul clings at last in a realm beyond sorrow and separation, held in "an embrace from which [the soul] is not severed by fulfillment of desire" (10.6). Augustine's God is, like a mother, the "fountain of life" (3.8) and "fountain of mercy" (6.16). In describing the vision at Ostia, Augustine says that he and Monica "laid the lips of our hearts to the heavenly stream that flows from your fountain, the source of all life which is in you" (9.10). He and Monica become as brother and sister nursing at the breasts of God. God's hand is "poised ready" to lift the child Augustine "from the mire" and wash him clean (6.16). This God is not a fallible, earthly mother who can die, nor the mythical mother of a lost Eden, but one filled with power, whose love can overcome sin and death.

In Augustine's conversion story (8.12), he leaves behind both his masculinity and his adulthood, returning to childhood to become the son of Continence, Charity, and Mother Church. He tells of sitting under the fig tree (which recapitulates the tree in Eden, and thus the childhood of the human race), being overcome by a great storm of tears because of his wordless desire for something he could not accomplish for himself (recalling the wordless tears and desire in his depiction of babies). Directed by the innocent voice of a child, he takes up the book of Scripture and reads it in a new way. In describing the baptisms of his little group of friends and family, he says that his son, Adeodatus, was "in your grace no younger than ourselves. Together we were ready to begin our schooling in your ways. We were baptized, and all anxiety over the past melted away from us" (9.6). He describes himself and his friends as "desperately seeking the way of happiness . . . like three hungry mouths, able only to gasp out our needs to one another, while our eyes were on you, waiting for you to grant us, in due time, our nourishment" (6.10). From his perspective as one of the redeemed, Augustine asks "even when all is well with me, what am I but a creature suckled on your milk and feeding on yourself, the food that never perishes?" (4.1). All these conversion motifs suggest a rebirth into a world in which language no longer implies separation but, through the Word of Scripture, brings innocence, peace, and real sustenance. This is the world unbound by time, one in which the soul takes the part, however briefly, of the New Jerusalem that Augustine evokes in *Confessions* 12, the "sublime creature" who never falls away from God, but is bound to him in love, drawing warmth and light from God "like a noon that never wanes" (12.15).

The alternatives Augustine offers to the reader are holding fast to this Mother God or relapsing into an existence that resembles the dark depths of the sea (13.2). Although he sometimes speaks of the Christian moving beyond the infant state and on to the "solid food" of difficult doctrine (13.18, 22), Augustine's depiction of his own life implies an end in a state of union and ease like that of a baby at the breast. This state is far removed from the world of separation, language, and "difficult doctrine." Augustine associates maturity with an all-consuming sexual desire, and he suggests a solution in the return to a "childhood" of relative innocence and dependence on God as Mother.

God as Lover, Augustine as Bride

The second rhetorical motif in the *Confessions* that serves to separate the positive attributes of the feminine from the problematic nature of woman is Augustine's appropriation of the position of the feminine-as-beloved for himself in relation to God as masculine Lover and Spouse. Although Augustine associates masculinity with reason and the spirit, he realizes that the Platonist *logos* doctrine of reason and enlightenment lacks something that is fulfilled in the Christian doctrine of the Incarnation, with its ties to humility and the body (7.9). He sees that even when men "by dint of study . . . have skill to number stars and grains of sand, to measure the tracts of constellations and trace the paths of planets," they cannot reach God by virtue of reason; they can only prepare by humility for God to come to them (5.3). Augustine associates masculinity with pride and ambition and realizes that it does not lead either to happiness or to holiness (6.6).

Augustine also associates masculinity with sin. In the *Confessions*, he refers to Adam as the "first sinner in whom we all died and from whom we are all descended in a heritage of misery" (10.20). Augustine's account of creation and fall in the *City of God* makes even more explicit his belief that all humanity inherits original sin through the male line, since all humanity derives from him (*City* 12.22). He carries the association of masculinity and sin into his own life story. He portrays his father, Patricius, the most important male figure in his early life, as prey to lust and unfaithful to his wife. Patricius was an unbeliever, and Augustine says that his mother "did all that she could to see that you, my God, should be a Father to me rather than he" (1.11). Monica's desire for an "immaculate conception" for Augustine suggests not simply a wish to protect him from Patricius's unbelief, but perhaps a desire to protect him from the taint of original sin passed through the male line.

The *Confessions* also explicitly associates the father with the son's budding sexuality and the lust that would torment him. At the first signs of Augustine's incipient manhood, his father rejoices in his son's virility and the fact that he will have grandchildren (2.3). Augustine, by contrast, associates his growing into manhood with the "brambles of lust" growing high above his head while his father stands by and does nothing to root them out (2.3). In that section he speaks of God as the "husband" of his soul (in the agricultural sense of husbandman), one who digs around vines and gets rid of brambles so that fruit can grow. He sees his own father as failing him and leaving him prey to empty lust, so that God must take the part of Father. Augustine associated his own fatherhood (and thus masculinity) with sin, attributing all that was good in his own son to God and saying that "there was nothing of mine in that boy except my sin" (9.6). Further, he makes his search for God outside himself symbolically parallel with the "outwardness" of male sexuality, saying, "I searched for you outside myself, and, disfigured as I was, I fell upon the lovely things of your creation" (10.27).

In another complex of images, Augustine associates his growth into adulthood, and his masculinity, with his skill at rhetoric. He also tells how words (and masculinity) finally failed him, while the "mute sufferings of my soul were loud voices" calling on God's mercy (7.7). He connects his parents' unconcern over his unchastity to their desire that he develop skill as an orator (2.2). His father "cared only that I should have a fertile tongue, leaving my heart to bear none of your fruits, my God" (2.3). Augustine thus associates, through his father's concerns, his tongue with his sexual organs. Patricius wants his son to be fertile both in begetting children and in worldly success. Augustine also describes how he "fell in with a set of sensualists, men with glib tongues who ranted and raved and had the snares of the devil in their mouths" (3.6). The literal penis in the fallen world is also outside the law of God. Man's reason no longer controls it, and original sin is literally transmitted through it. The seed that "flowed" from Adam has become "this bitter sea, the human race . . . never at rest from its surge and swell" (13.20; see also *City* 14.17–18). Through this rhetorical contrast, the mother's breast is a channel for the milk of God's care, whereas the penis is the channel for sin.

In contrast to the negative implications of the masculinity he inherited from his father Patricius as well as his father Adam, Augustine presents a positive picture of masculinity in Ambrose, the bishop of Milan. He speaks of his first encounter with Ambrose, "who was known throughout the world as a man whom there were few to equal in goodness. At that time his gifted tongue never tired of dispensing the richness of your corn, the joy of your oil, and the sober intoxication of your wine. Unknown to me, it was you who led me to him, so that I might be led by him to you. This man of God received me like a father" (5.13). As an advocate and example of celibacy and continence, Ambrose has removed himself from the world of male sexuality and ambition. In contrast to the "fertile tongue" that Augustine's own father wished for him so that he might attain worldly success (2.2–3), Ambrose's tongue is productive of the corn, oil, and wine of God's grace. In Ambrose, Augustine finds a father for his new life of continence and dedication to God, a new understanding of Scripture (5.14), and a new belief that rhetoric could be used in the service of God.

Having rejected the disturbing masculinity of the world and having not yet attained the "fertile" masculinity of Ambrose, Augustine identifies himself (and the male seekers to whom he addresses the *Confessions*) with the feminine.[9] Presenting himself as an exemplar of the sinner seeking God, he describes his own emptiness, his passivity, and his desire not to beget but to bear fruit to God. This characterization places him in a position that the larger culture as well as his own theology usually connected with women. Several factors contribute to these associations: the configuration of female sexual organs, the traditional view of women as the inferior and receptive partner in sexual activity, the subordinate position of women in society, their inferiority in the order of creation, and the widespread belief that women contributed only passive matter (not active form or intellect) to their children. In contrast to the power of God, however, all human beings are in the position of emptiness and need and thus associated with the feminine. Before the activity and providence of God, all humanity is passive. Images of Augustine as empty, divided, and scattered without God appear throughout the *Confessions* (for instance, 1.2, 4.1, 5.2, 9.1, 11.29). He asks, "What place is there in me to which my God can come, what place that can receive the God who made heaven and earth? . . . I should be null and void and could not exist at all, if you, my God, were not in me" (1.2). The "fruitful wastes of the desert" in which Antony finds God (8.6) is an image for both the emptiness and the potential of the feminine in relationship to God. In these paradoxical juxtapositions, Augustine both salvages and appropriates the stereotypical and less-valued qualities of the feminine, and in the process they lose a great deal of their negative charge.

Augustine also rhetorically places himself in the feminine position as the beloved or bride of God. The *Confessions* has been described as autobiography and as prayer, but it can also be seen as an extended conversation with a lover. Its tone of direct address and longing is strongly reminiscent of the Song of Songs, perhaps reflecting the influence of Ambrose's many sermons on that portion of Scripture. Augustine portrays his stance toward God as one of emptiness and yearning (for instance, 11.2, 1.2–5, 3.4). The conventions of the ancient Mediterranean world made a clear distinction between lover and beloved: the male lover took the active and dominant role, while the beloved (whether male or female) took the "feminine" role of passive recipient. Augustine consistently pictures God as the active lover and himself as empty and receptive, thirsting for God's love and grace. He eagerly awaits God's embrace; God is a jealous lover who will allow Augustine to find pleasure only in himself (2.2). God had prepared his soul to receive him by inspiring it to long for him (13.1). Christ is the lover who inflames the heart with words of love, the Bridegroom of his soul (4.15, 7.17, 13.15). In his search for God, Augustine says he "quivered with fear, yet at the same time . . . was aglow with hope," praying that God would set him on fire with love (9.4). He begs God to clasp him to himself and enter him (1.5), and describes God piercing his heart with the arrows of his love (9.2) and filling him (10.28). In Augustine's allegory of creation, he associates the masculine with reason and the feminine with desire. Finally, it is not through "masculine" reason or pride but through "feminine" humility and yearning of the heart that Augustine comes to God (8.4–6).

Conclusion

The *Confessions* contains a powerful rhetoric of the feminine. Augustine describes his life (and thus the life of the Christian) as a circle beginning and ending in blissful union with the mother. Humanity moves from an unremembered union with God in Eden, which Augustine suggests through the metaphor of the blissful oneness of mother and baby, to an unrealized (yet hoped for) union with God as Mother beyond the fragmentation and desire of the fallen world. Apart from the idealized mother who exists for the child, however, woman is other—an object apart from the male self. This woman serves Augustine as a synecdoche for all external objects that draw fallen humanity away from unity within the soul and unity with God. This synecdoche depends, in part, on Augustine's identification of woman with the lower attributes of the human person. The theology as well as the narrative of the *Confessions* subordinates women to men, consistent with Augustine's belief that they are inferior to men in the order of creation. He associates women with the instincts, the passions, and the body: things, good in themselves, which have become dangerous, since the male power of reason can no longer control them.

However, Augustine also recognizes that the virtues associated with woman's lower position in the cosmic hierarchy—emotion, humility, and passivity among others—are paradoxically necessary to his own salvation and that of the men to whom he addresses the *Confessions*. Unable to transcend what he saw as the ordering of creation and wary of the danger of woman as other, he separates woman from the feminine. He masculinizes or idealizes the female figures he considers virtuous. Then he appropriates feminine virtues for the higher, masculine level of the hierarchical scheme. While this might be considered a triumph for the feminine in some abstract sense, it leaves woman in an unfortunate position. She is still inferior, and she now possesses only half her being—the dangerous other. Just as Augustine progressively retreated into an all-male world in his life, so also he excludes women from the heart of the *Confessions*. Although he uses the rhetoric of the feminine to great effect, and although the figure of Monica plays a significant role in the narrative, the two core metaphors of the eschatological union with God subsume the feminine into the masculine, and by so doing, they augment the position that denigrates the feminine as such. In this view, only when the feminine is subsumed into the masculine does it become transformed and valued. These images are, first, the masculine God as Mother and Augustine as child, and, second, God as Lover and Augustine as feminine beloved.

The *Confessions* was certainly not the first document to incorporate these views of women or to appropriate the feminine in the service of male salvation. As one of the founding documents of Western culture, however, it has certainly had a great and long-lasting influence on the way both the church and the larger world have perceived women, represented them, and enculturated them. Whether or not Augustine intended all the meanings I have drawn out of his representations of women, and whether or not he would have approved of some of the results of those representations, the rhetoric of the feminine in the *Confessions* has had a lasting influence in the West. Augustine's work has often been implicated in the separation of soul from body, physical from spiritual, erotic from holy, and woman from man that have plagued the history of Christianity. Since Augustine's work does celebrate some aspects of the feminine, however, perhaps his rebellious postmodern daughters can enter into a dialogue with him and bring the revalued feminine—valued in its own right—back into the discourse and into the lived experience of real women's lives.

References

Augustine, Saint. *The City of God*. Translated by Henry Bettenson and with an introduction by John O'Meara. London: Penguin Books, 1984.
———. *Confessions*. Translated and with an introduction by R. S. Pine-Coffin. London: Penguin Books, 1961.
———. *On Christian Doctrine*. Translated by D. W. Robertson Jr. New York: Macmillan; London: Collier Macmillan, 1958.
Brown, Peter. *Augustine of Hippo: A Biography*. Berkeley and Los Angeles: University of California Press, 1967.
———. *The Body and Society: Men, Women, and Sexual Renunciation in Early Christianity*. New York: Columbia University Press, 1988.
Plotinus. *The Enneads*. Translated by Stephen MacKenna. 2d ed. Revised B. S. Page. London: Faber and Faber, 1956.

Notes

1. Saint Augustine, *Confessions*, trans. and with an introduction by R. S. Pine-Coffin (London: Penguin Books, 1961).

2. Peter Brown, *Augustine of Hippo: A Biography* (Berkeley and Los Angeles: University of California Press, 1967), 31.

3. Saint Augustine, *The City of God*, trans. Henry Bettenson and with an introduction by John O'Meara (London: Penguin Books, 1984). All references hereafter will be in the body of the text as *City*, by book and chapter number.

4. Quoted by Brown, *Augustine of Hippo*, 63 (*Letter* 245, 10).

5. Peter Brown, *The Body and Society: Men, Women, and Sexual Renunciation in Early Christianity* (New York: Columbia University Press, 1988), 396.

6. For Augustine's own account of his journey through Platonism, see *Confessions*, book 7.

7. In *On Christian Doctrine*, for instance, he connects the idea of the invisible things of God being understood by corporeal things (Rom. 1:20) with the Platonic idea of the material as corporeal signs reflecting the eternal reality of the One (*On Christian Doctrine* 1.4). Saint Augustine, *On Christian Doctrine*, trans. D. W. Robertson Jr. (New York: Macmillan; London: Collier Macmillan, 1958). All references hereafter will be in the body of the text as *Doctrine*, by book and chapter number.

8. Peter Brown notes that Augustine later referred to this period of his life "as a time of *Christianae vitae otium*" and links it to "the ancient ideal of *otium liberale*, a 'cultured retirement,'" (*Augustine of Hippo*, 115).

9. For a persuasive description of the male audience for whom the *Confessions* was written, see Brown's *Augustine of Hippo*, chap. 16, esp. 158 and 167.

4

Confessing Monica

Virginia Burrus and Catherine Keller

It is difficult to force Augustine to confess his mother fixation, partly because he is already so eager to do so. He is, after all, the man who virtually invented the closet, so that he could *come out* of its hollowed, hallowed interiority again and again, making a subject of his private perversions, flamboyantly exhibiting his stubbornly bent will. Monica is among the guilty pleasures enjoyed by the author of the *Confessions*. Moreover, unlike stolen pears, she is a love that the author cannot possibly renounce, a pleasure he cannot forgo. She emerges as the irrepressible subject of a holy life in a work that resists hagiography, as an irreducibly carnal figure in a tale that insists on love's sublimation, as Wisdom seductively incarnate in a book that has little to say about Jesus. Finally, she erupts, she *opens up*, as an excitingly fertile, disturbingly overdetermined, matrix of meaning, at the very place in the Scriptures where Augustine— sitting in silent contemplation—expects to find *nothing at all*.

This present meditation on the mother in Augustine's *Confessions* is written with two hands, one historical and literary, the other theological and exegetical. The text may, like *Confessions* itself, seem to divide naturally into two parts. Yet thoughts overlap, words interweave: it is finally impossible to say precisely where one subject begins and another ends.

Confessions is a woman's life. Is that so strange a claim? More paradoxical still, the womb of the life—cradled in the center of the text—is the account of the woman's *death*. It is in grieving his mother Monica that Augustine discovers his point of departure, just when we might have thought he was finished with his account. He departs, he begins again, then, in the middle—in *medias res*. (*Every beginning is also a departure— from something*). Grieving Monica, remembering his mother, delivering her eulogy to God in the pseudoprivacy of his ancient prayer closet, Augustine learns to read; he begins to write in earnest. *In principio Deus creavit*, runs the text. "In the beginning you made heaven and earth," he addresses the author of both Scripture and cosmos wonderingly (11.3).[1] Augustine creates too; he is also a writer: *he makes his confession* brashly "in this book before the many who will read it" (10.1). But perhaps we make too much of his sheer originality, his autogenerativity.[2] We forget—or fail to notice—that it is his mother who provides him the narrative material out of which to conceive time and space, to frame the very cosmos. Monica's life (centered on her death) gives him his opening, keeps his story of conversion open. Monica is Augustine's eternally unfinished business; she is present in all his beginnings.[3]

A beginning that is in the middle of the thing, an irruptive potentiality that resists narrative closure, Monica plots and is emplotted, simultaneously generates and disrupts story lines. Less an item than a happening, she *takes place* in the argument of Augustine's *Confessions*, and thus we must strive to understand *what that place is*. Present from the beginning (1.11), she meets her end (and in a sense also makes her formal debut) in book 9, where the narrative portion of the *Confessions* likewise concludes. There is a certain substitutionary logic to the mother's dying the death impossible for the author of an autobiography. The existence of book 9 nonetheless presents a dilemma, for book 8 already contains all the makings of another kind of ending, having staged the intense struggle of will that culminates in Augustine's dramatic "conversion" (the liberating death of his formerly enslaved self).[4] For the first-time reader, it must come as something of a surprise when Augustine extends his story into a ninth book that relates, first, his ascetic withdrawal and baptism and, second, his memories of the life of his mother. The centerpiece of these memories is a shared mystical experience occurring shortly before Monica's death and Augustine's oddly unexplained and open-ended departure for Africa at the portentous age of thirty-three. Such a dizzying spiritual encounter, following the dramatic experience of divine intervention in book 8's scene of conversion, seems excessive—more than the story demands, almost more than it can accommodate.

Yet, perversely, having scripted such a dubious *double climax*, Augustine may seem to add narrative insult to injury by going on to write a distinctly *anticlimactic* tenth tome. Previously swept along on the waves of the author's passionate recounting of the misadventures of his youth and the struggles of his conversion, tossed high by the unexpected thrill of his maternally mediated heavenly ascent, now as readers we find ourselves stalled on the vast, midlife calm of his mental abstraction. We may share Pelagius's outrage that Augustine is killing the tale in more ways than one: when viewed from the sober perspective of the morning after, conversion loses its sharp edge, the bloom of optimism fades, and old habits reassert their sway even in the life of a would-be saint.[5] (Who wants to read about *that*?) But books 9 and 10 are only the beginning of Augustine's refusal to allow his *Confessions* their proper end: three more seemingly superfluous books follow, as he makes yet another fresh start, now posing as biblical commentator in locating his account in the beginning, in Genesis, in the generation of world and written word. At this late point in the text, Augustine's snail's-pace advance through the first slim chapter of the capacious Book of books may seem to make not only a mess but also a mockery of the search for an end to the story of his life. Sucked into the ever-receding depths of Scripture's polyvalence, almost parodically prolific in his interpretive reinscriptions, Augustine the reader has, by any strictly linear measure of progress, come to a virtual standstill. Has the text, drained of desire, simply petered out?[6] Or, rather, as Augustine would have us understand it, has his own restless curiosity—tracked over time—been converted into eternal rest in the performative reading of the scriptural Sabbath?

The question is, Why *does* Augustine keep writing so far past his famous conversion? What—if anything—links the autobiographical books 1–9 of *Confessions*, which the tale of Monica finally overtakes, with the exegetical books 10–13, in turn *overtaken* by silent repose? (A repose that represents not, Augustine would urge, the stasis of death but instead yet another opening door [13.38]).

We can begin by observing that the reader's quest for the structured coherence of *Confessions* is inextricably intertwined with Augustine's narrated quest for Wisdom: "to love Wisdom herself, whoever she might be, and to search for her, pursue her, hold her, and embrace her firmly— these were the words that excited me and set me burning with fire" (3.4). As Danuta Shanzer interprets him, the author of *Confessions* constructs a deliberately enigmatic and suspenseful text by combining a proverbial "choice motif"—*Folly versus Wisdom*—with a "search motif"—*where is Wisdom to be found?* At least as early as book 3, when Augustine explicitly represents himself as seduced by Folly (3.6), "we are detectives with a Scriptural clue (Stultitia presupposes her opposite), and a Scriptural description or identikit picture of Sapientia, if we are prepared to use it to find or recognize her," Shanzer suggests.[7] Shanzer's reference to the "Scriptural clue" of book 3—namely, the allegorical figures of Folly and Wisdom in Proverbs 9—is itself a further clue but one that we, like the Augustine of book 3, have trouble putting to good use. Searching for the hidden Sapientia, we may not notice that she is there alongside Stultitia from the start: "And behold I saw something—or someone—neither disclosed to the proud nor laid bare to children, but humble in gait, sublime in accomplishment, and veiled in mysteries. And I was not the type who would be able to enter into her or to bend my neck to her guidance" (3.5). It is difficult to say at what point most readers realize that the Holy Scripture—for that is "who" is here described—does not merely offer clues but is also itself (*herself*) the answer to the riddle posed by the work: the Augustine of books 11–13, lost in silent contemplation of the biblical writings, absorbed in their depths, has indeed reached the end of the quest delineated in books 1–9. It is difficult to say at what point readers *also* realize that the end is always only beginning: there is no limit to knowing the beloved, to loving Wisdom, to interpreting a text. Perhaps we only recognize that Scripture is Augustine's Lady Wisdom when we too have become her lovers—readers sufficiently skilled as to be able to perceive the unity in a complex and open-ended work.[8] Some of us may have to read the *Confessions* again and again before we see the Lady at all.

Shanzer suggests that "Scripture's many faces, when she is seen as a woman, prefigure her many interpretations, when she is seen as a text."[9] One face that Shanzer fails to mention is the face of Augustine's mother. Indeed, Shanzer's framing of the autobiographical allegory of Folly and Wisdom developed in books 3–7 and culminating in the Herculean "choice" of book 8 seems to leave the minibiography of Monica in book 9 awkwardly caught, along with the rest of book 9 and book 10, in the liminal zone between the narrative quest and its exegetical consummation. Yet we would suggest that the "Life of Monica" is the crux of the narrativized enigma (*where is Wisdom?*), a riddle that is not so much solved as displaced—repeated and refrained—by the later exegetical performance (*she is [in] Scripture*). "Behold, moved by your prayers, I come to you, natural mother of all things . . . whose single divinity is venerated over the whole earth under many faces, varying rites, and changing names." Thus speaks the goddess in her seaside epiphany in Apuleius's *The Golden Ass*—a text that may be of special importance for understanding the structural significance of the figure of Monica in Augustine's *Confessions*. As John Winkler has argued, the eleventh and final book of Apuleius's novel, which contains the solemn manifestation of the many-named and many-faced goddess Isis, comes as a shock to a first-time reader of this witty and sophisticated text (*Golden Ass* 11.5). It also dramatically destabilizes the familiar parodic quest tale that is seemingly Apuleius's point of departure—namely Pseudo-Lucian's *Lucius, or the Ass*. "For if the ass-tale is a take-off on 'I went in quest of wisdom' narratives, then Apuleius has translated the parody, with all its ridicule of the quester intact, but has added at the end the very sort of epiphany and revelation that the parodied works contained."[10] Winkler emphasizes the uncertainty introduced by the supplemental Isiac book, which reinstates divine revelation in (relatively) "straight" terms at the conclusion, and outside the frame, of an (ambiguously) parodic narrative. The Apuleian novel, he argues, thereby refuses to adjudicate between competing truth claims and thus shifts the burden of decision to the reader, while at the same time making it clear that the decision lies outside the domain of rationally negotiable propositions. "*The Golden Ass* is an evocation of a religious experience bracketed in such a way that the reader must, but cannot, decide the question of its truth," Winkler suggests. "The implicit argument of the novel is that belief in Isis or in any integrating cosmic hypothesis is a radically individual act that cannot be shared."[11]

Augustine follows Apuleius's example, constructing a quest narrative that begins falsely with carnal curiosity and ends felicitously with divine disclosure.[12] Here—in contrast to his treatment of Virgil's *Aeneid*, for example—he lets a significant literary predecessor go utterly unnamed. This may be a necessary exercise of tact, where allusion so dangerously combines admiration with aggression. The Apuleian novel is quite possibly already making a mockery of Christianity,[13] and if Augustine subtly turns the tables in countermimicry, he cannot deny that there is also genuine flattery in his imitation. Apuleius seems to have written his novel less to propagandize the Isiac cult than to question the totalizing claims of all such cults, and Augustine arguably replays Apuleius's plot less to unseat a false goddess, Isis, and replace her with a true one, Wisdom, than to undermine an ironic agnosticism so as to assert the authority of divine revelation, not least by sternly imposing his "converted" perspective on the account of his earlier life. But how successful is he? As Winkler describes Augustine's *Confessions*, noting the contrast with Apuleius, "The present narrator invades his past as an enemy territory, using his god as a powerful ally to destroy the lingering vestiges of the pleasure he originally felt."[14] The contrast is real; nonetheless, we should not exaggerate the differences between these two literary works, the one a novel narrated in the first person and frequently read as autobiography (indeed, so read by Augustine himself), the other a novelistic autobiography occasionally labeled (as Augustine labeled Apuleius's work) a lying fiction.[15] Each pivots around a surprise ending that calls upon us to reassess the text retrospectively, thereby thematizing the necessity for artful interpretation—underlining the indispensability, and also the indeterminacy, of exegesis.

Winkler warns readers of Apuleius not to impose monologic and moralizing readings on a fundamentally complex and deliberately ambiguous text. Such a warning would likewise be well heeded by readers of the later North African. *Confessions* is seductive and hermeneutically challenging precisely where it is most powerfully empathetic—and most surprisingly noncommittal—in its replaying of the emotions of the author's earlier selves. Augustine sustains a remarkable level of ambivalence throughout the narrative books of his work—though unlike Apuleius he (narrowly) avoids parody. To cite merely a well-known example: his recollection of a boyhood theft of pears, frequently viewed as evidence of excessive critique of past behavior, skillfully introduces and interlaces moral judgment with vivid evocations of the fundamentally "good" pleasures that motivated the paltry crime—sensory gratification, social esteem, and above all "the delightful bond" of friendship (2.5). Much as Apuleius's narrator delivers a harrowing rendition of a "murder" that turns out to be no more than a slashing of wineskins (*Golden Ass* 2.32–3.10), here Augustine deliberately makes much ado about almost nothing. His purpose, it seems, is to cut moral transgressions down to their ordinary, nonheroic size while at the same time restoring a sense of their modest complexities. Likewise, Augustine's tender accounts of his various (with the exception of his concubine, homoerotic) "lovers" (for example, 4.8, 6.15) appear no more regretful than Lucius's enthusiastic recountings of his luscious nights with Fotis (for example, *Golden Ass* 2.16–17). (In fact, if we take Lucius's later recriminations of his mistress Fotis seriously, Augustine may be the less regretful).

Perhaps even more surprising (and even more often repressed) than the relatively forgiving, almost Apuleian eye that Augustine casts on his own past is the negativity that he introduces into the supplementary "book of the mother." As we shall see, he thereby sustains a positive ambivalence where we might expect (indeed, have been led by his interpreters to expect) a more reductively idealizing portrait to emerge. In this respect, book 9 of *Confessions* is as much a counterpart to the portrait of Venus in Apuleius's centrally embedded tale of Psyche and Cupid (*Golden Ass* 6) as it is an evocation of the final epiphany of Isis (*Golden Ass* 11). (Like Monica, Venus's opinion of what—or who—is best for her son initially differs from his own, but is subsequently revised).[16] The "ultimate" surprise ending of *Confessions*—showcasing an unambivalently positive representation of the divine female figure Sapientia/Scriptura that more closely matches Apuleius's Isis—is deferred to the last three books, which thus supplement the supplement. As in Apuleius's novel, the extended revelation—itself taking unexpected form—includes the equally unexpected message that no revelation is conclusive. Texts continue to give rise to interpretation. "For I know that what is understood in one way by the mind can be given multiple material significations; and what is given material signification in one way can be understood in many ways by the mind," muses Augustine. "For behold the simple love of God and neighbor—how it is given material expression in multiple sacraments and innumerable languages and, within each language, in innumerable turns of phrase!" (13.24).[17] It appears, then, that Augustine's *Confessions* only pretends to imagine itself the one and only, first and unique, thereby slyly challenging us to notice its deep dependency and intricate intertextuality. Augustine writes over the lines of other texts, both biblical and secular, as we have just seen. He has precursors, but we should not forget that he *also* has contemporaries. Others of the time—other Christians—are writing female biographies, inscribing the lives of women. They too are writing over the lines of other texts—tales of martyrdom and letters of consolation as well as stories of love. There is a trend, almost a fad. Gregory of Nyssa writes of his sister Macrina barely more than a decade before Augustine writes of his mother; Jerome writes of his longtime companion Paula a decade or so after *Confessions* is penned; nor are they the only ones doing it.[18] Augustine is not sheerly original, then; he inherits from the past and he is also in the thick of something ongoing. Like Gregory and Jerome, he writes from the perspective of a man grieving; like these other authors, he mourns a much loved woman, mourns a woman known for her grieving, thus grieves like a woman—reluctantly, and also excessively, with ambivalence. "The tears dried in my eyes. . . . It did not bring me to tears. . . . I did not weep." So he begins, only to reverse himself quickly. "The tears which I had been holding back streamed down, and I let them flow as freely as they would," Augustine next confesses, pleading that his reader not despise such womanish behavior but, rather, imitate it. "Let him not mock at me but weep himself, if his charity is great." (9.12)

Like Gregory and still more like Jerome, Augustine writes with tearful ambivalence of a woman, and he inscribes his ambivalence into the life. He writes with two hands, giving praise with one and taking it away with the other. The lives of women are not quite hagiographies, no matter who writes them. Monica, Augustine makes painfully clear, was no saint.[19] She had bad habits, perverse desires. "I cannot presume to say that from the time when she was reborn in baptism no word contrary to your commands ever fell from her lips," notes the son in the midst of his mourning. Since he is stating the obvious, why does he say it? "I will lay aside for a while all the good deeds which my mother did. For them I thank you, but now I pray to you for her sins" (9.13).

Indeed, Monica the well-intentioned sinner never quite gets it right, according to her son. Her life is always in need of revision; she is always in need of our prayers. We see this most clearly from the vantage point of her death, where Augustine, who has just promised to "omit not a word that my mind can bring to birth concerning my mother, your servant," now seems to have an oddly selective memory, zeroing in first on an account of childhood alcoholism framed by class conflict, on the one hand, and spousal abuse interlaced with intergenerational conflict, on the other, positioning his mother as a dubious pupil in a school of very hard knocks indeed. "Each day she added a few more drops to her daily sip of wine. 'But little things despise and little by little you shall come to ruin.' It soon became a habit, and she would drink her wine at a draught, almost by the cupful" (9.8).

Peter Brown notes that, in book 9's portrayal, "Monica, the idealized figure that had haunted Augustine's youth like an oracle of God, is subtly transformed, by Augustine's analysis of his present feelings upon remembering her death, into an ordinary human being, an object of concern, a sinner like himself, equally in need of mercy."[20] There have also, however, been earlier signs of Monica's flawed character in the text—leading little by little toward her "ruin" in book 9. Remember? As a young mother, she shuns the "better course" of an early baptism for her son and instead defers the rite, preferring that "the great tides of temptation . . . beat upon the as yet unmoulded clay rather than upon the finished image which had received the stamp of baptism" (1.12; cf. 5.9). When, after a visit to the public baths, her husband proudly reports "the signs of active virility coming to life" in their son, Monica again responds inadequately, worrying too little about Augustine's desires and too much about his career: "She was afraid that the bonds of marriage might be a hindrance to my hopes for the future, . . . my hopes of success at my studies." (Here Augustine's subsequent attempt to Christianize Monica's motive— because such an overt rationalization—merely calls attention to his mother's queer worldliness: "Both my parents were unduly eager for me to learn," he recalls, "my mother because she thought that the usual course of study would certainly not hinder me, but would even help me, in my approach to you") (2.3). Having left the tides of temptation to engulf her son, Monica unleashes a flood of her own into the text, worrying and weeping ceaselessly. "It cannot be that the son of those tears should be lost," a weary bishop finally snaps, a statement that she is pleased to accept as prophetic (3.12). If, as a mother, she is now metonymically defined by her tears, her sorrow begins to seem a bit much. A reader can almost imagine why Augustine sneaks away in the night, "leaving her alone to her tears and her prayers," boarding a ship for Rome—like Virgil's Aeneas giving Dido the slip. As Augustine represents it, even God's patience with the woman has grown thin by this point: Monica's excessive grief at Augustine's departure, "her too jealous love for her son," is identified as a divine punishment that fits the female crime of passion. Indeed, her maternal sorrow is itself the mark of sin, "proof that she had inherited the legacy of Eve" (5.8).

Crying is not all that is left to Monica, however. She still has scope to (mis)manage Augustine's life. Astonishingly, she has followed him all the way to Milan (6. 1)—no Dido, she, after all. Now, when it is too late, she finds her son a wife (6.13). Too late for Augustine, who has a long-time, devoted lover and a son. Too soon by at least two years for the prepubescent wife. Into the gap, a stop-gap mistress steps. (For, in preparation for his socially advantageous marriage, Augustine's common-law wife has been "torn from his side" and sent back to Africa; there, grieving like a widow and vowing chastity, *she* now plays Dido to his Aeneas, while his mother stands staunchly *at his side*, like Adam's rib. The unnamed concubine also plays an unsuccessful Psyche to his Cupid, with Monica in the role of Venus, most difficult of mothers-in-law.) Bereft of his soulmate and cleaving to alien flesh, Augustine suddenly finds his own sinfulness nakedly revealed. He cannot imitate the woman—his former lover—for whom his heart still bleeds. He cannot even wait for his new wife. The waves of longing for erotic intimacy with a woman beat upon him with the relentless force of an addiction, "an uninterrupted habit" (6.15). Little by little, he's been hooked, like Monica in the cellar with her sips of wine.

Augustine is not original, but he *is* creative. Writing the life of a woman, he gives birth to his own life. His *Confessions* is a "great book" but (like the life of a woman) not quite a hagiography. The saint's life is in his field of vision, but it is not his point of departure. When "a book containing the life of Antony" is read by another, Augustine leaves it lying just barely outside the frame of his text, a found object in another man's story of a stranger's conversion (8.6; cf. 8.12). His own life thereby also escapes the frame of holiness. It is—necessarily—unfinished. It is unfinished business, always beginning again. It is perpetually in the process of revision.

Augustine never quite sets it right. (This theologically weighty self-presentation is, after all, the root of his famous disagreement with Pelagius). For one thing, he keeps picking the wrong woman. First there was the Folly of Cicero, and then Mani. Now, so close to a proper Catholic orthodoxy, in his final nightmarish staging of Proverbs 9, he finds himself of two minds, struggling to decide between the austere beauty of Lady Continence (looking suspiciously like his virtuous African concubine) and the more local comforts of Mistress Habit, who beckons him to do "this thing or that"—"things so sordid and so shameful that I beg you in your mercy to keep the soul of your servant free from them!" the poor man cries (8.11). When Augustine eventually makes his choice for Continence, his mother, he tells us, is "overjoyed." "For she saw that you had granted her far more than she used to ask in her tearful prayers and plaintive lamentations" (8.12).

Is the reader surprised by Monica's spontaneous delight? We should not fail to note that, if the mother's sorrow has been exchanged for joy, it has entailed a complex conversion. Monica's tears have not been rewarded but chastened by gladness, her dream for the son of those tears not fulfilled but, little by little, revised. Augustine *insists* on it: "You 'turned her sadness into rejoicing,' into joy far fuller than her dearest wish, far sweeter and more chaste than any she had hoped to find in children begotten of my flesh," he assures his God (8.12).

"Time never stands still," writes Augustine (4.8). But once, before the end, they get it almost right, once time almost stands still. For a heartbeat—at the text's midpoint—Augustine and his mother rest together in the embrace of God's eternity: their lives truly coincide.[21] Leaning from a window overlooking a garden, they converse, he recalls. (It is in the days just before Monica's death, but they do not yet know that). The flame of their love draws them higher and higher: "And while we spoke of the eternal Wisdom, longing for it and straining for it with all the strength of our hearts, for one fleeting instant we reached and touched it." Afterward they imagine what it might be like to encounter God not through the veil of Scripture but directly voiced: "Suppose that we heard him himself, with none of these things between ourselves and him, just as in that brief moment my mother and I had reached out in thought and touched the eternal Wisdom which abides over all things" (9.10).

Augustine continues to long for the moment of naked truth, but the truth is that he has already touched his Bride. However briefly, he has reached out to Lady Wisdom, there in the window with his mother. Augustine is not ready to die, but he is nonetheless happy to be standing on the threshold with Monica. Where Macrina and Paula on their own deathbeds hasten to their heavenly bridegroom with joyous greeting, Monica uses her dying breath to renounce her desire to be buried next to her earthly husband (9.11). Is she saving herself for Christ or merely choosing Continence like her son? Choosing her continent son? Who is the Bride, who the Groom, in this strange woman's life? Augustine is grooming himself for Wisdom, but it is Monica who has accompanied him this far. It is Monica, the ever-revisable text, who enables him to recognize the woman with many faces. It is also Monica who teaches him how to submit to the chastening blows of divine desire (how to play the Bride). It is Monica who teaches him not only about sin but also about *charity*. One day the Lady will reveal herself to him nakedly (she may even come as his Lord).[22] Now he gazes upon her veiled form, he unfurls her pages, and it is his own naked hunger that is revealed. He sucks, he gulps, he devours the inexhaustible maternal body of text. ("But the very simplicity of the language of Scripture sustains them in their weakness as a mother cradles an infant in her lap" [12.27]). He consumes Wisdom's material feast of words. ("I had learned that Wisdom and Folly are like different kinds of food" [5.6]). He makes something new of the ancient writing. He makes something new of himself. Writing, he reads. Sucking, he feeds. He feeds us. We eat him. We are eating him, reading him now. We are eating, reading *her* now.

Monica is already there at the beginning, and she is still present in the many-faced and many-named scriptural Wisdom in whom Augustine rests at the end—sign of constant love, figure of ongoing metamorphosis, creature of both excess and deficiency. Beyond that, it is hard to say: she is elusive, adaptive, mobile, and multiple, a trickster skilled at evading domination, disguising desire, guiding by misdirection. She offers no easy solutions. *She demands a strong reading.*

She demands, she wills, by weeping. But it is the tears and cries of her son that lubricate our passage into the second half of his book (and of this essay). Upon emerging from book 10's labyrinth of time puzzles, in which temporality itself plays trickster, we find ourselves in the metaphys-ico-hermeneutical convolutions of the last three books. Here, in the in-terest of a theology of creation, narrative dries to a mere stream, to barely more than the first verses of the Bible. By the waters irrupts again the exhausting wrestling match with those first two verses of Genesis, as Au-gustine tries from every angle to guide and squeeze them into the estab-lished metanarrative of the *creatio ex nihilo*. That would be the driest dogma of them all, indeed the ultimate medium of theological dehydra-tion: the doctrine that rids us of the dark, chaotic waters, the *tehom* that flows in Genesis 1:2.[23] No wonder the torrents of sex, anguish, and ecstasy suddenly seem to have evaporated along with Monica herself. But not without a trace. The hungry mouth, the watering mouth, morphs into the mouth of the primal waters. Mysteriously, by way of Sapientia herself, the *Confessions*'s trail of iterative tears will open like an estuary into an evanescent ocean: a desert mirage? the mother herself? the matrix of a becoming-theology? To pick up the trail, let us sneak back to the funeral. The waters of that transitional text will churn up an unexpected net of connections, almost, indeed, of metonymic equivalences, between the tears and the tehom itself—and so will push us forward into the last triad of books, in which the iconic continuum of the *Confessions* will manifest itself: between tehom and a heaven with the face of Monica, her tears forever dried. "I closed her eyes, and a mighty sorrow welled up from the depths of my heart and overflowed into tears. At the same time, by a powerful command of my mind, my eyes drank up their source until it was dry" (9.12). The depth surges up irrepressibly: transmitted by touch from mother's eyes to son's, from death to life. A flood defies his self-control. The tears condense in themselves the salt water of the primal tehom. Luckily he masters the waters before any one notices: as Moses parted the sea with his rod, so Augustine commands the waters with his mind. He deciphers this paradigmatic act of manhood with phenomeno-logical precision. The organs are not puppets. Eyes and heart have wills of their own. The body can collude with the disorderly deep; it rebels against the mind's authority. Only with pain can he suppress the conspir-acy of body and tehom: "Most ill was it with me in such an agony!" When his son, Adeodatus, "burst out in lamentation," he is immediately silenced. The pain is passed to the next generation. To mourn the dead is unbecoming in a man, all the more in a Christian. Suppression of grief testifies to faith in eternal life. He resents the vulnerability but glories in suppressing it then and narrating it now: "But in your ears, where none of them could hear, I upbraided the weakness of my affection, and I held back the flood of sorrow. It gave way a little before me, but I was again swept away by its violence, although not as far as to burst into tears, nor to any change of expression" (9.12). The private turbulence of this inte-rior tehom is successfully kept locked behind the floodgates of his self-control. This Paulinized Stoicism absorbs the metaphysics of Being into the deep of a newly self-divided soul. Unchanged is the classical presump-tion that to be affected, to be *moved*, is to *be changed*—and so to occupy the passive/passionate feminine posture. He who surrenders to the fluid and the mutable fails to imitate the divinely unmoved, the impassionable One. Weeping eyes cannot host visions of immutability. Luce Irigaray draws the post-Freudian/preoedipal (or just: maternal) inference: "So the mother's child is engaged in stripping away the membranes, the inheritances that he finds too material. Subject to fading and death. And if this enlightened gaze was already rising above baser and darker attractions, it must also be purified of overly terrestrial sights, and equally he must give up his trust in so finite an organ as the eyes."[24] Nothing renders the eyes so organic, so material, so membranous, as their own flash floods. As Augustine resists the materiality of his maternal bond, the torrent pounds within his body. The oceanic imaginary nearly engulfs the text: "I fought against the wave of sorrow and for a while it receded but then it swept upon me again with full force." Yet his introspective analysis exceeds, or is deficient in, Stoic terms: "But I knew well enough what I was stifling in my heart. It was misery to feel myself so weak a victim of these human emotions, although we cannot escape then . . . and so I had the added sorrow of being grieved by my own feelings" (9.12). With psychological fidelity he captures his entrapment in this "two-fold agony." "Human emotions" of grief belong to the same continuum as lust: tehomic revolt—of himself against himself and against the divine order. Yet his stance is not that of simple judgment, but of a knowing ambivalence.

After all, tears, microcosms of the deep, were appropriate for his mother to shed—and for him, in his conversion, when he "probed the hidden depths" of his soul and "wrung its pitiful secrets from it." Having then aggressively deciphered the interior flux, "a great storm broke within me, bringing with it a great deluge of tears" (8.12). The psychic tehom repeatedly challenges his command—but in the case of his conversion, the challenge is divine. These secretions of conversion were "the sacrifice that is acceptable to you." Does a tehomic ambivalence persistently shadow his maternal ambivalence? If the unacceptable waters are those that flow from feelings of attachment to a creature—especially to a woman—rather than to the Creator, it happens nonetheless that these tears wash out the obstacle to intimacy with his creaturely mother.

When, later on the night of her funeral, alone, he gives vent to his grief, he acknowledges that he grieves for his own loss, thinking "about her sweet and holy care for us, of which I was suddenly deprived." In a stunningly unstoic moment of autocompassion, he writes that now he "took comfort in weeping in your sight over her and for her, over myself and for myself." "I gave way to the tears that I had held back, so that they poured forth as much as they wished. I spread them beneath my heart, and it rested upon them, for at my heart were placed your ears, not the ears of a mere man, who would interpret with scorn my weeping" (9.12).

Now he confesses: he could not face the scorn of other males. But this God does not suppress Augustine's feelings as Augustine suppressed his son's. The divine ear sprouts in the moist, visceral deep "beneath my heart."[25] It performs here as wise counselor. By listening to the sorrow—all the way down—it blesses the mourner. In the prehension of the heart floating restfully upon a tehomic waterbed, he prefigures the heart's rest in God. When the deep floods through the armor of the *apatheia* of elite Christian masculinity, he momentarily defies the totalizing male scorn. But does this exception—this sensitive male—prove the rule of patriarchy? Not the crude patriarchy of his abusive father, but the spiritual patriarchy—exalted by his mother?

We pick up the trail in book 11: "Hear me as I cry out of the depths." Thus Augustine finds himself struggling within the dark waters. He supplements the psalm: "For unless your ears are present with us in the depths, where shall we go?" (11.2). That Ear again, that so gynomorphic (vaginomorphic?) organ, blossoming in the primeval Deep. Like Nelle Morton's great Ear at the heart of the cosmos "hearing us to our own speech"—as women—Augustine's Ear attends him in his struggles.[26] They are rather more textual: he is not struggling with colonizing armies or patriarchs. He is mustering courage to originate his theology, which means for him to start from the Creation by solving the problem of origin itself. This is a hard shell to crack: When did evil get into a good creation? Is it in the chaos? But surely anything that exists is the good creation of an omnipotent Creator? He had been worrying way back in book 8, struggling since his conversion to believe in the ex nihilo (8.5). He reassures us that he got there.

If death let the deep gush through his eyes, let us now examine how it wells up in the ducts of his hermeneutics. When Augustine turns to the creation narrative, we should not be surprised that his real concern is not the materialization of the finite creation but rather, How can I be sure of my own immortality? Most riveting, then, is not so much what he wants the text to guarantee, or how he brings it valiantly into line with the Christian metanarrative, but the hermeneutical resonances released in the struggle, in the *distentio* and *intentio*, of his signifying practice. "The lowliness of my tongue confesses to your highness that you have made heaven and earth, this heaven which I see, this earth on which I tread and from which comes this earth I bear about with myself" (12.2). Yes, yes. But: "compared to you they are neither good nor beautiful nor real" (11.4). Even the prelapsarian earth feels burdensome. So external. (As may now this heavy hermeneutic, to you—you, reader: bear with us.) He asks eagerly: "But where is that *heaven of heaven*, O lord. Where is the heaven that we do not see?" (12.2). His desire is not now for life, but for life after death. The universe, however pretty, only interests him if it contains the immaterial heaven that God has—surely—made to house us beyond death: the goal of our earthly pilgrimage. But this yearning poses an exegetical dilemma: he must find this "heaven of heaven" within the Genesis narrative of origins. *Heaven* in the biblical languages means "sky." He therefore must find a way of installing his heaven of heaven *above* that shining but after all merely corporeal sky. The Bible, however, remains parsimonious in its allusions to an immaterial heaven or after-life.[27] What kind of hermeneutical depth can he plumb, to locate the higher "heaven" within this most original of texts? He presumes that God created not from any preexisting other, as in the *Timaeus*, nor out of any aspect of the divine selfsame, as with Plotinian emanations. *Non de Deo sed ex nihilo.* Therefore "heaven" must be understood as created. But more. "Doubtless that heaven of heaven, which you made in the begin-ning, is some kind of intellectual creature" (12.9). This is a problem. Genesis 1:1, which contains the crucial "heaven," functions as an intro-duction to the rest of the chapter; but the only subsequent reference to "heaven is the definitely material "firmament" of the second day—"God called the firmament heaven" (Gen. 1:2). Augustine zestfully takes up the challenge. He will need to argue that the "heaven" of the first verse is something altogether different from the "heaven" of the second day. So he suggests that the phrase "heaven and earth" in verse 1 signifies a still undifferentiated mix of both corporeal and spiritual potentiality. Then he can argue that the materially formed stuff of the sky (firmament) derives from this "heaven and earth"; but so does the invisible, incorpore-ally formed stuff of the "heaven of heaven." In order to pull off this exege-sis, he will make an intriguing use of the tehom of verse 2: "Lord, have you not taught me that before you formed this unformed matter and fashioned it into kinds, there was no separate being, no color, no shape, no body, no spirit? Yet there was *not absolutely nothing*: there was a *certain formlessness* devoid of any specific character" (12.3). Almost the hypothe-sis of *formation from* primal matter (rather than *creation of* all matter) recurs.[28] It is Augustine's preoccupation with the "certain formlessness," his pluralist meditation upon the complexity of this tiny text, which distinguishes his exegesis. Between the absence of the classical *nihil* and the presence of a finished creation, he spots it "in the transition from form to form." First he had been repelled: "My mind turned over forms foul and horrid in confused array, but still forms." These monstrous forms struck him, "as by something strange and improper" (12.6). But he realized that these were still forms. Only when he fixed his thought "*on the bodies themselves, and peered more deeply into their mutability,*" did he find the knots untied. "If it could be said, '*a nothing-something,*' or '*an is-is-not,*' I would say that it is such" (12.6). After tantalizing us with this *tohuvabohu* of text, however, he leaves us in the dark. Is this nothing-something too weird to write? His "heart" retreats into a "hymn of praise for those things which it cannot dictate." He won't share his queer pleasure with us. He tell us he is sparing us "all the knots which you [God] have untied for me concerning this question." Knotty secrets. Mum's the word?

Augustine's "heart" now dictates another unique hermeneutical strategy: to sketch his knotty filial love upon the face of tehom. The heaven of heaven, we learn, "is yet a partaker of your eternity, and because of its most sweet and happy contemplation of you, it firmly checks its own mutability" (12.9). That is, because this incorporeal creature "checks" its instability by "clinging fast" to the eternal God, it "partakes" of eternity. Thus it can offer Augustine's soul an eternal abode. The heaven of heaven therefore derives directly from the chaos of verse 2—the tehom.[29] The instant it was created, this heaven of heaven grabbed hold of God and clung for dear eternity. Thus it never became subject to mutability. In its state of formlessness, he avers, there can be no change—change is a contrast of forms. Therefore its formlessness allows him to argue cunningly for its immutability—an attribute otherwise reserved for God alone, as the eternal Being of form and order itself ("for in you there is no change, of form or motion" [12.11]). Augustine can thus argue that the "heaven" of verse 1 is "the first heaven, the heaven of heaven."[30] Becoming almost unreadable, he then supplies five alternative interpretations of the verse pair. He refutes none of them. In these choppy waters, he realizes that even among Catholic Christians, reasonable objections to his interpretation will obtain. It is here, while considering how to deploy the verse— "the earth was without form and invisible, and darkness upon the face of the deep"—that he bursts into delight rather than frustration at the tehom of the text itself: "Wondrous is the depth of your words" (12.14). Heaven, partaking in immutable eternity, while yet created as the chaotic, the aboriginal potentiality, echoes his joy. "Oh happy creature, if there be such, for cleaving to your happiness."

This "certain sublime creature that cleaves with so chaste a love to the true and truly eternal God" now shows her face. It is here where she—if there be such—appears as the Wisdom of Proverbs 8: "A certain created wisdom was created before all things, the rational and intellectual mind of your chaste city, our mother, which is above, and is free and eternal in the heavens" (12.14). So the female Wisdom *is* the "heaven of heaven"— or, metonymically, its mind. An iconography of incorporeal femininity bursts momentarily into view, variously intellectual, erotic, and filial in its absorption of Augustine's ecstatic hope.[31] "I will enter into my chamber and there I will sing songs of love to you, groaning with unspeakeable groanings on my pilgrimage, and remembering Jerusalem, with heart lifted up towards it." He merges its female subject with the feminine New Jerusalem.[32] "Jerusalem my country, Jerusalem my mother, and you who over her are ruler, enlightener, father guardian, spouse, pure and strong delight, solid joy, all good things ineffable, all possessed at once. . . . I will not be turned away until out of this scattered and disordered state you gather all that I am into the peace of her, the *mother most dear*" (12.16). What is distinctive, indeed as far as we know unique, in this conflation of Lady Wisdom with the bridal/maternal New Jerusalem is their manifestation as the upper waters. By personifying heaven, he is able to project onto this unfading face of the deep the unmistakable traits of his own most dear mother.

Monica is not just revised but also raised. From her death at the middle of the book—read her and weep—he opens her as the very corpus, the site, the matrix of all resurrection. Monica's best traits—her intelligence, fidelity, and "sweet and holy care," are iterated and amplified in the medium of the deep. She who adhered to a base husband now clings joyously to the ultimate husband. If Augustine had blessed his own mother to heaven, her traits now are now metonymically exalted as those of heaven itself. This poignant sublimation of the mother as "sublime creature" comes wrapped in the obscure correlation of the Christian heaven with the tehom. End things are swaddled in maternal sweetness, cradled in the waters of origin.

Yet this identification of tehom with heaven remains unstable: the waters still also signify, the shame of "our dark and fluid inner being." Fluidity, as mutability itself, denotes the very opposite of the eternal stability Augustine seeks. This *deeply* maternal ambivalence answers his need for immortality. In order to move from first to second verse in such a way as to save heaven and his soul from materiality, he needs the waters to signify "incorporeal" or "spiritual matter." So he leaves the "earth without form and invisible" to signify the "corporeal matter" from which the earth and the firmament were produced: " 'The earth invisible and without order' would be understood as corporeal matter before being qualified by any form, and 'darkness above the deep' as spiritual matter before any restraint was put upon its almost unbounded fluidity and any enlightenment from wisdom" (12.17). How does the "unbounded fluidity" of the primal sea become the eternally bounded and bonded stability of Mother Most Dear? His emphasis upon her light and stability, as participating in her High Husband's eternity, seems to belie her chaotic origin. But the following passage confirms our reading: "I have had much to say of the heaven of heavens, of the earth invisible and without form, and of the deep, showing how its darkness was in keeping with the spiritual creation, which in its formlessness, had no cohesion or stability. Such it would have remained unless, by being turned to God, . . . it had received beauty as well as life by the reflection of his glory. In this way the heaven of heavens came into being" (13.5). So then: the upper waters, at the moment of the dividing, become the heaven of heaven, the mother; while the lower waters beneath the firmament become the earth's seas. The "heaven of heaven" as mother/spouse or upper waters is thus distinguished from the sky, "which was later created between the waters above and the waters below" (13.5).[33] The "unbounded fluidity" is thus precariously congealed, its darkness radiated with divine light. Heaven awaits the restless soul, which like a child snuggles up to Mom, who has *her* arms around Dad. A cozy trinity. (What room could there be for Christ, except as hermaphroditically camouflaged in the "principium" of the beginning itself, as Sophia?) She abides forever the same, clinging to her husband, mirroring in her beauty his omnipotence—and thus wraps our finitude in immutable immortality. The most stable of families.

From the violent fountain of tears for Monica has cascaded an epiphany of the upper waters. But how can the signifier of the waters oxymoronically forfeit its fluidity? What are nonfluid waters—but ice? *La mère de glace.*[34] Her "almost unconstrained fluidity" gets immobilized, frozen in glory, before it can destabilize the subject of Western theology. Sophia, refashioned as the New Jerusalem, would become a politely feminine figure of speech for the City of God—a supernatural heaven, not a transformed earth.[35] Eschatology checks its "edge of social criticism" at her door.[36] Sublime, subjected, sublimated, and female: this hope, as he admits—thus enabling a pluralist hermeneutic that allows divergence

from his own theory—treads on thin ice. Separated from her wilder mate-
rializations, from the something-nothing of a watery "down there," from
the filth of bodily femininity, she cleaves to the higher masculinity.[37] She
offers embrace, comfort, home. Yet she embodies the supernal apathy of
the unmoved, the unresponsive Mover. Frozen, her fluidity denied, she
reroutes desire itself. The ice queen attracts the subject to himself—to
himself as one defined by an immutable masculine ideal. In her discussion
of Plato's cave, Luce Irigaray tracks the antecedent of what she marks as
a frozen femininity: "In other words, man does not get out of the maternal
waters here but, by freezing the path that would lead back to her, he gazes
at himself, re-producing himself in that paraphragm [parapet, outer raised
bank]."[38] In other words, the very path by which he flees from the mother,
that is, from his own fleeting creatureliness, is the frozen form of "her."
He cannot simply annihilate her without destroying himself. His specula-
tions, the abstracted vision of his immaterial and tearless eyes, require
the mirror of her unmoving surface: the concave mirror, the speculum.
He does not see her face, her *panim*. He sees his own. Yet even as this
freezing act repeats itself in the *Confessions*, unlike the *Republic*, indeed
not quite like the *Timaeus*, the waters actually appear in their cosmo-
gonic dignity and are celebrated—under strictly patriarchal conditions—as feminine. In his passion for the Father—"I glow and
shudder"—he almost melts down the ideal of the unchanging Same—
only to freeze it in the heavenly embrace of the Mother.

At such points of rhetorical liquefaction, where the ice thins out and
makes a precarious path upon the face of the deep, one could almost
retrace one's steps to an alternative Christianity. The fantasy of the path
not taken will not, however, lead to the next step: for instance, provide
a constructive theology of becoming, in which the Platonic privilege of
changeless being would thaw into a sustainable commitment to the creatures of the earth. Yet possibilities may survive in frozen form, like embryos, that would otherwise, in a more straightforward ex nihilo, have
been simply eliminated. The divine Wisdom we follow does not discard
her antique visage, captured in the brilliant mirror of the upper waters.

How might we begin to thaw out the theological potentialities of the
Augustinian Wisdom Mother? Is it a matter of *beginning* itself? Hannah
Arendt credits Augustine's doctrine of creation with her revolutionary
notion of "natality" (and "plurality") in public life.[39] *Natality* as a concept
allows her to challenge the Western, and especially the Heideggerian,
privilege of death or *mortality* as the source of both anxiety and action.[40]

Instead she lifts up "the fact of having become." The sheer species multi-plication of human beginnings becomes a trope for the shared human condition: "Beginning, before it becomes a historical event, is the su-preme capacity of man; politically, it is identical with man's freedom. *Initium ut esset homo creatus est*, 'that a beginning be made, man was created,' said Augustine. This beginning is guaranteed by each new birth."[41] In "beginning"—not origin—Arendt locates human freedom and thus the political will with which to resist totalitarianism.[42] According to Arendt's reading of Augustine, "This very capacity for beginning is rooted in natality."[43] The definition of our creaturely finitude through the beginning, the *initium* and thus the *novum*, sheds a new light on the moti-vation of the ex nihilo doctrine. Against Plato, in whom the lack of a strong beginning served profoundly conservative ends, she reads August-ine's beginning as a new beginning for thought.[44] Might we glean from her the possibility of an Augustinian freedom to resist domination: after all a certain edge of social critique? This possibility comes sorely barnacled by both the nostalgia for origins and the passion for ultimate stasis.

Yet a tehomic theology—a chaosophy—would recycle the creativity of the *Confessions* in order to deconstruct that abstract eternity and its omnipotent Origin. It would reroute the desire for the new, the energy of the initium. It may hear echoes of its beginning-freedom, this birth-right of resistance to totality, in the prolific flux of the Augustinian text. We natals need the nourishment. As the deafening (Augustinian) master narrative of creation, fall, and redemption itself falls away, we might hear unfamiliar voices amid the waves of his language. Within the sea of his own nothing-something, the improper, multiplying matrix of another birth, a wilder wisdom chaotically reappears. Not just the lachrymose mother or the frigid Sapientia—but *la mère qui jouit*.[45] She of many lan-guages, names, and sacraments, overflowing the division of history and theology—she may begin to satisfy a present hunger.

Dare we join Augustine in the prayer closet?

In you we oscillate like the tide. In us you flow like tears. In you we beat restlessly against the freeze-dried dogma. In us your parad/ice could melt with-out apocalyptic flood.

In you we fluctuate between tears and joy. In us your laughter wells warmly—proverbial Good Sport, divinely alluring Playmate, trickster Mother.

You are with us in all the beginnings. No longer clinging but flooding free—free not of the fragilities of the flesh, but of the shamed pastures of mat(t)er's frozen objectification.

You are with us in the *jouissance* of an end that is *always opening up*.

References

Arendt, Hannah. *Love and Saint Augustine*. Edited and with an interpretive essay by Jo-
    anna Vecchiarelli Scott and Judith Chelius Stark. Chicago: University of Chicago
    Press, 1996.
Asiedu, F. B. A. "The Song of Songs and the Ascent of the Soul: Ambrose, Augustine,
    and the Language of Mysticism." *Vigiliae Christianae* 55, no. 3 (2001): 299–317.
Brown, Peter. *Augustine of Hippo: A Biography*. Berkeley and Los Angeles: University of
    California Press, 1967.
Brown, William P. *Structure, Role, and Ideology in the Hebrew and Greek Texts of Genesis
    1:1–2:3*. Atlanta: Scholars Press, 1993.
Burrus, Virginia. *"Begotten, Not Made": Conceiving Manhood in Late Antiquity*. Stanford:
    Stanford University Press, 2000.
———. "An Immoderate Feast: Augustine Reads John's Apocalypse." *Augustinian Studies*
    30, no. 2 (1999): 183–94.
———. *The Sex Lives of Saints: An Erotics of Ancient Hagiography*. Philadelphia: Univer-
    sity of Pennsylvania Press, 2004.
Clark, Elizabeth A. "Rewriting Early Christian History." In *Theology and the New Histor-
    ies*, edited by G. Macy. Maryknoll, N.Y.: Orbis Books, 1998.
Courcelle, Pierre. *Les Confessions de Saint Augustin dans la tradition littéraire*. Paris: Études
    Augustiniennes, 1963.
Coyle, J. Kevin. "In Praise of Monica: A Note on the Ostia Experience." *Augustinian
    Studies* 13 (1982): 87–96.
Derrida, Jacques. "Circumfession." In *Jacques Derrida*, edited by G. Bennington and J.
    Derrida. Chicago: University of Chicago Press, 1993.
Ensler, Eve. *The Vagina Monologues*. New York: Villard, 1998.
Graybeal, Jean. *Language and "the Feminine" in Nietzsche and Heidegger*. Bloomington:
    Indiana University Press, 1990.
Irigaray, Luce. *Speculum of the Other Woman*. Translated by G. C. Gill. Ithaca: Cornell
    University Press, 1985.
Jantzen, Grace. *Becoming Divine: Towards a Feminist Philosophy of Religion*. Bloomington:
    Indiana University Press, 1999.
Keller, Catherine. *Apocalypse Now and Then: A Feminist Guide to the End of the World*.
    Boston: Beacon Press, 1996.
———. *The Face of the Deep: A Theology of Becoming*. London: Routledge, 2002.
Kristeva, Julia. "Stabat Mater." Translated by Léon S. Roudiez. In *The Kristeva Reader*,
    edited by Toril Moi. Oxford: Basil Blackwell, 1986.
Lionnet, Francoise. *Autobiographical Voices: Race, Gender, Self-Portraiture*. Ithaca: Cornell
    University Press, 1989.

May, Gerhard. *Creatio ex Nihilo: The Doctrine of "Creation Out of Nothing" in Early Christian Thought*. Translated by A. S. Worrall. Edinburgh: T. and T. Clark, 1994.

Mette, Hans Joachim. "Curiositas." In *Festschrift Bruno Snell zum 60. Geburtstag*. Munich: Beck, 1956.

Miles, Margaret R. *Desire and Delight: A New Reading of Augustine's "Confessions."* New York: Crossroad, 1992.

Morton, Nelle. *The Journey Is Home*. Boston: Beacon Press, 1985.

Rogers, Eugene F., Jr. *Sexuality and the Christian Body: Challenges in Contemporary Theology*. Malden, Mass.: Blackwell, 1999.

Schmidt, Victor. "Reaktionen auf das Christentum in den *Metamorphesen* des Apuleius. *Vigiliae Christianae* 51, no. 1 (1997): 51–71.

Shanzer, Danuta. "Latent Narrative Patterns, Allegorical Choices, and Literary Unity in Augustine's *Confessions*." *Vigiliae Christianae* 46, no. 1 (1992): 40–56.

Starnes, Colin. *Augustine's Conversion: A Guide to the Argument of "Confessions" I–IX*. Waterloo, Ontario: Wilfrid Laurier University Press, 1990.

Thandeka. *Learning to Be White: Money, Race, and God in America*. New York: Continuum, 1999.

Whitehead, Alfred North. *Process and Reality*. New York: Free Press, 1998. (Orig. pub. 1929.)

Winkler, John J. *Auctor and Actor: A Narratological Reading of Apuleius's "The Golden Ass."* Berkeley and Los Angeles: University of California Press, 1985.

Yanney, Rodolph. "The Sins of Saint Monica." *Coptic Church Review* 19, no. 3 (1998): 75–82.

Ziolkowski, Eric J. "St. Augustine: Aeneas' Antitype, Monica's Boy." *Literature and Theology* 9, no. 1 (1995): 1–23.

Notes

1. Translations of *Confessions* generally follow either R. S. Pine-Coffin (London: Penguin Books, 1961) or John K. Ryan (Garden City: Image Books/Doubleday, 1960). The Latin critical edition is *Corpus Christianorum, Series Latina*, vol. 27 (Turnhout, Belgium: Brepolis, 1981), 33.

2. It will become clear that we are by no means simply opposing—though we are "countering"—the insightful remarks of Francoise Lionnet, *Autobiographical Voices: Race, Gender, Self-Portraiture* (Ithaca: Cornell University Press, 1989): "Just as the universe was created out of nothingness, Augustine re-creates himself, the plenitude of his being, out of an experience of emptiness. This re-creation is mediated through the process of reading, which allows him to absorb in his human, historical, linear dimension the timelessness of eternal substance. The result of that re-creation is his own book, the *Confessions*" (63).

3. Need it be said? We take seriously Elizabeth Clark's critique of the positivistic trend in scholarship on Monica. Monica, as we encounter her in Augustine's *Confessions*, is always already a creature of text (as is her son, for that matter). "Confessing Monica," reading the text, we write her anew. See Elizabeth A. Clark, "Rewriting Early Christian History," in *Theology and the New Histories*, ed. Gary Macy (Maryknoll, N.Y.: Orbis Books, 1998), 89–111.

4. Book 8's conversion seems all the more *conclusive* in that it supplements and apparently perfects an earlier vision that followed his reading not of Scripture but of "some of the books of the Platonists" (7.9, 10)—a transient illumination of intellect that proves after all no match for daily

drag of habit (7.17). But see Lionnet, *Autobiographical Voices*: "It is through the death of the mother's body that Augustine can be resuscitated in spirit: the death of the mother is the culmination of his narrative of a life of sin and marks his liberation from earthly and bodily connections" (56).

5. Augustine notes elsewhere Pelagius's dismay upon reading *Confessions* 10, where he repeatedly addresses God: "Give what you command, and command what you will." In the same place Augustine recalls his emphasis in the *Confessions* on the role of "the faithful and daily tears of my mother" in securing his salvation, seeming to link divine and maternal grace very closely indeed (*On the Gift of Perseverance* 20.53).

6. This seems to be the opinion of Margaret R. Miles, *Desire and Delight: A New Reading of Augustine's Confessions* (New York: Crossroad, 1992), 129, who argues that in books 10–13 (in contrast to 1–9), the "author's pleasure and reader's pleasure do not coincide." "Longing for peace, he is pleasured by finding its trustworthy source. . . . Yet the *Confessions* does not reproduce Augustine's pleasure in his reader." Augustine, for his part, seems sure that his readers must share his delight in all thirteen books: "I know that they have given and continue to give pleasure to many of my brethren" (*Retractations* 2.32.1).

7. Danuta Shanzer, "Latent Narrative Patterns, Allegorical Choices, and Literary Unity in Augustine's *Confessions*," *Vigiliae Christianae* 46, no. 1 (1992): 45.

8. Cf. Francoise Lionnet's framing of the "unity" of the *Confessions*: "For Augustine, the project of narrating his own life is doomed to a dead end and must be redeemed by his reading of the sacred texts. This reading is a mode of revelation or illumination quite different from the experience of ecstasy (that is, the vision at Ostia or the unsuccessful attempts at atemporal contemplation of the 'One' in book 7, which momentarily abolish time and give him a taste of eternity)" (*Autobiographical Voices*, 39).

9. Shanzer, "Latent Narrative Patterns," 53.

10. John J. Winkler, *Auctor and Actor: A Narratological Reading of Apuleius's "The Golden Ass"* (Berkeley and Los Angeles: University of California Press, 1985), 273.

11. Winkler, *Auctor and Actor*, 179, 124.

12. Hans Joachim Mette, "Curiositas," in *Festschrift Bruno Snell zum 60. Geburtstag* (Munich: Beck, 1956), 228, proposes that the first ten books of Augustine's *Confessions* correspond to, and are intended to recall, the first ten books of Apuleius's *Golden Ass*—itself a crucial mediator of a negativized conception of "curiosity." Pierre Courcelle, *Les Confessions de Saint Augustin dans la tradition littéraire* (Paris: Études Augustiniennes, 1963), 103–7, extends the comparison of the treatment of curiosity and conversion in the two works, without, however, considering similarities in the texts' endings, in the use of female figures, or in the development of hermeneutical ambivalence—the aspects of primary interest to us.

13. Victor Schmidt, "Reaktionen auf das Christentum in den *Metamorphesen* des Apuleius," *Vigiliae Christianae* 51, no. 1 (1997): 51–71.

14. Winkler, *Auctor and Actor*, 141.

15. In the following passage Augustine simultaneously identifies *The Golden Ass* as autobiographical composition, by assuming the identity of the narrator Lucius and the author Apuleius, and insinuates doubts about its veracity: "This is what Apuleius, in the work bearing the title *The Golden Ass*, describes as his experience, that after taking a magic potion he became an ass, while retaining his human mind. But this may be either fact or fiction" (*City of God* 18.18). Modern scholars have hotly debated the question of whether *Augustine's* autobiography is "fact" or "fiction." (For one summary, see Colin Starnes, *Augustine's Conversion: A Guide to the Argument of "Confessions" I–IX* [Waterloo, Ontario: Wilfrid Laurier University Press, 1990], 277–89). Shanzer rightly questions the assumption underlying the sharp framing of alternatives—namely, that to invoke a literary topos is to engage in "falsehood": "We should not rule out the possibility that life may imitate literature" (Shanzer, "Latent Narrative Patterns," 43). One might further question her own easy distinction between "literature" and "life."

16. The links with the Apuleian Venus are strengthened by the links with the Virgilian Venus, as argued persuasively by Eric J. Ziolkowski, "St. Augustine: Aeneas' Antitype, Monica's Boy," *Literature and Theology* 9, no. 1 (1995): 11–23 (though we cannot agree with his idealizing reading of Augustine's portrait of Monica in book 9).

17. "Ecce simplex dilectio dei et proxitni, quam multiplicibus sacramentis et innuinerabilibus linguis et in unaquaqe lingua innumerabilibus locutionum modis corporaliter enuntiatur!" (13.24). Note the suggestive similarities between this passage in the last book of *Confessions*—which in context refers to the polysemy of Scriptura herself—and Isis's above-cited "syncretistic" self-description in the last book of the Apuleian text: "Cuius numen unicum multiformi specie, ritu vario, nomine multiiugo totus veneratur orbis" (11.5). The references to ritual and linguistic multiplicity are parallel; furthermore, if the Augustinian passage lacks reference to the goddess's many faces, he has already enacted that plurality within the text more broadly.

18. The context of earliest "women's lives" is explored further in Virginia Burrus, *The Sex Lives of Saints: Rereading Ancient Hagiography* (Philadelphia: University of Pennsylvania Press, 2004), 53–40. Cf. Virginia Burrus, *"Begotten, Not Made": Conceiving Manhood in Late Antiquity* (Stanford: Stanford University Press, 2000), 112–22, on the Macrinan life.

19. Derrida's reinscription of Augustine's text may be less disruptive than he indicates: "not that I dare link what he says about confession with the deaths of our respective mothers, . . . for my mother was not a saint" ("Circumfession," in *Jacques Derrida,* ed. Geoffrey Bennington and Jacques Derrida [Chicago: University of Chicago Press, 1993], 18–19). Of course, our claim that Augustine's text (like Derrida's) sustains an ambivalent portrayal of the maternal figure is by no means identical with the claim—simultaneously positivistic and misogynistic—that Monica was a bad mother, as reflected in, for example, Rodolph Yanney, "The Sins of Saint Monica," *Coptic Church Review* 19, no. 3 (1998): 75–82.

20. Peter Brown, *Augustine of Hippo: A Biography* (Berkeley and Los Angeles: University of California Press, 1967), 164.

21. Kevin Coyle's revival of the suggestion that it is only Monica who should be understood to achieve mystical heights at Ostia—a suggestion based in part on the improbability of "l'extase a deux"—is not without merit (J. Kevin Coyle, "In Praise of Monica: A Note on the Ostia Experience of *Confessions* IX," *Augustinian Studies* 13 [1982]: 87–96). At the same time, the perverse intimacy of the scene seems particularly well described by the phrase "l'extase a deux."

22. Book 11 of Apulieus's "goddess novel" ends, perplexingly, with a brief vision of the god Osiris. While describing his quest for Wisdom, Augustine is of course addressing himself to his "Lord God" throughout the *Confessions*. At the same time, the second-person address of the *Confessions* renders the divine addressee effectively gender ambiguous.

23. While most Christian theology continues to invest orthodoxy in the doctrine of *creatio ex nihilo*, it has come under fire on many fronts in the past century. Gerhard May, *Creatio ex Nihilo: The Doctrine of "Creation out of Nothing" in Early Christian Thought,* trans. A. S. Worrall (Edinburgh: T. and T. Clark, 1994), has made the decisive case for the faltering emergence of the full ex nihilo argument in the second century A.C.E., first in the writings of the Gnostic theologian Basilides. The church doctrine of *creatio ex nihilo* emerges only in the late second century, with Tatian and Theophilus of Antioch, and soon with Irenaeus. Ironically, it is the polemic against Gnosticism, especially in its Marcionite and Valentinian form, which drives "the defense of the omnipotence and unity of God," that "inevitably demands the proposition that matter also is created by God" (148). For a good summation of the exegetical case against the biblical origins of the ex nihilo, see William P. Brown, *Structure, Role, and Ideology in the Hebrew and Greek Texts of Genesis 1:1–2:3* (Atlanta: Scholar's Press, 1993).

24. Luce Irigaray, *Speculum of the Other Woman,* trans. Gillian C. Gill (Ithaca: Cornell University Press, 1985), 318.

25. The vicerality of the imagery offers a perfect illustration of Whitehead's "withness of the

body," indeed of causal efficacy, which he describes as a dark, obscure, visceral prehension, not the "vivid presentation" of "presentational" immediacy, that is, sense perception. See Alfred North Whitehead, *Process and Reality* (New York: Free Press, 1929/98).

26. Nelle Morton, *The Journey Is Home* (Boston: Beacon Press, 1985), 127ff.

27. Augustine does, however, glimpse it in the *Latin translation* of the psalter: "The heaven of heaven is the Lord's (*caelum caeli Domino*)." (Ps. 113.16/115.16) (*Confessions* 12.11).

28. He is not the first to work the layers and levels of materialization: the Plotinian philosophical framework highlights the transition from formlessness to form, from potentiality to actuality. Whether or not theologians had got on the ex nihilo bandwagon, they often understood the biblical chaos as a first stage, a formless matter waiting to be formed. Once the logic of ex nihilo had prevailed, it made sense to read the Elohim of Genesis as God creating this "unformed matter" as the material from which "he" would then press and shape the universe. The texts that argue most strongly for the ex nihilo, such as Irenaeus and later Athanasius, do not dally with this two stage theory but tend, rather, to repress the chaos altogether. See Catherine Keller, *The Face of the Deep: A Theology of Becoming* (London: Routledge, 2002), esp. chap. 2.

29. "This formlessness, this earth invisible and without form, is not numbered among the days. Where there is no form, no order, nothing comes or passes away." (*Confessions* 12.9)

30. It is "formed from the very beginning," while its earth is "invisible and without form" (So the argument from formlessness, which he needs in order to establish this pure and invisible potentiality that distinguishes the first heaven, cancels itself out. He also wants the reader to understand—though he cannot quite bring himself to say it, so badly does it jumble the signifiers—that the material sky, that is, the second "heaven," is derived from the "earth" of "heaven and earth," not from its "heaven.")

31. Eugene F. Rogers Jr., *Sexuality and the Christian Body: Challenges in Contemporary Theology* (Malden, Mass.: Blackwell, 1999), notes of this passage, "Augustine did not have to have read Freud to mix the yearnings of the spouse and the child that the Bible refuses to separate." While Rogers does not make an explicit link to the confessed homoerotic passion of Augustine's youthful "body," this proposition seems pertinent to its textualization: "Thus Christians have been free with erotic and romantic metaphors, and the eschatology that marries Christians foremost to god before each other could lead to the greatest romantic freedom of expression even, or especially, in such celibates as Augustine" (223).

32. If the *Confessions* is marked by a curious lack not only of explicit Christology but also of Mariology—places filled instead by the figure(s) of Monica/Wisdom—it is also strikingly lacking in references to the erotic bridal imagery of the Song of Songs, much beloved of ascetic commentators, including Augustine's exegetical "teacher" Ambrose (whose appearance in the guise of silent reader [6.3] prepares the way for Augustine's own readerly performance in books 11–13). As F. B. A. Asiedu, "The Song of Songs and the Ascent of the Soul: Ambrose, Augustine, and the Language of Mysticism," *Vigiliae Christianae* 55, no. 3 (2001), points out, the love lyrics of *Confessions* would seem to have cried out for an invocation of "the allegorical-mystical appropriations of the Song . . . , if Augustine had been so inclined" (299); yet Augustine positively avoids this well-worn exegetical path, as Asiedu demonstrates. Perhaps Augustine (in contrast to his more unambivalently ascetic colleagues) remains too uncomfortably aware of the place of "worldly" marriage and sexuality to allow easy appropriation of a sublimated bridal eroticism; perhaps, in addition, his textual representation of Monica/Wisdom (Tehom/New Jerusalem) here again rather strongly displaces prior scriptural figures.

33. Perhaps it is not so surprising that Augustine later admits to some discomfort with this freeflowing exegesis: "'The firmament' was made 'between the higher spiritual waters and the lower corporeal waters,' was said without sufficient deliberation. The subject, however, is exceedingly obscure" (*Retractations* 2.32.2).

34. Irigaray, *Speculum*, on Plotinus.

35. See Catherine Keller, *Apocalypse Now and Then: A Feminist Guide to the End of the World* (Boston: Beacon Press, 1996) and Virginia Burrus, "An Immoderate Feast: Augustine Reads John's Apocalypse," *Augustinian Studies* 30, no. 2 (1999): 183–94.

36. Thandeka, *Learning to Be White: Money, Race, and God in America* (New York: Continuum, 1999), 118ff.

37. The phrase "down there" comes charged with abjection from the tragic-comic soliloquy called "The Flood," referencing certain unspeakable feminine emissions, in Eve Ensler, *The Vagina Monologues* (New York: Viliard, 1998), 25ff.

38. Irigaray, *Speculum*, 351.

39. Hannah Arendt, *Love and Saint Augustine*, ed. and with an interpretive essay by Joanna Vecchiarelli Scott and Judith Chelius Stark (Chicago: University of Chicago Press, 1996), 122.

40. For a rich reconstruction of Arendt's "natality," see Grace Jantzen, *Becoming Divine: Towards a Feminist Philosophy of Religion* (Bloomington: Indiana University Press, 1999), 148ff. Jantzen reads Arendt through Irigaray and Levinas as she develops her own privilege of the "natal" versus the "mortal." Even without occluding the horizon of death, the feminist interpretation of Arendt's birth-trope emphasizes the finite and the fleshly (rather than Heaven) as the only Site in which the infinite occurs.

41. Arendt, *Love and Saint Augustine*, 147.

42. It is not as though the persistent theological dimension of Arendt's notion of "new beginnings" has been much in evidence among Arendt scholars. Joanna Vecchiarelli Scott and Judith Chelius Stark offer an incisive analysis of the difficulties posed by this early, Augustinian pre-Holocaust Arendt for the "Arendt canon." See their interpretive essay "Rediscovering Hannah Arendt," in Arendt, *Love and Saint Augustine*, 125–34.

43. Arendt, *Love and Saint Augustine*, 147.

44. Augustine's difference from Plato thus enables Arendt to articulate her difference from her mentor Heidegger: "Beginning as she meant to continue, Arendt immediately abandons Heidegger's death-driven phenomenology with Augustine as her guide" (Scott and Stark, "Rediscovering Hannah Arendt," 124).

45. "The mother who rejoices, enjoys, takes (erotic) pleasure . . ." We borrow the suggestive (and nearly untranslatable) French phrase from Jean Graybeal, *Language and "the Feminine" in Nietzsche and Heidegger* (Bloomington: Indiana University Press, 1990). Evoked is the Kristevan use of *jouissance*, which interrupts the Mary/Eve binary of asexual mother versus passionate woman, expressing her call for a postvirginal discourse of maternity, an "*herethics*" that "makes bonds, thoughts, and therefore the thought of death, bearable: herethics is undeath [a-mort], love. . . . *Eia mater, fons amoris*" (Julia Kristeva, "Stabat Mater," trans. León S. Roudiez, in *The Kristeva Reader*, ed. Toril Moi [Oxford: Basil Blackwell, 1986], 185).

5

O Mother, Where Art Thou? In Search of Saint Monnica

Rebecca Moore

Current feminist examinations of the hagiographies of notable women observe that women serve as the vehicles for delivering male-inspired and male-written messages. In one respect, that is inevitable, since men are writing about women and praising qualities that men find valuable. The description of Olympias, a virgin and companion of John Chrysostom, for example, reveals what religious men think is important in a woman: "a life without vanity, an appearance without pretense, character without affectation, a face without adornment . . . an immaterial body, a mind without vainglory, intelligence without conceit, an untroubled heart, [and] an artless spirit."[1] I locate these hagiographies within a genre I call "woman-of-worth" tales; that is, a category of accounts of praiseworthy females who serve as models for both women and men. This genre goes beyond mere saint making when the authors use women to present their own theological ideas. Literature of this type has little to do with history, and everything to do with theology and philosophy.

This is quite true of Augustine's accounts of his mother, Saint Monnica. There is good reason to question the historicity of Augustine's *Confessions* and *Dialogues*. Rhetorical and literary studies of the *Confessions* have demonstrated Augustine's debt to classical styles and forms. For example, the depiction of Monnica's frenzied grief over Augustine's departure from North Africa for Italy comes directly from the pages of his favorite author, Virgil, who outlined a similarly grief-stricken scene between Aeneas and Dido in the *Aeneid*.[2] Margaret Miles points out that Augustine was writing for a male audience, one that would have recognized his literary allusions, and not mistake them for history.[3] Hence, it seems as though the days when psychoanalysts could consider the *Confessions* a "case study," or when historians drew conclusions of fact, are over.[4]

Furthermore, Elizabeth Clark outlines the difficulties feminist historians have in reconstructing "real women" in late antiquity, given the current turn toward critical theory and poststructuralism.[5] Like Miles, she notes that the texts with which we work "are nothing if not literary productions." She warns against reading the vitae of female saints as history, and she asks the question this essay is asking, in this case about Monnica: "Can historians not retrieve the social-historical facts while discarding the miraculous and the phantastic?"[6] Her answer is cautionary. We cannot recover these saints "pure and simple," but they do leave traces behind.

What, then, if anything, can be known about Saint Monnica, given the limitations of genre, theory, and history? I believe that Edith Wyschogrod provides a possible approach when she describes the responsibility historians have to their subjects and the concomitant problem of telling the truth about the past.[7] If truth, by definition, corresponds to a reality, how can we gain access to that reality, especially in the case of Monnica, when it is mediated by time, dogma, and filial bias? In one sense, this obligation is impossible to fulfill: how can we ever truthfully write about the past? Yet historians are indeed responsible for giving voice to the voiceless. As Wyschogrod reminds us, "The historian's responsibility is mandated by another who is absent, cannot speak for herself, one whose actual face the historian may never see, yet to whom 'giving coun-tenance' becomes a task.'"[8] In other words, despite the radical skepticism that rightly exists today, historians have an ethical obligation to give voice to those unnamed or annihilated. Critical theories of history inter-rogate our claims about the past and challenge our very ability to make such claims. Wyschogrod dares to respond with an ethic that requires us to speak about the past based on our "eros for the dead," that is, our yearning for justice for them.

One place to begin the process of sketching an outline of Monnica is to locate her in Tagaste rather than Milan by spelling her name with two ns rather than one. Monnica's namesake, Mon, a North African goddess, suggests her family's origin in Numidia (modern-day Algeria). Peter Brown notes that "even Christian parents wisely dedicated their chil-dren" to the "Goddess of Heaven," a female deity linked to Carthage.[9] At the very least, Monnica's name and that of her grandson, Adeodatus, "reflect local, pre-Roman religious practice" that African Christianity did not always supersede.[10] It was practices such as these, however, that loomed large in Augustine's later political conflicts as bishop of Hippo.

If we are to "give countenance" to Monnica, we must revisit the *Con-fessions* and the *Dialogues* to see what traces of her might exist in these works of theology and philosophy (but not of history!). Although she warns of a theologized portrait of Monnica, Kim Power argues that Au-gustine presents his mother as an ideal Roman materfamilias, and as a model of simple Christian faith and piety (feminine), as opposed to having a more philosophically grounded approach to spirituality (mascu-line).[11] It is exactly these two qualities—motherhood and femininity—that the Christian woman-of-worth tale usually disparages. While the chronicles of other women-of-worth praise them for abandoning home and children to pursue a religious vocation, Augustine praises Monnica for *not* leaving her children, or at any rate, for not leaving him. She appears to be a woman who lives a fairly traditional life, up to a point, and does not sacrifice everything for a personal call to asceticism. While other women-of-worth speak like males rather than females, have a "manly faith," and know philosophy or biblical interpretation as well as, if not better than, their male counterparts, Monnica, as depicted by her son, has a humble, yet profound, faith. Even though he claims that his mother has the "strong faith of a man," Augustine also contrasts her innocent, God-given wisdom received through faith to the intellectual wisdom he and his colleagues have acquired through philosophy.[12]

In other words, Monnica is a woman-of-worth who remains maternal and female. This is true for her in the long section Augustine devotes to her in book 9 of the *Confessions* (7–13)—a kind of woman-of-worth tale—as well as for her in the rest of the *Confessions* and in the *Dialogues*. The characterization of Monnica as maternal and female may reveal traces of the woman herself because Augustine is using these categories to point out her weaknesses, her worldliness, her sinfulness. He sees his mother as weak because she remains motherly rather than ascetic; he sees her as female or "womanly," because she has a less sophisticated approach to questions of God and faith. She does not rise above the limitations of her gender or station in life, except when she is near death.

Moreover, it is only when she dies that Augustine is truly liberated from "earthly and bodily connections," in Françoise Lionnet's words. "It is through the death of the *mother's* body that Augustine can be resuscitated in spirit: the death of the mother is the culmination of his narrative of a life of sin." Monnica embodies Augustine's corrupt, worldly nature. Her death frees him from this identity, "an aspect of the self which must be effaced, erased, [and] obliterated, because it is none other than the 'sinning self.'"[13] James J. O'Donnell notes a triadic progression of fall and conversion in Augustine's account, which makes a similar point: "Augustine fell because he lost control of the image of god in himself: spirit first, son/word second, father third. He rose because he recovered that image in reverse order: father, son, and, finally, spirit."[14] In both instances, it is Augustine's recovery of spirit (and, one might add, father), through the death of his embodied self, that completes his conversion and ends the autobiographical narrative. Her son rejects what Monnica represents, namely, his sinful, *bodily* self.

I argue nevertheless that Augustine's critique of the maternal and the female as exemplified in his mother may provide glimpses of Monnica's actual countenance. We know that Augustine writes about his mother, and everyone else, to reveal his own life.[15] But rejecting all of Augustine's discussions of Monnica as theological or autobiographical constructs seems as rash as accepting all of them as historical. A middle way is to accept as possible what appears credible. This means setting aside incidents that have the odor of literature and philosophy, and scrutinizing the offhand details and critical remarks more closely. This approach looks at Augustine's garbage—what he throws out as unimportant or trivial—rather than considering what he has set before us for our admiration. We must also regard the latter, though, to see what may plausibly lie beneath the surface.

I look at Monnica, therefore, at her ordinariness, her infinite banality, within the context of woman-of-worth narratives.[16] She runs counter to the heroic type in many ways, and this places her in sharp relief. We may ask if she goes against type because Augustine is more faithful to the original. It seems noteworthy that few accounts of a woman-of-worth were written by a son or daughter. This does not in itself make the account more trustworthy, but does raise the possibility that maternal and female accurately characterize Monnica.

The Woman-of-Worth Rejects Motherhood

The writings of the church fathers are replete with misogyny; there is no need to repeat their denigration of women, of sexuality, and of the body here.[17] Even the vitae of exemplary women praise their subjects for atypical female behavior. I am calling these particular vitae woman-of-worth accounts. These women sacrifice almost everything to pursue a religious life. Home and family, children, and frequently wealth are left behind. Marcella, for instance, was a young Roman widow eulogized by Jerome for her refusal to remarry. She was so obedient to her mother that she sometimes did things that went against her own conscience, "content to throw away her money rather than to sadden her mother's heart."[18] The twenty-two-year-old Melania the Elder arranged for a guardian to care for her son before she left Rome for Alexandria and the desert ascetics.[19]

Such behavior characterizes the heroines of the *Christian* woman-of-worth, but not those of classical literature from Greece or Rome. The Roman *matrona* had been the ideal prior to the imperial adoption of Christianity. Motherhood was the primary role, and goal, for women in the Greek and Roman worlds. Even the vestal virgins, who renounced motherhood, served at the hearth of the goddess Vesta, which symbolized the great Roman family.[20] Although legal and social rights had improved for Greek women after the golden age of Athenian democracy in the fifth century B.C.E., the negative value assigned to unmarried girls remained well into late antiquity. This contrasts greatly with the Christian valorization of virginity, and its elevation above motherhood, as the preferred state for female Christians.

The Greek romances, appearing between the first century B.C.E. and the fourth century C.E., feature young virgins who protect their chastity at any cost, but only to prove themselves worthy of marriage in the end. Although the chastity stories in the Apocryphal Acts have been said to reflect these romances, Virginia Burrus challenges this view, finding their origins in popular folktales told by women.[21] In any event, there is a clear difference between the protagonists in these two sets of stories. Young women in the Hellenistic romances are chaste in order to be good middle-class brides.[22] Young women in the Apocryphal Acts, however, reject marriage. For example, Thecla, in the second-century Acts of Paul and Thecla, endures all sorts of torments to avoid marriage and to protect her virginity, even dressing up as a man so that she can travel freely.

Asceticism as a vocational choice for women flourished in the fourth and fifth centuries C.E. for a number of reasons, not least of which was the ascendancy of Christianity in the Roman Empire.[23] Moreover, "in a society in which sexuality is inextricably linked with patriarchal marriage, sexual repression might be viewed as a positive and liberating adaptation."[24] Fourth- and fifth-century vitae, therefore, describe daughters and sisters rejecting their families' plans in favor of asceticism. In addition, these stories extol married women and widows who leave worldly lives to establish monasteries in their homes, or to found new ones abroad. "A good pagan matron, like Cornelia, was supposed to produce as many children as possible," writes Augusto Fraschetti. "A Christian saint, once her wifely duties had been fulfilled, was expected to abstain from procreation."[25]

Forsaking one's family in order to pursue a religious life—with rare exception—was not a pagan value. But Jerome praises the holy women who abandon their children and the distractions of family life "in order to dedicate themselves to a 'higher purpose'—a life of spiritual perfection."[26] His letter to Eustochium on the death of her mother, Paula, details the latter's departure from Rome, "disregarding her house, her children, her servants, her property, and in a word everything connected with the world." Unlike Monnica, who weeps copiously upon Augustine's departure, Paula turns from her young son, whose hands are stretched out toward her, and from her daughter Rufina, who is sobbing silently, and directs her dry eyes toward heaven.[27] "Though it is against the laws of nature," Jerome writes, "she endured this trial with unabated faith; nay more she sought it with a joyful heart: and overcoming her love for her children by her greater love for God, she concentrated herself quietly upon Eustochium alone, the partner alike of her vows and of her voyage. . . . No mother, it must be confessed, ever loved her children so dearly. Before setting out she gave them all that she had, disinheriting herself upon earth that she might find an inheritance in heaven."[28]

In contrast to what appears typical of the genre, Augustine's woman-of-worth lives very much in the world. She is even a little *too* worldly in her ambitions for her son. Whenever he describes Monnica's practical activities in his own life—as opposed to his idealization of her role as God's faithful handmaid—he becomes testy and bitter. For example, though his parents make financial sacrifices to send him to school in Carthage, Augustine complains that it was for the wrong reasons: "Their only concern was that I should learn how to make a good speech and how to persuade others by my words."[29] He resents the fact that Monnica delays his baptism. Even when he is seriously ill as a child, and he "appealed to the piety of my own mother" to give him baptism, she refuses. Postponing baptism until adulthood was the norm at the time, however. Catechumens went through a lengthy period of instruction, often a year or more, before they would be baptized by immersion on Holy Saturday, and welcomed into the church on Easter Sunday with the laying on of hands by a bishop. In this case, Monnica's decision to defer the sacrament was not unusual in any way.

Augustine explains her refusal as an expectation that "if I continued to live, I should defile myself again with sin and, after baptism, the guilt of pollution would be greater and more dangerous."[30] Similarly, she wants to delay any nuptials, according to Augustine, preferring a concubine to marriage for him, concerned as she is about a hasty and disadvantageous partnership: "She was afraid that the bonds of marriage might be a hindrance to my hopes for the future."[31] These hopes center on success in this life rather than success in the afterlife. Monnica follows her son from Africa to Italy in her quest for the right kind of marriage and, presumably, grandchildren. Augustine detests this behavior.

Although to hear him tell it we might think that Monnica focuses all her attention and affection on her younger son, we can draw a few significant conclusions from other things he says. First, Monnica stays married and remains with her husband and children until her husband dies. She seems to enjoy Patricius, and she concurs with him in matters of child rearing, although as a Christian she provides religious instruction to the children. Unlike her peers, she avoids beatings from her husband. "Many women, whose faces were disfigured by blows from husbands far sweeter-tempered than her own, used to gossip together and complain of the behavior of their men folk," Augustine writes. "They used to remark how surprising it was that they had never heard, or seen any marks to show, that Patricius had beaten his wife."[32] Whether it was for the reason her son states—Monnica's submissive obedience to the will of her hot-tempered husband—is debatable. It does seem noteworthy, however, that she escapes the corporal punishment that accompanied family life in late antiquity. Similarly, conflicts between daughter-in-law and mother-in-law were typical at that time, but Monnica wins the affections of her husband's mother and eventually converts her to Christianity.[33]

Second, upon Patricius's death, Monnica goes to live with her son, the custom among Roman families. Although a *vidua* (a woman without a man) had more autonomy than girls or married women, she still required a guardian, despite the household and business responsibilities she might assume.[34] When she learns that her son is practicing Manichaeism, which she "loathed and shunned," Monnica refuses to live with him.[35] A dream persuades her, however, "so that she agreed to live with me and eat at the same table in our home."[36] Moreover, she continues to support his education, even after her husband dies.[37] When her son moves to Milan, Monnica follows, to arrange a suitable marriage. In Milan, Monnica establishes an independent relationship with Ambrose, the bishop of Milan.

While some analysts have seen this pursuit of her son as evidence of her obsessive nature, it seems more likely that Monnica is behaving in a traditional manner.[38] Family is the most important institution in Mediterranean culture, and honor is the most important value. In the typical woman-of-worth story, the female protagonist rejects the institution of family and the value of honor for the greater institution of church and the greater value of service or devotion to God. Monnica, however, remains committed to traditional ways. She attempts to move in with her son upon the death of her husband. She wants to arrange an advantageous marriage. These are all things a typical materfamilias would do.

Is this depiction merely Augustine's effort to create a model Roman wife and mother, as Power claims? If this is the case, Monnica is quite flawed, apparently behaving in an unseemly way in public on a number of occasions. The Stoic list of virtues and opposing vices encompassed prudence, self-control, courage, righteousness; and folly, intemperance, cowardice, and injustice.[39] By these standards, Monnica certainly does not appear to be a model, given her lack of self-control and her intemperance. Furthermore, chastity and modesty were the "most highly prized traits" in Roman society.⁴⁰ While Monnica's chastity is not in question, and she remains a *univira*—the wife of just one man—her public outbursts indicate a lack of modesty.

Is Augustine's portrait of Monnica part of his agenda to sacramentalize marriage, as Clark suggests? This seems a stretch, given his praise of virginity elsewhere. One might make an equally strong case for arguing that Augustine's agenda is to identify Monnica with the African Christianity that he is battling (see below).

Regardless of Augustine's purposes, I do think that we can identify some social-historical "facts" in these accounts. If we strip away the literary allusions, the hyperbole, and the theology to describe what Monnica actually does, we see that she fulfills her maternal and wifely obligations, unlike other women-of-worth. Today we might admire the female ascetics for bucking the patriarchal system and rejecting the roles that fathers, husbands, and sons had determined for them. Moreover, the uses to which Saint Monnica has been put by patriarchal religious authorities— long-suffering, living only for and through her children, having no independent identity—have been harmful to women's development and sense of self-worth. For instance, the cult of Saint Monnica in mid-nineteenth-century Paris brought together Christian mothers to pray and weep for their children.⁴¹ Viewed in her own time and place, however, minus the accretion of church dogma or patriarchal manipulation, Monnica might in fact be a model parent, or at least a good one: loving, caring, worried over her children's welfare, concerned about her husband and his family, anxious about both physical and spiritual well-being.

Even as a widow, an office in the early church that received special privileges and required special duties, Monnica remains maternal and worldly.⁴² Patristic literature is replete with stories of the *mulier sancta* who has been widowed: Paula, Marcella, Juliana, Melania the Elder, Olympias, and even Macrina (though technically she was only betrothed, and not married, when she was "widowed"). These holy women ran monasteries that oversaw the daily lives of consecrated virgins. For them, "widowhood, if strictly regarded, was a suitable channel for the ethos of holy renunciation and they augmented it by their example."⁴³

Monnica does not choose this path. She could justifiably have left her family behind and embarked upon a life of renunciation, but she does not. Instead, she faced the "horrors of widowhood," in John Chrysostom's words: "She has to correct the laziness of servants, and to be on the watch for their rogueries, to repel the designs of relations, to bear bravely the threats of those who collect the public taxes, and harshness in the imposition of rates."[44] Monnica does all that and more. Yet Augustine finds this despicable and carnal, rather than praiseworthy. Compared to the widows in the woman-of-worth tales, Monnica falls short.

The Woman-of-Worth Has a Manly Faith

Christian women in the fourth century achieved virtue (which contains the Latin word *vir*, or "man") by putting off their femininity and becoming male. The ultimate compliment of being "manly" was paid to a select few.[45] These included Melania the Elder, of whom Paulinus of Nola said, "What a woman she is, if one can call so virile [manly] a Christian a woman!" and whom Palladius called "that female man of God."[46] Palladius also complimented Olympias by calling her "a manly creature: a man in everything but body."[47] Gregory of Nyssa wondered if Macrina should even be termed a woman, "for I do not know if it is appropriate to apply a name drawn from nature to one who has risen above nature."[48] Even Augustine noted that he and his companions forgot, for a moment, that Monnica was a woman.[49]

These manly women are extremely wise, competing with men on the latter's own turf, namely, philosophical dialogues and biblical interpretation. Palladius describes Melania the Elder as "most erudite and fond of literature, and she turned night into day going through every writing of the ancient commentators"—indeed, reading three million lines of Origen, and two and a half million lines of Gregory, Stephen, Pierius, Basil, and others; moreover she did not read them only once, but many times.[50] Melania the Younger is a model of orthodoxy, a well-reasoned hater of heretics, although her hagiography shows her defending Origenism, Pelagianism, and Donatism.[51] Marcella interprets Scripture, according to Jerome, although she always frames her exegesis by claiming that it is simply what she has been taught by men.[52]

One of the wisest, and least female, of the women-of-worth is Macrina, the sister of Gregory of Nyssa. "Macrina is the virgin-philosopher *par excellence*. . . . [She] is a teacher, a leader and a mistress of Scripture."[53] She guides her own mother to philosophy, that is, the pure and simple life. She persuades their mother not to show any emotion when her brother Naucratius dies. On her own deathbed she displays no cowardice, but, rather, philosophizes "upon what she had chosen for this life, right from the beginning up to her last breath."[54] The evidence of her masculine mind is most apparent in On the Soul and the Resurrection, the dialogue Gregory composed that purports to describe their final conversation at her death. As Clark notes, "Macrina serves as a tool with which Gregory can think through various troubling intellectual and theological problems that confronted male theologians of his day."[55] The wise woman is a literary device, then, and one that should arouse caution, if not downright suspicion. This is true of a number of woman-of-worth texts, including Augustine's Dialogues, which feature Monnica in two of the pieces.

The Dialogues were written in 386 when Augustine was living with a group of like-minded men at Cassiciacum, a retreat in the countryside outside Milan. Monnica and Navigius, Augustine's brother, were also living with the group. Three treatises constitute the Dialogues: Contra academicos, De beata vita, and De ordine (Against the Academicians, On the Happy Life, and On Order). While the historicity of the Dialogues has been debated—with some even arguing that they are essentially stenographic transcripts of real conversations—many scholars assert that they are fiction, or rather, philosophy presented in the traditional form of a dialogue.[56] Let us accept the nonhistorical character of Augustine's Dialogues for now.[57] With that said, though, the Dialogues may in fact reflect a bit of Monnica, because Augustine again violates the conventions of the woman-of-worth genre by presenting Monnica as having a nonmasculine type of insight. It is true that Augustine reports that the group thought they had a man in their midst, given Monnica's wisdom and persuasiveness, but it is also true that he seems to present two models of spirituality: the experiential (feminine, as personified in Monnica) and the philosophical (masculine, as personified in himself and the other male members of his group).[58]

In De beata vita Augustine shows Monnica taking a leading role in the discussion of "the happy life." She asserts that no one can attain God without first seeking God.[59] Everyone possesses God, she believes, but God is favorable to those who live righteously and is hostile to those who live wrongly. She differentiates between possessing God and not being without God. "He who lives righteously possesses God, that is, has Him propitious to him; he who lives a bad life also possesses God, but as hostile to him. But," she adds, "whoever is still seeking God, and has not yet found him, has Him neither as propitious, nor as hostile, yet is not without God."[60] Monnica explains that wisdom is the one true wealth, and that want is actually foolishness, while fullness or plenitude is wisdom. Much of this sounds as though it could have come from Augustine's pen, as opposed to Monnica's lips. Where Monnica seems to glimmer a bit is when the dialogue concludes with her words of wisdom on the happy life, "the perfect life which we must assume that we can attain soon by a well-founded faith, a joyful hope, and an ardent love." While the words might be Augustine's—faith, hope, and love—the sentiment expressed, namely, that God is reached through traditional forms of piety rather than philosophy or study, might belong to Monnica. Certainly Augustine and his friends appear surprised at Monnica's simple yet profound wisdom.

Although Monnica plays a smaller role in *De ordine*, her presence and participation make the point that women need not be hindrances to philosophy.[61] In the *Confessions* her son blames the failure of a contemplative commune on the resistance of his friends' wives and concubines.[62] Furthermore, Augustine sees his own addiction to sex as an impediment to the pursuit of wisdom. In *De ordine*, however, her son not only uses Monnica's entrance to introduce the idea of women's contribution to philosophy, but he also directs a number of comments to her that undercut his own exposition on the liberal arts.[63] "She is the great exception," states O'Donnell, "the one who knows the essential things by direct experience that has no need for the *disciplinae*."[64]

Power writes that the *Dialogues* reveal "a clash of models of spirituality, the intersection of two very different ways of encountering the holy."[65] The *Dialogues* do seem to indicate a tension in Augustine regarding two spiritual paths: that of prayer and that of philosophy. As R. J. O'Connell notes, "For the Monnicas of this world, then, Christ now provides an alternative to the intellectualist way of the 'disciplines.' "[66] Monnica and other unlettered believers represent the way of prayer, while Augustine and his friends represent the way of philosophy and formal study. Augustine alludes to this when he writes, "That was the kind of person she was because she was taught by you [God] as her inward teacher in the school of the heart" (Chadwick's translation from book 9 of the *Confessions*).[67]

Monnica's approach to faith remains "female" in the sense that it is uneducated, intuitive, and guided by patriarchal church leadership. It is not male, because it lacks the philosophical and educational foundation men would have had: literacy, literature, and rhetorical studies. In Augustine's mind, men like himself would approach Christianity one way;

women would approach it differently. Despite these deficiencies, at Cassiciacum Monnica challenges her son's thinking on the nature of religious faith. And Augustine responds. As Mark Twain observed, when he grew older, his father got smarter. Monnica, and her type of faith, got smarter for Augustine, despite her female and weak nature.

Just as the *Dialogues* portray Monnica as a person of deep faith, so also does the *Confessions*, but with a difference. In the *Dialogues*, her faith is a source of wonder; in the *Confessions* it is many times a source of embarrassment for Augustine. For example, he notes the impatience of a certain bishop in dealing with Monnica's importunate attitude: "Leave me and go in peace. It cannot be that the son of these tears should be lost."[68] The fact that Monnica is reported to have contact with the unnamed bishop in North Africa, and with the bishop of Milan, Ambrose, raises the probability of her being a fairly religious woman. In Milan she is part of a sit-in at a church that was resisting a threat by Arian partisans. She is also advised by Ambrose to stop leaving food offerings for the dead in the cemetery, a ritual common in the African church.

Monnica's piety and practice seem to reflect the African Christianity that Augustine subsequently tried to replace with catholic, or Romanized, Christianity. Brown notes that Augustine and Aurelius, the bishops of Hippo and Carthage respectively, both attempted to stamp out drinking and feasting at tombs of the dead; while they may have succeeded in their own hometowns, the practice continued in other major African cities.[69] Although Augustine called the custom "pagan," it undoubtedly continued within the Donatist Church, in which his mother had grown up. Although Monnica complied with Caecilianist Christianity—a minority church movement that rejected the Donatists' insistence on the rebaptism of those whose sins required it—she continued her North African traditions until Ambrose admonished her to stop.[70]

It is not clear whether Augustine uses these accounts to promote his anti-Donatist agenda or to provide further evidence of his mother's simple nature. Clearly the stories are supposed to reveal how unsophisticated his mother is, and yet how faithful as well. Augustine does tell us that Monnica attended church "day and night," and that Ambrose praised her for her regular church attendance.[71] At these times her son even seems a bit proud of his mother. At the very least, however, her style of Christianity, along with her name, emphasizes her North African origins.

Another hint that reveals Monnica's African Christianity appears in the dreams and visions she has. "Dreams and trances were common: simple peasants would lie for days in a coma; and Monica [sic], as we have seen, placed great reliance on her dreams," explains Brown, writing of the "drastic" religion of the Christians in Africa.[72] Augustine describes her dream in which she sees a young man standing on a ruler next to her. The dream states, "Where you are, he is," and this reassures her.[73] Her intuitions are apparently so frequent that Augustine notes his mother's failure to have a positive vision about his impending marriage in Milan, and Monnica admits her inability in that instance to see clearly what was to happen. He also mentions the dream that enables her to calm a ship's crew during a storm at sea, and he alludes to other visions, admitting that he has not recorded all the visions that Monnica has.[74] Her reliance on dreams, then—rather than Scripture or doctrine—provides additional support for her African Christian origins.

Monnica's feminine and intuitive piety can be seen in her constant praying and attendant crying. In a previous article on Saint Monnica, I argued for the historicity of Augustine's depiction of Monnica's prayers and tears for his salvation, as the gift of tears, a mystical charism highly valued in the Eastern Christian church.[75] Now I am not so sure that it was anything more than a projection of Augustine's own deeply felt compunction over the life he led before his conversion.[76] One could argue, as I did, that given Monnica's sensible, practical nature in all other aspects of her life, she must have received a mystical gift, because the ceaseless crying is so foreign to her personality. In other words, she is subject to crying fits that are quite out of character, given her competence at household management and other practical matters. Lending some credence to the possibility that Monnica is in fact struck with uncontrollable weeping is the comment by the bishop, who remarks upon her many, many tears. Whether that is a single impassioned plea by Monnica, or one of many, we cannot know, although the *Confessions* provides at least eight instances of Monnica's crying and praying.[77] While her prayers characterize the institutionalized task of Christian widows to pray ceaselessly for benefactors, for sinners, for ministers, and others, we cannot know if this was the case for Monnica.[78] Certainly she stands in stark contrast to other women-of-worth who do not succumb to tears, such as Macrina, whom Gregory praises for refusing to cry upon the death of their brother.

Finally, we must not neglect the famous mystical experience at Ostia that Monnica shares with her son, although its historicity is certainly open to question.[79] "As the flame of love burned stronger in us and raised us higher towards the eternal God," writes Augustine, "our thoughts ranged over the whole compass of material things in their various degrees, up to the heavens themselves. . . . Higher still we climbed. . . . At length we came to our own souls and passed beyond them to that place of ever-lasting plenty."[80] At the conclusion of Augustine's description of the experience, he actually admits that "this was the purport of our talk, though we did not speak in these precise words or exactly as I have reported them."[81] And in the description of what they had heard from Wisdom herself (or, rather, himself in the text), he says, "*Suppose* that we heard him himself, with none of these things between ourselves and him." He concludes with another "*suppose* that this state were to continue" (my emphasis). Augustine is clearly telling the reader that the experience did not happen as he wrote it; yet just as clearly, it seems possible that he has had some sort of religious experience with his mother, perhaps in a time of prayer together, or in a discussion in which he saw her truly for the first time.[82] The world seems a "paltry place" compared to what they discuss, which is probably Monnica's impending death, since she falls terminally ill five days later. But even in this vision Monnica remains the female, sighing with happiness that she has seen her son become a "cath-olic Christian" before she dies.

The most we can say, then, is that Monnica appears to be a practicing Christian who takes her faith seriously and to deeper lengths once her children are grown. Like many Christian women in the pagan world, she succeeds in converting her pagan husband and her mother-in-law to Christianity. She raises her children in catholic Christianity, despite her neglect of their baptism, but retains some of her African Christian tradi-tions. She is in close contact with the bishops of two cities. She frequents the cemeteries in the ritual of providing food offerings for the dead. She aids Ambrose in resisting an Arian takeover. And she impresses her son as having a deep faith that equals, if not surpasses, his own, despite its lack of philosophical content.

Unlike her contemporary women-of-worth, Monnica does not found a monastery or convent. She is not wealthy, and although she is wise, it is not with the wisdom of the philosophers. She cares for her husband and loves her children. She weeps, unlike her female counterparts. In sum, Monnica remains female, for better or worse, throughout Augustine's ac-counts.

Conclusions

Augustine presents his mother as a less-than-perfect human being. When he exaggerates and emphasizes her faults to score his theological points, it seems as though some traces of a real person emerge, like shadows on a wall. He eulogizes her by recounting her childhood proclivity to tipple at the wine jar.[83] In fact, the reports of Monnica's qualities are more dubious than the accounts of her failings. For example, Monnica's unctuous advice to the wives of abusive spouses to keep quiet and obey their masters—that is, their husbands—sounds like something her son would say.[84] Not every account is believable or even intended to be biography.

Although Augustine seems aware of woman-of-worth stories, especially in the presentation of his mother in the *Dialogues*, he goes against the genre in a number of key ways. First, he criticizes Monnica, in a radical departure from traditional descriptions of praiseworthy women, which find nothing to criticize. Second, he shows her as both maternal and female throughout her life, in another difference from contemporary reports of model women. These deviations from type suggest that there might well be elements of truth in Augustine's portrayal of Monnica.

What I think we can say about Monnica, remembering our commitment to both truth and subject, is that she is a woman of faith whose family considerations keep her from choosing a completely ascetic life. We cannot examine her motives for making that choice—whether from worldliness, fear, maternal care, or excessive/obsessive love for her son. Given Augustine's critical stance toward her familial orientation, it seems as though he is lifting up her orientation as an object of criticism rather than praise. Her maternal character gets in the way of her spiritual development, according to Augustine. At the same time, however, he credits her maternal care as the vehicle through which God works to save him. For better and worse, she is a mother first.

Similarly, though Augustine praises Monnica's faith in the *Dialogues* in a backhanded way, the *Confessions* generally depicts her faith negatively: she participates in a cult of the dead, she neurotically (or devotedly) cries and prays over him, and she is in contact with church leaders who chastise her for her behavior. We cannot deduce much more than that Monnica did practice her faith, perhaps even as a witness to Roman Christianity in the face of a dangerous attack. It would be nice to think that she was a visionary and a mystic, but this image is vague and insubstantial.

This does not seem much to know about a woman who has been called everything from devouring and relentless to pious and self-sacrificing. We are only able to catch remote glimpses of Monnica in the interstices between Augustine's theological purposes and his literary devices. We see her through latticework in a distant garden, unsure of what is really there. Our desire to see the face of Monnica directly rather than through this barrier, and to hear her voice unmediated by any other, is an impossible goal. It nevertheless remains our responsibility to make the attempt.

Notes

1. *Life of Olympias, Deaconess*, trans. Elizabeth A. Clark, *Women in the Early Church* (Wilmington, Del.: Michael Glazier, 1983), 229.

2. Eric J. Ziolkowski, "St. Augustine: Aeneas' Antitype, Monica's Boy," *Literature and Theology* 9, no. 1 (1995): 1–23.

3. Margaret Miles, *Desire and Delight: A New Reading of Augustine's "Confessions"* (New York: Crossroad, 1992), 71, 80.

4. Garry Wills's biography of Augustine is the exception to this (*Augustine* [New York: Penguin, 1999]).

5. Elizabeth A. Clark, "The Lady Vanishes: Dilemmas of a Feminist Historian After the 'Linguistic Turn,'" *Church History* 67, no. 1 (March 1998): 1–31. See also "Rewriting Early Christian History," in *Theology and the New Histories*, ed. Gary Macy (Maryknoll, N.Y.: Orbis, 1999), 89–111.

6. Clark, "The Lady Vanishes," 19.

7. Edith Wyschogrod, *An Ethics of Remembering: History, Heterology, and the Nameless Others* (Chicago: University of Chicago Press, 1998). "Heterology" refers to "the historian who is driven by the eros for the dead and the urgency of ethics, and who speaks from out of the cataclysm that she cannot name" (xiii).

8. Wyschogrod, *An Ethics of Remembering*, xii.

9. Peter Brown, *Augustine of Hippo: A Biography*, rev. ed. with epilogue (Berkeley and Los Angeles: University of California Press, 2000), 21.

10. James J. O'Donnell, *Augustine: A New Biography* (New York: HarperCollins, 2005), 116.

11. Kim Power, *Veiled Desire: Augustine on Women* (New York: Continuum, 1996), 87–89, 91–92.

12. *Confessions* 9.4, *Sancti Augustini, Confessionum, Libri XIII*, ed. Lucas Verheijen, *Corpus Christianorum Series Latina*, vol. 27 (Turnhout, Belgium: Brepols, 1981). English translation in Saint Augustine, *Confessions*, trans. R. S. Pine-Coffin (New York: Penguin Books, 1961), 186.

13. Françoise Lionnet, *Autobiographical Voices: Race, Gender, Self-Portraiture* (Ithaca: Cornell University Press, 1989), 56 (emphasis in original), 32.

14. O'Donnell, *Augustine*, 70.

15. Miles, *Desire and Delight*, 82.

16. Marie-Odile Bonnichon uses the expression "infinitely banal" in "Pourquoi 'Sainte' Monique?" in *Histoire et culture chrétienne: Hommage a Monseigneur Yves Marchasson*, ed. Yves Ledure (Paris: Beauchesne, 1992), 25.

17. For discussions of misogyny in the early church, see Ross Shepard Kraemer and Mary Rose D'Angelo, eds., *Women and Christian Origins* (New York: Oxford University Press, 1999); Rosemary Radford Ruether, ed., *Religion and Sexism: Images of Woman in the Jewish and Christian Traditions* (New

York: Simon and Schuster, 1974); George Tavard, *Women in Christian Tradition* (Notre Dame and London: University of Notre Dame Press, 1973).

18. Saint Jerome, *Letters and Select Works*, trans. W. H. Fremantle, in *A Select Library of Nicene and Post-Nicene Fathers*, vol. 6, 2d ser., ed. Philip Schaff and Henry Wace (1893; repr., Grand Rapids: Eerdmans, n.d.), *Letter* 127.4, 254.

19. Palladius, *The Lausiac History*, trans. Robert R. Meyer (New York: Newman Press, 1964), 46.1, 123.

20. John Scheid, "Claudia the Vestal Virgin," in *Roman Women*, ed. Augusto Fraschetti, trans. Linda Lappin (Chicago: University of Chicago Press, 1994), 29.

21. Virginia Burrus, *Chastity as Autonomy: Women in the Stories of the Apocryphal Acts* (Lewiston, N.Y.: Edwin Mellen Press, 1987), 31.

22. Brigitte Egger, "The Role of Women in the Greek Novel: Woman as Heroine and Reader," in *Oxford Readings in the Greek Novel*, ed. Simon Swain (Oxford: Oxford University Press, 1999), 126.

23. Gillian Cloke, *"This Female Man of God": Women and Spiritual Power in the Patristic Age*, A.D. 350–450 (London: Routledge, 1995), 2.

24. Burrus, *Chastity as Autonomy*, 116.

25. Augusto Fraschetti, introduction to *Roman Women*, ed. Augusto Fraschetti, trans. Linda Lappin (Chicago: University of Chicago Press, 1994), 20.

26. Jane Tibbetts Schulenburg, *Forgetful of Their Sex: Female Sanctity and Society, ca. 500–1100* (Chicago and London: University of Chicago Press, 1998), 213.

27. Regardless of the historicity of this scene, see Ziolkowski, "St. Augustine"; what is significant is that Augustine says Monnica was crying and emotional, rather than reserved and dispassionate.

28. Saint Jerome *Letter* 108.6, 197.

29. *Confessions* 2.2; Pine-Coffin, 44.

30. *Confessions* 1.11; Pine-Coffin, 32. Augustine is so bitter about this he mentions it again in 5.9.

31. *Confessions* 2.3; Pine-Coffin, 46.

32. *Confessions* 9.9; Pine-Coffin, 195.

33. *Confessions* 9.9.

34. Fraschetti, introduction to *Roman Women*, 8.

35. Although this is not the customary interpretation of the passage, this is correct in the context, according to James J. O'Donnell, ed., *Augustine: Confessions; Introduction, Text, and Commentary*, 3 vols. (Oxford: Clarendon Press, 1992), 2.198. The Pine-Coffin translation provides this sense of the text as well.

36. *Confessions* 3.11; Pine-Coffin, 68.

37. *Confessions* 3.4.

38. See Walter Houston Clark, "Depth and Rationality in Augustine's *Confessions*," *Journal for the Scientific Study of Religion* 5, no. 1 (1965): 144–48; James Dittes, "Continuities Between the Life and Thought of Augustine," *Journal for the Scientific Study of Religion* 5, no. 1 (1965): 130–40; E. R. Dodds, "Augustine's *Confessions*: A Study of Spiritual Maladjustment," *Hibbert Journal* 26 (1927–28): 459–73; Charles Kligerman, "A Psychoanalytic Study of the *Confessions* of St. Augustine," *Journal of the American Psychoanalytic Association* 5 (1957): 469–84; Paul W. Pruyser, "Psychological Examination: Augustine," *Journal for the Scientific Study of Religion* 5, no. 2 (1966): 284–89; Philip Woollcott Jr., "Some Considerations of Creativity and Religious Experience in St. Augustine of Hippo," *Journal for the Scientific Study of Religion* 5, no. 2 (1966): 273–83. For salutary antidotes to these critical views of Monnica, see Donald Capps, "Augustine as Narcissist: Comments on Paul Rigby's 'Paul Ricoeur, Freudianism, and Augustine's *Confessions*,'" *Journal of the American Academy of Religion* 53, no. 1 (1985): 115–27 and Paula Fredriksen, "Augustine and his Analysts: The Possibility of a Psychohistory," *Soundings* 61, no. 2 (1978): 206–27.

39. Musonius Rufus, cited in Bruce W. Winter, *Roman Wives, Roman Widows: The Appearance of New Women and the Pauline Communities* (Grand Rapids, Mich.: Eerdmans, 2003), 61.

40. Fraschetti, introduction to *Roman Women*, 14.

41. Clarissa W. Atkinson, "Your Servant, My Mother: The Figure of Saint Monica in the Ideology of Christian Motherhood," in *Immaculate and Powerful: The Female in Sacred Image and Social Reality*, ed. Clarissa W. Atkinson, Constance H. Buchanan, and Margaret R. Miles (Boston: Beacon Press, 1985), 161.

42. For a discussion of the church office of widows, see Bonnie Bowman Thurston, *The Widows: A Women's Ministry in the Early Church* (Minneapolis: Fortress Press, 1989).

43. Cloke, *"This Female Man of God,"* 99.

44. Saint Chrysostom, *On the Priesthood*, trans. W. R. W. Stephens et al., in *A Select Library of Nicene and Post-Nicene Fathers*, vol. 9, 1st ser., ed. Philip Schaff (1889; repr., Grand Rapids, Mich.: Eerdmans, 1968), 1.5, 34.

45. Cloke, *"This Female Man of God,"* 214.

46. *The Letters of St. Paulinus of Nola*, trans. P. G. Walsh, vol. 2, *Letters 23–51* (New York: Newman Press, 1966), *Letter* 29, 105; Palladius *The Lausiac History* 9, 43.

47. Palladius *Dialogue* 56, quoted in Cloke, *"This Female Man of God,"* 214.

48. Gregory, Bishop of Nyssa, *The Life of Saint Macrina*, trans. Kevin Corrigan (Toronto: Peregrina, 1987), 26. Cloke renders this as "for I do not know if it is appropriate to describe her by her sex who so surpassed her sex," in *"This Female Man of God,"* 214.

49. *De beata vita* 2.10. *Sancti Aurelii Augustini, De beata vita*, ed. W. M. Green, *Corpus Christianorum Series Latina*, vol. 29 (Turnhout, Belgium: Brepols, 1970).

50. Palladius *Lausiac History* 55.3, 136–37.

51. Elizabeth A. Clark, "Piety, Propaganda, and Politics in the *Life of Melania the Younger*," in *Ascetic Piety and Women's Faith: Essays on Late Ancient Christianity* (Lewiston, N.Y.: Edwin Mellen Press, 1986), 66, 72.

52. Jerome *Letter* 127.7, 255–56.

53. Corrigan, *The Life of Saint Macrina*, 22.

54. Ibid., 47.

55. Clark, "The Lady Vanishes," 27.

56. Arguing for the historicity of the *Dialogues* is B. L. Meulenbroek, "The Historical Character of Augustine's Cassiciacum Dialogues," *Mnemosyne* 13 (1947): 203–29. The most convincing argument against is by John J. O'Meara, "The Historicity of the Early Dialogues of Saint Augustine," *Vigiliae Christianae* 5 (1951): 150–78. Othmar Perler provides a list of sources pro and con on the historicity issue in *Les voyages de Saint Augustin* (Paris: Études Augustiniennes, 1969): 183–84n4. Elizabeth A. Clark argues that Monnica at Cassiciacum serves Augustine's theological purposes, in "Rewriting Early Christian History," 101–3.

57. In a previous article I wrote on Saint Monnica, I tended to accept the historicity of the *Dialogues*. Now I am a bit more skeptical, having been persuaded by those who argue their adherence to the dialogue genre. See Rebecca Moore, "St. Monica and the Mystical Gift of Tears," *Magistra* 4, no. 2 (1998): 61–88.

58. *De beata vita* 2.10.

59. Ibid., 3.19.

60. Ibid., 3.21. English translation from "The Happy Life," trans. Ludwig Schopp, in *Writings of Saint Augustine*, vol. 1 (New York: Cima, 1948), 69.

61. Emilien Lamirande, "Quand Monique, la mère d'Augustine prend la parole," in *Signum Pietatis: Festgabe für Cornelius Petrus Mayer OSA zum 60. Geburtstag*, ed. Adolar Zumkeller (Würzburg, Germany: Augustinus Verlag, 1989), 3–19.

62. *Confessions* 6.14.

63. Sancti Aureli Augustini, *De ordine libri duo*, ed. Pius Knöll, *Corpus Scriptorum Ecclesiasticorum Latinorum*, vol. 63 (1922; repr., New York: Johnson Reprint, 1962).

64. O'Donnell, *Confessions*, 2.273, referring to *De ordine* 2.17.45–2.20.52.

65. Power, *Veiled Desire*, 88.

66. Robert J. O'Connell, *St. Augustine's Confessions: The Odyssey of a Soul* (Cambridge, Mass.: Belknap Press, 1969), 79.

67. Saint Augustine, *Confessions* 9.9, trans. Henry Chadwick (New York: Oxford University Press, 1991), 170.

68. *Confessions* 3.12.

69. Brown, *Augustine of Hippo*, 484.

70. O'Donnell, *Augustine*, 212–13.

71. *Confessions* 5.9 and 6.2.

72. Brown, *Augustine of Hippo*, 21.

73. *Confessions* 3.11; Pine-Coffin, 68.

74. *Confessions* 6.1. Pierre Courcelle, in *Recherches sur Les Confessions de Saint Augustin*, new ed. enl. (Paris: Éditions de Boccard, 1968), hypothesizes that Augustine wrote a short book about Monnica's visions (40n1).

75. Moore, "St. Monica and the Mystical Gift of Tears"; see n. 57, above.

76. Christians in the Eastern Church, where tears and great remorse were valued as gifts of the Holy Spirit, read Augustine widely, in part because of this very emphasis on compunction.

77. *Confessions* 3.11–12, 4.4, 5.7–9, 6.1, 8.12.

78. Thurston, *The Widows*, 96–105

79. Paul Henry, *The Path to Transcendence: From Philosophy to Mysticism in Saint Augustine*, trans. Francis F. Burch (Pittsburgh: Pickwick Press, 1981); from *La vision d'Ostie: Sa place dans la vie et l'oeuvre de Saint Augustine* (Paris: Vrin, 1938). The mystical experience described in the *Confessions* resembles other Neoplatonic descriptions of the soul's ascent to God.

80. *Confessions* 9.10; Pine-Coffin, 197.

81. *Confessions* 9.10; Pine-Coffin, 198.

82. Margaret More O'Ferrall says that Ostia was not mystical, but "rather an intense intellectual and emotional experience, clothed in Neo-Platonic language," in "Monica, the Mother of Augustine: A Reconsideration" *Recherches Augustiniennes* X (1975): 42–43.

83. *Confessions* 9.8.

84. Ibid., 9.9.

6

Not Nameless but Unnamed: The Woman Torn from Augustine's Side

Margaret R. Miles

Rather than re-establish those perceived as missing from the narrative as fully present, it might be of interest to account for the fact that the fragmented, erased, and ephemeral voices are nevertheless there, miraculously clinging to the rock of historical narrative like so many storm-battered mollusks.
—Irit Rogoff, "Tiny Anguishes: Reflections on Nagging, Scholastic Embarrassment, and Feminist Art History"

The woman with whom I was in the habit of sleeping was torn from my side (auulsa a latere meo) on the grounds of being an impediment to my marriage, and my heart, which clung to her, was broken and wounded and dropping blood. She had returned to Africa after having made a vow to [God] that she would never go to bed with another man, and she had left with me the natural son I had had by her (*ex illa filio meo*). . . . Nor was the wound healed which had been made by the cutting off of my [partner]. It burned, it hurt intensely, and then it festered and became more chilling and desperate.
—Augustine, *Confessions* 6.15

In his *Confessions*, Augustine famously grieved for a woman "torn from his side" by what he describes as his mother's desire that he make an advantageous marriage. She wanted him to marry an heiress, he wrote, "so that expense would be no burden."[1] The notoriously desirous Augustine represents himself as having no desire in the matter. Indeed, his mother and his partner seem, according to Augustine's narrative, to have engineered his desolation together. The passage seems to claim that his partner left him and her son voluntarily.

Revealed tantalizingly in a few brief passages in Augustine's *Confessions*, his partner of fifteen years and the mother of their son is an elusive figure.[2] She came to Milan from North Africa with Augustine. In the first year of their relationship, she bore their son, Adeodatus. She may have been a Christian, but the evidence is slender, largely consisting of the fact of her vow to remain celibate for the rest of her life. But she could also have been motivated to this choice by traditional Roman respect for a *univira*, or "one-man woman." There is no suggestion in the text that she and Augustine could or should have married. In the rigidly striated class structure of the later Roman Empire, a class difference meant that "formal marriage to her would have obliterated Augustine's social and vocational aspirations."[3] This summarizes what can be known about her from the only text in Augustine's voluminous writings in which she appears directly, the *Confessions*.

Problems, Methods, and Texts

A young woman who lived in late antiquity makes a brief appearance in a famous text. Her existence is not to be doubted. But her subjectivity, her passions and thoughts, are not represented. Indeed, the text's author, Augustine of Hippo, as well as numerous commentators across the centuries, present her briefly—if at all—as materializing specifically for the purpose of serving *his* passion: "In those years I lived with a woman who was not bound to me by lawful marriage; she was one who had come my way because of my wandering desires (*uagus ardor*) and my lack of considered judgment; nevertheless I had only this one woman and I was faithful to her."[4]

For Augustine's purpose of demonstrating his youthful sinfulness, his partner is essential to the text, yet she is tantalizingly inaccessible. Readers of Augustine's *Confessions* can do no more than glimpse her, and we cannot with confidence identify her influence on her well-known partner. Without using far too much imagination, we cannot reconstruct a fully fleshed character. The *Confessions*, in which she makes brief appearances is, after all, Augustine's autobiography.

Augustine's partner creates for a feminist historian some interesting historiographical questions. Most historians' interest in this "nameless woman" is limited to understanding her in order to understand Augustine better. Is there enough evidence of her to permit us to reconstruct *her* historical presence?[5] My answer will be yes and no. I will not be able to reconstruct her as an individual with subjectivity. I will, however, suggest that a reconstitution of her social niche in Roman North Africa goes at least part of the way toward recovering a picture of her. I will first pose several methodological and theoretical questions that challenge features of contemporary feminist historiography. Using textual criticism and historical reconstruction, I will then explore what *can* be learned of a woman who was present but unnamed in a highly influential late fourth-century male autobiography.

Let us begin by recognizing that Augustine's partner was not "nameless." Rather, Augustine did not reveal her name. Why? Cultural differences may be too profound and fundamental to warrant a guess. But there are more possible explanations than the few most frequently encountered. Feminist historians tend to think that Augustine withheld her name because of the misogyny they see in his later homosociality and commitment to celibacy.[6] Other historians usually interpret the fact in one of two ways. They either say that her name was withheld because the relationship was unimportant and insignificant, or they conjecture that Augustine sought to protect her. For example, Peter Brown finds historians' interest in Augustine's concubine "a very modern preoccupation," one that "Augustine and his cultivated friends would have found strange." For Brown, her primary role in Augustine's biography is that "this nameless woman bore Augustine's son, Adeodatus."[7] By contrast, John Noonan writes, "With delicacy he never gives her name."[8] However, it is at least possible that, for Augustine, her name remained, after a decade, too resonant with the pain of their parting to mention. Perhaps Augustine also remembered all too well the pleasures and delights of intimate relationship, and these memories threatened his new life as a celibate priest and bishop.

Whatever Augustine's reasons for omitting her name, her "namelessness" signals the absence of her subjectivity from the text. It would be tempting to name her, selecting a name from known North African Christian women's names of the period: Afrania, Antonia, Apollonia, Crispina, Demetrias, Donatilla, Ecdicia, Faltonia, Felicitas, Januaria, Juliana, Lucilla, Manlia, Marcella, Maria, Maxima, Monnica, Ostoria, Perpetua, Pompeiana, Potamia, Proba, Quartilla, Restituta, Sabine, Secunda, Sextilia, Tertulla, Thecla, Thelica, Verna, or Victoria. Rather than arbitrarily select a name for Augustine's partner, however, I must instead respect her "namelessness," acknowledging that her subjectivity is indeed lost to us, elided in Augustine's text, our only evidence of her existence. It would be presumptuous for an historian to attempt to reconstruct it. Too much imagination, projection, and speculation would be required.[9] Acknowledging this prompts me to reconsider two assumptions common to feminist reconstructions of historical women.

First, Irit Rogoff has suggested that when twenty-first-century historians relate to historical women on the basis of current sympathies, sensitivities, and projections, it is "narcissistic and self-referential." Empathy should not be privileged "as the primary principle of historical analysis." Further, she suggests that when we write about "fragmented, erased, and ephemeral voices" we cannot and should not "robustly reconstitute them." What we can do, instead, is to recognize that "without their vague and fragile presence at the margins, the stalwart presences at the center would lose much of their vitality."[10] We can then explore how this works in particular literary works.

Second, feminist historians tend to seek historical women who resisted victimization and found ways to achieve subjectivity and authorization for their work—individualists, in the context of their societies. In other words, we seek historical women characterized by those qualities that we—rightly or wrongly—believe ourselves to possess. Yet feminist historians, like historical women, are heavily inscribed by culture. In twenty-first-century media culture, in fact, a technology for socialization replaces and improves upon the capacity for socialization of face-to-face societies of earlier times. Socialization addresses not only behavior but also subjectivity, the way a person thinks herself, her society, and her world and her feelings about these. Social psychologist Rom Harré has written, "To think, to perceive, to be rational and to experience emotions are cultural endowments not native achievements."[11]

> The fundamental human reality is conversation, effectively without beginning or end, to which, from time to time, individuals make contributions. All that is personal in our mental and emotional lives is individually appropriated from the conversation going on around us and perhaps idiosyncratically transformed. The structure of our thinking and feeling will reflect, in various ways, the form and content of that conversation. . . . A person is not a natural object, but a cultural artefact.[12]

According to Harré, within the strong influence of cultural matrices, two prerogatives for developing personhood are available. These are "the capacity to act intentionally, in contrast to one's behavior emerging from a nexus of causal chains, and autonomy, in the sense of the capacity to adopt one principle rather than some other in the management of action."[13] These, we may note, are precisely the capacities Augustine described himself as lacking in relation to sexual desire and activity.[14] They are, however, capacities that even Augustine's slender text reveals about his partner. Her choices become evident to the reader of the *Confessions* when she and Augustine part. As I discuss below, by vowing future celibacy she exercised one of several options available to her. By framing her choice within her social and cultural situation, we will know all that can be known about Augustine's partner.

The Evidence

Scholars of Augustine often endeavor to understand his relationship with his partner on the basis of remarks made in his treatises on marriage, adultery, and virginity.[15] These treatises are invaluable for the occasional bits of information to be gleaned from them. But finally, what they give is Augustine's views, informed by his experience. If our primary interest is in his partner, they do not get us much closer to her. Moreover, many suggestions about his relationship are woven into treatises in Augustine's corpus that do not deal primarily with sex or marriage. In fact, we find small clues about Augustine's partner throughout his prolific writings. For example, his most concentrated discourse on relationship occurs in *The Trinity*, and although he seeks to understand the triune God in this treatise, his knowledge of relationship was informed by his own most intimate relationship. From these and other writings, we can infer, with more or less confidence, something about *his* experience. Having done so, however, we do not know any more about his partner. In short, textual evidence is elusive; it allows us only suggestions, questions, and occasional small partial insights.

However, Augustine's assumptions about sex and heterosexual relationship can be recovered from his writings. For example, as the quotations above from the *Confessions* demonstrate, Augustine largely reduced his relationship with his partner to sex. Later, in his treatise *On the Good of Marriage*, he includes neither love nor marital friendship with the three goods of marriage that he identifies: offspring, fidelity, and the sacramental bond.[16] Why? To alleviate his despair at losing her? To feel less guilt about dismissing her in favor of a temporary mistress and an advantageous marriage? To emphasize the complete reversal brought about by conversion? So that he can feel no responsibility for someone who offered him her body and her life and, when dismissed, returned alone to her home in North Africa?

One of the striking features of the *Confessions* is Augustine's assumption that he can define and describe his relationship with his partner from his perspective alone. Yet relationships are, by definition, two sided. To notice the absence of another perspective, another experience, is already to *miss* that perspective and experience. I would like to "unframe her from the constraints of victimhood," as Irit Rogoff wrote of another historical woman, to imagine her outside the terms of a powerful text that gives her "no place from which to speak."[17] I would like to do the same for Augustine's partner. She is too convenient a victim, framed within a narrative of the hero's journey to insight. Can she be seen in any other way than as a victim? The way to do this, I believe, is to place Augustine's partner in the social and cultural context in which she lived and within which her options were provided. Then her choices—albeit within a limited range—can be seen.[18]

In short, instead of seeking psychological explanations,[19] we must seek her niche in her society in her historical moment. We must ask, how did a newly powerful and upwardly mobile Christianity make use of gender to identify and define its values and authorization procedures?[20] For Augustine's partner was not a woman with a "lone individual plight, a singular drama," but, rather, a woman who occupied a cultural subject position shared by many women.[21] Instead of seeking her subjectivity where it does not exist, that is, in Augustine's text, I can use his text in two ways that Augustine almost surely did not intend. I can examine the social practices within which she made her choices, and I can compare her situation with that of the only other women the text allows us to glimpse: Monnica, Augustine's mother; the unnamed lover Augustine acquired after his partner returned to Africa; and the child heiress he intended to marry. How were these women differently positioned within nascent imperial Christian culture?

Women in Late Roman Society

First, the woman most fully represented within Augustine's *Confessions* was his mother. Augustine presented her as absorbed in securing for him social and professional advantages. He does not mention his siblings, who, readers are expected to infer, did not occupy Monnica's interest to any significant extent. There are, however, several passages in which he narrates episodes from Monnica's life that give us an invaluable picture of female culture in North Africa and imperial Milan. I will mention only one.

The passage to which I will refer has been discussed repeatedly in Augustine scholarship. I will not repeat these discussions, except to highlight the information they give about women's social expectations in the later Roman Empire.[22] Augustine described his mother's marriage to a man his reader must somehow try to picture as simultaneously extremely kind (*beniuolentia praecipuus*) and repeatedly unfaithful, hot-tempered, and inclined to physical abuse. Monnica escaped the bruises regularly worn by her women friends by practicing the advice she gave her friends.

> Many wives with husbands much milder than hers . . . went about with their faces disfigured by the marks of blows, and when they got together to talk they would often complain of the way their husbands behaved. But my mother, speaking lightly, but giving serious advice, used to say that the fault was in their tongues. They had all heard, she said, the marriage contract read out to them and from that day they ought to regard it as a legal instrument by which they were made servants; so they should remember their station and not set themselves up against their masters.[23]

Monnica further advised her friends not to contradict an angry husband, but to wait until he calmed down and then gently to explain the behavior that had aroused his anger. Blaming the victim and manipulation were Monnica's methods of avoiding marital conflict. The superior physical strength of most men, she believed, must be met by strategic accommodation. Domestic violence was apparently simply a fact of life for North African women. There is no evidence that Augustine's partner suffered from similar abuse; perhaps Monnica also taught her strategies for managing a man. But in a society in which intimate violence was to be taken for granted, no relationship could be free of its possibility and implicit threat.

The second woman who has a bit part in the *Confessions* was Augustine's second lover. Augustine wrote that after his partner's dismissal, "I had two years to wait before I could have the girl to whom I was engaged, and I could not bear the delay. So . . . I found another woman for myself—not, of course, as a wife."[24] This woman is the most mysterious of the women mentioned in the Confessions. Nothing is known of her but this one sentence. It was during or immediately after Augustine's less than two-year relationship with her that his conversion occurred. We do not know when, or under what circumstances, their relationship ended. Augustine may have taken her also as a concubine—he does not say—so that he would not be in danger of being charged with stuprum, or adultery.[25]

The third woman who appears in the Confessions is the young heiress to whom Augustine had proposed, and whose family had accepted him. Since the minimal age for marriage for Roman girls was twelve and the most common age was fourteen, the girl was probably between ten and twelve at the time she became engaged to marry Augustine.[26] To gain the advantages of marriage to a wealthy girl/woman, Augustine broke with his partner of fifteen years, the mother of his son.[27] We learn nothing about the religious commitments of the heiress and her family. All we know about her is that Augustine was interested in only, or primarily, her wealth.

The three women in sexual (or potentially sexual) relationships with Augustine were in very different social positions. The freedom with which Augustine was able to relate sexually to all of them serially must be seen as a context that significantly shaped the expectation each woman could hold. In a society in which women's circumstances were dictated by their relationship to a man, the flexibility of male sexual relationships meant that women's social positions were terrifyingly unstable. The only way for a woman to be in a strong position in the later Roman Empire was to own property, a relatively rare occurrence.[28] We cannot know whether Augustine's intended heiress might have eventually been in a position to compel his respect and to challenge his self-absorption, though arranged marriage at the age of twelve or fourteen would not seem conducive to developing a strong and independent spirit.

The success of a dominant male culture perhaps always requires a high degree of collaboration from women who are themselves excluded from the arenas in which social, political, and economic power is designed and administered. Michel Foucault defines "strong power" as power that attracts; "weak power" is forced to compel, having lost its attraction for a significant proportion of the population.[29] While male power is strong, many or most women concur with, work within, and support it. Contemporary feminists work hard to recognize historical women's creativity and energy in creating subcultures within which their needs and aspirations were more or less met. Yet there are all too many situations in which historical women's agency simply cannot be identified as anything but accommodation to the strictures of their social position.[30] Women's energetic initiative can be glimpsed, but women are often powerless to change dominant male assumptions and institutions. Often women's strategies can at best, like Monnica's, optimize women's positions on the margins of male culture.

The Christian Empire

Did the Christianization of Roman society offer women a new repertoire of choices? Did the instability of a historical moment in which the old values of empire were in conflict with new Christian values give women a wider range of opportunities? Christian asceticism and monasticism has been seen as offering women new and socially respected lifestyles.[31] Laws throughout the fourth century revised earlier restrictions on the length of time a woman could remain single after divorce or the death of her husband, allowing women to choose vowed celibacy rather than remarriage.[32] Ascetic women were free of the social expectation that they would marry and bear children, the primary role for women in late antiquity.[33] But what about women who married or became concubines, women such as those we meet in the *Confessions?*

The *Confessions* reveals a society in the making. Augustine converted to Christianity in the same decade—the 380s—in which Christianity was declared the official religion of the Roman Empire. He was part of a generation of young men who *formed* the Christian society whose values and institutions would survive the 410 c.e. fall of Rome. There was clearly a strong role for young men such as Augustine in the new Christian society. In the 390s they would elbow minority religions to the margins of society, rapidly removing Jews and adherents of Roman religions from public life.[34] "Multimedia" initiatives—laws, sermons, artworks, and mob violence—contributed to the formation of a Christian society that would be firmly in place by about 450 c.e.

Moreover, despite many enormous changes, the values and institutions Augustine and his friends constructed would survive far into the future; some institutions, such as monasticism, survive to the present. In short,

Augustine participated in, and narrated, the cultural excitements of the late fourth and early fifth centuries. He described vividly the intense emotions he experienced on hearing and reading of engaged couples who pledged celibacy and went to live in same-sex communities.[35] He repeatedly contrasted his own seriousness of purpose as a Christian with the social success epitomized and symbolized by a "good" marriage. Strong male friendships and excited plans for a male community free from worldly cares are a leitmotif throughout the *Confessions*.[36] Same-sex religious communities would quickly become stronger and more numerous, taking the place of imperial institutions in providing everything from social services to traversable roads in the medieval centuries.

Was there a new role for women in the Christian Roman Empire? Did Augustine's partner participate in the new excitements of the Christian empire? If she were indeed a Christian, the relinquishment of her sexuality would have placed her at the center of the ascetic movement, setting an example Augustine was not immediately prepared to follow but which he admired greatly. Furthermore, her role in the *Confessions* is central. The figure of Augustine's partner does more than contribute narrative vividness to Augustine's story. Her decision to remain celibate for the rest of her life also supported Christian rhetoric concerning the impossibility of great progress without correspondingly great sacrifice. From Augustine's perspective—and we do not have hers—she is the required living sacrifice, at first, by her absence, exacerbating the discomfort that led to his conversion, and later providing the example of celibacy that would be referenced many times in his writings. Augustine admired and extolled her as exemplary.[37]

But she was Augustine's sacrifice, *his* martyrdom. Even though she outdid him by vowing to have sex with no man for the rest of her days, his text swallows her act. Significantly, the language of tearing, wounds, dripping blood, and brokenness with which Augustine narrates his separation from her is the language of martyrdom. Without sacrificing her, he could not have aspired to "the highest peak of human heroism."[38] In Augustine's time, martyrdom, no longer a literal act, was reinterpreted in the Christian empire. In Athanasius's *Life of Saint Antony*, Antony, the prototypical ascetic, is described as practicing the "daily martyrdom."[39] In valuing martyrdom above all other Christian acts, Augustine was very much a North African, sharing with his compatriots respect for the ultimate sacrifice for faith.[40] Augustine's conversion, then, began with a martyrdom, extreme pain caused by "the cutting off of my previous mistress.

It burned, it hurt intensely, and then it festered, and if the pain became duller, it became more desperate."[41]

Augustine's partner converted to celibacy earlier than Augustine did, and at greater cost.[42] Hers was not simply a sacrifice of physical pleasure; it was also a critical social sacrifice in a society in which women's identity derived from their sexual arrangements. Augustine, by contrast, benefited socially from his vow of celibacy. He became a priest and a bishop at a time and in a place in which the church was a route to status and authority. She was sent away, but she went on her own terms.[43] Why did she not take her son with her when she returned to Africa? Did she despair of being able to support him when she herself would lack male protection? Did she unselfishly leave him to the parent who was expected to marry an heiress and thus would be able to bring the boy up with every advantage?[44] I address these questions by exploring further Augustine's partner's situation and her options within it.

Sexual Arrangements in Augustine's Society

I thought that I should be unbearably unhappy if I were deprived of the embraces of a woman. . . . I believed that continency was something that depended on one's own strength and I knew that I did not have enough strength for it.

—Augustine *Confessions* 6.11.

Two topics bear directly on the social world of Augustine's partner: concubinage and contraception. In "the Imperial period Roman marriage required no formal ceremony to be valid; cohabitation between eligible partners basically created marriage."[45] Beryl Rawson's investigation of the legal status of sexual arrangements in the later Roman Empire emphasizes that despite the ease of respected sexual arrangements, concubinage is not frequently attested for freeborn couples. Concubinage implied ineligibility for marriage, usually because of a class difference. The dissolution of such a relationship was similarly informal.[46] This informality, together with the severe penalty imposed by Augustus for adultery, namely, death by sword, combined to make sexual arrangements anxiety provoking.[47]

Concubinage and Marriage

In *Porneia: On Desire and the Body in Antiquity*, Aline Rousselle discusses the difficulty of describing Roman concubinage practices with precision.[48]

The evidence is fragmentary and sporadic. Historians are dependent for information on funerary inscriptions and "fragments of legal works written for the most part before the fourth century, and collected between 530 and 533 by a commission of jurists appointed by Justinian."[49] Also, changes occurred in the later empire, but on the basis of existing laws it is difficult to know whether laws were enforced or whether local practices actually conformed to the laws. Gillian Clark has also examined Roman law in relation to women, concluding that no generalizations can be made, because of local variations, inconsistencies in enforcement of recorded laws, and class differences. She writes: "We can sometimes see fragments of a pattern, but no overall design."[50]

However, C. N. Cochrane notes that under Theodosius (in the later fourth century), "the most significant departure [from Roman family law] was the disintegration, under Christian influence, of classical conceptions of the family and of family right."[51] The all-powerful paterfamilias of earlier times was gradually replaced by families with legal rights and protections.[52] One of the effects of this change was the greater legal protection of concubines' rights. By the end of the fourth century, a concubine "even had the right to inherit a modest part of her partner's estate."[53]

Rousselle also sees concubinage in a positive light, arguing that concubinage was "a free union in which the partners renounced the right to prosecute one another for adultery and to ask the tribunal to impose a punishment."[54] Concubinage involved fidelity and cohabitation. It ended when one or the other partner (usually the man), repudiated the relationship.[55] Lacking both the security and some of the restrictions of marriage, concubinage "should be seen as representing progress towards the right to enjoy a less unequal relationship [than marriage]."[56] Augustine recognized the less binding nature of concubinage; he says in a sermon, "Marriage is an iron fetter; other fetters can be loosed by us here in the church, but not this one."[57] Children born of concubinage belonged to the mother and carried her name. They were not eligible to inherit the father's property or goods.[58]

By Augustine's time, concubinage was an "official and respected condition."[59] Even the Christian Church recognized it, though it favored legitimate marriage, forbade a man to have both a wife and a concubine at the same time, and "required a baptized woman not to have known more than one man."[60] As a bishop, however, Augustine was judgmental of his earlier sexual arrangements. Opposed to concubinage, he advocated two choices in relation to sexuality, Christian marriage and vowed virginity.[61]

His view of "the good of marriage" lacks appreciation for anything but legitimate sex: "The crown of marriage is the chastity of procreation and faithfulness in rendering the carnal debt."[62] Only within marriage, and only for purposes of procreation, could sex be seen as even a limited good. For the older Augustine, in defiance of an accepted social practice, concubinage was sin.

However, he respected relationships that were faithful over a period of years. Without referring to his own relationship, he acknowledged that faithfulness, at least by the male partner, was unusual, when he commented in a sermon: "Women preserve chastity, which men will not preserve."[63] He repeatedly fulminated against the commonly accepted double standard: "I do not want Christian women to lie down under this. I solemnly warn you, I lay down this rule, I command you. I command you as your bishop; and it is Christ Who commands in me. God knows, in whose sight my heart burns. Yes, I say, I command you. . . . For so many years now we have baptized so many men to no effect, if there are none here who preserve the vows of chastity they took."[64]

Augustine's famous fantasies on the possibility of conception without the urgency of sexual desire[65] and immortality without death[66] serve his argument, against Manichaeans, for marriage as a good: "The bodies of the first marriage were both mortal at the first formation and yet would not have died, if they had not sinned. . . . Thus, even though through sexual intercourse generations of such bodies could have come into existence, which would have had increase up to a certain point and yet would not have inclined to old age, or they would have inclined as far as old age, and yet not to death."[67] It is not marriage, he was careful to say, even with its inevitable entailment of sex that brought death into the world, but sin.

Contraception

I learned by my own experience how great a difference there is between the self-restraint of the marriage covenant which is entered into for the sake of having children, and the mere pact made by two people whose love is lustful and who do not want to have children—even though, if children are born they compel us to love them.

—Augustine *Confessions* 4.2

When discussing contraception in late antiquity, it is important to keep in mind that contraceptive practices were not intended to improve women's lives. Rather, they "were essentially ways to avoid having to divide inheritances.[68] Nevertheless, the contraceptive practices of that society defined women's range of choices; they affected Augustine's partner as they affected all heterosexually active women.

Late fourth-century Christian attitudes toward contraception developed at the intersection of several influences. The widespread existence of contraceptive knowledge and methods was a fact of life in the later Roman Empire. As John Noonan writes, "The existence of contraceptive methods in the world from which the Christians came is established: by the [Hebrew Bible], by the Talmud, by Aristotle, by Pliny, by the physicians, and by imperial law. . . . Contraception was a social phenomenon in the Roman empire of which the Christians could not have been ignorant."[69]

However, Christians developed their attitudes toward contraception in the midst of polemics against their rivals, the Manichaeans, whom they accused of practicing sexual acts without procreative purpose. Writing sometime after 363 c.e. in Asia Minor, the Catholic bishop Titus wrote a treatise, *Against the Manichaeans*, in which he said, "Indulging in pleasure more frequently, [the Manichaeans] hate the fruit that necessarily comes from their acts; and they command that bodies be joined beyond what is lawful and restrict and expel what is conceived and do not await births at their proper time."[70] Noonan comments, "Sexual intercourse without procreative purpose and abortion are thus charged to the Manichees; *coitus interruptus* and anal intercourse may also be ascribed to them by the phrase 'beyond what is lawful.' "[71]

Because Manichaeans thought of the created world as the evil production of an evil Demiurge, they sought to avoid perpetuating it by procreation. Read with a hermeneutic of generosity, Manichaeans' acute sensitivity to the suffering of all living beings led them to seek to prevent the possibility of further suffering by infanticide or exposure, and even by the long suffering of human existence. However, in the context of the Roman state's interest in replenishing its population, Manichaeans represent a radical critique of both the Creator and the state.[72]

Two other debates influenced Augustine's views on marriage, concubinage, sex, and contraception. Without discussing them in detail, we must note that in the last decade of the fourth century, the monk Jovinian reacted against the "wave of ascetic enthusiasm which [had] spread throughout the Church."[73] Jovinian taught that marriage and virginity were equally conditions in which spiritual growth was possible. Augustine wrote in his *Retractations* that he had written *The Good of Marriage* specifically to oppose the "monster," Jovinian, who had "equated the merit of consecrated virgins and conjugal continence."[74] Apparently, if I may be pardoned an anachronism, Jovinian's teaching became a feminist issue. Women found in his teachings a greater respect for women. From the male perspective, respect for women rose and fell with respect for marriage.[75]

In 401 C.E., when he wrote *The Good of Marriage*, Augustine sought to refute Jovinian; in 419 when he wrote *Marriage and Concupiscence*, it was Pelagius he argued against. Against Pelagius (and later, Julian of Eclanum), Augustine argued that although marriage is a good, the pleasures of lust (*concupiscentia*), even though it produces offspring, is not itself a "natural good," as Julian claimed. For Augustine, the pleasure of sex is only to be tolerated when it is *led*, and modified by, the intention of producing children.[76]

Contraceptive Methods

Augustine and his partner were together for about fifteen years, from his sixteenth to his twenty-ninth year. Their son, Adeodatus, was born in the first year of their relationship (373 C.E.), and they had no further children. Interestingly, Augustine became a Manichaean in 373, the year of his son's birth, possibly attracted not only by the Manichaean solution to the problem of evil but also by its preference for preventing conception. Since he had acknowledged that he did not want children, the possibility may even be advanced to a probability.[77] The timing is telling. It is highly probable that Augustine and his partner practiced contraception for the remaining years of their relationship.

Human beings seem perennially to exhibit more hostility toward practices they themselves engaged in than those known only by hearsay. Long after his relationship with his partner ended, arguing against Manachaeism in his treatise *Marriage and Concupiscence*, Augustine excoriated the full range of late Roman prophylactic practices: "This lustful cruelty, or cruel lust, comes to this, that they even procure poisons of sterility [*sterilitatis venena*], and, if these do not work, extinguish and destroy the fetus in some way in the womb, preferring that their offspring die before it lives, or if it was already alive in the womb to kill it before it was born." Any of these practices effectively nullify a marriage, Augustine says. This is the only passage in Augustine's work that explicitly refers to artificial contraceptives.[78]

Augustine also refers to other contraceptive practices in his treatises on sex, virginity, and marriage. He claims to have heard at firsthand, during his time as a Manichaean, their teaching on the so-called rhythm method of contraception: "Is it not you who hold that begetting children is a greater sin than cohabitation? Is it not you who used to counsel us to observe as much as possible the time when a woman, after her purification, is most likely to conceive, and to abstain from cohabitation at that time, lest the soul should be entangled in flesh?"[79]

Conclusion

Desperately seeking Augustine's partner in a text that was not only uninterested in her, but actively presented her in a way that supported Augustine's present celibacy, has not been easy. At times I have lost the slender thread by which I hoped to pull her into view, and then, suddenly, it was all about Augustine, not about her. His flood of words tells us so much about himself, and so little about his lover of fifteen years. I have suggested that we can glimpse her through exploring the social arrangements that directed women's lives in the later fourth century. Her options, we saw, were not abundant, but she chose courageously when Augustine chose to end the relationship.

I have sketched her historical moment as a moment of social tension in which Christianity had become the official religion of state, and society was rapidly being organized according to new values. If my interest in her were primarily to better understand Augustine, it would be possible to examine the effects of their relationship on Augustine's theology. For example, I could suggest that Augustine may have learned at firsthand about humility—one of the central tenets of his theology—from his partner.[80] She apparently lived with Augustine without expectation, returning to North Africa without complaint when dismissed. This example of humility, seen at firsthand, could have been an even more vivid and immediate example of humility for Augustine than "the Word made flesh," which he says was initially so difficult for him to grasp.[81]

Or, if my interest were primarily in Augustine, it would also be possible to examine what we may consider Augustine's failures as the result of his inability to integrate sex into a loving and productive life.[82] I suggest that we might also see Augustine's failure to integrate intimate relationship as connected to his inability to understand concern and care for the world as a form for spiritual growth and insight. He did not offer models other than that of withdrawal from the larger society and centering "within" as the ideal for the Christian life.[83]

She disappears from our view, as she has disappeared from this essay, without a trace. On the one hand, she can be seen as the victim of new economies of emotional, religious, and social desire. On the other, and precisely within the excitements of her time and place, she outdid Augustine, the representative and prototype of Christian desire, by her choice for celibacy. Whether or not she was a Christian—the evidence is, in my view, inconclusive—she exercised her agency within a limited palette of possibilities. She could certainly have gone on either to marriage or to another concubinage relationship. But, even if she were not a Christian, to do so would have been to sacrifice Roman society's respect for the *univira*, or one-man woman. If she were Christian, entering a second concubinage under the strict requirements for women (only) for baptism and communion in the Christian Church would have sacrificed her good standing in the church.[84] We do not know whether she returned to North Africa to live in a religious community as Augustine did somewhat later. Let us conjecture that she did, for that is the only option offered by her society that would have permitted her to concentrate on the very aspect of her life that is most conspicuously missing in Augustine's *Confessions*, namely, her subjectivity.

Notes

1. *Confessions* 6.11. Translations of *Confessions* throughout are adjusted from Rex Warner, *The Confessions of St. Augustine* (New York: Mentor-Omega, 1963).

2. The term I translate as "partner" is usually translated as "mistress" or "concubine." Kim Power rightly points out that Augustine's preferred term was simply *unam* (the one), which seems to me closer to the most usual twenty-first-century term for persons in a committed relationship, "partners" (*Veiled Desire: Augustine on Women* [New York: Continuum, 1996], 95).

3. Power, *Veiled Desire*, 97; while class, based on wealth (and somewhat on education, as in Augustine's case), played a large role in forming social expectations in North Africa, as elsewhere in the later empire, apparently race did not. By late antiquity North African races—Punic, Berber, and "Ethiopian"—created a range of skin tones from very dark to light. Races were distinguished more by language than by color. The term *Berber*, for example, "was a collective term for tribes whose distinctiveness in fact countervailed their implied homogeneity" (G. W. Bowersock, Peter Brown,

and Oleg Grabar, eds., *Late Antiquity: A Guide to the Postclassical World* [Cambridge, Mass.: Harvard University Press, 1999], s.v. "Berber," 340).

4. *Confessions* 4.2. Centuries of scholars have accepted Augustine's self-presentation as a great sexual sinner. Presently, biographers tend to minimize his sexual experience. For example, Kim Power, in *Veiled Desire*, remarks, "Augustine's continence in a promiscuous world was remarkable" (98); similarly, Garry Wills, *Saint Augustine* (New York: Lipper/Viking, 1999): "His sexual activity was not shocking by any standards but those of a saint;" (xvii). The decisive examination of Augustine's sexual behavior is J. Roland E. Ramirez, "Demythologizing Augustine as a Great Sinner," *Augustinian Studies* 12 (1981): 61–88.

5. To my knowledge, only one article and one chapter in a book have sought to reconstruct Augustine's partner using historical evidence. These are Kim Power's "*Sed unam tamen:* Augustine and His Concubine," *Augustinian Studies* 24 (1993): 49–76, and the same author's chapter, "Augustine the Lover," in *Veiled Desire*, 94–107.

6. Aline Rousselle, *Porneia: Desire and the Body in Antiquity* (Oxford: Basil Blackwell, 1988), 182. Rousselle points out that no letters from women are included in Augustine's voluminous collected correspondence. He wrote fourteen letters to women, fewer than some of his contemporary celibate colleagues: John Chrysostom's correspondence includes fifty-three letters to women; Basil wrote thirteen letters to women; Jerome, thirty-four letters to women. Van der Meer emphasizes that Augustine rejected women when he rejected sex. In *Soliloquies* 1.10 Augustine wrote: "Nothing is so powerful in drawing the spirit of a man downwards . . . as the caresses of a woman and that physical intercourse which is part of marriage." Van der Meer, in *Augustine the Bishop* (London: Sheed and Ward, 1961), comments in a tone of grudging admiration: "These fierce words . . . came from the depths of his soul and he most strictly held to them. He went even further. No woman might set foot over the threshold of his house. No woman might speak to him except in the presence of some other person. . . . He did not even make an exception for his own elder sister and his nieces, all three of them nuns" (215).

7. Peter Brown, *Augustine of Hippo*, 2d ed. (Berkeley and Los Angeles: University of California Press, 2000), 50–51; also: "Augustine will lapse into a 'second class' marriage. . . . He will take a nameless woman as his concubine for the next fifteen years. . . . Whether he particularly enjoyed the experience is another matter" (27). Henry Chadwick, in *Augustine* (New York: Oxford University Press, 1986), calls Augustine's partner "his Cathaginian girlfriend . . . his common law wife" (15–16). As Rogoff remarks of another historical woman, Augustine's partner suffered from a "double betrayal": "Nor was her suffering and the indignity visited upon her by her deeply ambivalent and faithless lover any worse than that being visited upon her posthumously by. . . scholarship" (Irit Rogoff, "Tiny Anguishes: Reflections on Nagging, Scholastic Embarrassment, and Feminist Art History," *Differences* 4, no. 3 [1992]: 40).

8. John Noonan, *Contraception* (Cambridge, Mass.: Harvard, 1986), 125. Garry Wills, in *Saint Augustine* (New York: Lipper/Viking, 1999), finds it awkward not to have a name for Augustine's partner, and thus names her imaginatively: "To avoid clumsy titles, where *she has no name*, I shall call this woman Una (from *unam habebat*)" (my emphasis) (16).

9. Garry Wills makes this mistake in *Saint Augustine*. He reveals novelistic, as opposed to historical, interests by naming Augustine's partner and speculating on their meeting and courtship: "He was not merely persuading Una to live with him, but to make a break with her church (and, no doubt, her Catholic parents)" (17).

10. Rogoff, "Tiny Anguishes," 39, 40.

11. Rom Harré, *Personal Being: A Theory for Individual Psychology* (Cambridge, Mass.: Harvard University Press, 1984), 22.

12. Ibid., 20.

13. Ibid., 271.

14. But see *Confessions* 4.2. In a text in which Augustine "confessed" to many large and small

faults and "sins," it is striking (and not to be second-guessed), that he claims that he was faithful to his partner for the fifteen-year duration of their relationship. This was voluntary on his part; his culture and social niche would not have expected it. Augustine's faithfulness both undermines his claim to sexual addiction and his self-representation as a "great sinner" (Ramirez, "Demythologizing Augustine").

15. For an excellent example of this approach, see Elizabeth A. Clark, "'Adam's Only Companion': Augustine and the Early Church Debate on Marriage," *Recherches Augustiniennes* 21 (1986): 139–62.

16. Noonan, *Contraception*, 128.

17. Rogoff, "Tiny Anguishes," 43–44.

18. Wills probably overestimates her choices: "Can we say that he 'dismissed' her? She probably had some say in the matter" (*Saint Augustine*, 41).

19. As, for example, Kim Power does, both in "*Sed unam tamen*" and in *Veiled Desire*.

20. Robin Lane Fox characterizes Augustine and his friends as "overachievers" in the Christian empire in *Pagans and Christians* (New York: Alfred A. Knopf, 1987), 319 and passim; Peter Brown calls Augustine a "young man on the make" (*Augustine of Hippo*, 51).

21. Rogoff, "Tiny Anguishes," 42.

22. See, for example, Power's discussion of Monnica in her chapter "Augustine the Son," *Veiled Desire*, 71–93.

23. *Confessions* 9.9.

24. Ibid., 6.15.

25. Rousselle says that "only by becoming spouses or concubines can a free and responsible man or woman avoid being accused of adultery" (*Porneia*, 84).

26. "Marriage age varied according to class, region, and sex. Twelve was the minimum age for marriage for girls in Roman law" (*Digest* 23.2.4); Bowersock, Brown, and Grabar, *Late Antiquity*, 563.

27. Ramirez considers this action to be Augustine's most accurate claim to be a "great sinner." Although he questions that the young Augustine's sexual practices constituted "great sin" by contextualizing them within accepted practices of his society, he initially finds Augustine's abandonment of his partner morally culpable. Yet, by insisting that "it is a matter that must be judged entirely by the social rules which prevail at the time," he ends by denying that even this can be considered blameworthy (72–73).

28. Rousselle, *Porneia*, 100.

29. Michel Foucault, *Power/Knowledge*, ed. Colin Gordon (New York: Pantheon, 1972), 57.

30. It can be argued, of course, that no one has completely original agency, that everyone acts by bringing together in new combinations "provisions" found in her or his cultural repertoire. Yet it makes a great deal of difference whether one works with an enabling, authorizing cultural repertoire, or whether one necessarily works against the cultural grain, against a social positioning that marginalizes and invalidates one's agency.

31. See Peter Brown, *The Body and Society: Men, Women, and Sexual Renunciation in Early Christianity* (New York: Columbia University Press, 1988); Elizabeth A. Clark, *Ascetic Piety and Women's Faith* (Lewiston: Edwin Mellen, 1986); Kate Cooper, *The Virgin and the Bride: Idealized Womanhood in Late Antiquity* (Cambridge, Mass.: Harvard University Press, 1996); Susanna Elm, *Virgins of God: The Making of Asceticism in Late Antiquity* (Oxford: Clarendon, 1994); Margaret R. Miles, *Carnal Knowing: Female Nakedness and Religious Meaning in the Christian West* (Boston: Beacon, 1989); Aline Rousselle, *Porneia*; Rosemary Radford Ruether, "Misogynism and Virginal Feminism in the Fathers of the Church," in *Religion and Sexism* (New York: Simon and Schuster, 1974); Teresa M. Shaw, *The Burden of the Flesh: Fasting and Sexuality in Early Christianity* (Minneapolis: Fortress Press, 1998); and essays in Valantasis and Wimbush, *Asceticism* (New York: Oxford University Press, 1995).

32. "The *lex Julia* (59 B.C.E.) [had] required a widow to remarry within ten months, and a divorced woman within six months. The *lex Papia* (65 B.C.E.) extended this period to a year" (Rousselle, *Porneia*, 91).

33. For a discussion of the role of widows in the North African Church in the third century, see Peter Brown, *The Body and Society: Men, Women, and Sexual Renunciation in Early Christianity* (New York: Columbia, 1988), 148.

34. For a discussion of focused efforts to marginalize Jews during and shortly after Augustine's lifetime, see Margaret R. Miles, "Santa Maria Maggiore's Fifth-Century Mosaics: Triumphal Christianity and the Jews," *Harvard Theological Review* 86, no. 2 (1993).

35. *Confessions* 8.6.

36. Ibid., 6.14.

37. *Of Faith and Works* 19.35 (c.e. 413); translated in *Seventeen Short Treatises* (London: Oxford, 1847), 70: "In the case of a concubine, if she shall make profession that she will know no other man, even although she be put away by him unto whom she is in subjection, it is with reason doubted, whether she ought not to be admitted to baptism."

38. Brown, *Body and Society*, 397.

39. *Vita Antonii* 47: Anthony was "daily martyr to his conscience, ever fighting the battles of the faith"; see also *Barlaam and Joasaph*, ed. Woodward and Mattingly (London: W. Heinemann, 1914): "Monasticism arose from men's desire to become martyrs in will, that they might not miss the glory of them who were made perfect by blood."

40. See Margaret R. Miles, "Roman North African Christian Spiritualities," in *African Spirituality: Forms, Meanings, and Expressions*, ed. Jacob K. Olupona (New York: Crossroad, 2000), 355–56.

41. *Confessions* 6.15.

42. We do not know how she lived after her return to North Africa. She may have returned to her family, or it is possible that she could have been regarded as a widow and cared for by the Christian community of her village or town. Lacking a man, she would have had to throw herself on the mercy of family or community.

43. Is there perhaps a touch of sexual pride in Augustine's boast that she will have no other man after him?

44. Donald Capps, "The Scourge of Shame and the Silencing of Adeodatus," in *The Hunger of the Heart: Reflections on the Confessions of Augustine* (Society for the Scientific Study of Religion, Monograph Series no. 8, 1990), speculates that leaving Adeodatus with Augustine indicates "her anger and disgust, the vow never again to get involved in such a no-win situation" (89).

45. Beryl Rawson, "Roman Concubinage and other *de facto* Marriages," in *Transactions of the American Philological Association*, ed. Douglas E. Gerber (Case Western Reserve University, 1974), 279.

46. Rousselle writes of a "lack of formal acts to register the events of private life" (*Porneia*, 82).

47. Although it was never repealed, Rousselle notes that this penalty was "rarely applied, particularly to women, until the time of Constantine" (*Porneia*, 88n51).

48. See also Susan Treggiari, "Concubinage," *Papers of the British School at Rome* 49 (1981), 59–81.

49. Rousselle, *Porneia*, 80.

50. Clark elaborates: "Every scrap of material should come labeled with date and place of origin, purpose and prejudices, social level" (Gillian Clark, *Women in Late Antiquity: Pagan and Christian Lifestyles* [Oxford: Oxford University Press, 1993], 139).

51. Charles Norris Cochrane, *Christianity and Classical Culture* (Oxford: Oxford University Press, 1940), 326

52. However, Augustine still thought of fathers as "giving orders to" extended families consisting of family members and slaves (*De civitate dei* 19.16).

53. Kim Power, "*Sed unam tamen*," 63n20.

54. Rousselle, *Porneia*, 80.

55. "The fact that it was easier to bring a concubinage to an end and to show the legal dissolution of the relationship than it was to dissolve matrimonial ties did not make it any easier for those who were dependent to this degree on a man's decisions" (Rousselle, *Porneia*, 97).

56. Rousselle, *Porneia*, 100. If a woman who had been a concubine lacked economic independence, however, it is difficult to see how concubinage represented progress toward more mutual
relationships.

57. *In Ps.* 149.15

58. Rousselle, *Porneia*, 91.

59. Ibid.

60. Ibid., 105.

61. Augustine describes his own earlier situation in *De bono coniugali* 5, acknowledging that a
relationship of mutually vowed faithfulness in which there is no avoidance of conception might even
be called marriage (*nuptiae*). Yet he is strongly judgmental of his own role in the relationship: "For
if a man lives with a woman for a time, until he finds another worthy either of his high station in
life or his wealth, whom he can marry as his equal, in his very soul he is an adulterer, and not with
the one whom he desires to find but with her with whom he now lives in such a way as not to be
married to her." His judgment is somewhat more lenient on his partner: "The same is true for the
woman, who, knowing the situation and willing it, still has relations unchastely with him, with
whom she has no compact as a wife. On the other hand, if she remains faithful to him and, after he
has taken a wife, does not plan to marry and is prepared to refrain absolutely from such an act, surely
I could not easily bring myself to call her an adulteress; yet who would say that she did not sin, when
he knows that she had relations with a man though she was not his wife." In *Serm.* 312.2, he again
refers to his earlier situation when he says: "If you have no wives, you may not have concubines,
women you will later dismiss in order to marry a wife."

62. *De bono conjugali* 11; I disagree with Frederic Van der Meer's assessment of Augustine's
teachings on marriage, that is, that "he is to be reckoned among the great eulogists of Christian
marriage" (*Augustine the Bishop*, 186).

63. *Serm.* 82.2.

64. Ibid., 392.4, 6, quoted by Peter Brown, *Augustine*, 244.

65. *De civitate dei* 14.26: Augustine's fantasy of conception without pleasure in *City of God* 14.23
imagines sex without lust: "The sexual organs would have been brought into activity by the same
bidding of the will as controlled the other organs. Then, without feeling the allurement of passion
goading him on, the husband would have relaxed on his wife's bosom in tranquility of mind . . . [the
two] united for impregnation and conception by an act of will, instead of by a lustful craving." In
Marriage and Concupiscence 53 (written at approximately the same time), he has thought of an
amusing analogy for lustless conception: ejaculation could, like urination, be accomplished "at the
bidding of the will."

66. *De bono conjugali* 2.2. Woody Allen's "I don't want to be immortal through my work; I want
to be immortal by *not dying*. I don't want to live on in the hearts and minds of my countrymen; I
want to live on in my apartment" is a profoundly Augustinian fantasy. Augustine writes in the
passage cited: "For if to the garments of the Israelites God granted their proper state without any
wearing away during forty years, how much more would he grant unto the bodies of such as obeyed
his command a certain most happy temperament of sure state, until they should be changed for the
better, not by death, whereby the body is abandoned by the soul, but by a blessed change from
mortality to immortality."

67. Ibid.

68. Rousselle, *Porneia*, 195.

69. Noonan, *Contraception*, 28–29.

70. Titus of Bostra *Against the Manichees* 2.33, quoted by Noonan, *Contraception*, 114.

71. Ibid.

72. Peter Brown, *The Body and Society* (New York: Columbia, 1988), describes the life expec-
tancy of citizens of the Roman Empire "at its height in the second century A.D." as less than twenty-
five years. "For the population of the Roman Empire to remain even stationary, it appears that each

young woman would have had to have produced an average of five children." In order to accomplish this replenishment of Roman citizens, women started young: "the median age of Roman girls at marriage may have been as low as fourteen" (6).

73. David G. Hunter, "Resistance to the Virginal Ideal in Late-Fourth-Century Rome: The Case of Jovinian," *Theological Studies* 48 (1987): 45.

74. *Retractationes* 2.48.

75. Jerome *Adversus Jovinianum* 2.47; I am simultaneously amused and offended by the many indexes in scholarly books that say "marriage, see women" (or "women, see marriage"), equating, as did Augustine and his contemporaries, marriage and women!

76. *De nuptiis et concupiscentia* 13.

77. Augustine often refers to anal intercourse as a method of contraception. In *De bono coniugali* 11 he writes: "But when the husband wishes to use the member of his wife that has not been given for this purpose, the wife is more shameful if she permits this to take place with herself rather than with another woman." Augustine returns several times in this short treatise to "that use which is contrary to nature." The treatise is a fascinating mosaic of recognizable autobiography, advocacy for marriage, and condemnation of practices that prevent conception. Indeed, the reader is left wondering whether his repetitious injunctions against anal intercourse suggest that this might have been the young Augustine's preferred contraceptive method; see also *De nuptiis et concupiscentia* 35.

78. *De nuptiis et concupiscentia* 1.17.

79. *De moribus manichaeorum* 18.65. Perhaps this ancient teaching that a woman's most likely time to conceive is immediately after her menstrual period is the origin of the old joke "What do they call people who use the rhythm method? Parents!"

80. He came, however, to rank humility very highly in the Christian life: "The way is firstly humility, secondly humility, and thirdly humility" (*Epistula* 118.3).

81. *Confessions* 7.19.

82. Elizabeth A. Clark, "Adam's Only Companion," 139; Clark argues that if Augustine had developed "unswervingly" the implications of his statement (in *De civitate dei* 14.11) that Adam sinned because he "refused to be separated from his only companion, even if it involved sharing her guilt," he would have come to "a notion of marital friendship unique for his time and place."

83. Margaret R. Miles, *Desire and Delight: A New Reading of Augustine's "Confessions"* (New York: Crossroad, 1993), 98–99. See Philip Cary, *Augustine's Invention of the Inner Self: The Legacy of a Christian Platonist* (New York: Oxford, 2000), 5; Cary argues that Augustine created the "inner self" as unshared space. Earlier philosophers, like Plotinus, had thought of the inner self as common space, the site of relationship to the universe. Augustine famously asks, "What do I seek? God and the soul. Nothing more? Nothing more" (*Soliloquies* 1.1).

84. Augustine, by contrast, improved his moral standing in the eyes of the church by sending his concubine away and planning marriage. Brown quotes Pope Leo I: "To abandon one's concubine in order to take a wife in legitimate matrimony was 'not bigamy, but a sign of moral improvement" (*Augustine of Hippo*, 79). The older Augustine will urge other men to do the same (*Serm.* 224.3).

7

Augustine's Letters to Women

Joanne McWilliam

Augustine wrote several letters to women, these making up only a small part of his epistolary corpus. They differ little, if at all, in range of content and tone from those written to men. There are letters of condolence, letters of advice, letters on the religious life, and letters (the majority) covering two or three of these categories. There are, finally, letters of theological import. The only category missing is, not surprisingly, that to do with public life. But *Letters* 124 and 126 deal with ecclesial affairs that became public and in which Albina, to whom they are written, seems to have played a role. I do not consider here all of Augustine's letters to women but have taken examples from each of these categories.[1] In these examples we see him dealing with issues of ecclesiastical, doctrinal, and pastoral import. The letters provide pictures of his interactions with Christian women during the three and half decades of his episcopate and his attitudes toward them. Augustine took the women and the issues and questions contained in their letters seriously. He thinks them capable not only of deep and prayerful spiritual lives but also of sound practical judgment and exemplary leadership both in their families and in religious communities. He gives serious and specific advice on how they should fulfill these roles. Despite his respect for women's capabilities, it is clear that he expected them to heed his advice and admonitions.

There are several letters of condolence. *Letter* 263 (dated 425–30) is one of the last Augustine wrote. He begins by accepting a gift from "the eminently religious" Sapida. We know from a sermon that he did not usually accept those gifts that were suitable for him alone, but sold them and gave the proceeds to the poor (*Sermon* 356, Benedictine edition), but he makes this exception as a gesture of comfort (1). The gift is a tunic and his reluctance indicates that it was rich in fabric or ornamentation. But it had belonged to Sapida's dead brother, Timotheus, and she has told Augustine that his wearing it would afford her "no small consolation" (1).[2] He will, he tells her, wear it "out of affection" for her brother, who had been a deacon in the church of Carthage. The letter continues along more ordinary consolatory lines. Sapida's heart is pierced and her tears are its blood (language reminiscent of *Confessions* 6.15), but her brother's love for her and hers for him outlives death and "is hidden with Christ in God." Sorrow is natural and right, but that of a Christian should not be too lengthy, particularly in the hope of the bodily resurrection that will come.

Letters 92 and 99, to Italica, are a pair and more interesting than *Letter* 263 (except for the light this last sheds on Augustine's attitude to his clothing and to gifts). *Letter* 92 (408) replies to a request for a letter on the occasion of Italica's husband's death. After a conventional and somewhat perfunctory paragraph, Augustine turns quickly to one of his favorite themes—the superiority of spiritual to bodily sight. This topic takes up the rest of the letter, making it a precursor of the much longer 147. *Letter* 99, written a year later to the same woman, is different in subject and tone. In the course of business correspondence over a house, Augustine learns that things are not going well in Rome (it would be sacked the next year). He had previously heard only "vague rumours," "much less calamitous than [what] we hear now" (1). For whatever reason, he has been kept in ignorance of the true state of affairs and regrets it. He writes: "[Pain] suffered by one member is mitigated when all the other members suffer from it. And this mitigation is effected not by actual participation in the calamity, but by the solacing power of love. . . . The tribulation is borne in common by all, seeing they have in common the same experience, hope, and love, and the same divine Spirit." It is interesting that one of the great consolations in bereavement or tribulation—knowledge that the sorrow is shared—is given not for Italica's husband (perhaps Augustine did not know him), but for the threat of invasion. (The letter anticipates the widespread shock and grief that would engulf the Roman world when the city was sacked a year later.)

A series of three, *Letters* 124, 125, and 126 (all written in 411) deals with ecclesiastical business and politics. *Letter* 124 is directed to Albina, Pinianus, and Melania and *Letter* 126 to Albina alone (she is referred to as Your Holiness throughout). *Letter* 125 to Alypius, bishop of Thagaste, is a complaint against Albina and fills in the background. Albina was the daughter-in-law of Melania the Elder and the mother of Melania the Younger, who was married to Pinianus. The family, wealthy and influential, was one of many that had fled Rome in 408 because of the threat of barbarian assaults and by 410 had settled in Thagaste (Augustine's hometown). All three letters concern the efforts of the church in Hippo to ensure that Pinianus settle there instead of Thagaste.

The first letter starts with an effusive lead-in (which incidentally provides a sidelight on Augustine's dislike of cold weather). He is in "a fever of distress" because of not being able to visit with Albina's family. He does not want to go to Thagaste and leave his somewhat fragile congregation in Hippo, which takes offence when he is absent. Nor can he invite them to Hippo: there has been a smear campaign against him (the subject not specified here) that will spiritually kill the perpetrators. Hippo, in his opinion, is at that time unworthy to receive Albina and her family.

Letter 125 casts some light on the unsavory situation and raises questions about where Augustine thinks the unworthiness lies. While not addressed to Albina, it is certainly about her. The church in Hippo very much wanted Pinianus to settle there and be ordained for that city. Augustine has promised Pinianus that he (Augustine) would not be party to an ordination against Pinianus's will. Accusations and counteraccusations fly back and forth, in both Hippo and Thagaste. First, Augustine seems to be vying with Alypius about who is the more offended. Augustine judges that he is because Alypius's detractors are the common people, whereas Augustine's are Albina and the like. He is "the victim of . . . suspicions from those who are the light of the church" (2). Albina has apparently accused the people of Hippo of avarice in trying to lure the wealthy Pinianus (and his family) there. But Augustine sees in this overt accusation a covert accusation of himself. It is not clear, in fact, how open the allegation was. In this letter Augustine, telling Alypius of Albina's charge against the people of Hippo in desiring Pinianus's residency and ordination, "were moved not by his fitness for office, but by regard for his ample means" (2). Augustine goes on to say: "Nevertheless, she *almost openly* [emphasis mine] said that she had the same suspicion of myself, and not she only, but also her pious son-in-law and daughter who, on that very day, said the same thing in the apse of the church" (2). However, in *Letter* 126 to Albina herself, he says (in a tone I can read only as sarcastic) that "it was not possible for you to combine modesty and freedom more happily than when, instead of stating your sentiments against the bishop, you left them to be discovered by indirect inference" (10).

Letter 126 is an attempt by Augustine to justify himself in Albina's eyes, but he seems to protest too much. It is clear that Pinianus did not want to be ordained and that Albina and Melania shared his resistance. Nor did Pinianus wish to commit the family to Hippo. What if the barbarians invade, he asks, and Melania intervenes to say that the climate is unhealthy (4). The tone of *Letter* 126 is self-righteous, more in sorrow than in anger, and occasionally sarcastic. It is notable that Augustine's anger (he gives every indication of anger, though he denies it) is directed against Albina, not Pinianus, whose refusal is the root of the controversy. Albina, Augustine says, is bitter, and he will not increase her agitation "by giving in to indignation because of that which [he has] suffered in this affair" (1). He defends both himself and the people of Hippo. They are not avaricious and covetous. He blames Albina (and presumably her family) for suspecting that Pinianus is wanted in Hippo for the largesse he may dispense there (a suspicion the reader cannot help but share): "They did not ask from you [Albina and her family] pecuniary advantage, but testified their admiration for your contempt for money" (7). Worse, the bishops are seen as covetous and censured for that by Albina. Augustine protests the odium aimed at bishops, who must manage church property. They not only are innocent of financial malfeasance, but must also be seen to be innocent: "God is my witness that, for the whole management of those ecclesiastical revenues over which we are supposed to exercise lordship, I bear it only as a burden which is imposed by love of the brethren and fear of God" (9). It would counter historical evidence to see Augustine as personally money minded (see *Letter* 263, above), but every bishop needs money for his diocese.

A large part of the letter discusses the question of oaths and their binding quality. Augustine regards an oath as binding even when taken under duress. Pinianus took an oath in which he vowed that "if, at any time, he should be pleased to consent to accept clerical office he should do so only in Hippo" (3). Albina blames Augustine for "not interfering to forbid [Pinianus's] oath" (14). In Augustine's eyes, she has inferentially threatened his good name and so compelled an oath in turn from him. This is the heart of the matter: Albina has forced Augustine into a position where he finds it necessary to proclaim his innocence by oath. In "compelling" this oath Albina has committed "a much more grievous wrong" than Augustine did in commanding an oath from Pinianus (8). (In fact, it appears that he did not so command, although under pressure to do so from a riot in Hippo [6]). More to the fore in Augustine's defense is offended dignity: how can this woman and her family accuse him, indirectly or directly, of improper concern for money? "You have desired unquestionably to correct us" (9).

Albina, a Roman aristocrat and probably toughened considerably by her exile, was not afraid to take on a provincial bishop. She had settled in Thagaste as a matter of convenience and clearly did not want to tie her family there or to Hippo permanently (they left for Jerusalem in 417). It is interesting that throughout Augustine addresses Albina, although Pinianus himself was wealthy and presumably capable of making his own decisions. He comes across as caught between two strong, not to say forceful, personalities—Augustine and Albina.

Letter 208 (423) is, as Augustine himself described it, "partly consolatory, partly hortotary," and is addressed to a woman named Felicia, who has clearly been a Donatist (1). It is evident from this letter that Augustine is dealing with the ongoing challenges of integrating Donatists into the Catholic Church twelve years after the judgment against them by Count Marcellinus, the emperor's representative. Augustine expresses sympathy with Felicia in her consternation at encountering "a bad pastor" in the Catholic Church, reminding her that good and bad are found in both the leaders and the led and that this mixture will endure to the end of time (3). Felicia is reminded that Christ "has reserved the work of final separation" for himself and that the Catholic Church, unlike the

Donatist, is not confined to North Africa. Further, even bad shepherds "teach that which is good though they do that which is evil" (4). It becomes apparent at the end of the letter that Felicia was one of those "compelled to enter" (see *Letter* 185 to Boniface, chapters 22, 23, 33, and passim) and that, because of her experience in the Catholic Church, she is repenting her decision. Augustine does not fault Felicia for her criticisms, but takes the opportunity to remind her that in the final accounting all will be sorted out according to divine wisdom and justice. He is concerned to offer this spiritual direction to a woman who is perplexed and dismayed about the moral state of the Catholic clergy. Her loyalty, Augustine reminds her, is not to priests or bishops, good or bad, but to Christ in the Catholic Church: "For if you should depart this world separated from the unity of the body of Christ, it will avail you nothing to have preserved inviolate you virginity" (7). The letter ends with Augustine's request for a reassuring answer. He wanted to be sure that he had convinced Felicia.

There are two letters to nuns, 210 and 211. The first is to "the holy mother, Felicitas [the successor to Augustine's sister as superior of the convent], brother Rusticus and the sisters who are with them." The second is to the nuns of the same convent, who were restless and dissatisfied with Felicitas's government. *Letter* 210 avers that adversity can be as much "a gifting of God when He warns" as "prosperity is . . . when He comforts" (2). The adversity in this case seems to be quarrels in the house, specifically reproofs not accepted in the right spirit. The one who gives the rebuke is admonished not to become quarrelsome in turn, but to return love for hatred: "Be more earnest to dwell in concord than to vanquish each other in controversy" (2). *Letter* 211 is written in the same context, but is addressed to the nuns of the convent. The first four chapters are devoted again to rebuke. News of the unrest has been so widespread that it has come even to Augustine's absent ears. His presence, however, would not have been helpful: "I must have found you such as I did not desire, and must myself have been found by you such as you did not desire" (1). He would not have sided with the rebels seeking a new superior; the revolt is imitating that of Judas, the traitor (4).

The so-called Rule (chapters 5–16) may tell us a good deal about women's religious houses at the time, although it is difficult to know how typical these particular rules were.[3] In any case, they give a clear picture of Augustine's ideals for these particular women. They also, in passing, indicate the degree to which women from all classes entered religious life and the dangers of class distinctions following them there. Augustine was clearly aware of the problems engendered by these distinctions and advises the nuns how to behave to ameliorate the situation.

The first rule enjoins common property, not in the sense of equal shares to all, but (with a reference to Acts 4:35) "to every one according to her need" (5). Augustine warns both against those who brought wealth to the community considering it still their own and, less conventionally, against those who came from poverty finding happiness "within the monastery [in] food and raiment such as was elsewhere beyond their reach" (5). A parallel admonition is that the latter must not be proud of their association "with persons whom they would not have dared to approach in the outer world" and the former are told that they should "glory in the fellowship of their poor sisters" rather than "the rank of their wealthy parents" (6). Class distinctions go beyond attitude: some women were "weak in consequence of their early training" and they might receive more or better food and clothing (9). Others, "whose training has made them more robust," should be happy in the vigor of their constitution, which gives them "greater strength to bear hardships" (9). Relaxation in fasting and other austerities is there for the sick (9); other members of the community should fast, but not to the detriment of their health. And there is to be no snacking (8).

What will most strike the twenty-first-century first-world woman are the rules on bathing and laundry. The superior is to set the laundry schedule, lest "undue solicitude about spotless clothing produce inward stains upon your souls." Except for the sick, there is not to be "constant washing" and baths are allowed once a month. There is a rule to please any librarian: "Let manuscripts be applied for at a fixed hour every day, and let none who ask for them at other times receive them" (13). There is, unfortunately, no indication of what those manuscripts were, but this rule shows that at least some of nuns were literate.[4]

The nuns are urged to be regular in prayer, and there are a couple of interesting chapel rules. The chapel must not be used for anything but prayer and—inhibiting the more vocal—there is to be no extra chanting (7). There is to be a common wardrobe and the women are to take whatever clothing is issued, not seeking to please. It seems their hair was dressed in nets and when they go out (never alone) their heads are to be covered with a heavy veil. Clearly the expeditions outside the convent were of great concern to Augustine.

The single topic given the most space in this letter is "wanton eyes"

(10–11). No fixed regard is to be afforded a man, for looking can awaken desire (10). Augustine is concerned not only lest women traveling outside the convent be the passive object of male gaze, but that the nuns themselves may be tempted to "fasten their glances upon a man" (10) and so seek to have his eyes turned on them. It is not surprising that Augustine warns the nuns against encouraging men's sexual interest but it is also noteworthy to see how much potential sexual initiative he recognizes in them.

The letter ends with repeated exhortations to avoid quarrels and to obey the superior and the group is instructed that this treatise is to be read once a week as a mirror for self-examination.

Finally, there are three letters specifically to give spiritual or theological advice (although snippets of such advice are woven into most of the letters). Such instruction can be found elsewhere in Augustine's writings, but I want particularly to draw attention to the absence of condescension in these letters. Augustine is convinced that these women are not only willing but also able to learn. The degree of familiarity with the Bible he assumes is also noteworthy.

The first is *Letter* 130 (412) to Proba, another refugee from Alaric's invasion of Rome. Proba was "the widow of the richest man in the Empire, the mother and aunt of consuls."[5] There was hardly a more prominent and highly ranked Roman family than the Anicii. Proba was accompanied by her daughter-in-law, Juliana, and her granddaughter, Demetrias (more about her below). In those uncertain and chaotic times, Proba had become alarmed by reading the text from Romans 8:26 ("We do not know how we ought to pray"), and she asks Augustine for advice. In his response he does not fob her off, dismissing her concerns and anxieties, and his answer is far from simplistic. *Letter* 130 is a thorough and sophisticated treatise on petitionary prayer.

"The Christian soul ought to feel itself desolate" (2.5). Although rich, Proba is not to find security in wealth nor in her family's safety and status, but in God. Augustine notes that Proba, unlike other wealthy Christians, has not given her money to the poor because she still has financial obligations (out of "some consideration of duty to your family" [3.9]). It is borne in on the reader again how important a role money played in the relations between the refugee families and the North African church. That so many were wealthy should cause no surprise: the poor, even the middle class, in Italy could not afford to flee overseas to secure refuge. But Proba's money must not be spent for pleasure, she is told, only for health, and there is nothing wrong in praying for health for herself and her family (3.7). What else may be prayed for? Honor and power? Yes, if in seeking them "they may promote the interest of those who may be [your] dependents" (6.12) or to do some other good. "A competent portion" (6.12) of money may be prayed for, but no more (6.12). Those who have these goods may pray to keep them; those who do not, to achieve them (6.13). Augustine reminds Proba that the Lord's Prayer contains all she need ask for (21).

All these petitions have come under the umbrella of "a happy life" (4.9). Will these benefits suffice? The happy life is having all one wishes to have and wishing to have nothing that one ought not to have (5.11). Augustine repeats virtually the same definition of happiness given in *On the Happy Life* twenty-five years earlier but his purposes in this letter are more particularized.[6] He is concerned here to address this one person, taking into account her questions as well as the specific circumstances of her life. He makes important connections between spiritual instruction on the nature and practice of prayer and moral principles about the proper understanding of and path to true happiness. The objects of prayer outlined above are "dross in comparison with obtaining eternal life" (7.14). Everything, including human relationships, must be referred to God: "We love God for what He is in himself and our neighbours for his sake" (7.14). Perfect happiness will not come in this life, but Proba must pray always for that eternal happiness. But why direct petitionary prayer to One who knows all our needs? Because prayer is for the benefit of the one who prays.

One of the most interesting aspects of this letter is its moderate tone. Proba is not urged to give all her money away. She is reassured that it is legitimate to pray for health, honor, power, and money above the poverty level. She is to leave time for other necessary and good works and is told that the short, spontaneous prayers of "the brethren in Egypt" are a good exercise (10.20). There are no recriminations, hidden or overt, here. The relationship between Augustine and this household was very different from that with Albina's. In this case, Proba has maintained the proper relationship of deference to Augustine in his position as bishop and spiritual leader. She had not presumed to criticize or embroil Augustine in conflicts played out in public view. And for his part, Augustine is on far less contentious ground with this letter, a straightforward instruction on the nature and practice of prayers of petition.

Letter 147, On the Vision of God, was sent the following year (413) to

Paulina, who had written to ask Augustine "about the invisible God and whether He can be seen by bodily eyes." This is a letter not about petitionary but contemplative prayer. There is little if anything here which had not been said before (see *Letter 92*), even as early as the Cassiciacum writings, but here aspects of prayer are gathered together and expanded to make it one of his most considered writings on the subject. This long letter is often described as a treatise; it is an important one, and addressed to a woman. Augustine asks Paulina not to "depend on his authority" (2), but on that of Scripture, and the letter is a mosaic of biblical, especially New Testament, quotations.

He begins by telling Paulina that she will find meditation and prayer more helpful than intellectual probing. This is not condescension because she is a woman; he would have said the same to a man. Echoes of *On the Trinity*, on which Augustine was working at the time, are heard as he reminds Paulina that we see God in this life not with bodily eyes, but "with the gaze of the mind, as everyone sees himself inwardly, when he sees himself living, wishing, seeking, and knowing" (3). But is this interior sight, which lacks the form and color that even memory possesses, enough to convince us that God can be seen? Citing Matthew 5:8, "Blessed are the clean of heart, for they shall see God," Augustine begins to explain his theory of the vision of God. He provides an extensive analysis of the meaning of this text, replete with other passages from Scripture and citing examples of Old Testament figures such as Moses who had extraordinary experiences of God's presence (32). This is not the place for a lengthy study of Augustine's letter (already done many times), but a few salient features are worth noting. It includes the distinctions between empirical knowledge (where we are our own witness) and knowledge based on authority (relying on the word of others, whatever their degree of human authority, culminating in sure knowledge based the absolute authority of Scripture).

Belief is a kind of knowledge, but, unlike memory, it is not being mentally conscious of something, but *gazing*. This gaze in this life rests not on God's substance but on whatever form in which God chooses to appear (for example, the theophanies of the Old Testament, citing Ambrose's *Exposition of the Gospel According to Luke*). The ability to effect this gaze of the mind depends both on living out the epistemological distinctions Augustine makes here (and which he plays out much more fully in *On the Trinity*) and on the moral preparation that he sums up with repeated references to the "clean of heart" from the Beatitudes.

Augustine also invokes the theme that is central to his explorations in *On the Trinity*: humans as the *image of God* (44). As well, in explaining our knowledge of God, Augustine acknowledges our need of the Spirit to realize that there is something beyond that which is experienced by sensible knowledge, and of the Word who as image declares God to our mind (29).

Contrary to what some say, our knowledge of God does not lead to becoming what God is. But when we "see God invisibly, we will be joined to God incorporeally" (37). Augustine then turns to the nature of the resurrected body (a subject he will explore at greater length in *Letter* 148 and book 22 of *On the City of God*).[7] The risen body will remain a body, not become a spirit, he opines, acknowledging that here he is going against "custom." After citing various views on the matter (including those of Ambrose and Jerome), Augustine reiterates his confidence in Paulina's abilities to weigh these difficult matters by writing that the views of the experts should not be accepted with the same weight as the authority of Scripture and that "those otherwise minded may try to see with the mind what is true, and to seek God in the simplicity of their hearts" (54). Augustine gives no indication that Paulina is not capable of such seeing and seeking. The letter ends rather abruptly by Augustine's reminding Paulina that a clean heart is necessary to see God, leaving the matter of the resurrection to another time.

And finally there are "the letters to Demetrias" or, more accurately, to Demetrias at one remove. They again tell us something of Augustine's relations with the wealthy Roman exiles and, even more, of his deep concerns about Pelagius's teachings. Demetrias was a young woman of the distinguished Anicii family, a granddaughter of Proba (*Letter* 130), who had decided to adopt the religious life. The family requested letters of counsel for her from Jerome, Augustine, and Pelagius and the letters are addressed to her grandmother and her mother.[8] Jerome described her decision, among other hyperbole, as "lessening the calamity of the fall of Rome" (*Letter* 130, 1). Augustine's first letter after hearing the news, written in 413 to Proba and Juliana, was more restrained than Jerome's, the plaudits more conventional. Reflecting a contemporary controversy in which Jovinian, a Roman monk, maintained that the efficacy of baptism was such that the ascetic life in itself does not denote greater holiness than other ways of Christian life. Augustine assures Demetrias's grandmother and mother that (Demetrias) "will be above the rest in holiness," advising them that they can "enjoy in [Demetrias] what was lacking" in themselves (*Letter* 150). There is a hierarchy in Augustine's heaven.

The second letter, written in 416, names Alypius as coauthor but the language and theology are Augustine's throughout. This letter (188) was written to Juliana (Proba had died in the meantime) and in the three years since his previous one to them Augustine has shifted his focus from the value of asceticism to that of divine grace. After the formal and congratulatory opening, the tone of the letter differs markedly from that of *Letter* 150. Pelagius (who also opposed the Jovinian position) had written in 414 to Demetrias (the letter has been called his "manifesto"). He begins and argues at some length for the strength of human nature as created and instructs her in her capabilities. She must not be hindered in her calling, thinking it to be impossibly difficult. And her choice is one of free will (Jerome also stressed free will in his letter). Demetrias must realize, Pelagius argues, that she would not "be able to have the good she willed unless she was so created to be able to have evil as well."

If Pelagius's letter had been written to evoke a horrified Augustinian response (it was not), it could not have succeeded better. It was important to Augustine that he convince the Anicii of Pelagius's error; both wanted the support of that family. Augustine therefore vigorously warns Demetrias against Pelagius's teachings. He charges that Pelagius is encouraging her to be "ungrateful to God," not acknowledging that her vocation to the ascetic life is a gift of God, but thinking it is the result of her own choosing (very much Pelagius's point). Augustine says that that Pelagius's opinions "oppose the grace of God" (2). He acknowledges that Pelagius speaks of grace, but his words are "so ambiguous that they may have reference either to nature or to knowledge or to forgiveness of sins" (8). This hardly does justice to the Pelagian passage, "See what Christians are able to do, whose nature and way of living is taught in even better ways by Christ, and who are also aided by the help of divine grace."[9] Augustine grounds his refutation of Pelagius largely in texts of Scripture (from the Gospels, the Epistles, Wisdom literature, and the Psalms). Ever the rhetorician, Augustine states that he will not assign particular motives to Pelagius so that he not seem "to judge rashly men's inner motives." But despite Augustine's overt refusal to question Pelagius's motives, he in fact does just that. He calls Pelagius a "flatterer" (6) and a "deluded admirer who tells her [Demetrias] that she has this [continence] from herself" (14). Finally, Augustine expresses the hope that Demetrias has read Pelagius's letter with tears and lamentations, "praying in faith [to the Lord] that these words are not her own, but another's" (3.9). He asks, as he did in the letter to Felicia, to be reassured that wrong opinions are not held and that Pelagius's errors are rejected by Juliana, Demetrias, and the rest of the family.

What conclusions to be drawn from this survey of Augustine's letters to women are those suggested at the beginning of this essay. They are not condescending, nor are they patronizing. As stated at the outset, Augustine's letters to women show him using a variety of approaches to the questions and issues that his women correspondents presented to him. He is at times consolatory, admonitory, instructive, supportive, and direct in his assessment of their dilemmas and the solutions he provides. He takes them and their questions seriously and he gives thought to his answers. In fact, one of his most extensive explorations of the vision of God and contemplative prayer is addressed to a woman. There is no doubt that Augustine considered her capable of both, with the assistance of God's grace. Whatever Augustine thought of women's bodies, he did not discount their intellectual interests and powers.

Notes

1. E. Anne Matter, in "*De cura feminarum*: Augustine the Bishop, North African Women, and the Development of a Theology of Female Nature," *Augustinian Studies* 36, no. 1 (2005): 87–98, and included in the present volume, provides a helpful list of all the letters Augustine wrote to women and the main topics.

2. The English translation of the letters used is that of the *Nicene and Post-Nicene Fathers*, vol. 1, *The Confessions and Letters of St. Augustine* (Buffalo, 1886), sometimes slightly altered, except that of *Letter* 147, which is from *The Fathers of the Church*, vol. 20, *St. Augustine: Letters*, vol. 3 (New York: The Fathers of the Church, 1953), 131–64.

3. See George Lawless, "Regula," *Augustine Through the Ages: An Encyclopedia*, ed. Allan D. Fitzgerald (Grand Rapids, Mich., 1999), 707, 709. Lawless points out that the letter is not now considered a structural unity, but as breaking between chaps. 4 and 5.

4. For a discussion of the literacy and the social influences of Augustine's women correspondents, see Catherine Conybeare, "Spaces Between Letters: Augustine's Correspondence with Women" and Mark Vessey, "Response to Catherine Conybeare: Women of Letters?" in *Voices in Dialogue: Reading Women in the Middle Ages*, ed. Linda Olson and Kathryn Kerby-Fulton (South Bend: University of Notre Dame Press, 2005), 57–72, 73–96.

5. Peter Brown, *Augustine of Hippo: A Biography* (Berkeley and Los Angeles: University of California Press, 1969), 340.

6. By the end of the dialogue *On the Happy Life*, Augustine and the other discussants come up with this definition of happiness: "This is the happy life: to recognize piously and completely the One through whom you are led to truth, the nature of the truth you enjoy, and the bond that connects you to the supreme measure" (4.35). In the paragraph prior to this definition, they agree

that as long as they are still seeking in this life, even with the help of God, "we are not yet wise and happy."

7. In his *Retractations* Augustine refers to this letter and its subject matter in this way: "I have written a book on the vision of God, in which I undertook a careful examination of the future nature of the spiritual body at the resurrection of the saints, and whether and how God, who is a spirit, can be seen by a body. But that very difficult question at the end I explained as best I could in Book 22 of *The City of God.*" *Retractations* (2.41). See also Augustine's extensive discussions on the activities that will occupy the saints in heaven in his *Commentaries on the Psalms* (83.8, 85.24).

8. See Joanne McWilliam, "Letters to Demetrias: A Sidebar in the Pelagian Controversy," *Toronto Journal of Theology* 16/1 (2000): 131–39.

9. Pelagius *Ad Demetriam* 8, see also 19.

8

De cura feminarum: Augustine the Bishop, North African Women, and the Development of a Theology of Female Nature

E. Ann Matter

Because of his enormous profile in the development of Western Christian thought, Augustine has often been evaluated and judged more by his legacy, that is, how he has been received, than by what he actually said and did.[1] Of course, in some ways this is his own fault, since, even in his own lifetime, through vehicles such as the *Confessions* and the *Retractations*, he provided an ex post facto filter through which his own works were seen. James J. O'Donnell has recently suggested that one could tell a rather different version of Augustine's later life, especially his conflicts

This essay was first published in *Augustinian Studies* 36, no. 1 (2005): 87–98.

with the Donatists and Pelagians, if one were not to automatically begin with the framework of the *Confessions*. Instead, O'Donnell suggests that we could use the impressive and understudied collection of extant letters, most of which date from after 395, when Augustine was first elected bishop in Hippo, to make a new narrative of what, as O'Donnell puts it, "Augustine didn't confess."[2]

This is a tantalizing idea, one that I would like to apply to an area of Augustine's influence on the Christian tradition in which the *Nachleben* has surely outshouted the murmurs of the life: Augustine's theological formulations about the role and nature of women.[3] The problem of "Augustine on women" has been one of the more lively debates among contemporary scholars of Christian antiquity, and it is fair to say that there is a variety of opinion on the subject. Even among explicitly feminist women scholars, there are broad differences in opinion, from those who are committed to defending Augustine as a relatively positive voice on women in his context (Børresen, Soennenecken),[4] to those who explain his seeming harshness as a consequence of asceticism and sexual renunciation (Clark and Richardson, Truax, Weaver and Laporte, Van Bavel, McGowan),[5] to those who (again, in varying degrees) essentially blame him for the heritage of women's inferiority in Western Christianity (Pagels, Clark, Miles, Ruether, Daly). Elaine Pagels's widely read critique of Augustine centers on an analysis of the cultural implications of the doctrine of original sin, especially the role of the story of the Fall in Genesis 3. Pagels lays the blame for Christian sexual repression and misogyny squarely on Augustine, positing that Augustine's pessimistic views of sexuality, politics, and human nature would come to dominate in Western culture, and that "Adam, Eve, and the serpent—our ancestral story— would continue, often in some version of its Augustinian form, to affect our lives to the present day." In other words, for Pagels, it is not what Augustine intended, but what he left as a legacy that really counts.[6] From these scholarly voices, it is an easy step to the more popular feminist historiography that simply assumes that Augustine is the source of misogyny in Western culture as a whole.[7]

As David Hunter has amply shown, a far harder position on women's ontological inferiority was struck by Ambrosiaster, an aristocratic Roman cleric writing in the 380s, who is explicit in claiming that Genesis 3 shows exactly that women are not in the image of God.[8] Ambrosiaster's influence was particularly strong in the tradition of canon law, and so had a tangible impact on the ecclesiastical regulation of Christian women.

Augustine, in contrast, in the tradition of Clement of Alexandria, equates the "image of God" with the human mind, a move that makes it harder to deny women a part, except perhaps with respect to their embodiment. In spite of the fact that he was comparatively positive about women's ontological equality in his own time, most scholars of women in Christian history have tended to agree with Pagels, blaming Augustine for women's inferior role in the tradition.

In all this polemic, it is often the case that the analysis (psycho or other) begins with the youthful Augustine as autobiographically portrayed in the *Confessions*. But I would like to try something else in this essay. Rather than approaching Augustine's views of women through his autobiographical accounts of tormented relationships with his mother, the indomitable Monica, and with the unnamed companion of his young adult years, what picture of the role of women emerges from the life of the busy bishop of Hippo, in both his letters and the important theological treatises? And, most intriguing to me, could the concerns evident in the bishop's letters give us some ideas about the theological formulations that have been the source of such a painful legacy? In suggesting this strategy, I do not mean in any way to deny that Augustine's words have been used against women in Christian culture; it is obvious that they have. But in keeping with the themes given above, I want to investigate what Augustine's role as a Roman African bishop had to do with what became "Augustine on women" and how this influenced the construction of a Western Christian theology of "women's nature."

Now, concentrating on Augustine's letters can be challenging in a number of ways. In the first place, compared to other more philosophically sophisticated treatises, the letters are woefully understudied in the secondary literature. Even as Catherine Conybeare has pointed out, the letters Augustine wrote to women are tantalizing hints of the rich and complex relationships he had with Christian women and of the level of literary and theological training of his female correspondents.[9]

The traditions of manuscript and printed transmission of the traditional 270 letters in the corpus are also less well understood. And then, of course, there is the collection of twenty-nine new letters (twenty-six by Augustine) discovered by Johannes Divjak in 1981 to add a new dimension to the idea of neglected texts.[10] Out of all these letters, Kim Power says, only twenty-three are written to women, a number that can be immediately reduced to seventeen if we count only letters written only to women, not to women together with their husbands or other male relatives.[11] Chart 1 shows this—actually, I found twenty-four letters that should be considered, plus two letters to men that closely accompany letters to women. Only one of these is from the new collection.

This chronological arrangement of the letters suggests that Augustine's correspondence with women falls into several groups. From 395 until 409, there are a number of letters to Paulinus of Nola and his wife, Terasia, an ongoing correspondence that is actually between the two men and only includes Terasia tangentially, even though Augustine always addresses her with respect.[12] Augustine's first known correspondence with a woman, Italica, can be dated to this period. Italica was a Roman matron to whom Augustine wrote two letters of consolation, one for the loss of her husband (*Letter* 92) and the other after she has written three times in alarm over news of terrible things happening in Rome (evidently the siege of Alaric, *Letter* 99). In both letters, he urges Italica to keep focused on eternal life and the Beatific Vision of God, the only real consolations for sorrow and grief in this world. It would be interesting to know more about who Italica was and why Augustine praises her as "worthy to be honored in the love of Christ," and "most devout servant of God, most worthy of holy praise among the body of Christ."[13] What we do know, though, is that the concern of the last letter addressed to her, the Visigoth threat that resulted in the sack of Rome in 410, makes an important background for the next group of letters to women.

From 410 until 418, Augustine carried on a lively correspondence with a number of extremely wealthy noble women who had taken refuge in North Africa after the sack of Rome. Two well-known families stand out in this story as refugees to North Africa who brought with them enormous wealth and influence and some theological positions as well.

The first were descendents of Melania the Elder, a hero of Christian asceticism who had been a friend of Rufinus and Evagrius of Pontus, and had built an important monastery on the Mount of Olives in Jerusalem in the last decades of the fourth century.[14] Her daughter, Albina, together with Albina's daughter Melania the Younger and Melania's husband, Pinian, took refuge in Thagaste and wanted to see Augustine. In *Letter* 124, Augustine wrote to them that he was physically unable to travel during the winter months. The following two letters, to Alypius, bishop of Thagaste (*Letter* 125), and to Albina (*Letter* 126), tell the rest of this intriguing and amusing story. The family eventually came to Hippo, and, while there, they attended services in Augustine's church. The people of Hippo were so impressed by Pinian's piety (and perhaps his wealth), they raised a clamor that he should be ordained a priest for their church. Pinian refused, but the crowd would not let him go until he had taken an oath that he would not leave Hippo and that, if he were to be ordained a priest, it would be nowhere but at Hippo. The following day, the family returned to Thagaste, arguing that an oath taken under duress does not count, and accusing the citizens of Hippo of avarice. Augustine's letters to Alypius and Albina attempt to refute this charge and try also to hold Pinian to his vow to stay in Hippo. The family ends up in Palestine, however, where both Pinian and Melania the Younger enter religious life.[15]

One thing this story underlines is that the bishop of Hippo was not always able to control the Roman refugees who were flooding North Africa. This was true theologically as well; in fact, it is this influx of wealthy refugees that bring to Augustine's attention the extent to which Pelagius had become a spiritual leader of the Christian elite in Rome. This particular family had long been associated with theological movements of the fringes of orthodoxy: Melania the Elder had been close to major figures in the Origenist controversy, from which optimistic theological framework, Elizabeth Clark has argued, it would not be difficult to turn to Pelagianism. In fact, Melania the Younger, Pinian, and Albina actually meet with Pelagius in Palestine and defended him in a letter to Augustine.[16] Peter Brown has suggested that part of the reason that Augustine delayed his attack on Pelagius until 415 was because of these wealthy patrons.[17] The influence of this family on Augustine's views of Pelagius continued: he later wrote a treatise about the relationship of Pelagius to the orthodox church in response to a letter from Melania the Younger (*Grace and Free Will*).

Another important Roman family who ended up in North Africa after the sack of Rome included Proba and Juliana, a mother and daughter-in-law of a noble Roman family, the *gens* Anicii. Augustine's *Letter* 130 to Proba is a discussion of prayer, and *Letter* 131 offers advice for facing physical adversity. Two letters have to do with Juliana's daughter Demetrias, who had astonished the Roman nobility by consecrating her virginity to God and taking the veil (*Letters* 150, 188). The second of these, *Letter* 188, asks about a book that had supposedly been sent to Demetrias and that expresses Pelagian sentiments. Augustine wanted to know who had authored this book; in his later work, *The Grace of Christ*, Augustine identifies it as Pelagius's *Liber ad Demetriadem*.[18] In *Letter* 188, Augustine argues forcefully that Demetrias's vow of chastity itself was a gift from

God, not an action of her own will. For this family in particular, August-ine seems to want to argue for an anti-Pelagian view of asceticism: his treatise on consecrated widowhood (*The Good of Widowhood*) was dedi-cated to Juliana.

Other letters in this chronological period also focus on issues of conti-nence, renunciation, and chastity. *Letter* 147 to Armentarius and Paulina urges them to stick with their mutual vow of chastity, even though they had asked to be released from it. And *Letter* 147 to Paulina, the longest of Augustine's letters to women, is actually an eloquent exposition of the Vision of God, how one can see God with the eyes of the soul and through the vehicle of prayer. Paulina is called in this letter "religiosa famula Dei," which suggests she may have been a nun.

Religious life is the dominant theme of the next group of letters, dating from 421 to 424. Specifically, Augustine is concerned here with concord in monastic communities and purity in the church community. *Letter* 210, to the abbess Felicitas and the priest Rusticus, is an episcopal admo-nition about the dangers of rancor and contention in religious communi-ties. *Letter* 211 seems to suggest that Augustine's widowed sister had been the head of a house of consecrated women in Hippo and that, upon her death, there had arisen disputes about the passing of authority in the community. The second part of this letter is a set of rules for monastic life; this is the framework for the Augustinian *Rule*, a textual anomaly that has spurred vigorous scholarly dispute by George Lawless and others, about whether this letter is the original *Rule*, or an adaptation of one written for men.[19] In another letter, 208, to the Virgin Felicia, Augustine admits to her that many of the clergy are corrupt and bad men, but urges her to not abandon the church. Augustine says she must simply listen to wicked leaders, but she should not follow their example. One of the newly discovered letters of Augustine, *Letter* 20* to Fabiola, also dates to this period. It tells the interesting tale of the scandals perpetrated by Antoninus, whom Augustine had chosen as coadjutant bishop of Hippo in the area called Fussala, once a Donatist stronghold. Antoninus, who had engaged in every sort of dishonest behavior on both personal and professional levels, was taking refuge with the lady Fabiola in Rome.[20] Once again there is an interesting question of the limits of Augustine's authority with the aristocratic and elite Christians.

Finally, let us consider briefly the letters to women that are essen-tially undated; that is, all that is known is that they date from after Augustine was made bishop in 395. They cover a variety of topics: Augustine consoles Sapida, a virgin mourning the death of her brother and accepting the tunic she had woven for him (*Letter* 213), and writes to Florentina on the true teacher and the nature of study (*Letter* 266). *Letter* 262 to Ecdicia is a more difficult problem. Ecdicia, a married woman who had taken a vow of continence, had consulted Augustine on the difficult problem of her husband's adultery (*Letter* 262). In this letter, Augustine chides a married woman for taking on an ascetic life against her husband's will. Ecdicia, Augustine argues, is ultimately responsible for her husband's adultery, since she drove him to take a mistress. The very fact that this story evoked such a reaction from Augustine suggests the tensions ascetic women were creating in fifth-century Christian society.

Several of these letters show the same concerns with defense against heresy that we have seen in the correspondence with the Roman refugees. *Letter* 265 to Seleuciana about the baptism of Saint Peter argues that, indeed, Peter was baptized, in contradiction to what Seleuciana had been taught by a certain Novatian. And he writes to a pious noble woman named Maxima (*Letter* 264), whose province was overrun by spiritually arrogant men who sowed error and misused the goods of the church. Augustine does not mention the specifics about the province, or the errors, but the theme is very familiar.

A number of concerns emerge from these letters, taken as a whole. First, of course, is the role of rich women in the spread of Pelagian ideas in North Africa—as though the Donatists had not been trouble enough! Problems about purity in both Donatism and Pelagianism speak to these issues, since Augustine the bishop was determined to teach about a church of sinners indeed, but one in which the ultimate cause for all good is the grace of God. This accounts for his continual urging that his correspondents look beyond this earth to the ultimate goal of salvation. These were also themes in letters to men, of course, but for women, especially the women of the Augustinian legacy rather than the Augustinian correspondence, the stakes are higher.

If we compare the treatises Augustine was writing during these years, especially the ones that are at the source of the "Augustine on women" question, we find some interesting ideas. First, there is *The Literal Meaning of Genesis*, written between 401 and 415, where the superiority of man to woman is established physically, intellectually, and spiritually (*Literal Meaning of Genesis* 11).[21] Then, in his *Questions on the Heptateuch*, dated 419, he says women were made to serve men (1.153), a sentiment he must have nurtured as he penned his admonitory, persuasive, sometimes even wheedling letters to noble women.

But it is in *The Trinity* where we find big problem passage in chapter 12, where Augustine seems to say that women are in God's image only when they are considered "humanity" along with males, but not in some sort of essence as female human beings (see Chart 2 for the Latin of this passage): "The woman together with the man is the image of God, so that the whole substance is one image. But when she is assigned as a helpmate, which pertains to her alone, she is not the image of God; however, what pertains to man alone, he is the image of God just as fully and completely as he is joined with the woman into one" (*The Trinity* 12.7.10).

I began this essay with a list of modern scholars who have been concerned with the legacy of this passage, which may be called the *locus classicus* of the "Augustine-on-women" problem. Many have argued that Augustine fought against expected societal norms to insist that women also participate in the category *homo* and, therefore, in the image of God. But they tend to attribute Augustine's hesitation about women's physical equality to the fact that his relationships to women were marked by the restraint to be expected of an ascetic celibate. I would like to suggest that this also seems to be related to the problems of church discipline and the theological disputes that he had to deal with during these decades as bishop of Hippo.[22]

Augustine's letters to women show his kindness and consideration of women's questions—Italica's existential angst, Proba's desire to pray, the nuns' concern for community. But the background of these letters must have been deeply frustrating to him. *The Trinity* was written over long period, perhaps started as early as 399, and still worked on until 422/6. Would it be surprising to find the full bitterness of Pelagian scandal, including the role played by women patrons, reflected there?

If so, so what? Does it make any difference if we can explain the evolution of Augustine's thought on women, and even the "Augustine-on-women formula," in the context of his struggles with Donatist and Pelagian communities in the last years of his life? I would argue that it does make a difference, both on the level of microhistory and on the level of macrohistory. Microhistorically, it removes us from a fixation on Augustine's self-portrait of a man obsessed with sex and his mother and allows us to consider his views on the nature of women in the context of his other theological preoccupations. In other words, Augustine's ideas about women developed in a particular context in which he was struggling with particular theological constructs and should not be essentialized either as abnormal psychology or as truth.

On a broader basis, of course, this example brings home the point that this is always true, that no theological framework can be divorced from the particularities of the world that shaped it. This is a lesson that institutional Christianity is still struggling to learn. In any case, the idea that Augustine's view of women is linked to his worries about the purity of the church and the struggle to find a coherent explanation for the continuing presence of sin in the world is certainly something he did not confess.

CHART 1
Augustine's Letters to Women

Date	Letter	Addressee(s)	Topic
395	31	Paulinus and Terasia	A. has been elected bishop
397	42	Paulinus and Terasia	Send P.'s work against pagans
404	80	Paulinus and Terasia	Perplexity about will of God
408	92	Italica	On the vision of God
[408	92A	Cyprian	Please take letter to Italica]
408/9	95	Paulinus and Terasia	Life to come and Resurrection
408/9	99	Italica	Consolation over sack of Rome
410/11	124	Albina, Pinian, Melania	Refugees at Thagaste, A. cannot visit
[411	125	Alypius	Disputes Albina's suspicions]
411	126	Albina	Controversy about Pinian
410 end	127	Armentarius and Paulina	Vow of continence
411	130	Proba	True happiness and Pater Noster
412/13	131	Proba	Consolation on poor health
413/14	147	Paulina	On the Vision of God
413/14	150	Proba and Juliana	Demetrias took the veil!
417/18	188	Juliana	Anti-Pelagian
421/22	20*	Fabiola	Antoninus, bishop of Fussala
ca. 423	208	Felicia, Virgin	Priestly scandals
ca. 423	210	Felicita and Rustico	On harmony in community of nuns
ca. 424	211	Nuns of Hippo	On monastic order—Rule
after 395	262	Ecdicia	Marital fidelity and obedience
after 395	263	Sapida	Gift of tunic woven for her brother
after 395	264	Maxima	Errors of Christians
after 395	265	Seleuciana	Baptism of Saint Peter
after 395	266	Fiorentina	On the true teacher
after 395	267	Fabiola	Souls on earth consoled

CHART 2
Important Treatises That Deal with Women

401–15	*The Literal Meaning of Genesis* 11.42 man made before woman men superior to women Eve responsible for Fall
419	*Questions on the Heptateuch* 1.153 women made to serve men
399–422/26	*The Trinity* 12.7.10: mulierem cum viro suo esse imaginem Dei, ut una imago sit tota illa substantia: cum autem ad adjutorium distribuitur, quod ad eam ipsam solam attinet, non est imago Dei; quod autem ad virum solum attinet, imago Dei est, tam plena atque integra, quam in unum conjuncta muliere. The woman together with the man is the image of God, so that the whole substance is one image. But when she is assigned as a helpmate, which pertains to her alone, she is not the image of God; however, in what pertains to man alone, he is the image of God just as fully and completely as he is joined with the woman into one.

Notes

1. I thank Catherine Conybeare, David Hunter, and Susanna Elm for their suggestions for revision of this essay.

2. This is developed in James J. O'Donnell, "Augustine's Unconfessions," in *Postmodernism and Religion* (Bloomington: Indiana University Press, forthcoming); and James J. O'Donnell, *Augustine: A New Biography* (New York: Ecco Books, 2005).

3. On Augustine's attitude toward women in general, see Kim Power, *Veiled Desire: Augustine on Women* (New York: Continuum, 1996); E. Ann Matter, "Women," in *Augustine Through the Ages: An Encyclopedia*, ed. Allan D. Fitzgerald et al. (Grand Rapids, Mich.: Eerdmans, 1999), 887–92; and Matter, "Christ, God, and Woman in the Thought of St Augustine," in *Augustine and His Critics: Essays in Honor of Gerald Bonner*, ed. Robert Dodaro and George Lawless (London: Routledge, 2000), 164–75.

4. Kari Elisabeth Børresen, *Subordination and Equivalence: The Nature and Role of Woman in Augustine and Thomas Aquinas*. trans. C. H. Talbot (Washington, D.C., University Press of America, 1981); and "In Defence of Augustine: How *Femina* is *Homo*," in *Augustiniana* 40 (*Festschrift für T. J. van Bavel*) (1990), 411–28; S. Soennenecken, *Misogynie oder Philologie? Philologisch-theologische*

Untersuchungen zum Wortfeld "Frau" bei Augustinus. Kontexte: Neue Beitrage zur Historischen und Systematischen Theologie 13 (Frankfurt: Peter Lang, 1993).

5. Elizabeth Clark and Herbert Richardson, *Women and Religion: A Feminist Sourcebook of Christian Thought* (New York, Harper and Row, 1977); A. Truax, "Augustine of Hippo: Defender of Women's Equality?" *Journal of Medieval History* 16 (1990): 279–99; F. E. Weaver and J. Laporte, "Augustine and Women: Relationships and Teachings," *Augustinian Studies* 12 (1981): 115–31; T. J. Van Bavel, "Augustine's View on Women," *Augustiniana* 39 (1989): 5–53, and "Woman as the Image of God in Augustine's 'De Trinitate XII,'" in *Signum Pietatis: Festgabe für Cornelius Petrus Mayer OSA zum 60. Geburtstag*, ed. A. Zumkeller (Würzburg, Germany: Augustinus Verlag, 1989), 267–88; R. J. McGowan, "Augustine's Spiritual Equality: The Allegory of Man and Woman with Regard to *Imago Dei*," *Revue des Etudes Augustiennes* 33 (1987): 255–64.

6. Elaine Pagels, *Adam, Eve, and the Serpent* (New York: Vintage, 1988), quotation from 150; Elizabeth A. Clark, *Women in the Early Church*, Message of the Fathers of the Church, vol. 13 (Wilmington, Del.: Michael Glazier 1983); Margaret R. Miles, *Augustine on the Body*, American Academy of Religion Dissertation Series 31 (Missoula, Mont.: Scholars Press 1979), quotation from 131; Margaret R. Miles, *Carnal Knowing: Female Nakedness and Religious Meaning in the Christian West* (Boston: Beacon Press, 1989); Rosemary Radford Ruether, *Sexism and God-Talk: Toward a Feminist Theology* (Boston, 1983), 63, 85–87; Mary Daly, *The Church and the Second Sex* (New York: Harper and Row, 1968).

7. Julia O'Faolain and Lauro Martines, *Not in God's Image: Women in History from the Greeks to the Victorians* (New York: Harper and Row, 1973).

8. David G. Hunter, "The Paradise of Patriarchy: Ambrosiaster on Woman as (Not) God's Image," *Journal of Theological Studies*, n.s., 43 (1992): 447–69; see Ambrosiaster, *Quaestiones veteris et novi testamenti: Q. 21*, ed. A. Souter, *Corpus Scriptorum Ecclesiasticorum Latinorum*, vol. 50, 47–48.

9. Catherine Conybeare, "Spaces Between Letters: Augustine's Letters to Women," with a response by Mark Vessey, in *Voices in Dialogue: New Problems in Reading Women's Cultural History*, ed. K. Kerby-Fulton and L. Olson (Notre Dame: Notre Dame University Press, 2005).

10. *Corpus Scriptorum Ecclesiasticorum Latinorum*, vol. 88 (Vienna, 1981), English translation by R. B. Eno, *Saint Augustine, Letters*, vol. 6 (1*–20*) (Washington D.C.: Catholic University of America Press, 1989) and the scholarly study *Les lettres de Saint Augustine decouvertes par Johannes Divjak: Communications presentees au colloque des 20 et 21 septembre 1982* (Paris: Etudes Augustiniennes, 1983).

11. Power, *Veiled Desire*, 109.

12. For a discussion of the correspondence with Paulinus and Terasia, see Power, *Veiled Desire*, 110–11.

13. "In Christi caritate honorandae," *Letter 92*, salutation; "Religiosissimae atque in Christi membris merito sancteque laudabili famulae Dei," *Letter 99*, salutation. For English translations of these letters, see *Saint Augustine, Letters*, vol. 2 (83–130), trans. Sister Wilfrid Parsons, *The Fathers of the Church*, vol. 18 (New York, 1953), 50, 139.

14. See Peter Brown, *The Body and Society: Men, Women, and Sexual Renunciation in Early Christianity* (New York: Columbia University Press, 1988), 279–84.

15. Elizabeth A. Clark, "Piety, Propaganda, and Politics in the *Life of Melania the Younger*," in *Ascetic Piety and Women's Faith: Essays on Late Ancient Christianity* (Lewiston: Edwin Mellen Press, 1986), 61–94.

16. Clark, "Piety, Propaganda, and Politics," 74–76. See Augustine *De gratia Christi* 1.1–2 for the report of this letter.

17. Peter Brown, "The Patrons of Pelagius: Roman Aristocracy Between East and West," in *Religion and Society in the Age of Saint Augustine* (New York: Harper and Row, 1972), 214–15; Brown, *The Body and Society*, 410–12.

18. Augustine, *De gratia Christi* 1.23 (PL 44, 372ff.).

19. L. Verheijen, ed., *La règle de Saint Augustine*, vol. 1, *Tradition manuscrite*; vol. 2, *Recherches historiques* (Paris, 1967); on this topic, see also A. Zumkeller, *Augustine's Rule: A Commentary*, trans. M. J. O'Connell, ed. J. E. Rotelle (Villanova, Pa., 1987); and G. Lawless, *Augustine of Hippo and His Monastic Rule* (Oxford, 1987).

20. The Divjak letters are found in *Corpus Scriptorum Ecclesiasticorum Latinorum*, vol. 88 (Vienna, 1981). See also the discussions of W. H. C. Frend, "Fussala: Augustine's Crisis of Credibility (Ep. 20*)" 251–65 and Serge Lancel, "L'affaire d'Antoninus de Fussala: Pays, choses et gens de la Numidie d'Hipone saisis dans la duree d'une procedure d'enquiete episcopale Ep. 20*," 267–85, both published in *Les letters de Saint Augustin decouvertes par Johannes Divjak* (Paris: Etudes Augustiniennes, 1983).

21. All dates are taken from James J. O'Donnell, *Augustine: Confessions*, vol. 1, *Introduction and Text* (Oxford: Clarendon Press, 1992), lxvi–lxix.

22. It is interesting to note that Hunter suggests that Ambrosiaster was similarly motivated to insist on women's subordination to men in response to wealthy Roman women who were engaged in sexual renunciation and ascetic practices ("The Paradise of Patriarchy," 466–67). Hunter's discussion of Jerome's attitudes toward women and how they were mitigated by consecrated virginity is also interesting in comparison to Augustine's problems with the female followers of Pelagius (460–61).

9

Augustine on Women: In God's Image, but Less So

Judith Chelius Stark

Does Augustine consider that women, as well as men, are made in the image of God? The number and variety of articles that deal with this vexed and difficult question have increased greatly over the past thirty years. Any consideration of this topic must at the outset acknowledge the very early and groundbreaking work of Kari Elisabeth Børresen, who considered this question in *Subordination and Equivalence: The Nature and Role of Women in Augustine and Thomas Aquinas* (1968).[1] Since then Børresen has written extensively on the topic and has more recently moved away from seeing "Augustine's definition of female subservience as a God-willed part of the creational order" to a more positive assessment of Augustine on this point.[2] However, she also qualifies this assessment by stating that her "more *positive* assessment of Augustine results from a more *negative* judgment of his doctrinal framework, namely, the malecentred *conformity* of both scriptural texts and their subsequent interpretation."[3]

Two recent studies, one by E. Ann Matter and the other by David Vincent Meconi, provide readers with excellent reviews of the literature on this question and take a stand on the issue.[4] Both authors argue that Augustine considers women to be made in the image of God, but only in the spiritual sense. Meconi develops a fully textual argument and claims that Augustine is not nearly so reluctant to accord women full imago status as other writers and critics maintain.

These two authors, Børresen, and others have contributed a great deal to the debate thus far and support the view that Augustine accords women imago status, at least in a spiritual sense.[5] Nonetheless, this essay shows that in other senses, that is, precisely as women—embodied, gendered, and sexually differentiated—Augustine does not consider women *as women* to be the image of God and certainly not so fully as men. Moreover, not surprisingly, Augustine does not attach these same qualifications (considered by Augustine to be impediments) to men in any of the discussions that he conducts about their status as image of God. Men are always accorded full status as image of God without any hesitation or further debate on Augustine's part. Previous studies do not fully address these issues in comparative ways, nor do they fully draw out the implications of Augustine's own statements on women and their status, especially in light of the conditions he stipulates for women.

This study addresses a number of questions arising from the stipulations Augustine makes about women: first, why are women considered to be made in God's image in a spiritual sense and with multiple conditions attached to this status; second, why does Augustine qualify the imago status for embodied, gendered women when he does not do so for men; and third, what implications can be drawn from Augustine's own thinking about the stipulations he makes about women and their imago status? In this essay I focus primarily on Augustine's great work *The Trinity*, especially book 12, from which most of the earlier studies take their starting point. In an important section of book 12 Augustine attempts to reconcile Paul's First Letter to the Corinthians 11:7–8 with Genesis 1:26–27. This is the key text on the question about women's imago status in *The Trinity* that must be addressed and analyzed. However, in addition to analyzing this central text, it is important to understand the setting, the tone, and the broader arguments that Augustine is making in book 12 within which his comments and dilemmas about women appear. Some relevant texts from other of Augustine's writings are also brought to bear on this analysis. His project in *The Trinity* provides the bigger picture for his comments on women. An overarching principle in *The Trinity* is Augustine's support for the Nicene formulation of the Trinity as divine unity expressed through the absolute equality of the Father, Son, and Spirit. The three-ness in unity was the bedrock understanding of the Trinity that Augustine explored and expounded against the lingering elements of Arianism (with its view of a kind of divine subordination of the Son to the Father and a different sort of divinity for each) that still persisted in late fourth and fifth century Latin Christianity. The value of Augustine's contributions to these ongoing debates in *The Trinity* cannot be overstated, but they are not the major focus of this chapter.

Nevertheless, the implications of Augustine's own project are drawn out here, especially with regard to the relationship (including notions of equality, eternity, and love) among the three entities of the divine Trinity as the reference point for understanding human beings and their capacities. I also examine here what Augustine leaves unsaid and what moves he makes in the argument at various crucial points about women and their imago status. We will then see that, although Augustine had the conceptual tools and lines of argument available to affirm the image of God in women in a much less conditional way than he did, he did not do so. Why does he fail to affirm women's imago status when his own project in *The Trinity* gave him a powerful paradigm with which to overcome the hierarchical thinking and rigid dualities that led to his narrow and highly qualified view of women? As these tensions in Augustine's thinking are brought into sharper focus, this study shows that there are ways out of Augustine's dilemma embedded in his own texts, even though he himself failed to make use of the solutions that were available to him in his own thinking.

Imago Dei: Language and Distinctions

There is scarcely a phrase containing more resonance and layers of meaning in the entire corpus of Augustine's works than the phrase "image of

God." During his long writing career, spanning more than forty years, Augustine analyzed this phrase from Genesis 1:27 in many of his writings. He wrote extensively on the creation story in Genesis, including entire texts and major parts of his longer works: *Genesis Against the Manichaeans* (389), *Literal Commentary on Genesis* (393, unfinished), *Confessions* 9–13 (397–401), *Literal Commentary on Genesis* (410–15), and *The City of God* 11 (418). Some of Augustine's views on these texts changed over the years, whereas on other points, he remained highly consistent. For our purposes it is interesting to note that in his early work *Genesis Against the Manichaeans*, Augustine has already moved away from understanding humans as image of God as analogous to the Son as image of the Father to the emphasis on humans as image of the Trinity. It is this latter position that comes to pervade his thinking and writing from then on. Moreover, in *The Trinity* (400–420) the image of God concept plays its most central role as the key and access point to understand the interior life of human beings and human beings' relatedness to God, as well as the interior life of God (to the extent that humans are able to do so in this life). In the *Confessions* Augustine acknowledges his debt to Ambrose, who had helped Augustine understand the true meaning of the text from Genesis 1.[6] First, Augustine had to come to the realization that God is not a physical being, but is a completely spiritual substance. Only then could he appreciate wherein the image of God resides in human beings. Second, he understands that the image of God resides in the human mind and is fully spiritual; as he writes in *The Trinity*, "After all, reason and the authority of the Apostle [Paul] declare that man is made in the image of God, not according to the form of the body, but according to the rational mind" (12.7.12). Grounded in his analysis of Genesis 1, Augustine affirms the special status of human beings by taking up the fact that they are the only created things given the designation "image and likeness of God" in the first creation account. As consistent with patristic scriptural exegesis, Augustine considered Moses to be the author of the complete book of Genesis, as well as the whole Pentateuch (*Confessions* 12.20.29). Of course, Augustine could not have benefited from modern biblical scholarship that has identified two separate creation accounts in Genesis 1 and 2, and so he read the text as one account, with all the difficulties and challenges to consistency that such a reading entails.[7]

Even though he never made this distinction explicit, it is important to see that Augustine has two overarching ways of understanding the imago status of human beings—the ontological and moral dimensions. Each of these is now considered in turn.

Ontological Dimensions of Image of God

In its very essence, the human individual is constituted in the image of God, which, as we have seen above, is of a spiritual nature and resides in the rational part of its being. Augustine often emphasizes that it is this rational part of the person that makes the individual uniquely human, separating humans from the rest of the animal kingdom. Human beings, nonetheless, share powers and capacities with other animals, but rationality is both what sets us apart from other animals and what constitutes that part of us that images God. In addition to the fact that rationality constitutes the nature of what we are as human beings, it provides us with the fundamental orientation at the core of our being. Because humans are made in the image of God, in their very essence they are cast toward God, their creator, in a fundamental relatedness. Just as human beings have relationship to God as their very essence, Augustine will discover that relationship is the inner life of human beings and, indeed, is the inner life of the Trinity itself. How this dynamic of relationship plays out in humans, in God, and between human beings and God, will be explored in greater depth and detail below. For now, it is simply important to note that although the human person on the level of being is complete in and of itself (made of body and soul), it is not absolutely independent or autonomous.[8] Rather, the human's ground of being as image of God is relatedness to God and, in fact, participation in the very being of God: "The mind is God's image precisely in that part in which it is capable of God, able to participate in God. This great good is possible only because of the mind's being in the image of God" (*The Trinity* 14.8.11). This is a tall order for human beings and one that, according to Augustine, they more often than not fail to live up to; hence his many and extended musings on the story of Adam and Eve and their defiance of God in the Garden of Eden. This brings us to consider how Augustine understands the moral dimensions of humans as the image of God.

Moral Dimensions of the Image of God

In addition to Augustine's view that the imago status of human beings is their fundamental reality and orientation, he also sees human fulfillment

(what he calls *beatitudo* or the *beata vita*) as the full recovery and achievement of their true nature as image of God. Again, the story of Adam and
Eve is the founding narrative of the creation and subsequent fall of
human beings into sin. As a result of this fall, the image of God becomes
distorted and blurred. The coming of Christ is the central event in
human history, leading to the restoration and recovery of the image for
all who accept and believe in Christ's saving power.

Although human beings can never completely eradicate their imago
status on the ontological level, they are capable of a tremendous distortion of the image in the moral sense by committing sinful deeds through
the exercise of free will. Again the temptation of Adam and Eve gives
Augustine the basic narrative through which to articulate his understanding of human beings' ability to use their God-given free will to act in
defiance of God's commands. As a result of these choices, human beings
are separated from God and find it increasingly difficult to effect a return
to God, as Augustine himself discovered before his conversion (*Confessions* 8.9.21–11.27). What also results is the distortion of the imago status
of human beings in their futile efforts to "be like God" on their own
terms. In Augustine's analysis of his infamous theft of pears, he calls his
sin "the dismal imitation of omnipotence" (*Confessions* 2.6.14). An irony
underlying the narrative of the Fall is that human beings were already
made in the image of God, whereas the serpent's temptation presents Eve
with the prospect (delusional though it is) of "being like God" on her
own terms. In contrast to this pride, Augustine finally understands toward
the end of his conversion accounts in *Confessions* 7 and 8 that humility
and the acceptance of a dependent relationship with God are keys to his
conversion back to God. Pride steps out of the order created by God and
so brings moral discord into the world, whereas humility accepts and lives
within the order established by God. As a result, the imago status of
human beings is both sustained and enhanced, drawing them ever closer
to God through the complex interplay of divine grace and human
willing.[9]

The Trinity: *Plan and Objectives*

Augustine's extended and intricate discussions in *The Trinity* do not lend
themselves to brief synopses. That being said, if there is one fundamental
principle that is the bedrock of his work, it is this: God is absolutely

simple, immutable, and spiritual and God is also three as Father, Son, and Holy Spirit. With such a long work (fifteen chapters/books) written over an extended period of time (probably from about 400 to 420 C.E.), Augustine is responding to, drawing on, and refining some of what had been written and declared through church councils about the Trinity, as for example, at the Council of Nicaea (325 C.E.). One of the central doctrines that Augustine is exploring in *The Trinity* is the divine nature of all three persons—Father, Son, and Holy Spirit—as one God, not three Gods. Among other issues, Augustine is drawing out the implications of the declarations of the Council of Nicaea that rejected the Arian view that the Son possesses a different sort or lesser kind of divinity than the Father. In his introduction to his translation of *The Trinity*, Edmund Hill writes this about the Arian debates that concerned Augustine:

> The definition of the Council of Nicaea in 325 did not solve the problem [the nature of divinity of the Father and the Son] for the orthodox; it only forced them to realize that there was a problem to solve, by affirming that the Arian solution was unacceptable. It declared that the Son is in no sense a creature, and that therefore the generation of the Son is something quite different from creation; and that the Son is as fully and equally God as the Father, that he is consubstantial, *homo-ousios*, with the Father.[10]

Augustine's insistence on the utter one-ness of God and yet with real (not just nominal) distinctions among the Father, Son, and Spirit needs to be set in the context of these Arian and post-Nicene debates, along with acknowledging Augustine's substantial contributions to a theology of the Trinity for Western Christianity. For some understanding of Augustine's importance on this doctrine, Hill's introduction to the translation of *The Trinity* serves as a very useful and informative starting point.[11] These debates and discussions to which Augustine contributed so enormously are not only abstractions about theology and the uses of philosophy to understand the divine nature, they also form the wider setting within which Augustine explored human beings as the image of the triune God. In all the discussions that follow in this chapter, this divine reference point needs to be kept firmly in mind; it is where, for Augustine, these discussions of human beings in all their capacities must ultimately lead. As Hill remarks in his introduction, Augustine combined the "economy of salvation" with his efforts to approach the Trinity as the subject of "metaphysical" speculation and, for these reasons, Augustine's great work remains unsurpassed in Christian theology.[12]

Augustine divides *The Trinity* into two parts: in books 1–7 he discusses the various ways of approaching the triune nature of God and books 8–15 contain a thorough exploration of human beings as the "image of God." Even with such an exhaustive exploration, Augustine (the lover of words) is keenly aware of the limitations of language and of the human mind to grasp fully the nature of God, even as imaged in human beings (15.27.48–50). We are ultimately caught up short, but the effort still is worth making, for as Hill notes, "God's image is looking for God. The only proper way for an image to find its exemplar is for it to realize its likeness."[13] Augustine's writings in *The Trinity* and other texts on the structure and functioning of the human mind are complex, detailed, and extensive. The richness of his analyses, especially in *The Trinity* books 8–15, cannot be discussed here in their fullness. The focus for the rest of this chapter is on Augustine's writings on the human mind insofar as they illuminate his discussions of women and their imago status. To do this, some points are made in the following section about Augustine's project in *The Trinity* book 12 as a whole and then with regard to his discussion about women.

Women in *The Trinity* Book 12

Augustine's overall project in the second half of *The Trinity* is to elaborate a series of trinities in the human person through which the divine trinity may be glimpsed. Not all the trinities he discovers reflect the image of the divine, but he develops a thoroughgoing analysis of human beings to give as complete a picture as possible of the mind at work. This enables him to decide which of the many trinities he locates actually constitutes the image of God in humans. In books 9 and 10 Augustine names and describes the trinity as found in the human mind (*mens*) and by the end of book 10, he comes to his most persistent elaboration of the mind as memory, understanding, and will (*memoria, intellectus,* and *voluntas*). In book 11, he develops the trinities of the outer man that do *not* constitute an image of the divine trinity. He develops these as a prelude to book 12, in which the many mental activities of the inner man are brought forth. Augustine continues this analysis through book 13. Then in book 14 he picks up the inner mental trinity of memory, understanding, and will and shows how their fundamental origin and orientation are in remembering, understanding, and loving God.[14] This, however dimly and obscurely, constitutes the imago status for human being (*homo*). Where and how do women fit into this complex and elaborate analysis?

Clearly the question of women's imago status is not the central focus of book 12 (or any part) of *The Trinity*, but book 12 contains the most important and contentious texts about women and their possible status as image of God. Actually, the fact that Augustine deals with the question in such indirect and oblique ways is, in itself, revelatory. No doubt it shows that of all the many questions and issues that engaged Augustine's restless and ever-curious mind throughout his long writing career, the ones concerning women and their imago status were not the most compelling for him. Women move into Augustine's field of vision largely insofar as they are included in his discussion of other topics, such as sexuality, chastity, virginity, and marriage. From these discussions it comes as no surprise that Augustine does not deal with women in their own right so much as he does in their various prescribed roles in relation to men—as mothers, wives, virgins, or widows. Here is Augustine's advice to a young man dealing with a strong and commanding mother (reminiscent for Augustine, most likely, of Monica): "What is the difference? Whether it is in a wife or a mother, it is still Eve, the temptress, that we must be aware of in any woman."[15]

However, even though women's imago status may not be the most burning question for Augustine, what he has to say about it still has relevance, as evidenced in recent feminist scholarship on his writings and because of his enormous stature in Western Christianity. In both regards, it is well worth analyzing what Augustine had to say about women, even as he does so obliquely and in analogical language, and to consider what appears in his texts by inference and implication, as well as what would not bring himself to say directly about women's imago status.

Of the many and complex elaborations of trinities that Augustine develops in book 12, three points are the main focus of this section: first, those views of the imago status that are rejected by Augustine; second, the complex and controversial sections in which Augustine discusses women and men in reference to the texts in Genesis and First Corinthians and the consistency (or not) between them; and third, inferences that can be drawn from Augustine's statements on women as image of God.

First, in this section of *The Trinity* Augustine rejects at least three different views of what constitutes the imago status of human beings. He does not consider the human family made up of father, mother, and children to be adequate for the discovery of God's image in human beings. He rejects the view that there may be any strict correlation between the human family and the Father, Son, and Spirit. He does so for scriptural reasons and also because "such things may be offensive in carnal affairs by arousing thoughts of physical conceptions and births" (5.5). Augustine hastens to add that those of pure mind may be able to think of these things purely, while "to the impure whose mind and conscience is defiled, nothing is pure" (5.5). Augustine concludes this section with the injunction "Let him so accustom himself to find traces of spiritual things in material things that, when he shall begin to ascend upwards from them under the guidance of reason, he may arrive at that unchangeable truth itself through which all things have been made, and may not take with him to the highest things that which he loathes in the lowest" (5.5). Augustine rejects another reading of Genesis 1:26–27—one that implies a primordial hermaphrodism, as in "Male and female he created them." By conflating the two creation accounts, Augustine appeals to Genesis 2:24, in which Adam and Eve are created separately as two distinct individuals who then cleave to each other as "two in one flesh" (6.8). The last view rejected by Augustine entails seeing man as representing the mind and woman as representing the body. He rejects this view as well because many of the powers of the human body are also found in other animals and so the image of God cannot be found there, even though Augustine probably knew about this reading of the Genesis text from one of Ambrose's works.[16]

Mind, Image, and Gender

Augustine begins to use gendered language early in book 12 as he draws distinctions between two parts of the mind: the part that is concerned with temporal things, which he considers rational and not shared with other animals, and the other part, which considers intelligible and unchangeable truths. This latter part directs and should control the other part of the mind. Then Augustine makes the correlation to the "helper" that was drawn from the first man and that is like the part of the mind that assists in dealing with temporal matters. It is important to note that as early as his writing *Genesis Against the Manichaeans* (389), Augustine is using gendered language and notions of superiority and control for both the activities of the mind and for the relation between man and woman.[17] As Augustine notes in this section of *The Trinity*, the activities of the mind differ in their objects, while the mind retains its fundamental one-ness so that "it is not separated as to sever unity" (3.3). Just as Adam and Eve are "two in one flesh" (Gen. 2:24), Augustine asserts that the activi-ties of the mind belong to the mind as a unified entity. His quest for the imago status leads him to search for the image of God in the entire mind as a unified entity. This emphasis on the unified mind with a diversity of functions (activities) looks promising as an initial step to understand the imago status through the diverse actions of the mind, including those associated with Eve and woman. But perhaps then Augustine sees where this may lead and introduces the following qualification:

> A trinity has to be discovered in the whole nature of the mind in such a way that if, on the one hand, temporal activity stops—it is only for this that an assistant is needed and that something of the mind is drawn off to administer these lower affairs—this trinity is found in one quite simply undivided mind; and if, on the other hand, one makes this distribution of functions, only in that part which is concerned with the contemplation of eternal things can one find something that is not only a trinity but also an image of God; while in that part that is drawn off for temporal activity one may perhaps find a trinity, but certainly not the image of God. (5.5)

How revealing it is that the part of the mind represented by Eve and woman is the part that does not reflect the image of God. If in this text Augustine had stayed with the emphasis on the unitary nature of the human mind and its various activities as a *trinity* and as *the image of God*, the door would have remained open for him to affirm women's imago status unequivocally, even in this symbolic or analogical way. However, it looks as though once Augustine opened this door in his thinking and took a quick glimpse inside, he could not bring himself to leave it open and explore the consequences of his own thinking. What a tremendous loss to the history of this debate that he could not or would not do so.

Let us now turn to the central and controversial texts from book 12 (sections 7.9–12) to sort out how Augustine understands women's imago status and the qualifiers he uses in his argument. First, a few clarifications are in order. Augustine's overall project in the second half of *The Trinity* (8–15) is the search for the image of God in human beings. Just as in the first books of *The Trinity*, he does not want to sacrifice the supreme unity of the divinity to a kind of tripartite emanation theory or to give any support to the Arian view of differing notions of divinity for the three in one God, he takes great pains to emphasize the essential oneness of the human being who engages in any number of "trinitarian" mental activities. In book 12 he is further exploring the image of God as found in the "inner man." His emphasis is decidedly on *mens* (the mind) and its activities in contrast to the gendered body of human beings. The mind alone as a spiritual entity is the location of the image of God. Furthermore, there are at least three ways in which Augustine uses the term *woman* in these central sections of book 12. First, he refers to woman as she appears in the two creation accounts in Genesis—"Male and female he created them" (Gen. 1:27) and as Eve drawn from the side of Adam as his "help-mate" (Gen. 2:22–23). As noted above, Augustine did not consider these as two different accounts and so conflates them and considers them as one story. Second, *woman* also means actual real women of flesh, blood, and gender living in the world here and now. Third, Augustine uses *woman* to symbolize the lower intellect that deals with temporal matters (see above). Each of these meanings should be kept in mind in order to sort out Augustine's complex and, at times, convoluted analysis. Finally, it is obvious that Augustine's overriding interest in this section is to render consistent the text from Paul's First Letter to the Corinthians (11:7–10) with the text from Genesis 1:26–27.

Now to the texts in some detail to see what Augustine writes and also what he fails to write at crucial points in his discussion. This central section immediately follows Augustine's rejections of the human family as the image of God in human experience. He reiterates that the imago status is not to be understood as three separate human beings, as in the family structure. To support this view Augustine cites 1 Corinthians 11:7, writing, "The man ought not to cover his head, because he is the image and glory of God. But the woman is the glory of man." He follows this citation with the following comments: "If the woman according to her own person completes the image of the Trinity, why is the man still called that image when she has been taken from his side? Or even if one human person out of three can be called the image of God, as each person in the exalted Trinity is also God, why is the woman also the image of God? For this is also the reason why she is commanded to cover her head, which he is forbidden to do because he is the image of God" (7.9). This text forms the end of the argument against seeing the family structure as the image of God. What is notable about this text is the way Augustine states his musings on women's imago status: he puts it in the hypothetical, "If the woman in her own person completes the image . . ." (7.9). Augustine's emphasis is clearly on asserting man as the image of God even when the woman has been taken from his side. His emphasis is *not* on asserting women's imago status in her own right, which he could easily have done at this point. He does so only in the weaker sense by putting it in the form of a question: "Why is the woman too not in the image of God?" Immediately after asking the question, Augustine answers it by citing Paul's text once more for emphasis, leading to the inference that, since woman is not so fully image of God as is man, "she is told to cover her head which the man is forbidden to do because he is the image of God" (7.9).

In the paragraph that follows, Augustine recognizes the dilemma he has created by introducing the text from 1 Corinthians questioning women's imago status. How will Augustine attempt to harmonize Paul's text with Genesis 1:26–27? Let us watch the show and notice the way Augustine slides between the various uses of the term *woman* in these sections. It is clear that he wants to adhere to the overarching principle that men and women are both image of God in some senses. He writes, "It says that what was made to the image of God is the human nature that is realized in both sexes, and it does not exclude the woman from being understood in the image of God" (7.10). In what sense, then, is woman, too, made in the image of God? In the spiritual sense, from which, as Augustine writes, she is not to be "excluded." Again Augustine could have written this much more affirmatively, but he did not do so. In the following few sentences he discusses the punctuation of the text from Genesis 1:26–27 and returns once more to the disparity with Paul's text from 1 Corinthians 11. Then he writes:

> The solution lies, I think, in what I already said when discussing the nature of the human mind, namely, that the woman together with her husband is the image of God, so that the whole substance is one image. But when she is assigned as a help-mate, a function that pertains to her alone, then she is not the image of God; but as far as the man is concerned, he is by himself alone

> the image of God, just a fully and completely as when he and the
> woman are joined together into one. (7.10)

Augustine first introduced gendered language as a way to understand the
activities of the mind divided into the higher intellect that gazes upon
the eternal and unchangeable and is associated with man and the lower
intellect that deals with temporal matters and is associated with woman
(book 12.3.3, 4.4). In that earlier section of book 12, the primary terms
of the comparison are the activities of the mind that Augustine is trying
to explain, for which he then uses the language from the second creation
account in Genesis 2, in which woman is drawn out of man to be his
helper. In the current setting, Augustine has switched the terms of the
comparison in the sense that his primary task is to make 1 Corinthians
11:7 compatible with Genesis 1:26–27 about whether women as well as
men are the image of God. To solve this quandary, he appeals to the
distinction he made earlier to explain the workings of the human mind;
now, the comparison goes the other way. Augustine never questions
whether men are fully God's image. Man is fully God's image either when
he is considered on his own or when he is joined to woman. Either way,
he wins. The problem arises about women in this setting because of Augustine's effort to find a way to harmonize 1 Corinthians 11:7 with Genesis 1:26–27. For her part, only when woman is joined to the man is she
considered to be the image of God, just as only when the lower intellect
is joined to the higher is it considered to be the image of God. There is
no question that when the higher intellect is consulting the truth, it
alone is the image of God. The analogy that Augustine used earlier in
book 12 to explain the functioning of the human mind by an appeal to
Scripture using *man* and *woman* in symbolic ways to represent the parts
of the mind now in this section becomes the center of the argument to
show that woman's imago status needs torturous qualifications to accommodate Paul's view in 1 Corinthians 11:7.

In the following two paragraphs Augustine shifts the argument back to
a consideration of the human mind and reinforces the distinction made
earlier that only the higher activities of the mind hold the image of God
and that the lower part when acting alone and is "directed to the handling of inferior things, is not the image of God" (7.10). Augustine then
issues a warning about the dangers that the lower intellect presents to
the higher intellect and that Paul's reference to women being veiled is
the way to express the importance of the higher intellect keeping the

lower intellect under its control. Furthermore, Augustine refers to Paul's distinction between male and female in the 1 Corinthians text as referring to the "mystery of a hidden truth," by which he seems to mean the importance of the power and control exercised by the higher intellect in directing the lower intellect in the performance of good works in the world. Augustine confirms that the image of God (ontologically speaking) is found "not according to the form of the body, but in the rational mind" (7.12) and that one needs to be renewed in the image of God (morally speaking) through baptism into Christ and by performing good works (again citing some texts from Paul's Epistles). Once more (as above in section 7.9), in the form of a question and using the language of exclusion, Augustine asks, "Who is it then who would exclude women from fellowship, since they are co-heirs with us of grace?" (7.12) If the answer is "Paul," as seems likely from 1 Corinthians 11, Augustine uses Paul's own words in Galatians 3:26–28 to mitigate that exclusion: "For you are all sons of God through faith in Jesus Christ. For whoever has been baptized in Christ, has put on Christ. There is neither Jew nor Greek, there is neither slave nor freeman, there is neither male nor female. For you are all one in Christ Jesus" (7.12). After quoting this text in full from Paul to answer Paul, Augustine asks, "Surely this does not mean, does it, that believing women have lost their bodily sex?" (7.12). Although Scripture scholars disagree about what exactly Paul meant by these verses in Galatians, one point at least seems clear: as a result of "baptism into Christ," the ordinary categories that were used in the ancient Mediterranean world to "place" people—religion, status before the law as a slave or a free person, and sex differences—are transcended or nullified. Some scholars have argued for a stronger interpretation of this text by claiming that Paul is questioning the institution of slavery and even the accepted view of the natural inferiority of women to men; others see it in light of tensions in traditions preceding Paul to which he was responding and that he was trying to overcome.[18] However, even if Paul did not intend to support the abolition of slavery or to challenge sexual discrimination in the "oneness of Christ," it is important to see how Augustine uses this citation from Galatians in his argument at this point in his text.[19]

Since Augustine has raised the question about whether this text means that "believing women have lost their bodily sex" (7.12), this thought occurs to him as a real possibility. The sentence that follows provides the clue to the direction of his argument: "But because they [women] are being renewed to the image of God where there is no sex, it is there where there is no sex that man [*homo*] was made to the image of God, that is in the spirit of his mind" (7.12). So, in effect, Augustine's answer to Paul is "Yes, she has lost her bodily sex." This is the price that women must pay to be considered the image of God. This price is not exacted from men, at least not in the same ways. In a more positive vein, Augustine reminds his readers that the image of God resides in the mind, where there is no sexual differentiation. All well and good, if Augustine had also highlighted sexual difference and gendered embodiment as much for men as he does for women. Not surprisingly, he does not do so. If Augustine had ended his discussion at this point with the citation from Galatians, again it would have left the door open for a much more positive, complete, and egalitarian articulation of women's imago status. But he does not end there. He returns to 1 Corinthians 11:7 to wonder why the man does not cover his head because he is the image and glory of God, while woman ought to because she is the glory of man. Here is his answer: "It is only because she differs from the man in the sex of her body that the part of the reason which is turned aside to regulate temporal things is symbolized by her corporeal veil. So the image of God does not reside except in that part of the mind of man in which it clings to the contemplation and consideration of eternal reasons, which not only men but women also possess" (7.12). Augustine's emphasis here is important, since he pointedly does *not* say that because of sexual differentiation or embodiment in general, men and women both are not in the image of God. No, this is reserved for only women. Augustine's effort is to accommodate 1 Corinthians 11:7 to Genesis 1:26–27 and clearly the problem lies with the bodies of women and not men's bodies. Not only that, the symbolically "male" part of the mind (higher intellect) is never called into question as image of God the way the "female" (lower intellect) is. Augustine conflates the symbolic and actual uses of the terms *man* and *woman* in this last section and then somewhat begrudgingly acknowledges that women as well as men possess the whole mind, including the higher intellect, with its orientation toward the eternal and the unchanging.

Augustine returns full circle to the overarching principle with which he began this section, namely, that women and men both possess the higher intellect that is capable of eternal truths and in which the image of God resides. However, Augustine had to engage in some fancy intellectual headwork and scriptural interpretation to get there. Along the way, women had to pay the price of giving up their gendered embodiment in

ways that were not called for in men. Only after women have been neut-
ered, so to speak, can Augustine safely agree that women also possess that
part of the mind wherein the image of God resides. But he fails to take
the next step to give the positive, unequivocal statement that, therefore,
women too are made in the image of God. Furthermore, if Augustine's
argument had not been so driven by his need to establish consistency
between the two texts from Scripture, he might have been able to affirm
women's imago status without all the twists and turns that this project
entailed for him. Unfortunately, he foreclosed an avenue of thinking as
soon as it opened up for him under the cover of reaching for scriptural
consistency.

After Augustine's grudging acknowledgment that women, too, possess
the higher intellect in which the image of God resides, the following
quarter of book 12 is devoted to a series of warnings and admonitions
about not allowing the lower intellect (the "woman" part) seize control
of the mind from the higher intellect (the "man" part): "If that which
presides as the masculine portion in the watch-tower of counsel does not
check and restrain it [the "woman" part of the mind that deals with
temporal matters], then it grows old among its enemies . . . and that
vision of eternal things is withdrawn from the head itself, which in company with its spouse eats what is forbidden, so that the light of its eyes is
not with it" (8.13). The following six sections of book 12 are replete with
the dangers and enticements through which the lower intellect
("woman") can drag down the higher intellect ("man") into the sensuous
delights of temporal things. Augustine's language in this section draws
heavily on the story of the first sin and its consequences in Genesis 3. He
identifies pride and greed as the roots of evildoing and as temptations for
the soul to love its own power and to reject God's commands. This fault
would seem to lie in the decision of the higher intellect, and even when
this part of the mind goes astray through a kind of ignorance of temporal
matters, Augustine readily excuses this error: "This is a sin apart from the
body, and is not be put down to fornication, and is therefore very easily
forgiven" (10.15). Augustine is not so forgiving or understanding, however, of the "woman" part of the mind:

> But when the soul, greedy for experience or for superiority or for
> the pleasure of physical contact, does something to obtain the
> things that are sensed through the body to the extent of setting
> its end and its proper good in them, then whatever it does it does

> basely and commits fornication, sinning against its own body. It drags the deceptive semblances of bodily things inside, and plays about with them in idle meditation until it cannot even think of anything divine except as being such, and so in its private avarice it is loaded with error and in its private prodigality it is emptied of strength. (10.15)

This disaster occurs when the "male" part of the intellect yields control and supremacy to the "female" part that the higher intellect should be directing to deal with temporal matters. At all costs, the order and hierarchy must be maintained, but once the disorder had occurred, the soul cannot "go back up again having squandered and lost its strength, except by the grace of its maker calling it to repentance and forgiving its sins" (11.16). No easy forgiveness and understanding here.

After all the dire warnings and descriptions of the consequences of entanglements with the temporal, sensuous world, Augustine has a brief and more positive appraisal of the activities of the higher and lower intellect. He identifies *sapientia* (wisdom) as the object of the former and *scientia* (knowledge) as that of the latter. Each is necessary for the conduct of human life, but the order and hierarchy must be maintained at all costs so that the lower intellect remains subservient to and under the control and direction of the higher intellect. Augustine sums up his thinking in this section:

> In this explanation we have sought a certain rational marriage between contemplation and action in the mind of the individual man, since the functions are divided between these two, while the unity of the mind is preserved. It also adheres to the historical truth of that account about the first two human beings, the man and the woman, from whom the whole human race is propagated. But it need only be listened to, insofar as it helps us understand that the Apostle [Paul] intended something to be sought in each individual human being, though as regards the different sex of the two human beings, he assigns the image of God only to the man and not to the woman. (12.19)

Here Augustine shows, by implication, what happened in the past and what will continue to happen if the "woman" part of the mind (and by extension, woman) is no longer controlled by the higher (male) intellect.

Once again, Augustine chose not to take the opportunity to affirm women's complete and unqualified imago status. He might have done so at least in the symbolic sense of emphasizing more fully the important role that the lower intellect plays in dealing with temporal matters and in the acquisition of a specific kind of knowledge about the physical world. In Augustine's evocation of Neoplatonic metaphors of ascent, it is, after all, from the physical world that the ascent begins and for this task the lower intellect plays a unique and vital role. Augustine himself comes to admit this, but only after he has made sure that his readers have seen the dangers and enticements of the world in all its ambiguous wonder.

In the last few paragraphs of book 12, Augustine discovers another trinity involving the higher intellect that focuses on the eternal and the lower intellect dealing with the temporal and the will that joins the two. Here again Augustine could have affirmed both the trinity and the imago status that would have included the lower intellect (symbolized by woman). For, in fact, without this part of the mind acting on temporal things, Augustine's entire project is doomed to failure even on its own terms.

Implications and Conclusions

Even after all this, toward the end of book 12 Augustine is uncertain about the correct interpretation of 1 Corinthians 11:7. He cites the text and again forecloses the opportunity to affirm women's imago status fully and without any conditions. Again, it is instructive that he does not do so. Since he has interpreted Paul's text in a symbolic sense to apply to the various functions of the mind, he has given himself the opening to affirm women's imago status in the full ontological and spiritual senses. He does not complete this train of thought but moves quickly into the moral realm to exhort his readers to adhere to the moral project of conforming one's mind according to God's "eternity, truth and love." As a good rhetorician, most likely he realized his use of aposiopesis, a device in which a thought is suddenly broken off in midstream as the speaker is unwilling or unable to complete it. So Augustine switches to the moral project as a cover for the uncompleted thought about women's imago status. He could have moved either to affirm their status in a full and unqualified way or to qualify it further. Even in the language of the moral project to which he has switched, as it were, in midthought, he once again admits the use of the lower part of the intellect to deal with changeable and corporeal things, but again only with the language of admonition and warning. Augustine admits that we cannot live without being involved in the material world, but be careful, he warns, "not to set up such things as the final goal and twisting our desire for happiness toward them, and that whatever we do in the use of temporal things under the guidance of reason, we do it with our gaze fixed on the eternal things which we are to attain, passing quickly by the former and setting our hearts on the latter" (13.21). In playing out the correlations that Augustine constructs, it is clear what his preferences are: the eternal and the unchangeable are to be preferred to the temporal and changeable world, the higher part of the mind (the "man" part) is preferred to the lower ("woman") part, wisdom is preferred to knowledge, and man is preferred to woman. As he writes in the final section of book 12, "Wisdom is concerned with the intellectual cognizance of eternal things and knowledge with the rational cognizance of temporal things, and it is not hard to decide which should be preferred and which subordinated to the other" (15.25).

Augustine has admitted that women as human beings (homo) are made in God's image—in the ontological and spiritual senses, but not as women per se (femina). This emphasis on the spiritual imago status is consistent with Augustine's hierarchical way of thinking about reality and what is to be valued and for what reasons. Recent authors, such as Van Bavel, Cline-Horowitz, and Meconi, have argued for the imago status of women in the spiritual realm, which, after all for Augustine, is the one that really matters.[20] Even though woman is in a spiritual sense included in homo as image of God, according to Børresen, the results are decidedly mixed: "Augustine's backdating of women's salvational Godlikeness to the order of creation only serves to dissociate spiritual equivalence from female subservience, so that women's subordination in church and society remains normative."[21] In the context of Augustine's model of hierarchy, preference, and subordination, what real significance is there that women have imago status in the spiritual sense and not as women? Through this move, Augustine not only maintains and bolsters the hierarchical, value-laden model he inherited from the Neoplatonists, he also cuts off a fruitful line of thinking about the material and social world where women and men of flesh and blood, mind and heart live their lives. And it is from this world that such women and men begin the human journey that may lead them back to God. Augustine's failure to integrate more fully the spiritual and the physical lies at the heart of his enterprise and it plays out not only in issues concerning women, sexuality, and the family, but also in questions about power, politics, and society. What real difference does it make that women as human beings are made in God's image in the spiritual sense if such status has little or no bearing in the physical, temporal, and social world? The imago status of women is acknowledged but only after they have paid the price of having to prescind from their bodies and their sexuality. This is not a price that Augustine has exacted of men. It could be argued that at least Augustine has provided the grounding for a fuller articulation of women's imago status by placing it in the spiritual realm, which is, after all, the most important reality for him. Even granting this point, Augustine has done this in the most minimal way possible, according women some acknowledgment as human beings, but providing very little leverage to challenge women's subordinate status in the social, political, or legal realms. In fact, given the language of hypothesis and exclusion that Augustine used in the section cited above from *The Trinity*, an emphasis on women's imago status was not an issue for which he was going to provide full and unqualified support. If anything, the series of qualifications that Augustine employs when he discusses this topic makes it clear that even if women are in some sense made in God's image, even for this much, they must pay the price of being disembodied and degendered in ways that are never required of men. Kim Power notes the enormous implications that follow from Augustine's position:

> The question of the *imago Dei* is of vital importance to theology and spirituality because our subjective and objective images of God are interdependent and reciprocal. What is rejected as less than human will not be present in our image of God. What is feared as vitiating will not be present in our image of God. Rather God's image may be created from the distortions deep within the human person. Augustine's rejection of the spiritually feminine in God, and therefore his rejection of all creatureliness, all temporality, all contingency, all emotion from the divine image in the human person prescinds from the subjective *imago Dei* all that is distinctively human. Taken to its logical conclusion, the person is most like God who is least like a human being—finite, fallible and contingent. . . . And if woman *qua* woman bears the image

of God, then the Augustinian notion of God must also undergo amplification and enrichment.[22]

Taking his cue from the second creation account in Genesis 2:20–25, Augustine's descriptions of women in this section of *The Trinity* are replete with terms that point to women's position as dependent on, derived from, and different from men (and not only with regard to sexual differentiation). To use the language made famous by Simone de Beauvoir, Augustine clearly considers men to be the norm and women to be "other." And the comparison only travels one way: women are compared with men, who are the standard. Men are never compared with women in any sort of mutual or reciprocal ways. Given Augustine's disposition toward hierarchical thinking, it comes as no surprise that he constructs the comparisons and contrasts between men and women vertically and not horizontally. Clearly, he is not comparing equals in any real sense. In the hierarchy of the higher intellect over the lower intellect, Augustine is very much concerned with how the lower power may seduce and bring down the higher. There is very little, if any, acknowledgment on Augustine's part of the indispensable role played by the lower intellect in acquiring knowledge about the world and in initiating the process of ascent. Augustine pays attention to the world largely as the starting point from which to move beyond the world. If the lower part of the intellect is like Eve, Adam's helper, it is not all that clear what kind of help this part of the mind provides. If anything, Augustine casts the lower intellect more as a hindrance to the higher intellect, and a very significant one, and not as being all that helpful to it. Augustine overemphasizes the dangers and difficulties of the lower intellect's involvement with the temporal, changeable world and very much underrates its contributions to the mind's work and to the human project of returning to God from the starting point of this world. James O'Donnell notes the deep divides that Augustine's views have created for the rest of the tradition:

> Deeply rooted in Augustine's version of Christianity (and in western ways of Christianity ever since) is a divide that appears in various ways: body and spirit, science and religion, therapy and punishment. . . . The danger of such a separation needs to be seen. For such spiritualization will support complicated, and to most eyes, pathological disenfranchisement of the body, sexuality, and women in mainstream western cultures. Much of the labor

expended on elaborating incarnational spirituality and other recent theological ventures could have been saved had the fundamental and unnecessary lines not been drawn long ago.[23]

These divisions, distortions, and underemphases are most unfortunate,
and not only because of the "labor lost," but even more so because of the
destructive effects on real women's lives for thousands of years. These
failures become especially clear when one considers what riches Augustine discovered in the inner life of the mind throughout the second half
of The Trinity. He was on to something there that could have provided
him with a paradigm and a different set of principles for understanding,
not only the inner life of the mind, but also something truly revolutionary
about the nature of human relationships. In her work, Børresen sees an
opening for what she calls ongoing "reinculturation of theology" by challenging and enlarging Augustine's discourse about women's status as
image of God. While being open about Augustine's negative influence on
the tradition, Børresen also considers work on these texts as fruitful and
transformative. She notes, "Patriarchal gender hierarchy, which in his
society was affirmed as normative a priori, is here corrected by God's
enhancement of women's humanity, in spite of their inherent femaleness.
From a present feminist standpoint, Augustine's 'feminism' appears
thwarted by his malecentred spiritualism. Defeminised equality by means
of sexless imago Dei is today overcome by updated, inclusive Godlikeness
as equally pertaining to women and men, in their holistic diversity."[24]

Embedded in the life of the divine trinity and in the inner life of the
mind in which Augustine discovers and enunciates the divine image in
humans, are the principles of equality, reciprocity, mutuality, and interrelationship. Both the life of God and the inner life of humans have these
qualities as constitutive of their very essence. Augustine's descriptions of
the inner life of humans are brimming with the intricacies of the mind's
workings as memory, understanding, and will in their interplays and in-
terconnections without reducing the mind and its activities to a faculty
psychology and without sacrificing the elemental unity of inner human
life. Nor does hierarchy or rigid subordination enter into his thinking on
these points. In these ways, his anti-Arian intentions in The Trinity may
come to serve wider purposes of inclusion and correcting his "malecentred spiritualism." Augustine comes up with a wide assortment of trinitarian activities of the mind, extensively elaborated without ever being
exhaustive. Just as the human mind could ring the changes of its own

inner workings virtually without ceasing, how much more so with the inner life of the triune God. Augustine writes toward the end of book 15 about seeing God face to face in the next life:

> But when the sight comes that is promised us face to face (1 Corinthians 13:12) we shall see this trinity that is not only incorporeal but also supremely inseparable and truly unchangeable much more clearly and definitely than we now see its image which we ourselves are. However, those who do see through this mirror and in this puzzle, as much as it is granted to see in this life, are not those who merely observe in their own minds what we have discussed and suggested, but those who see it precisely as an image, so that they can in some fashion refer what they see to that of which it is an image. (15.25.44)

We are left to imagine and to work out what might have happened had Augustine drawn out the implications of his own paradigm of interrelationship, based on equality, mutuality, and reciprocity, that he discovered as the inner life of God. He brought these insights to bear on the inner life of human beings, but not to human beings themselves and their relationships. He who was able to elaborate so fully and wondrously on the first two themes could not bring it to the third point. Had he done so for human interrelationships, the consequences and significance for the real lives of women, and men too, would have been radically different and greatly improved, and especially so for women. Women would then have been considered, along with men, to be made fully in God's image and likeness. Full stop. No qualifications or hesitations. Our contemporary work on Augustine draws out the consequences of his own thinking, even if he himself did not think them through or dare to do so. If he could not have developed these implications for all sorts of cultural and social reasons, there is nothing stopping us from so doing and thereby reaping the benefits for women more fully than Augustine could ever have imagined.

Notes

1. Kari Elisabeth Børresen, *Subordination et équivalence: Nature et rôle de la femme d'après Augustin et Thomas d'Aquin* (Oslo-Paris, 1968); updated as *Subordination and Equivalence: The Nature and Role of Women in Augustine and Thomas Aquinas* (Washington, D.C., 1981).

2. Kari Elisabeth Børresen, "In Defence of Augustine: How *Femina* Is *Homo*," in *Collectanea Augustiniana: Melanges T. J. Van Bavel*, ed. B. Bruning, M. Lamberigts, and J. Van Houtem (Louvain: Leuven University Press, 1990), 411.

3. Ibid.

4. E. Ann Matter, "Christ, God, and Woman in the Thought of St. Augustine," in *Augustine and His Critics*, ed. Robert Dodaro and George Lawless (New York: Routledge, 2000), 170–74. David Vincent Meconi, "*Grata Sacris Angelis*: Gender and the *Imago Dei* in Augustine's *De Trinitate XII*," *American Catholic Philosophical Quarterly* 74, no. 1 (2000): 48–62.

5. Tarcisius J. Van Bavel, "Woman as the Image of God in Augustine's *De Trinitate XII*," in *Signum Pietatis: Festgabe für Cornelius Petrus Mayer OSA zum 60. Geburtstag*, ed. A. Zumkeller (Würzburg, Germany: Augustinus Verlag, 1989), 281–82, 286. See also Kim Power, *Veiled Desire: Augustine on Women* (New York: Continuum, 1994), 136–68.

6. Augustine, *Confessions*, trans. Henry Chadwick (New York: Oxford University Press, 1992), 6.3.4.

7. Raymond E. Brown, Joseph A. Fitzmyer, and Roland E. Murphy, eds., *The Jerome Biblical Commentary* (Englewood Cliffs, N.J.: Prentice Hall, 1968), 3–4; 10–12.

8. The question of Augustine's view of the human person as an entity composed of body and soul is a complex one that cannot be fully discussed here. His thinking is certainly indebted to a number of earlier traditions, including Neoplatonism (Plotinus and Porphyry), Stoicism, and other early Christian writers. Perhaps Augustine's most famous definition of the human being as "a soul using a body" (*On the Morals of the Catholic Church* 1.27.52) points to at least two important directions in his thinking on the matter: that humans are composed of the two aspects, body and soul, and that there is a hierarchy encoded in his observation that the soul uses the body and not vice versa. In another text, *The Magnitude of the Soul*, Augustine remarks that the soul is a "rational substance that is designed to rule the body" (13.22). In later works, especially *The Trinity*, his analysis stresses more of the unity of the human being, but he never completely works out the ways in which body and soul fully fit together. In a way, one could argue that the solution is postponed to the next life with the resurrection of the body, which will entail a reunion of the resurrected body with the soul. At that point, the body will be a "transformed" physical body, but will still be physical in some senses of the term. This strategy, of course, does not solve the question. In fact, it makes it even more mysterious and problematic.

9. The relationships between grace and free will in Augustine's thinking are also complex and impossible to summarize in a short note. Nevertheless, readers may take note of the following aspects of this complex issue: the nature and effectiveness of grace, its status as a gift from God, its role in assisting sinners perform meritorious actions, its relationships to both free choice of the will (*liberum arbitrium voluntatis*) and freedom (*libertas*), and God's grace before the first sin of Adam and Eve and in the aftermath of sin. Some of Augustine's texts in which he discusses these aspects of the questions are *Free Choice of the Will*, *Confessions*, *On Nature and Grace*, *Enchiridion*, *The City of God*, *Admonition and Grace*, and *Commentaries on the Psalms*. As might be expected, the secondary literature on these topics is also vast.

10. Edmund Hill, introduction to Augustine, *The Trinity*, trans. Edmund Hill (Hyde Park, N.Y.: New City Press, 1991), 43.

11. Ibid., 18–59.

12. Ibid., 46–47, 56. Hill cites a lengthy passage from *The Trinity* 1.7.14 to show the extent to which Augustine's task is informed by Scripture, his predecessors' works, and his own speculative interests, 46.

13. Ibid., 54.

14. Let it be noted that Augustine is very careful to avoid a crude and reductionist view that would posit some sort of one-to-one correspondence between, on the one hand, human memory, understanding, and will with, on the other hand, the members of the Trinity, as Father, Son, and

Spirit. Augustine's final triad of memory, understanding, and will are carried through into book 15 as the pervasive rendering of what constitutes the image of God in humans. But even here, the analogy is hardly perfect. The final "trinity" in humans is in the human being, but is not identical to it. However, as Augustine writes, "but that Trinity, of which the mind is an image, is nothing else in its totality than God, nothing else in its totality than Trinity. Nor is there anything pertaining to God's nature that does not belong to that Trinity; and the three persons are of one nature, but not as each individual is one person" (15.7.11). The absolute one-ness and simplicity of God is of utmost importance for Augustine to underscore.

15. Augustine, *Letter 243*, trans. Sr. Wilfrid Parsons (New York: Fathers of the Church, 1956), 225.

16. Ambrose, *On Noah and the Ark*, 92, in J.-P. Migne, ed., *Patrologiae Cursus Completus: Series Latina* (Paris, 1878–90), vol. 14, col. 424. Augustine's reading, understanding, and interpretation of Scripture is a long and complex story that spans his lifelong quest to answer questions about God, creation, the nature of good and evil, and humanity's place in the world. As early as age nineteen, when he was first inspired to a life of philosophy by reading Cicero's *Hortensius*, Augustine turned to the Scriptures but was deeply disappointed because they lacked the style and elegance of Latin literature (*Confessions* 3.5.9). Then Augustine spent ten years as an auditor with the Manichaeans, who had their own idiosyncratic brand of scriptural interpretation in which they rejected the Old Testament entirely and read the New Testament very selectively. They were especially attracted to some of Paul's Epistles, since his views on light and darkness and the flesh and the spirit could be read according to Manichaean dualism. When Augustine arrived in Milan, hearing Ambrose preach on the Scriptures gave him his first glimpses of understanding those texts in figurative and spiritual ways (*Confessions* 5.14.24). Not only did this open Augustine's ears and mind to a whole new way of reading Scripture, it began to provide him with powerful resources to challenge and then finally reject the Manicheans, along with their approach to Scripture.

17. Augustine writes in this early work: "Hence, Scripture begins to explain how the woman was made. It says that she was made as man's helper so that by spiritual union she might bring forth spiritual offspring, that is, the good works of divine praise, while he rules and she obeys. . . . For there was still need to bring it about not only that the soul rule over the body, because the body has the position of servant, but that virile reason hold subject to itself its animal part, by the help of which it governs the body. The woman was made as an illustration of this, for the order of things makes her subject to man" (*Genesis Against the Manichaeans*, trans. Roland J. Teske [Washington, D.C.: Catholic University of America Press, 1991], 2.11.15).

18. For some sense of the debates on this issue from Galatians 3:26–28, see Dennis Ronald MacDonald, *There Is No Male and Female: The Fate of a Dominical Saying in Paul and Gnosticism* (Philadelphia: Fortress Press, 1987); Hans Dieter Betz, *Galatians: A Commentary on Paul's Letter to the Churches in Galatia* (Philadelphia: Fortress Press, 1979), 185–201; Charles B. Cousar, *Galatians* (Atlanta: John Knox Press, 1982), 85–89; Scot McKnight, *Galatians: The* NIV *Application Commentary* (Grand Rapids, Mich.: Zondervan, 1995), 199–203. In his book Betz mentions those scholars who have seen a Gnostic influence of the androgynous Anthropos morph into a Christ-Anthropos in a number of Pauline texts and have argued for seeing the abolition of sex differences in this text from Galatians based on the figure of an "androgynous Christ-figure" (196–97, 199–200). At the outset of his book MacDonald reviews the variety of ways scholars have interpreted this text (2–14) and then argues that "both Paul and the primary transmitters of the saying were committed to sexual equality but in radically different and theologically incompatible ways. . . . In its denial of sexual differentiation the saying spoke of the individual soul's achievement of the divine image, immaterial and sexually unified. Paul, however, subtly altered the wording of the saying and profoundly altered its ethical consequences. As it now stands, the denial of social divisions in Galatians 3:28 is the apostle's own original declaration and not an echo of a more socially egalitarian tradition still audible in spite of Paul's attempts to muffle it" (15).

19. Augustine has also cited the text from Galatians 3:28 earlier in the final book of the *Confessions* (13.23.33) where he discusses the creation accounts from Genesis. At that point, he is interpreting the notion of humans having dominion over the rest of creation and ascribing to them a kind of "spiritual judgment" that other creatures do not possess: "For 'you made man male and female' in your spiritual grace to be equal, so that physical gender makes no distinction of male and female, just as there is 'neither Jew nor Greek, neither slave nor free person' (Gal. 3:28). So spiritual persons, whether they preside or are subject to authority, exercise spiritual judgment" (13.23.33) Later in *The Trinity* Augustine has the opportunity to use the text from Galatians as a counterweight to the text from 1 Corinthians 11:7, but unfortunately fails to do so. In fact, as this section of book 12 unfolds, he uses the text from 1 Corinthians 11 to trump Galatians 3 and not the other way around.

20. This is the line of argument that is developed in some way or other in the articles cited below, that is, that Augustine at least considered women to be in God's image in a spiritual sense. After all, they claim, he took the analysis to this point. In this essay I argue that it was not far enough and that Augustine's failure has had profound implications for the tradition in Western Christianity and on Western culture as a whole. See Tarcisius Van Bavel, "Woman as the Image of God in Augustine's *De Trinitate* XII," in *Signum Pietatis: Festgabe für Cornelius Petrus Mayer OSA zum 60. Geburtstag*, ed. A. Zumkeller (Würzburg, Germany: Augustinus Verlag, 1989) 267–88; David Vincent Meconi, "*Grata Sacris Angelis*: Gender and the *Imago Dei* in Augustine's *De Trinitate* XII," *American Catholic Philosophical Quarterly* 74, no. 1 (2000): 48–62; Maryann Cline Horowitz, "The Image of God in Man—Is Woman Included?" *Harvard Theological Review* 72, 1–2 (1979): 200–204.

21. Kari Elisabeth Børresen, "In Defence of Augustine: How *Femina* Is *Homo*," 417.

22. Power, *Veiled Desire*, 221–22.

23. James J. O'Donnell, *Augustine: A New Biography* (New York: HarperCollins, 2005), 191.

24. Børresen, "In Defence of Augustine," 425.

10

To Remember Self, to Remember God: Augustine on Sexuality, Relationality, and the Trinity

Julie B. Miller

The general emphasis on relationality and experience in feminist theology has engendered a thorough examination of Christian teachings on two seemingly unrelated topics in recent years: the Trinity and sexuality. In the former instance, Christian feminist theologians have repeatedly turned to the doctrine of God, and specifically to the Trinity, in attempts to forge new, liberating models of relationality in contrast to the often authoritarian, hierarchical, and individualistic models offered by malestream theology. While some theologians have denied the possibility of recouping this doctrine for feminist purposes, others have seized upon the intrinsic internal relationality of the Trinity in order to "make the doctrine of the Trinity exemplify the kind of relations, and the kind of society, that we most admire."[1] In the latter case, with regard to sexuality, many theologians have attempted to recoup the positive aspects of sexuality and eroticism, the most maligned but also, seemingly, the most intensely intimate, powerful, and "relational" of all human experiences.[2]

Not surprisingly, then, several feminist theologians have taken up the complex task of examining what, if anything, the experience of sexuality and the doctrine of the Trinity have to do with each other.[3] As Sarah Coakley has suggested, there appears to be an intrinsic, yet "messy," entanglement between our experience of sexuality and our experience of God.[4] And Margaret Miles has argued that "the sexual is a way the soul speaks."[5] If this is so—and even if it is only so in the traditional Augustinian Christian construction of it—it is incumbent upon theologians not only to understand and to critique how sexuality and the divine have been related through traditional patriarchal theologies, but also to construct new paradigms for both in order to allow for a more just and liberating experience of sexuality and divinity for women and men alike.[6]

In the past forty years or so, many traditional scholars have used psychoanalytic theories to unravel the apparent correlations between Augustine's seemingly abject fear of intimate relations (resulting from the overbearing presence of his mother, Monica) and his construction of a "fail-safe" God, yet none of these has ventured so far as to depict in detail how this fail-safe God has been constructed.[7] Hence, it is my intention in this essay to explicate just how Augustine's doctrine of the Trinity is ultimately reflected in his experience of sexuality, and vice versa. Thus, I examine the connection between Augustine's formulation of God as a trinity of memory, understanding, and will and his anxious suspicions of intimate human relations, including, but not limited to, sexual relations. It is my belief that by depicting God as a trinity that is perpetually remembering, knowing, and loving itself, Augustine belies his fear of relations that obliterate the self, relations in which one forgets and loses oneself. Since Augustine believes this loss of self is most apparent in sexual relations, actual human sexual relationships are deemed highly ambivalent in his theology.[8] However, he maintains and uses both the model and vocabulary of passionate, sexual pleasure to express his euphoric experience of spiritual connection with God. It appears that, for Augustine, in the safety of divine-human relation, in which neither party is vulnerable to the loss of self, unabashedly passionate and, some might say, even erotic relations between God and human can exist. Unfortunately, for Augustine, at least, the same passionate experiences cannot be shared between two human beings, for these relationships inevitably end in loss.

It is my further intention not only to explicate how his teachings on both these subjects have been significantly shaped and constructed by the discourse of Neoplatonism, but also to offer a feminist psychological critique of Augustine's early relationship with his mother in order to suggest an alternate reading of that relationship to the ones offered by traditional neo-Freudian analyses. In this essay I argue that neither Neo-platonic theory nor the patriarchal culture in which Augustine and Monica lived and breathed could sufficiently allow for a full-bodied love of God, let alone a full-bodied love for another human being, particularly a person of the opposite sex.[9] Together, these factors not surprisingly re-sulted in a self-contained trinity and an abject fear of intimate human relationships.

Augustine as Addict

Much ink has already been spilled on the topic of sex in Augustinian thought. As Peter Brown notes, when it comes to Augustine's views of sexuality, we tend to believe that "we know what he said; and we feel in no uncertain terms that he should not have said it."[10] Carter Heyward is even more blunt: "Augustine, Bishop of Hippo, was the first theologian to systematize erotophobia—fear of sex—as a staple (arguably *the* staple) of christian [sic] orthodoxy."[11] In linking sexuality with the transmission of original sin and thereby denying the possibility of good, life-enhancing sexual pleasure, Augustine denied the possibility that sexual love could be a legitimate and profound expression of one's desire for intimate con-nection with one's beloved, let alone an expression of one's desire for God.[12] But in his systematic attempts to work out why this is so, he reveals a profound experiential similarity between his sexual desire and his desire to rest completely in God. Unfortunately—for Augustine him-self and for the generations of Christians who have been influenced by him—he could not overcome the breach he felt between these two de-sires. If the feminist theological emphasis on the goodness of both sexual-ity and divinity is true, it is therefore important to examine why

Augustine could not do so and what implications this had for his formulation of the doctrine of God, the Trinity.[13]

In *Desire and Delight*, Margaret Miles's 1992 study of Augustine's *Confessions*, Miles suggests that Augustine was so negative about sex because
he was what contemporary readers might call a "sex addict."[14] Because of
his inability to control his own sexual impulses, he found it necessary to
deny himself all sexual pleasure in order to attain any semblance of an
integrated life.[15] However, specifically because of the tremendous power
of Augustine's sexual desires and the intensity of his sexual pleasure, Augustine structured his formulation of spiritual pleasure on the model of
male sexuality, with "its rhythm of collecting and spilling," swelling and
pouring forth.[16] The language of sexual desire was apparently the only
language powerful enough to capture the depth of Augustine's desire for
God, and he used this language throughout his writings. But since his
personal experience of sexual passion ultimately caused him much discomfort and anxiety, continence, "the hoarding of seminal fluid," the
collecting and gathering up of one's self, of one's vital energies, became
for him "the practice and paradigm of an integrated life."[17]

However, I would like to push this discussion in a slightly different
direction by asserting that sex was problematic for Augustine not necessarily because he was a sex addict, but because he was, more fundamentally, what one might call a "love addict." That is, in his most intense
and early relationships, Augustine poured out his soul upon his beloved;
in so doing, he tended to "lose" himself in these relationships. This tendency to invest all of himself in relationships and to "forget himself" in
the intensity of his affection set the stage for pain and confusion when
his beloved was torn away from him. Hence, in his mature years, he strove
to avoid all such relations.

Loss of Self and Other in Augustine's Relationships

For example, in his *Confessions* Augustine poignantly tells the story of his
pain and anguish at the death of his childhood friend, the one man who
was "sweet to me above every sweetness" (4.4.7).[18] Reflecting back on
this experience twenty years after the fact, the intensity of his emotions
are still evident: "In me there had arisen I know not what sort of affection
. . . for most heavily there weighed upon me both weariness of life and

fear of dying. I believe that the more I loved him, the more did I hate and fear death, which had taken him away from me, as my cruelest enemy. I thought it would speedily devour all men, since it had been able to devour him. I marveled that other men should live, because him, whom I had loved as if he would never die, was dead" (4.6.11). When his "second self" was wrenched away from him, everything lost its meaning, and Augustine nearly lost his will to live: "I carried about my pierced and blood-ied soul, rebellious as being carried by me, but I could find no place where I might put it down" (4.7.12). This friend had been "more real and more good" to Augustine's soul than God had ever been, and he raged at the world in the face of his loss, "hating all things because they no longer held him" (4.4.9). Ultimately, Augustine admits he had lost himself in this relationship, stating, "I thought that my soul and his soul were but one soul in two bodies. Therefore, my life was a horror to me because I would not live as but a half" (4.6.11).

While much has been made of Augustine's relationship with his mother, Monica—analyses that we will examine in the final section of this essay—for our purposes at this point it is necessary to note simply that at her death he exhibited a similar grief and sense of loss of self. As with his experience at the death of his childhood friend, at the death of his mother many years later, we see him struggling again with his anguish, ashamed at its intensity. However, this time he purports to know why he is suffering so: his passionate affections were a result of disordered love and therefore a result of human weakness: "I upbraided the weakness of my affection, and I held back the flood of sorrow. . . . It distressed me greatly that these human feelings had such sway over me, for this needs must be according to due order and our allotted state. . . . My heart was wounded through and my life was as if ripped asunder. For out of her life and mine one life had been made" (9.12.31, 30). Unable to break the force of "habitual" attachment to his loves, to maintain the "due measure between soul and soul, wherein lie the bright boundaries of friendship" (2.2.2), he had given too much of himself. And in the death of his be-loved, part of his very self was lost.

Interestingly, we hear very little concerning Augustine's one long-term, committed sexual relationship. But the little he does reveal is tell-ing. When his partner was "torn away" from his side because she was an impediment to a more socially acceptable marriage, he felt much anguish: "My heart still clung to her: it was pierced and wounded within me, and the wound drew blood from it. . . . Not yet healed within me was that

wound which had been made by the cutting away of my former companion. After intense fever and pain, it festered, and it still caused me pain,
although in a more chilling and desperate way" (6.15.25). In discussing
this one intimate sexual relationship, Augustine suggests that part of
himself had been "cut away," but he does not go so far as to suggest that
he "lost" himself in his beloved, that the two had become "one," that he
was but a "half." Rather, he chooses to describe himself as wounded and
bloody, yet seemingly whole nonetheless. In the end, he blames the pain
and suffering of *this* loss on his sexual addiction, not on his capacity for
unbounded love: he denies that he had given himself up in this relationship, stating that he was "not so much a lover of marriage as a slave to
lust" (6.15.25). He interpreted the pain that he felt in losing his lover
and his subsequent turn to another mistress for comfort not as an understandable response to the loss of a committed, long-term partner and the
desire for connection with another. Instead, he saw in his actions an
unnatural desire for sexual pleasure, for the "slimy desires of the flesh and
. . . youth's seething spring" (2.2.2).

It is this model, then, of unhealthy lust, of concupiscence, in which
one anxiously seeks after and pours oneself onto those objects—including
persons—unworthy of one's full attention and love, that Augustine subsequently uses to interpret all his relationships. Augustine was convinced
that in intimate relationships, if we do not maintain the "due measure"
or proper emotional distance from the other, we lose ourselves. He also
believed that in sexual relations—more specifically, in sexual orgasm—we lose ourselves completely.[19] Sex, then, became the symbolic
focal point for Augustine's anxieties concerning this more diffuse and
profound fear of loss in intimate relations. This loss is what he spent the
rest of his life trying to avoid; this loss is what his doctrine of the Trinity
is predicated upon.

The Trinity of Memory, Understanding, and Will

Augustine develops this principle of human relations as inevitable loss of
self through his various formulations of the story of the Creation and Fall.
Correlatively, he develops a method of escape from this loss through his
understanding of the image of God as reflected in the human soul as a
trinity of memory, understanding, and will. In his attempts to work out

both the significance and purpose of the two sexes, the meaning of sexuality itself, and the ultimate cause of the Fall, Augustine delineates his nuanced yet tortured understanding of the human person as a soul subject to the loss of itself through its very attachments to other persons: through the development of his doctrine of the Trinity as reflected in the human soul, he shows us how we can return to God, fully mindful and fully whole.

Augustine's debt to Neoplatonic philosophy, and particularly to Plotinus, is evident in his preconversion renderings of the relationship between the human soul and God, or the One.[20] Plotinus's teachings on the triad of the One, Intelligence, and Soul provided Augustine with a rational, relational schema with which to understand the human soul's relation to the cosmic One, or God. According to this philosophy, the process of creation is one of emanation and return, a process by which the "potent simplicity of the One 'overflows' into Intelligence, and Intelligence overflows into Soul."[21] In response to this outpouring, all created things desire to return to the One, "to return to the fullness of being of which it is an outflow."[22] The fulfillment of the self in the One is, in effect, the blissful loss of self as a separate or individuated entity and a return to the One. In fact, in emanation theory—in contrast to creation ex nihilo—the return of the soul/self to the One, as difficult and demanding as it might be, is not fraught with the sense of fear and loss that we see later in Augustine's work on this point in his recast Christian Neoplatonism. It is only in the soul's return to God that the soul will find peace, happiness, and contentment. If it fails to do so, the soul will be forever frustrated in its attempts to satisfy its desires through unworthy and finite objects. The soul's anxious desire to return to the One, to God, is poignantly reflected in Augustine's famous sentiment that "our hearts are restless until they rest in You."

Yet Augustine's conversion to Christianity necessitated a revision of this Neoplatonic approach to the One, for Christian doctrine asserted that God's nature was not a monad, but, rather, a trinity. While throughout his writings Augustine speculated on several versions of this trinity, in his mature reflections found in *The Trinity*, he settled upon the notion of the human as the image of God in a trinity of memory, understanding, and will.[23] He reasoned that since humanity was created in the image of this God, we must be able to discover within the self the very nature of the trinity. Reflecting on the workings of human rationality, Augustine believed he discovered the imprint of the trinity in the workings of the human mind, or memory.[24]

Memory, for Augustine, encompassed much more than current understandings of the word suggest. Instead of simply implying the notion of recall, as we might think of it today, for Augustine, memory was more akin to perpetual self-reflexivity and self-identity, a self-presence constantly aware of and hence knowledgeable of itself. Further, although the memory, understanding, and will appear to be three different capacities of the human soul, Augustine asserts that they are really one; yet, as one, they also exhibit distinct qualities while sharing in the qualities of each other: "For not only is each [capacity] comprehended by each one, but all are also comprehended by each one. For I remember that I have memory, understanding and will; and I understand that I understand, will and remember; and I will that I will, remember and understand; and at the same time I remember my whole memory, understanding and will" (*Trinity* 10.11.18). In this construction of the soul as a perpetually self-aware, self-loving, and self-knowledgeable one-in-three, Augustine believed he glimpsed the image of the trinity. What is most important, however, is that in turning inward, toward knowledge of ourselves, we ultimately find knowledge of God. For as Augustine attests, "This trinity of the mind is not on that account the image of God because the mind remembers itself, understands itself and loves itself, but because it can also remember, understand, and love God by whom it was made" (*Trinity* 14.12.15). Being in full possession of ourselves, wholly self-aware and self-knowledgeable, we are then able to be fully knowledgeable of God, and to thereby love God, as is our duty.

Thus, Augustine argued that souls, made for God, can only be fully satisfied if they are wholly attuned to and present to God. They can only be aware of God if they are mindful of him, and they can only be mindful and knowledgeable of God if they *will* to be so. They can only be mindful of God if they are mindful of themselves as creatures of God made in God's image. If at any point the soul turns its attention to objects or persons other than God, the soul will lose the self-conscious awareness of God; having no memory of God, it cannot know or love God, or itself. Hence, to give undue attention to bodily concerns or even to other people leads to forgetfulness of both oneself and God. It leads one to "waste" oneself on trivial matters and to thereby diminish one's potential happiness and harmony.

The Fall

For Augustine, this capacity to waste or lose oneself only becomes a problem as a result of the Fall; in paradise, God, soul, and body were all related in a perfect, complete, albeit hierarchical, harmony. Before the Fall, Adam and Eve were wholly mindful of God and their subordinate nature to him. Keeping God always in their memory, they had knowledge of God; knowing God and his goodness, they willed to continue in his restful, peaceful presence. However, because of a "spontaneous falling away" of the *will* to love God above themselves, Adam and Eve lost the knowledge of God, and in so doing, they lost themselves. As the "weakest link," as it were, in the triad of the human soul, the will's fall ushered in the loss of both the memory and knowledge of God and of itself. With this loss of unity in the trinity of the soul, the image of God within it became dim indeed, and all personal, social, and sexual relations reflected this loss.

In book 12 of *The Trinity*, Augustine offers one of his most nuanced understandings of the human soul and its fall from grace by interpreting the creation of Adam and Eve as the allegorical story of a single soul in light of a threefold division of the human person. Adam, representative of higher reason, needed a helpmate suitable to him to regulate the soul's necessary dealings with material and temporal things. Eve, symbolic of lower reason, was thus taken from his nature, his "rib," to perform this task. The two together, then, form one mind/soul, and together they represent the soul as the image of God, a creature that is subject to the higher authority of God and Eternal Truth.

In the Fall, however, the original harmonies among the human soul, the body, and God were destroyed. Adam, higher reason, succumbed to the persuasive words of Eve, lower reason, who in turn had given in to the serpent, the symbol of bodily passion. In so doing, Adam disobeyed the command of God, destroyed the peace of paradise and the natural harmony that had existed within the individual person. By abdicating his position of authority, Adam allowed sin—experienced as disorder, disharmony, discontent, and ultimately, the forgetting of God—to enter the world. The human person has thus been forever after "ruled" by its lower reason, which is attached to the temporal things of this life, rather than ruled by the wisdom and love of God ascertained through the use of one's higher reason.

Elsewhere, Augustine augments this allegorical interpretation of the Fall, understood as the story of a single soul, with a social interpretation. In it he depicts the Creation and Fall as illustrative of ideal—and subsequently imperfect—human relations, most specifically, sexual relations. In *The Literal Meaning of Genesis* Augustine asserts that Eve was created for the sole purpose of bearing children. He comes to this conclusion by reasoning that a male "helper" would have been more suitable to Adam if he had been in need of aid in tilling the soil or even simply in need of comfort and companionship. He claims, "How much more agreeably could two male friends, rather than a man and a woman, enjoy companionship and conversation in a shared life together." Thus he states, "I do not see in what sense the woman was made as a helper for the man if not for the sake of bearing children" (9.5.9). In this scenario, Eve is not simply symbolic of the inferior portion of the soul but also symbolic of woman's—all women's—inferior social status. Moreover, this inferiority is understood to be an intrinsic part of God's divine, harmonious order, an inferiority found even in paradise.

Holding this belief that Eve was created solely for the purpose of procreation, Augustine asserted that sex would have taken place in paradise—a rather bold proposition at the time—but without the "tumultuous ardor of passion" in which it is presently experienced (9.3.6). He explains these mechanics in *The City of God*: "Those parts, like all the rest, would be set in motion at the command of the will; and without the seductive stimulus of passion, with calmness of mind and with no corrupting of the integrity of the body, the husband would lie upon the bosom of his wife. . . . No wild heat of passion would arouse those parts of the body, but a spontaneous power, according to the need, would be present" (14.26).[25] What is significant here, I believe, is that in this passage, Augustine does not suggest that sexual relations are of a different order from other human relations. Rather, he is proposing that sexual relations are the same as, and perhaps even the paradigm of, all social relations in paradise. Harmonious, properly ordered, and fundamentally passionless, all sexual relations would remain subject to the will of God, and, since this was proper to the hierarchy that God created, to the will of the male; that is, when Adam decided it was time to have a child, he and Eve would have intercourse. The sexual experience, like all other social experiences, would be pleasant, controlled, and harmonious. All emotions would be in accord with reason, resulting in complete tranquillity of soul. No sadness, no "foolish joy," no excessive passion would intrude upon this peaceful pleasure. Rather, "true gladness" would "ceaselessly flow from the presence of God, who was loved out of a pure heart, and a good conscience, and faith unfeigned" (14.26). The sexual affections would never be unruly, or "out of control." Insofar as Adam and Eve remained steadfastly cognizant of God and obedient to God's will, this harmony would exist. However, the harmony of these glad yet passionless social relations was permanently ruptured by the will's "falling away" and disobedience to God.

In light of our discussion thus far, it should not be surprising to discover that according to Augustine, the disobedience of Adam and Eve was precipitated not by an arrogant sense of rebellion or even a ravenous sexual appetite but, rather, by a previously existing disorder of the affections and an undue attachment of one to the other: Adam, spurning God, accepted the forbidden fruit from Eve because he "could not bear to be severed from his only companion" (City 14.13). It was not that Adam was deceived and believed that Eve's words were true, but that he, "by the drawings of kindred yielded to the woman, the husband to the wife, the one human being to the only other human being" (City 14.11). Adam and Eve had somehow become too dependent on each other, too lost in the other. Moreover, while in the City of God it is Adam who is described as being too attached, in The Literal Interpretation of Genesis, Augustine states that it is Eve who is the lost one. Here, Adam eats the fruit because he did not wish to make Eve unhappy, "fearing she would waste away without his support, alienated from his affections, and that in this dissension would be her death" (11.42.59).

In either case, the first couple, in "loving too much," reflected a new paradigm of human relations in their fallen state, in which human attachments entail not only the loss of knowledge of God but the loss of self. By loving each other too much, they brought the pain and suffering of the loss of self into the human condition; ultimately, they also ushered in death, the most complete and terrifying loss of self known to humanity. Indeed, Augustine understands the destruction and suffering caused by the intimate attachment between these lifetime companions quite literally as a fall into "nothingness," though not into complete oblivion. God was merciful: "Man did not so fall away as to become absolutely nothing; but being turned toward himself, his being became more contracted than it was when he clung to Him who supremely is. Accordingly, to exist in himself . . . to be his own satisfaction after abandoning God, is not quite to become a nonentity, but to approximate to that" (City

14.13). By clinging to each other and forgetting God, Adam and Eve nearly lost themselves completely.

Punishment of the Soul

As just punishment for their disobedience to his "very brief and very light precept," God abandoned the soul to itself, to live in bondage to itself (*City* 14.15). This bondage consisted of two factors: the soul's disobedience to itself and the body's disobedience to the soul. In the former instance, no longer are the higher and lower reason in harmony. Rather, they fight against each other, resulting in the "sickness in the mind" that God has allowed. In his *Confessions*, Augustine gives a moving depiction of this torment of the soul:

> Whence comes this monstrous state? Why should it be? Mind commands body, and it obeys forthwith. Mind gives orders to itself, and it is resisted. Mind gives orders to the hand to move, and so easy is it that command can scarce be distinguished from execution. Yet mind is mind, while hand is body. Mind commands mind to will: there is no difference here, but it does not do so. . . . I say that it commands itself to will a thing: it would not give this command unless it willed it, and yet it does not do what it wills. (8.9.21)

In this state, the soul is in constant conflict with itself. Emotions rage against reason, reason battles with the heart, the soul succumbs to worldly temptation in spite of itself. In such a state, the human person can find no peace.

While Augustine is clear that the disobedience of Adam and Eve was caused by disobedience in the soul, and hence it is fitting that the soul should war constantly against itself, Augustine purports that the effects of our disobedience to God are demonstrated even more vibrantly in the rebellion of the body against the will. Moreover, while most of our bodily parts remain in the service of the will and rarely give us any trouble, there is one site in which the disharmony of the soul and body is conspicuously felt: the sexual organs. More specifically, the penis.[26] This disobedience was experienced immediately after Adam and Eve disobeyed God:

"They experienced a new motion of their flesh, which had become disobedient to them, in strict retribution of their own disobedience to God. For the soul, reveling in its own liberty and scorning to serve God, was itself deprived of the command it had formerly maintained over the body" (City 13.13). According to Augustine, no other experience is quite like that of the sexual organ's rebellion against the will. Even when one is moved to extreme anger and violent passion, the body is still under the command of the will, "for he who in his anger rails at or even strikes someone, could not do so were not his tongue and hand moved by the authority of the will" (City 14.19). Not so with sexual passion. Even when one wants to move the penis at will, in accord with his lust, he is at times unable to do so: "But even those who delight in this pleasure are not moved to it at their own will. . . . But sometimes this lust importunes them in spite of themselves, and sometimes fails them when they desire to feel it, so that although lust rages in the mind, it stirs not in the body" (City 14.16). The war within the soul is played out on the battlefield of the body.[27] The human person, unable to control its passions and its body, unable to do what it wills, inflicts pain upon itself, on its most intimate relationships, and on society as a whole.[28]

The Constitution of the Soul

At this point it is necessary to examine more closely why God's "abandoning the soul to itself" should cause so much pain and suffering—even death—in the human realm. In her article "Vision: The Eye of the Body," Margaret Miles describes the significance of Augustine's belief that the soul is ultimately formed and shaped by the objects on which it focuses its visual attention. She describes the classical belief that there is a "visual ray" generated by the mind that literally connects the mind to the objects that it sees. In this "seeing" comes "understanding." Moreover, the object seen is permanently drawn into the soul as the soul literally absorbs the image of the object into itself. This image is retained in the memory, the seat of all knowledge and hence, of the self. According to Augustine, then, vision "is a two-way street." In forming images made "out of itself," the soul "gathers them into itself, for in forming them it gives them something of its own substance; it also retains that by which it may freely judge of the nature of these images" (Trinity 10.5.7).

Further, the soul is considered to be a malleable, fluid sort of entity. Not the "bounded self" assumed by twenty-first-century people, the self is rather a constant flow of vital energies.[29] These energies, this self, must be consciously formed. Hence, Augustine sees the "formless flow" of the male "loss of seed" in ejaculation and of female menstruation as a symbol of the mind, which "without the force of discipline" will remain "unseemly fluid and dissipated."[30] By turning from God and relying only on itself, the mind will be scattered and spilled, emptied of itself and wasted away. Spending itself on objects of the external world, it quite literally loses itself, being formed in their image instead of the image of God. The mind can no longer remember its true nature. If it cannot remember itself, it cannot know itself; if it does not know itself, it cannot know God, and the self is lost.

Augustine vividly describes the experience of this dissipation, this loss of self and of God, that occurred in his adolescent relationships: "[Lust and desire] clouded over and darkened my soul . . . and swept my feeble youth over the crags of desire and plunged me into a whirlpool of shameful deeds. . . . I wandered farther away from you, and you let me go. I was tossed and spilt out in my fornications; I flowed out and boiled over in them, but you kept silent" (Confessions 2.2.2). Becoming a "land of want" to himself, he continued to "foam over" and "waste himself" upon sensuous and temporal pleasures. As he departed from God and entangled himself in earthly delights, the passions of his lusts had free rein over his reason. In this state of disorder, his emotions could only "tear the mind apart and dissipate it, making life most miserable."[31] Augustine believed that quite literally, as the mind slips away from itself and loses itself, it risks losing everything, including eternal life. He illustrates at length how this forgetting of oneself happens in even seemingly "trivial" matters: "Out in the field . . . a chase [between a dog and a rabbit] will perhaps draw me away from some important thought and draw me to itself. . . . Unless you show me my weakness, and quickly warn me, either to rise up to you from the sight through some reflection, or to spurn the whole incident and pass by it, I stand there vacant-minded. . . . My life is filled with such incidents, and my one hope is your exceeding mercy" (Confessions 10.35.57).

If such dissipation can occur through mundane acts, how much more intense is this vacant-mindedness, "forgetting" of oneself, in sexual orgasm? In this experience, lust takes possession of the body and "moves the whole man," resulting in the most intense of all physical pleasures;

significantly, the intensity of this pleasure is so great that "at the moment of time in which it is consummated, all mental activity is suspended" (*City* 14.16). In his writings in response to Julian, Augustine argues that the sexual experience is qualitatively different from that of eating because of the inability to think during the former:

> We often not only think, but even dispute, about important matters at feasts, even between morsels of food and sips of drink; we pay close attention when listening and speaking; we learn what we wish to know, or recall if it is read to us. But that pleasure about which you argue with me so contentiously, does it not engage the whole soul and body, and does not this extremity of pleasure result in a kind of submersion of the mind itself, even if it is approached with a good intention, that is, for the purpose of procreating children, since in its very operation it allows no one to think, I do not say of wisdom, but of anything at all?[32]

Later on in his argument with Julian he invokes Cicero to shore up his argument that even pagan philosophers agreed with his premise:

> You give elegant praise to your protégé when you truly say that one cannot think about anything else during intercourse. This is entirely true. What can one think about when the very mind with which he thinks is so absorbed in this carnal pleasure? He whose words I quoted in the foregoing book [Cicero] spoke well when he said: "When its activity is most intense, it is most hostile to philosophy. Intense pleasure of the body is incompatible with great thought. What man, under the power of this the most intense of pleasures, can use his mind or carry on a process of reasoning, or think about anything at all?" Not even you could have made a more serious charge against the lust you praise except by admitting that in its onslaught no one can think about what is holy.[33]

Hence, for Augustine, even a righteous man who thinks about procreation prior to intercourse "cannot think about this when experiencing it."[34] We quite literally "lose our minds" completely in orgasm and, in so doing, we lose ourselves. As such, we also forget God.[35] Since forgetting God is the root of all misery, it is certainly best to refrain from all sexual activity, if one is able.[36] In doing so, one will be better able not only to maintain control of one's bodily passions, but also to maintain possession of oneself. For Augustine, sexual pleasure just is not worth the risk, for, as he queries, "In what way, pray, can anyone possess something if he has lost his mind?" (*Trinity* 14.14.19).

As I have shown in the preceding discussion, Augustine firmly believed that if not properly monitored, one always "loses" oneself in intimate relationships. For "love is generally needy and poor, so that its outpouring makes it subordinate to the objects it loves."[37] Sexual relationships predicated on sexual desire are simply the most complete and intense human relationships and therefore the most vulnerable to this type of loss. Since the soul takes on the shape and form of the objects upon which it pours its affections and attention, it becomes dependent on them to the point where it cannot even recognize itself if these objects and their images are stripped away.[38] That is why the death of a beloved friend or the loss of a favorite object can be so disorienting and painful. As Augustine experienced it, when one pours oneself out in such a manner, one is really emptying oneself of one's very life and soul. Thus one must reverse this pattern. By "cleansing the eye of the mind" and gathering oneself up from the wreckage of one's relationships and turning inward, one can begin to truly nourish the soul on true food, which is God.

Continence as Remembrance

This process of turning our affections and longing toward God is what Augustine calls continence. It is essentially an activity of remembering. By re-collecting ourselves, gathering ourselves, essentially "pulling ourselves together" we stop the outward flow of our soul's energy. Through the practice of continence, "he who was lost is found." It is thus in the activity of remembering, which occurs in the "fields and spacious palaces" of memory,[39] that one "encounters and recalls" oneself (*Confessions* 10.8.12, 14). One gains true knowledge of oneself as dependent wholly upon God. In fact, when one turns inward into one's memory, one discovers that all knowledge resides in the memory; moreover, all knowledge is an activity of re-membering, of continence.

In the *Confessions* Augustine discusses this phenomenon at length. Delving into the deep caverns of the memory he ascertains that it contains knowledge that he had never "learned" before, knowledge that had never been implanted by means of "the portals of [his] flesh" but that he recognized as true even so (10.10.17). But this recognition of knowledge and truth is not a spontaneous process. Rather, it takes a lot of work. It takes thought and action: "By acts of thought we gather together and collect as it were things that memory contained here and there and without any order, and then observe them and see to it that they be placed near at hand as it were in that very memory, where they previously lay scattered and neglected. Thus they will occur easily to the mind already made familiar with them" (10.11.18). This is a process that must be constantly renewed: "If I cease to recall these things for a short space of time, they are again submerged and slip down into still deeper hiding places" (10.11.18). Subsequently, we must constantly collect, gather, and remember that which we desire to have present to ourselves. We know things by remembering them; if we fail to remember, we no longer have knowledge of them.

As previously mentioned, in *The Trinity* Augustine pushes this further. In his musings on how the human self can indeed reflect the image of God, he recognizes that the memory, understanding, and will must all work together if we are to have any knowledge at all. One cannot know a thing unless one also *remembers* and understands it; one cannot understand a thing unless one also knows it and *wills* to understand it, nor can one will something unless one remembers and *understands* what one wills (10.11.17). These three are "mutually referred to one another," and as such are "not three substances, but one substance" (10.11.18). Augustine has discovered in the mind what he considers to be the very image of God imprinted on our souls.

How, then, do we gain knowledge of this God if not from our memory? In his attempt to go beyond memory to find God, Augustine realizes he cannot do so, for "if I find you apart from memory, I am unmindful of you. How then shall I find you, if I do not remember you?" (*Confessions* 10.17.26). He concludes that God "deigns" to reside in our memory; if he did not, we could not know him. We could not enjoy the happy life that consists of rejoicing "over you, to you and because of you: there is no other" (10.22.32). Thus even before we "consciously" remember him, God resides in our memory. All we need do is have the will to think on him, to remember him: "When I shall cleave to you with all my being, no more will there be pain and toil for me. My life will be life indeed, filled wholly with you" (10.28.39). In order to remember God, we must "collect" and remember ourselves. For if we forget ourselves, we forget God, and in this double act of forgetting, we become miserable and lost.

The model of continence, then, takes on added significance. It is not simply the practice of monitoring our sexual and other passions by which we lose ourselves. Rather, it is a means of self-integration and self-control precisely because it is a method of gathering, of re-collecting, of re-membering one's self. Through continent behavior one can ensure that one will not "pour out" oneself onto the sand. By constantly re-collecting oneself, one will never lose oneself. It is not surprising, then, that only in this re-collection of oneself, this re-membering of oneself, that one will reflect the image of God in which one was created, the God who perpetually remembers, knows, and loves himself. And just as God does not risk losing himself when he loves us, in loving this God we no longer risk losing ourselves. It is to this point that we now turn.

The Mindful Love of God

As I have demonstrated above, Augustine used the model of sexual orgasm and male ejaculation to describe the inevitable loss of self and subsequent pain and suffering that occurs when one inordinately loves objects or persons unworthy of one's full attention. Yet as Margaret Miles has demonstrated in *Desire and Delight*, Augustine also models his notion of spiritual pleasure around the panting and sighing, swelling and spilling of male sexual pleasure. The language he uses to express his love for God is laden with passionate sexual imagery. Some of his most beautiful prayers resemble the anguished utterances of a lover bursting with desire for the beloved. In the *Confessions* he exclaims: "You have blazed forth with light, and have shone upon me, and you have put my blindness to flight! You have sent forth fragrance, and I have drawn my breath, and I pant after you. I have tasted you, and I hunger and thirst after you. You have touched me, and I have burned for your peace. . . . O Love, who are forever aflame and are never extinguished, O Charity, My God, set me aflame!" (10.27, 10.29). Yet in this love of God, even in the highest moments of contemplative joy, Augustine does not lose himself or "forget" himself. Reflecting on the vision of God he shared with his mother at Ostia, he does not describe an ecstatic eclipse of the soul, an apophatic transcendence of reason and comprehension. Rather, he describes it as a moment of "understanding," the attainment of eternal Wisdom in a "swift thought" in which he heard God's Word uttered by God himself (*Confessions* 9.10.25). With no "tumult of flesh" or earthly sounds to hinder him, Augustine attained a moment of clear understanding and insight. He remained wholly in himself, as God filled his soul with Wisdom and light.

What Augustine experienced and what his philosophy subsequently explained is that we cannot love God unless we are mindful of him, unless we remember him and know and understand that we remember him. And we cannot be mindful of God unless we are mindful of ourselves, for otherwise we would not know that we knew and loved God. Thus, the joy we experience in the love of God is the very antithesis of that experienced in the height of sexual pleasure. For while in orgasm "all mental activity is suspended" and we thereby forget ourselves completely in that instant, in the contemplative love of God, we are more present to ourselves than we have ever been before. It is in loving God that we most fully reflect the image of God in which we are created, a God who is always present to himself because he is always knowing, loving, and remembering himself. Mirroring this God, we are fully present to ourselves.

Moreover, in this love of God, one is freed to experience both culturally masculine and feminine aspects of love and the erotic. Augustine states that it is his desire to be receptive, to be "ravished," to be "subdued" by his lover. In "stretching out desire as widely" as he can, he offers his "bosom and lap" to his lover. Becoming submissive, becoming "feminine," he readies himself to be "entered" and to receive his God.[40] In short, he becomes the bride to Christ's bridegroom. In turning to that which is higher, instead of that which is "lower" as one does when one loves another's body or another's imperfect soul for its own sake, Augustine does not risk losing himself; rather, he can finally express the full vitality of his passion. He can then, indeed, ascend, arise, "enter in to the Joy of the Lord," to pour himself out on this receptive lover, in whom he will be "absorbed" and hidden away "within its deepest joys" (*Confessions* 9.10.25). Evidently for Augustine, if God is one's lover, one can be penetrated and poured forth simultaneously and yet not disappear. One can experience the wonder of spiritual, erotic union.

As we have seen, one does not "lose" oneself when one gives oneself to God, the one for whom we are made, that which is superior to oneself. But the question remains: How, then, can God give himself to us? How can God "pour himself out" into human flesh and human soul and not risk losing himself, emptying himself into something lower than himself, something that cannot possibly contain it, as is the case when humans spill their souls into bodies and other humans?

The answer, simply, if rather crudely, is because God is God. Nothing is impossible for God. But more specifically, God is a Trinity that is always remembering, knowing, and loving itself. There is nothing God can do to change this fact. God can never forget himself. In all his activities, God is constantly "in possession" of himself, always united, always one, always three. God is always mindful of himself. In the incarnation of the Word, therefore, the Son did not lose himself, although he emptied himself into human flesh.[41] By emptying himself into human form, he did not lose his divinity but, rather, took on our humanity in order that he could become an example for us by which we could perceive and understand our need to return to God (*Trinity* 7.3.5). In like manner, the Holy Spirit, who inflames our soul with longing for God by "diffusing" God's love into our hearts, is not made "less" than itself by this action, although through it, the whole Trinity is "poured forth in our hearts" and "dwells" in us (*Trinity* 15.18.32). Hence, even though God is poured upon us and into us, he is not "scattered about." Even though he fills all things with himself, he is not dispersed and dissipated. He remains all in all (*Confessions* 1.3.3). God and humans can therefore enjoy the fullness of passionate love for each other without the fear of death and annihilation.

Psychological Analyses of Augustine's Relationships

Augustine's anxious fear of human relations has not gone unnoticed by his many psychoanalytic interpreters.[42] While the temptation toward psychoanalytic reductionism is a risk in any such interpretation, given the feminist insistence on the relationship between experience and ways of knowing and theologizing, the attempt to understand the deep-seated, perhaps unconscious, reasons *why* Augustine experienced intense relationships as ones of loss may prove fruitful, not only in our attempt to understand Augustine, but also in our hopes to create the conditions necessary for both just interpersonal relationships and empowering constructs of God.[43]

Thus far, theorists who have offered psychological readings of Augustine tend to emphasize either his early oedipal conflict and his undue

attachment to his mother or the preoedipal narcissistic wounds he endured in childhood as a result of thwarted trust and emotional neglect.
While it is not possible to offer here a lengthy discussion of each of
these approaches, suffice it to say that the oedipal reading tends to view
Augustine as a man fearful of intense personal relationships because of
Monica's persistent possessiveness and control, which led to his incom-
plete individuation from her; the narcissistic reading finds Augustine to
be fearful of intense personal relationships because Monica's manipulative "possessiveness could not be an adequate substitute"[44] for Augustine's
infantile need "to be held internally and externally."[45] Hence, lacking
the experience of "loving attention from his parents," Augustine never
fully learned to love and to be loved, never trusted that the Other would
return the love he gave in kind.[46] He therefore eschewed intense emotional attachments, preferring to distance himself from them and to keep
himself free from the pain these relationships would inevitably entail.

What is clear to the perceptive feminist reader of these accounts is
that in such readings, Augustine's psychological problems appear to rest
squarely on the shoulders of Monica, the "manipulative," "possessive,"
"domineering," "rigid, "constrictive," "controlling," and "devouring"
mother to whom he ultimately surrendered through his conversion to her
beliefs, her church, and her God.[47] Even accounts such as that proffered
by J. G. Kristo, who attempts to make sense of Augustine's psyche
through the use of Nancy Chodorow's analysis of the (patriarchal) relationship between mother and infant, paint Monica as an unloving and
unempathetic creature intent solely on living her life's ambitions through
her son.[48] Although such a rendering should not be surprising to one
even cursorily familiar with the most popular schools of twentieth-century psychology, it is still rather depressing to find that the limitations
(but not the brilliance) of Augustine's life and work are a result of his
mother's apparently overwhelming faults. But if we were to take seriously
the insights of feminists such as Chodorow who have struggled to unravel
the oppressive and debilitating underpinnings of Western (Christian) relational patterns and psychology and then apply a feminist critique to
Augustine's life and work, we may yet gain an understanding of Augustine's psychological makeup and a view toward a "way out" for the rest of
us.

In her work *The Bonds of Love*, Jessica Benjamin offers us such a possibility. According to Benjamin, most psychoanalytic theories are founded

on the premise that the child's primary psychological goal is to separate and individuate itself from the overwhelming oneness and unity with the mother it experiences as an infant. In this model, the assumption is that unity and relationship are the primary, if infantile, experience; autonomy and independence are the mature ends in which successful psychological growth results.[49] In other words, relationship is the problem, autonomy is the solution. Classic theories thus view individuation as a process of "disentanglement" from the infant's original symbiotic state with the mother. They therefore "cast experiences of union, merger, and self-other harmony as regressive opposites to differentiation and self-other distinction" (46, 47). Permeable boundaries and experiences of union and connection with the other are not seen as positive, mature, and healthy responses to life lived in community with other subjects but are, rather, viewed as threats to the tenuous, autonomous self. As Benjamin states, "Merging was a dangerous form of undifferentiation, a sinking back into the sea of oneness—the 'oceanic feeling' that Freud told Romain Roland he frankly couldn't relate to. The original sense of oneness was seen as absolute, as 'limitless narcissism,' and, therefore, regression to it would impede development and prevent separation" (47). Most important for our purposes, Benjamin notes that "in its most extreme version, this view of differentiation pathologized the sensation of love: relaxing the boundaries of the self in communion with others threatened the identity of the isolate self. Yet this oneness was also seen as ultimate pleasure, eclipsing the pleasure of difference. Oneness was not seen as a state that could coexist with (enhance and be enhanced by) the sense of separateness" (47). Augustine's fear of oneness and the subsequent "loss of self" this entailed—as well as his continuing use of erotic language of euphoria and joy in regard to his relation with God—are quite readily understood through such a theory, particularly if we assume that Monica was a peculiarly self-involved, overwhelming, devouring oedipal mother.

However, what is ignored, or better, assumed, in such traditional theories is that for the infantile mind, the mother is merely an object to be conquered and controlled; it is the father who offers the infant a model of subjectivity and independence—and a way out of the overwhelming, smothering oneness it feels with the mother. The mother, not viewed as a subject in her own right, as an Other capable of surviving infantile anxiety and rage, is subsumed into the infant's own psyche. Thus, the infant is left alone in the tyranny of its own psyche, until the father steps in.

The father, seen as a subject separate from the infant self, offers the infant a strong, stable Other who can hold the infant's rage and ego and "survive" intact. Through its encounter with the father, the infant learns that it is not alone in the world. Through the father the infant learns that there is a reality outside of itself with which it can and must engage. Hence, through its subsequent identification with the father, the infant learns to separate itself from the all-encompassing grasp of the over-whelming mother. The infant moves from oneness to autonomy, and in so doing, the infant grows, matures, and becomes a successful subject in its own right. Any threat to this individuation causes serious anxiety and fear; hence, intense mutual relation is suspect and to be avoided. Needless to say, this process is all the more pronounced in the male infant.[50]

However, Benjamin argues that given their intricate analyses of infantile development, traditional psychological theories lack an equally powerful analysis of "the structure of gender domination" that undergirds Western rationality and psychology.[51] As the Other in western culture, woman—and in particular, the mother—has not been perceived as a "vitally real presence but a cognitively perceived object" (78). And this is not only the view of the infant but of the mother herself. A woman's learned reluctance to assert her own subjectivity and her "willingness to offer recognition without expecting it in return" results in the infant's inability to perceive her as a subject in her own right, a subject capable of representing a world outside of the infant's own ego (78). Whence the infant's fear of being subsumed in this "oceanic oneness" with the mother and its anxious strivings toward differentiation through identification with the father and rejection of relationality and connection.

Benjamin argues that this lack of recognition of the subjectivity of women, and particularly of mothers, is what has been missing, not only in traditional psychoanalytic theory, but also in the social and personal lives of women: in other words, this is *what happens in real life*" (214). The child is only capable of perceiving the mother "as a subject in her own right if the mother *is* one" (214). Historically and psychoanalytically reduced to a "mere extension of a two-month-old" (23), women and mothers have not been recognized as full subjects in their own right and oftentimes do not even see themselves as such. Hence, they are unable to successfully provide the subjective recognition a child needs but are instead reduced in the child's mind (and in society's and often her own) to a mere object. The give-and-take of recognition is thus unable to fully take place in the infant-mother relationship. The child becomes overwhelmed by the all-encompassing ego/mother and seeks escape through the separation and rejection of the mother signified by moving toward the father.

Theologically, as in the case of Augustine, we should not be surprised, then, to find the need for a "fail-safe" yet distant God upon whom one can wholly depend, but in whom one will not be "swallowed up" and destroyed, a God whom one can love but, in loving, one will not "lose" oneself. Following this traditional, malestream assumption, James Dittes argues that this is, in essence "*the* religious quest": to find something in which the human soul can "lodge itself, vigorously, intensely, intimately . . . safely."[52] Ultimately, the soul yearns to "pour itself out—but not upon the sand." The desire to be "totally present, unreservedly committed to another, 'all there' in firmly reliable bond, to love God with the whole heart, whole soul, whole mind . . . [to] trust unconditionally and absolutely—this is the religious impulse." The assumption here is that the soul "*must* make absolute investment" (emphasis added) in someone or something.[53] In other words, in this traditional malestream reading, it is the very nature of the soul to seek an absolutely trustworthy and fail-safe bond with another, in which no loss of self or pain will interfere. And this is what Augustine sought, and found, in his doctrine of the Trinity.

But, Benjamin asks, what if the mother can and does recognize and assert her own subjectivity? What if she demands and receives recognition by the infant as a subject separate from itself, yet a subject related to the infant in caring, mutual connection? What then? Would the infant necessarily fear connection as an adult? Would it eschew that "oceanic feeling" of love and oneness as a regressive, fear-inducing threat? Would it necessarily seek a sense of *absolute* trust and safety in a powerful but distant Other? Or might the infant learn to live in connection with others, albeit a tenuous one at that? Might it not seek connection with others in the midst of pain of loss, knowing that loss is not the end of the story and that connection will come around again? Might it not seek a God who also feels pain and loss, but who maintains connection nonetheless? Her answers are quite enlightening with regard to our current discussion.

The key to Benjamin's theory is the notion of intersubjectivity; key to intersubjectivity is the notion that the task of psychological growth and maturation entails not only the task of individuation but also the task of retaining connections to other subjects. Building on nonpsychoanalytic models of development such as Piaget's, intersubjective theory sees the infant as "active and stimulus-seeking" rather than as a passive entity seeking only the release of tension through the satisfaction of innate needs through the object of the mother. Rather, the innate sociability of the infant and its desire to relate to the world *as* world, as other than itself, is assumed. In this view, the individual grows and develops in relation to other subjects; the infant is not a single monad that views the outside world—and most specifically, the mother—as an object, as part of its own self. As Benjamin notes, central to this perspective is that "the other whom the self meets is also a self, a subject in his or her own right. It assumes that we are able and need to recognize that other subject as different and yet alike, as an other who is capable of sharing similar mental experiences. Thus, the idea of intersubjectivity reorients the conception of the psychic world from a subject's relations to its object toward a subject meeting another subject."[54] In this view, then, "the infant is never totally undifferentiated (symbiotic) with the mother, but is primed from the beginning to be interested in and to distinguish itself from the world of others" (18). In accepting this already innate sense of individuation in the infant, the psychological task then becomes twofold. No longer is it seen simply as the need to individuate and separate from others, as in the traditional model. Rather, the task now is to separate but also to remain connected to others. As Benjamin notes, the issue is "not how we become free of the other, but how we actively engage and make ourselves known in relationship to the other" (18).

Within this intersubjective theory, the importance of being recognized *as* a self by another self is fundamental to growth and development. The process of recognition is essentially a reflexive one. As a child grows and begins to assert itself, it comes to view itself as a creative, effective agent as it is recognized as such by another subject: "recognition is the essential response, the constant companion of assertion. The subject declares, 'I am, I do,' and then waits for the response, 'You are, you have done'" (21). Benjamin argues, however, that what most theories of recognition miss is the need for *mutual* recognition between subjects. As Benjamin puts it, it is as if the child notes to itself, "reality recognized me so I recognize it—wholly, with faith and trust, with no grudge or self-constraint" (41). For recognition to "work," to carry the force powerful enough to sustain the self's need for it, not only do we need to be recognized *by* the other, but we need to recognize the other "as a separate person who is like us but distinct" (23). The child must therefore see the mother as a subject in her own right, rather than as an object or extension of itself. If the mother is not viewed as such—as was quite possibly the case with Monica—recognition by her will not be enough for the child to feel that it has been recognized as an agent and a self, capable of acting on and in the world: an Augustinian fear of intimacy and an Augustinian doctrine of God would likely result.

This Augustinian solution is understandable for two significant reasons. First, such an exchange between mother and child is not without tension, or paradox, as Benjamin refers to it. Second, within patriarchal culture, this tension is quite often broken; substituted for it is the seemingly less anxiety-producing dynamic of dominance and subordination. Indeed, this exchange is in itself structured on tension, on the careful negotiation between self and other, or better, self and another equally important self. It is predicated on the necessity of both self-assertion and recognition by another. To be a self necessitates that other selves have power to recognize us as selves. As selves, as individuals, we are dependent upon others to recognize us as such, and vice versa, and this necessitates that we recognize the other *as* other, yet an other capable and willing to share in and to understand my feelings and thoughts. One must acknowledge that "sameness and difference exist simultaneously in mutual recognition" (47). In sharing an exchange of mutual recognition, such as in the game of peekaboo, both infant and mother engage in the back-and-forth of self-assertion and mutual recognition. And in the recognition of themselves as interconnected yet distinct persons, they also find pleasure (30). Yet, perhaps most important for our purposes, such an intersubjective exchange is also predicated on a certain sense of loss and of the "complexity of life outside the garden" (223). For example, Benjamin notes that for a new mother this necessitates the recognition that " 'you' who are 'mine' are also different, new, outside of me. It thus includes the sense of loss that you are no longer inside me, no longer simply my fantasy of you, that we are no longer physically and psychically one, and I can no longer take care of you simply by taking care of my self" (15). Indeed, while this dynamic may most easily be seen and explained in the experience of the new mother, Benjamin shows how all experiences of mutual recognition entail a bit of this me/not me dynamic: "You belong to me, yet you are not . . . part of me. The joy I take in your existence must include *both* my connection to you and your independent existence—I recognize that you are real" (15). I need you, yet I cannot control you. And even if I succeeded in controlling you, you could no longer meet my needs.[55] In every encounter with you, you remain separate, distant; I cannot have you. And that is okay. It is, in fact, this distance that is the ground for our connection. Without distance, without separation, without loss, we would be one, and, as one, as "monad," I would be alone. Desperately so.

But with this distance, this separation between selves, intense, erotic attunement and connection with another can take place. Benjamin argues that if mother and child successfully negotiate the need for mutual recognition, connection will not be a seemingly life-threatening occurrence for adults; neither will loss. Rather, such persons will be able to maintain "more permeable" boundaries and to enter into states such as erotic love in which there is a "momentary suspension of boundaries" between myself and another, where one can let go and "lose" oneself in another in the safety of knowing that one will not be swallowed up or "lost": "The capacity to enter into states in which distinctness and union are reconciled underlies the most intense experience of adult erotic life. In erotic union we can experience that form of mutual recognition in which both partners *lose themselves in each other without loss of self*; they lose self-consciousness without loss of awareness. Thus early experiences of mutual recognition already prefigure the dynamics of erotic life" (emphasis added).[56] In such a view, sameness and difference, self and other, are held together yet apart in the act of mutual recognition. Oneness and separation coexist and, indeed, enhance one another (47).

The psychological task then becomes how to balance self and other, connection and loss—not wholly to disentangle oneself from the other or to avoid loss at all costs (46). For in recognizing the other, the self must "relinquish its claim to absoluteness." It must recognize that I am *not* the "king of the world." Nor are you. In this state, loss—of control, of you, of desires and dreams and hopes—is inevitable. But this loss is not the end of the world, nor of me. For I still exist, even in my vulnerability and pain. I still exist, in the mutual recognition I continue to maintain with you, with others, with the world. Loss is not the end of me, or of you. It is, rather, the foundation upon which we can be found again. For, while the logic of paradox acknowledges that the breakdown of recognition will occur, it also recognizes that recognition can once again be renewed (223).

Hence, Benjamin argues that such a theory—and, more important, practice—allows us to "counter the argument that human beings fundamentally desire the impossible absoluteness of oneness and perfection." Rather, we can see that "things don't have to be perfect, that, in fact it is *better* if they are not. It reminds us that in every experience of similarity and subjective sharing, there must be enough difference to create the feeling of reality, that a degree of imperfection 'ratifies' the existence of the world" (47). In such an interchange of assertion and recognition, two selves are not merged, and as such, they do not feel threatened by the exchange, but, rather, feel "fed" by it, "getting nourishment from the outside, rather than supplying everything for oneself" (47). The self indeed is experienced not as a monad but as a self that can interact with and rely upon others for sustenance and connection.

The implications of this psychology for a theology of relationality and trinity are immense. While Augustine has given us a clear example of the type of God-construct that may result from a cultural situation in which women and mothers are not accorded full subjectivity but are, rather, reduced to objects in the mind of their sons and their society, the possibilities for a different construction of God, one formed in the full recognition of women's subjectivity, are only beginning to take shape. Perhaps, if and when women en masse are seen and begin to see themselves as subjects, if and when relation and connection are understood to be fundamental to psychological and spiritual maturity, if and when separation and loss are viewed as inevitable and necessary conditions for connection, if and when oneness and difference are seen to coexist and even to mutually enhance each other—then, perhaps we will be able to envision a God that need not be absolute, distant, and "fail-safe." Perhaps we can then begin to envision a God who can hold us in our pain and loss, but who can also enable us to connect again, to love again, to lose again. I suspect that this God will bear little resemblance to Augustine's self-contained trinity of memory, understanding, and will.

Conclusion

As Sarah Coakley has noted, in the Western Christian tradition there exists an "unresolved antimony between the (acceptable) erotic desire for the divine on the one hand, and actual relations with people of the opposite sex on the other."[57] Augustine and his teachings have much to do with this. While I do not necessarily agree with Coakley that there are "*intrinsic*, if initially puzzling, connections between sexuality, spirituality and the Christian doctrine of the Trinity" (emphasis added), I do agree that *Augustine* made such a connection, albeit an implicit one, and therefore it is virtually impossible for Western Christians since his time to unravel this "'messy entanglement' of sexual desire and desire for God" that has become so much a part of the Christian tradition.[58]

As Peter Brown has noted, Augustine always longed for clear and unproblematic relationships, but for him, sex always seemed to get in the way. Carrying with them "the leaden echo of true delight," sexual relationships never fully satisfied.[59] Augustine could not imagine how sex could enhance a human relationship, because for him, it never did. He desired to give his whole self and soul to another and this he found impossible to do through the medium of the human body. Somehow, something always got lost in the translation. This loss was himself. But, as I have shown, we need to deepen this analysis. It is not simply that sex gets in the way; it is, rather, that the pain and confusion of the loss of one's self, which undergirds Augustine's whole doctrine of God and philosophy of human relationships, is symbolized and concretized in the act of sex. For this reason, sex was to be avoided.

Further, the matter of which came first—the philosophy or the experience—is akin to the old problem of the chicken and the egg. On the one hand, Neoplatonic philosophy was a valuable tool in helping Augustine understand this loss. Believing that the soul is meant to return to its creator, he could readily explain the feelings of frustration and lack associated with intimate human relationships, including sexual ones. By declaring true love to be that in which we love the soul of another *not in themselves* but simply as a means of loving God, he was able to "step back" from the intensity of personal relationships and gain some semblance of peace. This necessarily entailed his refraining from sexual relations, for they were the primary way in which we lose ourselves in another.

Moreover, with this philosophy, Augustine did not need to forego the passion of sexual relations altogether. In developing the doctrine of the Trinity as a unity of memory, understanding, and will, he ingeniously compensated for the gap between Neoplatonic philosophy and the Christian teaching of the Incarnation and the Gift of the Holy Spirit, for Christians believed that God poured himself out into humanity, but did not diminish himself in any way. In taking up aspects of Neoplatonic emanation theory, the return of the soul to the One/God need not be experienced as loss and diminishment, but in reality as its true destiny and ultimate fulfillment. By adopting this notion of the Trinity, Augustine could make sense of this seemingly self-emptying gesture. And he could retain the passion of his desires. Since he, as an image of God, would remain mindful of himself in his love for God, he did not risk the pain of loss he associated with intimate human relations. No longer need he fear the pain of human desire so eloquently expressed throughout his works.

Yet, on the other hand, one might well argue (as many feminist scholars before me have done) that Neoplatonic philosophy was a cause of, not a solution to, Augustine's problem. Primarily, in a world and culture in which women were not encouraged to view themselves as subjects in and of themselves and in which they were not viewed as such by others, we have the necessary if not sufficient conditions for the psychostructural construction of a fearful, anxious, monadic, "masculine" self, incapable of sustaining and withstanding the inevitable tension and loss of human relationships. Further, if one believes, as I do, that our experiences are shaped in part by the discourses and worldviews in which we participate, then Augustine's deployment of a thoroughly hierarchical model of relationships could not *but* lead him to the sorts of theological conclusions he makes. Since Augustine was wholly convinced that the body was an inferior, if necessary, aspect of the self, and because he was unable to view women as equal partners in relationships, it is not surprising that he could not experience joy and peace in his passionate sexual experiences. Moreover, if we use a model of a malleable soul subject to dispersion, it is not surprising that his most passionate and intimate experiences were experienced as a "loss of self," and that this loss was not embraced as a natural, potentially enriching aspect of the human condition but, rather, as one to be avoided at all costs. However, at this point, more foregrounding of the Neoplatonic notions of emanation and return to the One/God in his theology might have mitigated some of his anxieties about the loss of self in the process of return through human connectedness and then to the ultimate union with God. Finally, it is clear that his doctrine of the Trinity, understood as "mind" never vulnerable to the loss of itself, is derived from and is in reaction to his very personal and painful experiences, yet personal experiences most likely shared with other men and women in his patriarchal society and culture.

Ultimately, Augustine longed for safe, passionate relations, sexual and otherwise, that entailed no fear of loss, no possibility of pain. The Christian Neoplatonic philosophy to which he adhered and the doctrine of God that he constructed offered him a way to deal with the inevitable pain of loss. However, it did so at the expense of intimacy and love. What

Augustine expresses so eloquently in his tortured attempts to understand how one loses oneself when loving another is the real vulnerability and risk we take when we allow ourselves fully to love another person. To love and to feel as if one is lost in the other, that "the two have become one," always entails a risk, a chance that the other will be taken from us or leave of his or her own accord. In the end, it was the pain of *this* loss of loved ones—of his childhood friend, his mother, his sexual partner—that ultimately led Augustine to recognize how closely tied and mingled his life, his soul, had become with those he loved. It is this loss, this grief, that he struggled to avoid for the remainder of his days and that kept him at an emotional distance from those he loved.

Feminist scholars who hope to rehabilitate sexuality and the trinity from the grips of an Augustinian framework can, I believe, still learn something from Augustine if we listen attentively to the pain of loss to which he speaks. Unlike Augustine, however, we must face head-on the vulnerability, risk, and pain that are part and parcel of loving relations, including sexual relations. We therefore cannot make facile assertions about the inherent goodness, divinity, or sacramentality of sexual relations and the erotic.[60] To do so is to ignore not only the experience of loss that accompanies the death or departure of a loved one, but also the experience of loss in every form of relationship, the experience of two individuals "missing" each other even when connecting, of one's beloved being just beyond one's grasp. But it is also to ignore the experiences of those many women and men for whom sex is not a safe, divine, or sacramental experience but is, rather, an experience of betrayal and violation.[61] Moreover, we cannot speak of the trinity simply as a model of "organic" connection or of "perfect" harmony and unity among equals.[62] Feminist attempts to use the notion of trinity as a model in which diversity may be found in unity, and vice versa, in which uniqueness and individuality can coexist, in which mutuality with respect for difference can be held together: all these would benefit in taking seriously the further insight offered us by Benjamin, that such "harmony" and unity, mutuality and connection, always entail the risk—no, the inevitability—of loss and pain, of misconnection and nonrecognition as well. But, if connection is maintained and the subjectivity of all is admitted and encouraged, such loss need not be a devastating one. Rather, it can be held and healed through subsequent reconnection and recognition.

Margaret Miles maintains that Augustine, despite his vigorous denials, illustrated that "the sexual is a way the soul speaks."[63] But for him, bodily, physical eroticism was a taste of death; the sex and the passion it evoked had to be spiritualized. Those who maintain that human sexuality and intimate relations can in fact be passionate experiences of life, not death, as well as experiences of the divine, not the degenerate, must work to make this so: our first step will be to work toward the acceptance of women's full subjectivity. In so doing, we must also work to incorporate both the anxieties of "losing oneself" in a beloved and the pain of grief at the loss of love into a full-bodied, full-souled theology of sexuality. In so doing, our theologies of God and the Trinity cannot but be wholly transformed as well.

Notes

1. Mary Daly, Gyn/Ecology: The Metaethics of Radical Feminism (Boston: Beacon Press, 1978), is the quintessential example of this feminist critique and dismissal of the Christian Trinity, asserting that "it is 'sublime' (and therefore disguised) mythos, the perfect all-male marriage, the ideal all-male family, the best boys' club, the model monastery, the supreme Men's Association, the mold for all varieties of male monogender mating" (38). However, she does not forego the notion of "trinity" per se, as she recoups the "Triple Goddess" tradition from which she believes the Christian Trinity derives. See Pure Lust: Elemental Feminist Philosophy (Boston: Beacon Press, 1984). For the latter approach see Jane Williams, "The Doctrine of the Trinity: A Way Forward for Feminists?" in Women's Voices: Essays in Contemporary Feminist Theology, ed. Teresa Elwes (London: Marshall Pickering/ HarperCollins, 1992), 31.

2. The feminist literature reexamining the Western construction of sexuality is immense. In the field of theology, see especially the work of Carter Heyward, Anne Gilson, James Nelson, Kathleen Sands, Pamela Cooper-White, Marie Fortune, Carol Adams, Margaret Miles, Sheila Briggs, Rita Nakashima Brock, Marvin Ellison, Christine Gudorf and Mary Pellauer, among many others.

3. See Sarah Coakley, "'Batter My Heart . . .'? On Sexuality, Spirituality, and the Christian Doctrine of the Trinity," Graven Images 2 (1995): 74–83 (reprinted from the Harvard Divinity Bulletin, 23, no. 3/4 (1994): 12–17) and "Creaturehood Before God: Male and Female," Theology 93 (1990): 343–54. For other such attempts, see also Sally McFague, Models of God: Theology for an Ecological, Nuclear Age (Philadelphia: Fortress Press, 1987); Rita Nakashima Brock, Journeys by Heart: A Christology of Erotic Power (New York: Crossroad, 1995); Carter Heyward, Touching Our Strength: The Erotic as Power and the Love of God (San Francisco: Harper and Row, 1989); Kathleen Sands, Escape from Paradise: Evil and Tragedy in Feminist Theology (Minneapolis: Fortress Press, 1994); Mary Grey, "The Core of our Desire: Reimaging the Trinity," Theology 93 (1990): 363–72.

4. Coakley uses this phrase quite often to discuss the complexity of this relation. See Coakley, "'Batter My Heart . . .'?" for one such example.

5. Margaret Miles, Desire and Delight: A New Reading of Augustine's Confessions (New York: Crossroad, 1992), 76. Here Miles is quoting James Hillman, Myth of Analysis (Evanston: Northwestern University Press, 1972).

6. I maintain the belief that human sexuality and eroticism are culturally constructed. The emphases of particular cultures determine what will be deemed erotic within that culture. Much work in feminist theory has been focused on demonstrating how sexuality has been constructed as

negative and evil in Western culture; these scholars then attempt to show that sexuality is indeed divine, or at least divinely inspired. However, I believe that we cannot simply assume the divine nature of eros, especially in the face of abundant evidence to the contrary, as manifested in sexual violence and exploitation. Instead, we must work to make sexuality an expression of the divine. The reformulation of Christian doctrines of the Trinity is one important step in this process.

7. For example, see James E. Dittes, "Augustine: Search for a Fail-Safe God to Trust," in *The Hunger of the Heart: Reflections on the "Confessions" of Augustine*, ed. Donald Capps and James E. Dittes (West Lafayette, Ind.: Society for the Scientific Study of Religion, 1990).

8. Augustine, in dialogue with Julian, clearly demonstrates his position that marriage is a good instituted by God and that married sexual relations are therefore good as well, if and only if they are intended for procreation. However, he consistently maintains that the sexual desire, or concupiscence, that motivates these sexual acts is sinful; indeed, in his more polemical moments, he argues vociferously that this sexual desire is in fact evil, albeit forgivable, if experienced and acted upon within the marriage relation. Julian, I believe, may very well have been intending to confront this ambivalence, deeming that such sexual desire was not inherently sinful nor evil but, rather, a "good" passion created by God for the purposes of progeny. For a thorough explication of Augustine's position on the evil of concupiscence and the good of marriage, see *Against Julian*, trans. Matthew A. Schumacher, *The Fathers of the Church*, vol. 35 (New York: The Fathers of the Church, 1957) and *On Marriage and Concupiscence*, in *St. Augustine's Anti-Pelagian Works*, ed. Philip Schaff (Grand Rapids, Mich.: Eerdmans, 1956). For many of Augustine's essential writings on human sexuality and marriage, as well as discussions of the salient points in these texts, see Elizabeth Clark, ed. *St. Augustine on Marriage and Sexuality* (Washington, D.C.: Catholic University of America Press, 1996).

9. As I examine in this essay, intimate relations between men and women are particularly difficult to sustain because of the lack of subjectivity accorded to women in patriarchal societies. Love between two men was much more easily understood in Augustine's thought, for men were thought to be equals, while women were God-ordained inferior helpmates.

10. Peter Brown, "Augustine and Sexuality," in *Protocol of the Forty-sixth Colloquy*, ed. Mary Ann Donovan (Berkeley, Calif.: Center for Hermeneutical Studies in Hellenistic and Modern Culture, 1983), 1.

11. Carter Heyward, *Touching Our Strength: The Erotic as Power and the Love of God* (New York: HarperSanFrancisco, 1989), 89.

12. See Augustine's anti-Pelagian writings and treatises against Julian for his understanding of how original sin is "transmitted" from one generation to the next. Augustine fundamentally believed that in the fall of the first humans, the human will was essentially wounded, and it could no longer maintain control over its fleshly and concupiscential passions. This lack of control is most profoundly experienced in the lack of control over one's sexual organs, and hence, for Augustine, this shameful concupiscence is the primary signifier, if you will, of our fallen and wounded nature. See *Against Julian* and *On Marriage and Concupiscence*.

13. While rejecting the notion of Augustine as sex addict, Willemien Otten argues that "it is important to regard Augustine's reflections on sexuality and sexual sin not as separate from his theological and doctrinal reflections, but rather as preceding them or perhaps underlying them." Her concern is with analyzing how Augustine's reflections on sexuality influence and shape his notions of Christian community. While Otten argues for a more integrated and less problematic understanding of Augustine's sexuality than I do, the underlying argument is quite similar. If sexuality had been as important to Augustine as it appears to be, then we should not be surprised to see similar analyses and concerns reflected in his doctrinal teachings. See Willemien Otten, "Augustine on Marriage, Monasticism, and the Community of the Church," *Theological Studies* 5, no. 3 (1998): 385–406.

14. Miles, *Desire*, 38. The language of addiction understood in a contemporary, psychological manner is surely not one that Augustine himself would have used, but I believe it can be a useful lens through which to examine his conceptualizations of his own sexual experience and love rela-

tionships. However, it is important to note that the concept of sexual addiction need not presume that Augustine necessarily engaged in numerous or "promiscuous" sexual relationships. Rather, the notion of addiction signals a preoccupation with sex and sexual desire around which the addict organizes his or her experiences and actions. One certainly can be a celibate sex addict, much as a recovering alcoholic who is sober may continue to organize his or her life around alcohol, albeit the avoidance of it. Likewise, the notion of being addicted to love does not necessarily manifest itself in an individual's engaging in a pattern of serial love relationships but can, as I argue, manifest itself in opposite terms. That is, because of the pain of loss caused by the ending of love relationships, the addict may avoid actual relationships in the hopes of avoiding the pain associated with them.

15. Ibid., 70.

16. Ibid., 14.

17. Ibid., 98.

18. All quotations are from *The Confessions of St. Augustine*, trans. with an introduction and notes by John K. Ryan (Garden City, N.Y.: Doubleday, 1960.)

19. Augustine discusses this phenomenon in *The City of God*, trans. Gerald Walsh and Grace Monahan (New York: Fathers of the Church, 1952), 14.16. I explore this assumption and its implications for his doctrine of the trinity in detail in a later section of this essay.

20. See Catherine Lacugna, *God for Us: The Trinity and Christian Life* (San Francisco: HarperSanFrancisco, 1991) for a particularly lucid explication of the various philosophical influences upon Augustine's thought.

21. Andrew Louth, *The Origins of the Christian Mystical Tradition: From Plato to Denys* (Oxford: Clarendon Press, 1983), 38.

22. Ibid., 39. One may very well argue that the whole of Platonic philosophy is itself based upon this male experience of sexual swelling and release. But the passion with which Augustine attends to this experience is unique and ultimately led to the Western Christian identification of self with sexuality not found in earlier Platonic musings. For more, see Peter Brown, *The Body and Society: Men, Women, and Sexual Renunciation in Early Christianity* (New York: Columbia University Press, 1988).

23. All quotations are taken from The Fathers of the Church, *The Trinity*, trans. Stephen McKenna (Washington, D. C.: Catholic University of America Press, 1992).

24. For an informative discussion of the importance of memory in Augustine's theology, see John A. Mourant, *Saint Augustine on Memory* (Villanova, Pa.: Augustinian Institute, 1980).

25. All quotations are taken from The Fathers of the Church edition of *The City of God*, trans. Gerald Walsh and Grace Monahan (New York: Fathers of the Church, 1952). See also Augustine's anti-Pelagian writings for a detailed account of how sexual concupiscence functions in the marital relationship and in the transmission of original sin. See *Against Julian* and *On Marriage and Concupiscence*.

26. Margaret Miles has convincingly demonstrated that Augustine uses a male model of sexuality, although he assumes it to be true for females as well. I believe that a disconcerting demonstration of this universalizing of the male (and, perhaps, simply of Augustine's own) experience can be found in chap. 1 of the *City of God*. Here Augustine is counseling nuns who had been raped by invading forces during the sack of Rome. Assuming that all sexual activity is pleasurable, he applauds those nuns who could resist the temptation to give into the "pleasure" of rape and suggests that the rape may be for their own good, keeping them humble and warding off the sin of pride. Obviously, he has no understanding of the often painful aspect of sex for women and the overwhelming violence of rape.

27. Margaret R. Miles, "The Body and Human Values in Augustine of Hippo," in *Grace, Politics, and Desire: Essays on Augustine*, ed. H. A. Meynell (Calgary, Alberta: University of Calgary Press, 1990), 60.

28. According to Augustine, all human relations are in disarray. War, slavery, and the tyrannical

rule of emperors have been allowed by God as punishment for this disobedience and as a necessary means of social control. One is not even able to trust one's friends, as friendships are full of "slights, suspicions, quarrels, war today, peace tomorrow" (*City* 19.5). Love of friends as well as family can only cause us pain.

29. Miles, *Desire*, 93, 94.

30. Augustine, *The Good of Marriage*, in *Treatises on Marriage and Other Subjects*, ed. Roy J. Deferrari (New York: Fathers of the Church, 1955), 39.

31. Augustine, *Two Books on Genesis Against the Manichees*, in *Saint Augustine On Genesis*, ed. Thomas P. Halton (Washington D.C.: Catholic University of America Press, 1991), 79.

32. *Against Julian*, trans. Matthew A. Schumacher, *The Fathers of the Church*, vol. 35 (New York: Fathers of the Church, 1957), 228.

33. Ibid., 284.

34. Ibid.

35. While the nuances of Augustine's notion of memory are not the main point of this essay, it is important to note that his suggestion that we suspend all mental activity and "lose our minds" in sexual orgasm—and therefore forget God as well—is an apparent contradiction of his belief that all knowledge, including knowledge of God, always already resides in the caverns of our memory; hence, it would follow that it is never possible to completely obliterate God from our memory, although it is possible to not be actively aware of this knowledge at any given point. As John Mourant explains, Augustine's fear that we might actually be able to completely obliterate God from our memory is a failure of his distinguishing "between forgetfulness and the things that are forgotten. Forgetfulness is just as characteristic of the mind as is memory." Further, in forgetting, "what I remember is the act of forgetting or a particular item of knowledge but not complete forgetfulness which would be oblivion and the very contradiction of memory. For that which is wholly absent in the sense of privation, amnesia or oblivion, is not present for the mind to remember" (*Saint Augustine on Memory*, 19). Hence, in his intense anxiety over the loss of our minds during orgasm, Augustine apparently forgets his own construction of memory and the impossibility to totally obliterate God from the mind. If he had remembered this crucial point, he may not have been quite so afraid of orgasm and the apparent loss of self experienced therein.

36. *The Good of Marriage*, 13.

37. Augustine, *The Literal Meaning of Genesis*, ed. Johannes Quasten (New York: Newman Press, 1982), 1.7.13.

38. Margaret Miles, "Vision: The Eye of the Body and the Eye of the Mind in Saint Augustine's *De Trinitate* and *Confessions*," *Journal of Religion* 63 (1983): 128.

39. Miles, *Desire*, 105.

40. Barry Ulanov, *Prayers of St. Augustine* (Minneapolis: Seabury Press, 1983), 84, 85. However, it is necessary to note the dangers of assuming any essential or natural link between the "feminine" experience of sexuality and the experience of subordination and violence inherent in the rhetoric of ravishment. This is exactly the construction of female sexuality that feminist theologians and secular theorists have been challenging for decades. See, for example, Catherine MacKinnon, *Toward a Feminist Theory of the State* (Cambridge, Mass.: Harvard University Press, 1989); Susan Estrich, *Real Rape* (Cambridge, Mass.: Harvard University Press, 1987); Diana Russell, *Making Violence Sexy: Feminist Views on Pornography* (New York: Teacher's College Press, 1993); Susan Brownmiller, *Against Our Will: Men, Women, and Rape* (New York: Simon and Schuster, 1975); Andrea Dworkin, *Our Blood: Prophecies and Discourses on Sexual Violence* (London: Secker and Warburg, 1988); Joanne Carlson Brown and Carole Bohn, eds., *Christianity, Patriarchy, and Abuse* (New York: Pilgrim Press, 1989); Marie Fortune, *Sexual Violence: The Unmentionable Sin* (New York: Pilgrim Press, 1983); Elisabeth Schussler Fiorenza and Mary Shawn Copeland, eds., *Violence Against Women*, Concilium 1994/1 (Maryknoll: Orbis Books, 1994); and Renita Weems, *Battered Love: Marriage, Sex, and Violence in the Hebrew Prophets* (Minneapolis: Fortress Press, 1995), among others.

41. However, in a certain sense, the Son is "less" than himself: "In this form He has been found to be not only less than the Father but also of the Holy Spirit as well, and not only that, but He has been found to be even less that Himself, not of Himself who was, but of Himself who is, because by the form of a slave which He received, He did not lose the form of God" (*Trinity* 2.1.2)

42. See, for example, the works of James Dittes, Donald Capps, David Burrell, E. R. Dodds, Charles Kligerman, and J. G. Kristo.

43. David Burrell makes an insightful distinction between the use of psychoanalytic theory as a heuristic device to aid understanding versus the use of it to explain fully Augustine's life and work. The latter does a grave injustice to the intricacies of Augustine's theology and should be avoided. Yet, if used as a heuristic device, such theories can perhaps illuminate Augustine's thought for twenty-first-century readers steeped in these discourses. See David Burrell, "Reading the *Confessions* of Augustine: The Case of Oedipal Analysis," in *The Hunger of the Heart: Reflections on the "Confessions" of Augustine*, ed. Donald Capps and James E. Dittes (West Lafayette, Ind.: Society for the Scientific Study of Religion, 1990).

44. J. G. Kristo, *Looking for God in Time and Memory: Psychology, Theology, and Spirituality in Augustine's "Confessions"* (New York: University Press of America, 1991), 24.

45. Volney Gay, "Augustine: The Reader as Selfobject," *JSSR* 25/1 (1986): 66.

46. Quotation from Kristo, *Looking For God*, 24.

47. For these and other unflattering characterizations of Monica, see the essays in *The Hunger of the Heart*, ed. Donald Capps and James E. Dittes (West Lafayette, Ind.: Society for the Scientific Study of Religion, 1990), particularly the articles by Paul W. Pruyser, David Burrell, and James Dittes. In this same volume, Charles Kligerman, "A Psychoanalytic Study of the *Confessions* of St. Augustine," paints a particularly negative Freudian portrayal of Monica as "a woman superficially sweet and mild, but capable, with an air of moral superiority, of sustaining unrelenting pressure." A "frigid, hypermoral" woman, Monica was "frustrating" to her husband but engaged in "erotic," "stormy emotional scenes" with Augustine and turned to him in an "engulfing type of seductiveness."

48. While Kristo makes use of Chodorow's analysis of the psychological effects of mothering on small children, he appears unaware of Chodorow's own critique of the ideological and social conditions that perpetuate "patriarchal" mothering patterns in women and the negative psychological issues which may result from it.

49. Jessica Benjamin, *The Bonds of Love: Psychoanalysis, Feminism, and the Problem of Domination* (New York: Pantheon Books, 1988), 25. Further references to this work appear parenthetically in the text.

50. Both Nancy Chodorow and Jessica Benjamin—as well as many Freudian theorists—discuss how the mechanism of differentiation is experienced differently by boys and girls. While girls can and are encouraged to identify with the nurturing gender characteristics of the mother, the boy cannot do so if he intends to maintain his gender superiority (and his genitals, or so he fears). Hence, the problem of individuation and the threat of the all-encompassing mother is more pronounced in boys than in girls.

51. Benjamin, *The Bonds of Love*, 188. Further references to this work appear parenthetically in the text.

52. Dittes, "Augustine," 258.

53. Ibid.

54. Benjamin, *The Bonds of Love*, 20. Further references to this work appear parenthetically in the text.

55. In discussing the dynamics of Nietzsche's master-slave dialectic, a dialectic arguably foundational to Western constructions of gender identity in which the male is the master, the female the slave, Benjamin notes how this dialectic breaks down in the very moment the master achieves his goal of making the slave a total object. In this instant, the slave no longer possesses any capacity to

acknowledge or recognize the master *as* master and the master therefore loses all identity as a master. It is only in the maintenance of the other's subjectivity, however minimal, that our own can be recognized as well. For a complete discussion of this dynamic, see Benjamin, *The Bonds of Love*, chap. 2. For an analysis of the master's need for an "uppity" slave for the dynamic to work, see also Lynn Chancer, *Sadomasochism in Everyday Life: The Dynamics of Power and Powerlessness* (New Brunswick: Rutgers University Press, 1992).

56. Benjamin, *The Bonds of Love*, 29. Further references to this work appear parenthetically in the text.

57. Sarah Coakley, "Creaturehood Before God: Male and Female," *Theology* 93 (1990), 343–54, quote from page 344. The heterosexist bias of this model is exemplary of the problems which occur when attempting to essentialize and spiritualize sexuality in the hegemonic Western Christian tradition. See my comments in n. 6, above.

58. Coakley, " 'Batter My Heart . . .'?" 74, 76.

59. Peter Brown, *The Body and Society: Men, Women, and Sexual Renunciation in Early Christianity* (New York: Columbia University Press, 1988), 388, 394.

60. I believe it is necessary to take seriously the constructed nature of sexuality and to avoid assertions such as those found in much *eros* theology that assumes the inherent goodness and divinity of the erotic. For such a characteristic formulation, see especially the works of Carter Heyward.

61. The literature on sexual violence against women is extensive, and studies have shown that approximately 25–35 percent of women and 10 percent of men will be victims of sexual assault in their lifetimes. The most recent study of which I am aware suggests that the sexual abuse of boys may be even higher than ever thought, with an estimate of one in three girls and one in every six boys experiencing some sort of sexual abuse as children. This reality must be taken seriously if we are to adequately reconstruct our notions of sexuality and its relation to the divine. See Michel Dorais, *Don't Tell: The Sexual Abuse of Boys* (Montreal: McGill-Queen's University Press, 2002).

62. Mary Grey, *The Wisdom of Fools? Seeking Revelation for Today* (London: SPCK, 1993), 99; Anne M. Clifford, *Introducing Feminist Theology* (Maryknoll, N.Y.: Orbis Books, 2001), 115.

63. Miles, *Desire*, 76. Here Miles is quoting James Hillman, *Myth of Analysis* (Evanston: Northwestern University Press, 1972).

11

The Evanescence of Masculinity: Deferral in Saint Augustine's *Confessions* and Some Thoughts on Its Bearing on the Sex/Gender Debate

Penelope Deutscher

I

Over the past twenty years, a substantial amount of feminist debate has centered around what has become known as the sex/gender distinction—a distinction originally employed to assert that what is regarded as conventional feminine behavior is not the inevitable result of being a "biological" woman, but is, rather, the product of social forces and is therefore mutable. Since this essay is not specifically about that debate, I

This essay was first published in *Australian Feminist Studies*, vol. 15, 1992 (41–56).

direct the reader to a recent edition of *Australian Feminist Studies* for its description of the history of this distinction.[1] There, an introduction and four essays serve to remind us of the extent to which sex/gender has not ceased to trouble Anglophone feminism, despite the fact that the presumptions that underpin the distinction have long and variously been criticized.[2] Soon, no doubt, the question of why sex/gender has continued to be so troublesome for feminism will become as debatable a topic as was the original distinction itself.

I am interested in what seems to have become a by-product of the sex/gender debate: attempts by some to sustain a terminological distinction between the terms *man* and *masculine*, or *woman* and *feminine*, in their theoretical work. The sex/gender debate seems to have fostered a conviction that it is important not to "confuse" the usage of the term *woman* with that of *femininity*, and similarly *man* with *masculinity*.[3] If so, then we might regard it as a legacy of "sex/gender" that confidence is indirectly thus expressed in the possibility of sustaining a terminological distinction between these terms. Yet this confidence I refer to is strangely articulated and a little uneasy. For example, it is expressed by criticisms that certain feminist theorists have confused or "fudged" these terms: *woman*, *female*, and *feminine* and *man*, *male*, and *masculine*—sometimes despite their own intentions. Behind each accusation seems to lie an indirect confidence in a terminological clarity that has become obscured by the hapless theorist.[4]

This is not to deny that the texts cited by such critics do contain a constant terminological slippage of the sort described. Yet the ubiquity with which feminism confuses, and accuses itself of confusing, these terms suggests that the problem does not lie with the accidental theorist so much as with the terms themselves. Perhaps, in other words, it is the terms, and not the theorists, that are structurally confused.[5] One problem with the accusatory trend is that it shifts the focus away from examining the reasons why the confusion is unavoidable.

In this essay, I do not discuss the history of the sex/gender distinction, but rather the history of philosophy. I examine the work of Augustine in order to propose a functional interconnection between the terms *man* and *masculinity*, *woman* and *femininity* that occurs in the kind of structure where man defers to his "god." Through the discussion I hope to suggest some reasons why it is no accident that these terms cannot be distinguished with any stability, and to ask what we reinforce when we indirectly suggest that they can be.

II

There has been some blurring between two trends in recent feminist philosophy, between, on the one hand, "sex/gender" arguments about the relationship between "woman" and "femininity," and, on the other hand, "dichotomous theory" analyses of "masculine/feminine" oppositions. According to the latter, masculine identity has been constructed in and is dependent on its dichotomous opposition to the feminine in the context of a series of affiliated, sexed oppositions. Sometimes, such readings have followed the Pythagorean table by representing these opposed identities in columns of oppositions that might be headed "man"/"woman" *or* "masculine"/"feminine," thus:

man/woman
(or) masculine/feminine
reason/emotion
rational/irrational
mind/body
culture/nature
subject/object
presence/absence
valued/devalued

. . . and so on.[6]

Why is there indecision about whether to title the left-hand side "man," or "masculinity"?[7] The influence of sex/gender might have some theorists feeling they prefer the supposed "gender" term *masculinity* in order to reinforce the proposal that these are not man's "essential" attributes. For different reasons, theorists who follow the movement of these oppositions in the history of philosophy would not restrict the table to the title "man/woman," since they would not want to limit the discussion to the ways that philosophers speak specifically about "men" and "women" but would include, for example, the ways that a philosopher might conceive man as transcending the *feminine*. We might want to title the left column "man" *and* "masculinity," since it does refer to both. It refers to an aspiration, articulated through ruse and violence, that the category "man" coincides with his identity as "masculine," and that "woman" coincides with "femininity."

At the point of an uncertainty about whether such a table should be headed "masculine/feminine" or "man/woman" or both of these, we negotiate an intersection between a concern of the sex/gender debate (the relationship between "woman" and "femininity") and a concern of dichotomous theory (the opposition between "masculinity" and "femininity"), raising a question about the relationship between them. How, in other words, does the interconnection between the terms *man* and *masculine* relate to the opposition between "masculinity" and "femininity"?[8] In this essay I suggest that the latter "opposition" operates through the blurred movements of the former interconnection. I find myself forced always to hover uneasily between referring to "the masculine/feminine opposition," and referring to "the" "man/woman opposition" and am interested in the reasons why it is necessary to say both at once.

III

The thesis of this essay is that we can understand the interconnection between "man" and "masculine" in the opposition "man"/"woman" by understanding these oppositions as being "theologically" grounded. It will be seen that *theological* is used here in a particular sense. The term is used to refer to the deferral of "man" toward a god, a divine realm, or a transcendent point—truth, or origin: a point that is radically "not-man," but toward which man gestures, or with which he identifies. Sexual oppositions can be "theological" in this sense even when not deriving from "religious" texts, and their mobilization of "theological thinking" can be most surreptitious. In the analysis of sexed dichotomous oppositions in the history of philosophy, the recurring series of philosophical texts that tend to be discussed are of some kind of overtly "religious persuasion."[9] However, one tends not to see this theological orientation entering very much into the feminist discussion of those oppositions, except when that discussion is itself overtly religious in focus.[10] This is an unremarkable oversight, since the point has been to analyze masculine/feminine, and not divine/masculine dichotomies.[11]

But since the philosophy texts that feminism rereads do lean—in both indirect or direct ways—toward a theological persuasion, it seems that feminism has already been dealing, implicitly, and sometimes unwittingly, with theology. So this is not a point about whether feminism "should" interest itself in theology. Since there are feminisms that do recommend such an interest, I should make clear that this is not one of them. Rather, I am suggesting that we recognize ways in which the masculine that is opposed to the feminine is a masculine already deferring toward a divine ideal. How might our analysis of man/woman require some consideration of how we are already dealing with the idea of "god?" I use the term *god* as a paradigm for the kind of "not-man-yet-man's ideal" realm also grounding sexed dichotomies in nonreligious texts. Because of its role as a paradigm, I here consider an overtly religious philosophical text.

To begin, we might try the experiment of trying to fit Augustine's god in relation to the table of sexed oppositions. It is not an inappropriate experiment: it does seem that one should be able to place this god somehow in relation to that table, for he bears an explicit relation to ideas of masculinity and femininity—he is, for example, obviously represented as a paternal figure, as god-the-father. Yet where we do try his inclusion, it is most disruptive. Although aspects of god have certain connotations of gender, we nevertheless find that he cannot be associated with either the feminine or the masculine with any stability. First, as disembodied, positively valued, and the origin of meaning and truth, god does not incarnate the concept of traditional femininity. Yet, second, neither can he be aligned with the masculine, because some distinction is always upheld *between* man and god. How then to represent god in relation to the opposition between masculinity and femininity? Feminism would need to account for how the masculine has been opposed to the divine and yet *also* opposed to the feminine. We would need to ask how we should understand the relationship between the divine and feminine "columns": is man a middle point or third term between god and woman?

Perhaps we should regard "god/man" as a distinction between ideas of superhuman and human masculinity? Here, despite the distinction between them, god still would join man on the "left hand" masculine side in opposition to the feminine. But when god is considered to form a dichotomous opposition to man, this also seems to shift man to the feminine, "right hand" side, in relation to god. This occurs where man is represented as embodied, material, and weak in relation to god. Does this make god/man a kind of *equivalent* of man/woman? If so, should we say that in the god/man opposition, man becomes aligned with woman and that the distinction between man and woman is thereby disrupted? However, we must also note that since both god and woman are opposed to man and defined as "not-man," there is a sense in which they too can be considered as aligned.[12]

These preliminary suggestions indicate ways in which this god disturbs sexed oppositions. At the point at which we must represent a division within the masculine side between "superhuman" (divine) and human masculinity, we seem to see the dyadic table structured with a "third" dichotomous side and rendered a three-column structure: "god/man/ woman," or "divine/masculine/feminine." This is the moment of the table's own structural incoherence. A third "side" does not fit dichotomous understanding and makes the other two sides more supple. In other words, in relation to the "divine" column, the masculine is both identified with the divine and also rendered feminine. Man's opposition to the feminine is both undermined and reinforced.

This point will be seen to rely on certain deconstructive approaches and extends beyond arguing that the "problem" for feminism is dichotomous opposition. Looking at the ways in which god has both a necessary relation to (reinforcing notions of ideal masculinity) and disrupts the masculine/feminine opposition shows that the "problem" is not dichotomous representations of masculinity and femininity, men and women. The dichotomy is in itself "problematic" in the sense of its necessary "incoherence"—its double moves and double logic.

So it could be said that this god rather *confuses the issue* between man and woman, and between masculinity and femininity. However, this question is confusing and disruptive in a way that is informative of, rather than a distraction from, the latter. In regard to the terminological slippage inherent to the terms *man/masculine, woman/feminine*, I suggest that questions of god and theology are pertinent to such slippage.

IV

Consider the account given by Augustine in his *Confessions* of the relationship between masculine and divine identity.[13] Unlike philosophers who have wanted to suggest some kind of affinity between man and god, Augustine particularly insisted on their difference, on the radical nondivinity of man and the radical nonmasculinity of god. Since each was to be understood as the negation of the other, we could describe the relationship as constituting an either/or dichotomy.

But his story is not so simple. For one thing, Augustine is troubled by the scriptural account of man as being made in god's "image" (*Confessions* 6.3 [136]). If the Bible says that man is made in god's image, how can they be understood as the antithesis of each other? So he explains that this reference must be understood in a "spiritual" rather than a literal sense. For the Bible, says Augustine, often contrary or illogical, needs frequently to be understood as having this kind of double meaning, and this has occurred because of the need to explain in simplistic terms that will be comprehensible to the uneducated layperson as well as to the scholar sensitive to theological subtleties (5.14 [131], 12.12, [313], 12.27 [328]). But for all the neatness of this explanation, an account of god and man as being aligned, rather than radically different, keeps creeping back into Augustine's account.

It is in his account of the relations between woman and man that this becomes apparent. At first sight, matters between these two protagonists seem very familiar. Woman has been made for man and is physically subject to him, "just as the active appetite is made subject, so as to conceive right and prudent conduct from the rational mind" (*Confessions* 13.32 [367]). The problem, although Augustine does not indicate it as such, lies in the question of why and on what grounds man is superior to woman. Reason over nature, apparently. However, Augustine does not take for granted the standard by which reason is master over nature. It is here that we start to see god disrupting matters, as Augustine appeals to him to support this hierarchy and the primacy of man:

> In [animals] reason has not been placed in judgment over the senses and their reports. But men can ask questions, so that they may clearly see the invisible things of God "being understood by the things that are made." (*Confessions* 10.6 [235–36])

> We see . . . man, made to your image and likeness, and by this, your own image and likeness, that is, by the power of reason and intelligence, set over all non-rational animals. (*Confessions* 13.32 [367])

Here man, it is true, is the superior animal on earth because of his power of reason and understanding. However, on this account the power of reason does not have "intrinsic" primacy. In other words, the primacy of reason over nature, and of man over irrational animals, is not internal to the oppositions "man/animal" or "reason/nature"; rather, reason is valued because it renders the (male) possessor most like god and allows one to read the world as his material Scripture. So while Augustine will posit man as superior over woman because he is more closely aligned with reason, this superiority of reason and hence man's superior position is dependent on the positioning of god.[14]

But let us take note of what has happened here. In explaining the superiority of the "man of reason," Augustine is reliant on the image of a god to whom this man is close, in whose image he has been made.[15] So rather than explaining away the reference to man being made in god's image, he now *relies* on this idea. It would be incorrect to take at face value Augustine's presentation of man and god as radically opposed, because we must also take into account his presentation of them as aligned in opposition to creatures affiliated with nature. With this second refrain, god, although the radical opposite of man, also forms with him a kind of continuum along which a life-giving god is even more than man's life-giving soul rather than being "not man": "But I say to you, O my soul, that you are already my better part, for you quicken the body's mass and give it life, and this a body cannot give to a body. But your God is for you even the life of life" (*Confessions* 10.6 [235]).

On Augustine's account, god is both "not-man" and "like-man." The positions of god and man are sustained by that contradiction. Man is only valuable insofar as he is like god, but god can only be identified insofar as he is not like man.[16] So, to achieve the value of reason and the identity of man, a kind of "double move" must occur, where man owes his worldly primacy to his identification with the divine, and so that identification is asserted. Yet the divine, on which man's identity is parasitic, owes its identity to its difference from man, and so the association between god and man must also be rejected.

Since in relation to man, god has a kind of dual identity (both like and unlike), what would happen if we tried to relate god to the man/woman dichotomy? The difficulty is that god could not here either be aligned with man, or be opposed to man, because both these representations would be true. God seemingly needs to be represented twice on our table: once in alignment with man in opposition to woman and nature, and also once in opposition to man as "not" everything that man is.[17]

And since god's relation to man is dual and self-contradictory, then under what we might call these theological conditions, it might be no surprise that man's identity is itself similarly structured. Indeed, perhaps we have become too familiar with the account of the identification of man with mind, reason, value, presence, being, superiority, mastery, and dominance, to the point of neglecting his alter ego. It is worth bearing in mind that the personage "man" I reintroduce here has had no less of a career in the history of philosophy. Here is Augustine speaking of his relationship as a man to god:

> I do this service by deeds as well as by words: I do this "under your wings," with too grave a peril unless "under your wings" my soul had been subdued to you and my infirmity made known to you. I am but a little one . . . (*Confessions* 10.4 [232])

> I despise myself before your sight, and account myself but dust and ashes. (*Confessions* 10.5 [233])

Despite the fact that god does guarantee man's position as the "man of reason," nevertheless, in relation to god, man is also humble, submissive, lowly, weak, a child, despised, mere dust and ashes. Not only is he devalued and cast in a lowly position, but where he becomes "dust and ashes," he is considered to be a kind of human clay. Since it is god who provides his animation, he is, in other words, identified not with reason but with materiality here.

And if, while identities are revolving about, it seems that woman, at least, is the one constant, fixed point—most devalued and aligned with animals on the lowest rung of the divinely ordered ladder—then we must also remember Augustine's "second" woman, whose position is no less indebted to god:

> For in this way you made man male and female in your spiritual grace, where as to bodily sex there is neither male nor female, because there is neither Jew nor Greek, neither slave nor freeman. (*Confessions* 13.23 [356])

> Because of her reasonable and intelligent mind she would have equality of nature. (*Confessions* 13.32 [367])

Where Augustine casts woman as irrational, her position as inferior is ensured by the god who legitimates the standard by which man is superior by virtue of the rational faculty that allows him to approach god. Yet Augustine also writes that it is god who guarantees that all those of rational intelligence are created as one, and that therefore man and woman are created as one.

So, what I have been drawing out of this theological text is the way that it presents us with a god, a man, and a woman, each of whom has both a dual and a self-contradictory identity. God is both like-man and not-man; man is identified with reason (and valued) in opposition to materiality and yet he is also identified with materiality (and devalued) in opposition to god; and woman is both subject to man as a natural impulse is subject to reason, and equal to man since equal in reason.

Moreover, these self-contradictions can be understood as necessary, and not incidental, to the identity of each. First, I have already suggested that god must be both like-man and not-man. This is because god's identity is established via his position as not-man, an identity with which man at the same time identifies in his own capacity as like-god. So second, this structure will mean that man must be both feminine and masculine, identified with both the material and the immaterial. Following the path of this equivocation, since the "man of reason" is masculine insofar as he is like-god, his identity is therefore dependent on the establishment of god's identity. Although god does seem to be identified as not-man, this is however a paradoxical identification, since man is an "empty" term (dependent upon the establishment of god's identity). So, where god is identified as not-man, we find that man gives this content by being rendered *feminine,* and the dichotomy between man and woman must be forsaken. In other words, where we are told that god is not-man, we are told that god is not-*material,* not *embodied,* not-*emotional,* not-*passionate,* not-*feeble.* It is for this reason that we can point out this second equivocation: we say that it is necessary (if paradoxical) for man to be feminine, in order to be masculine. It is as feminine that man negatively gives god the identity he himself identifies with as masculine.

Insofar as god therefore both ensures man's identity as masculine and merges him with the feminine, he both ensures and undermines the basis for man's superiority over woman. So, last, we can point out this third equivocation: while ensuring the femininity of woman, god yet renders her masculine. Following the path of this third dual identity: while Augustine associates man with mind, and woman with body or nature, the position of both relies on the positioning of god. As we have seen, mind is valued over body or nature because it allows one to approach god through the reading of his message. Yet the legitimation provided by god involves a contortion. By that standard, Augustine invokes the primacy of mind over body. Yet in so doing, he is necessarily led into an account of bodily inferiority: since body is mere physicality, it does not affect the quality of the mind within. Taking such a tack, also necessary to institute the primacy of mind and legitimate the position of man, Augustine is led to consider that the difference between man and woman is "merely" bodily.

This is why Augustine must tell us both that woman is inferior "by body," and yet also that her bodily difference cannot render her inferior. Indeed, it would be incorrect to say that Augustine is "forced" to tell us of male and female being treated as one. The connotation of duress would be inappropriate, since here it is via the claim that man and woman are "created as one" that reason gains its position as the trait significant where body is not. Only through having so used woman to help establish the primacy of reason will Augustine disassociate woman from it. Woman has been included with man as "reason" to then be devalued in opposition to him as "not-reason."

The man of reason has always been acknowledged as also a bodily and material man. Indeed, Descartes's very insistence on the reliability and primacy of reason is connected to his own account of the threat posed by man's body, a capsule always threatening to overwhelm mind/man with desires, passions, and confusion unless reason be exercised with vigilance. Here, however, we might rethink the way that Augustine's man of reason also "happens" to be represented as material man, his irrational woman as rational, and his "unlike-man" god represented as "like-man." I have suggested these dual identities are functional, rather than accidental.

In other words, a means is suggested by which we might rethink our understanding of the man of reason's anomalies. For example, we cannot explain anomalies whereby this man is considered to be material and feminine by talking about the difference between representations of man and the symbolism of masculinity. In other words, it is not that masculine identity is symbolically associated with reason while men are sometimes conceded to be empirical, material beasts, or men of body. Rather, via the structure I have discussed, it is instead *only* by *not* being the man of reason (for example, by being positioned as material and feminine in relation to god, and by conceding that woman is the "woman of reason") that man is established as the man of reason. Another way of saying this is that it is not *despite* but *because of* the dual and self-contradictory identities of god, man, and woman that the man of reason is established.

This begins to suggest a certain inadequacy about the use of the table of dichotomous oppositions to represent this kind of structure. I originally asked how we might place Augustine's god in relation to that table and suggested that it would be a placement difficult to effect, since god would have to appear twice—once in opposition to the masculine side, and once in alignment with it. However, I suggested that this confusion might be informative of the table of sexed oppositions. The difficulties involved in our pinning down god relate to the fact that neither man nor woman is any the easier to pin down. None of these terms is discrete, separate, or fixed—rather, they are structurally confused. Their representation as aligned, fixed, and rigid binary oppositions is inappropriate. How instead to represent the structure that the table of dichotomies misses and elides? How instead to represent this structure by which the masculine side, rather than pertaining to man while the feminine side pertains to woman, has to incorporate the feminine to achieve the effect of a masculine identity, and where woman is sometimes rendered masculine to achieve the effect of her feminine identity?

V

For feminist theorists, the desire to establish the difference between the terms *sex* and *gender* involved the desire to distinguish the "biological" and the "social": although this was not Augustine's problem, there is a different sense in which his theology does mobilize a difference between *sex* and *gender*, if we understand this to mean the difference between *man* and *masculinity*. I do not mean that these terms are coherently distinguished in Augustine's text. Rather, Augustine's text mobilizes the non-coincidence of man and masculinity—a different kind of "difference" between the two—allowing a *slippage between* them, and that it is via that slippage that the text achieves the effect of the identities of man and god.

Certainly, in the *Confessions* Augustine does not overtly discuss the distinction between man and masculinity. Nevertheless, the difference between "man" and what "man" is identified with is crucial to the identity of "man" in this text. On the basis of the self-contradictions of god, woman, and man, how is it that the identity of the man of reason is effectively produced? The implicit distinction, or difference, between man and masculinity (the identity of man) is operative in this regard. Masculinity is a most facilitating and flexible concept because of the slippage by which it defines man by not coinciding with, indeed by being different from, the term *man*. This distinction enables man to be accounted for as *in excess of that with which he is identified*. We have seen that man must share the attributes associated with the feminine—emotions, passions, embodiment—if the divine is to be the point on which man's masculinity is parasitic. It is the man/masculine distinction that is able to account for or encapsulate the fact that man must be "contaminated" by the feminine to be distinguished from it.

This distinction divides off and displaces onto the feminine whatever of man exceeds that with which man is identified, whatever of man is regarded as exceeding his own masculinity. So here, where the relationship between "man" and the masculine is shifting and flexible, we will see that the term *feminine* must also have an extreme flexibility. Moreover, while masculinity defines man by being different from man, indicating not man but the supposed essence or kernel of man, it facilitates this by deferring that identity. Where masculinity indicates man's identity by not coinciding with it, it does so by rendering that identity a receding, vanishing point. And so we are confronted with "evanescent man."

To follow this recession, let us start by examining the mind/body opposition that is usually and simply represented as aligned with (or underneath) the man/woman opposition. How might we understand these sexed dichotomies as operative in Augustine's text? The problem with such a two-column representation is that it does not describe the way that, where man is aligned with mind, mind/body is a division of, or split between, masculine and feminine *within* the term *man*. Here, it is as body that man exceeds the masculine and so body is displaced onto the feminine. However, it would also be incorrect to represent *mind* as the fixed masculine term. For example, Augustine describes mind as infiltrated by its bodily housing, filled with passions, desires, everyday matters, and incorrect thoughts; a muddled storehouse of images delivered to the mind or memory by the senses (*Confessions* 10.14 [243], 10.8 [236–38], 10.33 [261]). Materiality occupies the masculine again—that is to say, at the point of mind also, man exceeds rather than coincides with the masculine. So here, we see the kernel of man recede a little further off again. What is essential to man, what is masculine, now recedes to the reason that sorts through the everyday mental morass. Nevertheless, no more than mind is reason the fixed point of masculinity: man's reasoning mind joins body on the side of material discarded in relation to the soul, which survives beyond the earthly confines of the body and so achieves a greater disembodiment than reason.[18] So the point of masculinity moves toward a divine point, involving a progressive displacement onto the feminine of what of man is "not-masculine." Indeed, there is a point in Augustine's text where in relation to the soul, the feminine has become a category inclusive of mind and reason.

In relation to the soul, mind, inclusive of reason and inferior mental content, is part of man's materiality, abandoned at death. Yet not even soul guarantees man coincidence with the point of god it approaches. Man must always fall short of god, and this is how Augustine specifically accounts for the relationship. As soul we will dwell in god's heaven of heavens—but never quite be at one with god (*Confessions* 12.9–11 [310–12]).

Since Augustine associates women with nature and materiality, we may say that the material excess by which man is constantly overflowing the masculine point that identifies him is feminized. This material excess is the extent to which man does not coincide with god. Yet within Augustine's terms it is impossible that man should coincide with god, for the necessary difference between man and god (upon which god's identity is based, upon which man is parasitic) would then be lost. The point of pure masculinity that defines man and by which the feminine as "not-man" is devalued, must be positioned as a point inaccessible to man. Despite the fact that god has been defined as "not-man," man is only truly masculine insofar as he approximates god. So for all that god is "not-man," paradoxically it is god who is positioned at the point of pure masculinity. So the recession, while rendering an illusion of masculine identity as mind, or reason, does so by moving toward a point never arrived at. All that is progressively isolated from man and devalued as "not-man" is displaced onto the feminine. Man is defined by a term he is nevertheless not, and never at one with, defined by a term that is but a shifting recession to a point with which it never coincides. So the feminine, being the extent to which man falls short of god, is thereby a term flexible enough to include all that we typically define as masculine: reason, mind, man.

Discussing the self-contradictory identities of god, man, and woman, I asked how they acted to produce an identity that has been termed the "man of reason"—the illusion that masculine identity is ordered in terms of those sexed, dichotomous oppositions. So in summary:

First, the terms *man* and *masculinity* must be dislodged so that masculinity can define man without coinciding with man. This allows man to be identified seemingly with a fixed part of himself (the kernel of man), while this kernel is a shifting vanishing point. In this receding movement, the feminine is a devalued category in relation to a man who himself also always falls short of the identity the feminine is devalued for not being.

Second, Augustine is only able to value the privileged masculine term in each shift, and devalue all that the privileged term is opposed to, because of the illusion of and identification with a point not attainable. So, to sustain the effect of man's identity, there must be the positioning of a divine point that is nevertheless incoherent as the ultimate masculine point.

And third, there must be a field of feminized materiality, that, far from coinciding with the term *woman*, must be a term elastic enough to encompass every aspect of man displaced from man in the illusion of recession to his own identity. In this sense we can say that enveloped within the category of the feminine will be whatever of the masculine the feminine is also opposed to and devalued in terms of body, of course, but also mind and even, at a certain point, reason.[19]

So, we have considered slippages between "man" and "masculinity" in Augustine's *Confessions*. But what of the sex/gender debate? Perhaps while discussing the "man/masculine" distinction, we may have ended up saying something useful about "theology," at work in the distinction between man and masculine. I should again say that I am thinking not of the protagonists of the sex/gender debate itself, although to follow the operation of deferral in that debate could be an interesting enterprise. Rather, I am thinking of the by-product of that debate—an idea that one *should* be able to distinguish sex and gender, man and masculinity, man and what is attributed to man.

For, on the strength of the movement of slippage between man and masculinity, we can rethink our idea of what it is to employ "theological thinking." Slippage produces the effect of sexed identity, and this structure depends not so much on a figure or personage as on the deferral of masculinity toward a divine field that it both must and must not be identifiable with. As part of such a structure, *man* and *masculine* are blurred terms, interdependent, intersliding, impossible to pin down or to separate, since masculinity defines man without coinciding with him, while receding from him.

Indeed, we might start to suspect that theological thinking of the deferring kind discussed here is lurking somewhere in the background when we stumble across distinctions between man and masculine, woman and feminine, that are blurred and shifting, strangely elusive. For reason, or whatever kernel that man is identified with and valued in terms of, is never intrinsically valuable—it always relies on a legitimating prop. The hierarchy of man/woman oppositions must always be supported. If it is not in terms of the reading of a message from god, such hierarchies still point toward some kind of transcendence. The primacy of man and reason defers toward the realm of *logos*, or the realm of truth.[20] And as such, the point made early in this essay can now be changed. It is not that philosophy constructs sexed identity through a structure of deferral *and* that philosophy has often been theological, although this is certainly true. Rather, it is *insofar* as philosophy has constructed sexed identity in this way, that we can describe it as theological, relying on the pursuit of and recession toward some transcendent point that the masculine both is not at one with and yet is identified in terms of.

This discussion set out not from the sex/gender debate proper but from the terminological slippage between woman and feminine, between man and masculine, between sex and gender that, I would argue, inevitably occurs. I embarked from what might be described as a "post sex/gender" faith in a potential terminological clarity that seemed to inspire the accusations of the hapless theorist who confuses the terms. It is not that I disagree that the terms have been confused and their deployment confusing. Rather than belonging to the theorist, the confusion is inherent to the terms themselves. My point has been neither that they are not distinguishable, nor that they are. The terms are different in the sense that they do not coincide. But the noncoincidence of man and masculinity allows the effect of man's *seeming* to coincide with masculinity. Since it is via the dislodgement of man and masculinity that the illusion of their coincidence is rendered, we can say that the terms are separate, yet not separable, interconnected but not at one. It is because masculinity is dislodged from, is different from, man, and yet is not separable from man, that it is possible for man to seem to be identified by a masculine identity he does not arrive at, and thus the illusion of man's coincidence with the masculine is effected. This does not say much about the various claims about the interrelation between something called "biology" and something called the "social."[21] But we should not confuse the reasons why theorists wanted to distinguish those terms, with the reasons why *man* and *masculine, woman* and *feminine* are not distinguishable terms in our work. Working with terms that are structurally confused, we should not wonder at our failures to distinguish them coherently.

Notes

1. See Anne Edwards, "The Sex/Gender Distinction: Has It Outlived its Usefulness?"; Genevieve Lloyd, "Woman as Other: Sex, Gender, and Subjectivity"; Denise Thompson, "The 'Sex/Gender' Distinction: A Reconsideration"; and Moira Gatens, "Woman and Her Double(s): Sex, Gender and Ethics," all in *Australian Feminist Studies* no. 10 (1989): 1–47. In particular, Anne Edwards provides a history of the use of the sex/gender distinction in feminism.
   [The phrase "recent edition" has been retained here to indicate that this essay was written in the thick of the sex/gender debate of the early 1990s.—Ed.].
2. For the argument that theorists of gender tend to formulate consciousness and body as arbitrarily connected and as passive and neutral tabulae rasae receiving postnatal social inscription, see, for example, Moira Gatens, "A Critique of the Sex/Gender Distinction," in *Beyond Marxism? Interventions After Marx*, ed. Judith Allen and Paul Patton (Sydney: Intervention, 1983). Jane Flax, "Postmodernism and Gender Relations in Feminist Theory," *Signs: Journal of Women in Culture and Society* 12, no. 4 (1987): 620–42, points out, "Initially, some feminists thought we could merely separate the terms sex and gender. . . . It became clear that such an (apparent) disjunction, while politically necessary, rested upon problematic and culture specific oppositions, for example, the one between 'nature' and 'culture' or 'body' and 'mind.' . . . New questions emerged: does anatomy (body) have no relation to mind? What difference does it make in the constitution of my social experiences that I have a specifically female body?" (635–36). Judith Butler, *Gender Trouble: Feminism and the Subversion of Identity* (New York: Routledge, 1990), argues that "gender ought not to be conceived merely as the cultural inscription of meaning on a pre-given sex. . . . Gender is not to culture as sex is to nature; gender is also the discursive/cultural means by which 'sexed nature' or 'a natural sex' is produced and established as prediscursive, prior to culture" (7).
3. For example, Toril Moi, *Sexual/Textual Politics* (London: Methuen, 1985), describes it as a "[long-]established practice among most feminists to use 'feminine' (and 'masculine') to represent social constructs (gender) and to reserve 'female' (and 'male') for purely biological aspects (sex)." Presuming it to be the equivalent of the sex/gender distinction, she describes the distinction between feminine and female, masculine and male, as "a fundamental political distinction." "It is in the patriarchal interest that these two terms (femininity and femaleness) stay thoroughly confused. Feminists, on the contrary, have to disentangle this confusion" (65).
4. Instances would include Anne Edwards's suggestion that while Ann Oakley explicitly intends to sustain a sex/gender distinction, she constantly confuses the terms. See Ann Oakley, *Sex, Gender, and Society* (Aldershot, U.K.: Gower/Temple Smith, 1972), as discussed by Edwards, "The Sex/Gender Distinction," 2. Toril Moi accuses Hélène Cixous of "slippage from 'feminine' to 'female' (or 'woman')" (Moi, *Sexual/Textual Politics*, 113); and similarly this is the "source of unease" in Cixous's work for Morag Schiach: "Their 'Symbolic' Exists, It Holds Power—We the Sowers of Disorder Know It Only Too Well," in *Between Feminism and Psychoanalysis*, ed. Teresa Brennan (London: Routledge, 1989). Both Marion Tapper and Denise Russell have accused Genevieve Lloyd, *The Man of Reason: "Male" and "Female" in Western Philosophy* (London: Methuen, 1984), of confusing her references to conceptions of femininity with her references to women.
   Tapper articulates her concerns thus: "It is clear that Lloyd is working with a distinction between sex and gender, that she is concerned not simply with the problems women face but with conceptions of femininity, their relation to conceptions of human ideals and their function in the subordi-

nation of women. But it is sometimes difficult to determine which of these issues is being discussed. This is partly because of the fluctuating terminology, between maleness, manliness and masculinity, and their correlates, femaleness, womanliness and femininity" (Marion Tapper, reviewing Lloyd, *The Man of Reason*, in *Public/Private* [Sydney: Local Consumption], 6 [1985]: 126–27).

Denise Russell is similarly concerned about "a confusion between sex and gender which is problematic throughout the book. . . . Lloyd blurs the sex/gender distinction more often than the authors she is discussing," although Russell does concede that "a rationale could be provided for keeping the sex/gender distinction fuzzy" (Denise Russell reviewing Genevieve Lloyd, *Australiasian Journal of Philosophy*, no. 64, suppl. [1986]: 139).

5. Although many theorists now insist on the structural blurring of sex and gender, accusations persist that writers have mistakenly blurred these terms.

6. The original discussion of the table of oppositions, formulated by the Pythagoreans as "two columns of cognates" to suggest the ten principles constituting the world, is found in Aristotle, "Metaphysics," trans. William David Ross, in *The Works of Aristotle*, vol. 8 (Oxford: Clarendon Press, 1928), A. 5 986a. Tables showing series of aligned binary oppositions reappear in modern feminist debate; for example, see Hélène Cixous, "Sorties," in *New French Feminisms: An Anthology*, ed. Elaine Marks and Isabelle de Courtivron (London: Harvester Press, 1981), 90; Val Plumwood, "Ecofeminism: An Overview and Discussion," in *Australiasian Journal of Philosophy*, no. 64, supplement (1986): 131; Alice Jardine, *Gynesis: Configurations of Woman and Modernity* (Ithaca: Cornell University Press, 1985), 72.

7. Cixous in "Sorties" describes her table with the opposition Man/Woman. Toril Moi describes Cixous's table as consisting of the left-hand "masculine" side and the right-hand "feminine" side, and then says that any of the oppositions of the table can be traced to the hidden underlying "male/female" opposition (*Sexual/Textual Politics*, 104–5). For Val Plumwood, in "Ecofeminism," the oppositions are associated with "masculine/feminine," while for Alice Jardine in *Gynesis*, the table is headed "Male/Female."

8. Feminist theorists have described the sexed binary opposition(s) as consisting of superior and inferior sides. The woman/female/feminine side is cast as the privation or "-A" of the man/male/masculine "A" side. The masculine side appears to have a stable and positive identity independent of its opposition to its feminine, binary opposite. However, feminists have argued, rather, that the masculine side is indebted to and produced by that opposition, that it exists only via the exclusion or foreclosure of a feminine identity exceeding the scope of the "-A" and that the terms are thus interconnected so that one can only discuss them as discrete "identities" by abstraction. This kind of analysis can be pursued in works such as Luce Irigaray, *Speculum of the Other Woman*, trans. G. C. Gill (Ithaca: Cornell University Press, 1985); Elizabeth Grosz, *Sexual Subversions: Three French Feminists* (Sydney: Allen and Unwin, 1990); Jardine, *Gynesis*; and Flax, "Postmodernism and Gender Relations." It is in the light of various analyses of the interconnection of the man/woman opposition as productive of those terms that I consider the blurred interconnection of man and masculine/woman and feminine as facilitative of the effect of a man/woman or masculine/feminine opposition.

9. Works, anthologies, and collections that select from the series Plato, Aristotle, Augustine, Aquinas, Descartes, Locke, Rousseau, Kant, and Hegel include Martha Lee Osbourne, ed., *Women in Western Thought* (New York: Random House, 1979); Mary Briody Mahowald, ed., *Philosophy of Woman: Classical to Current Concepts* (Indianapolis: Hackett, 1983); Carol McMillan, *Women, Reason, and Nature: Some Philosophical Problems with Feminism* (Oxford: Basil Blackwell, 1982); Susan Moller Okin, *Women in Western Political Thought* (Princeton: Princeton University Press, 1979); Lorenne Clarke and Lynda Lange, eds., *The Sexism of Social and Political Theory: Women and Reproduction from Plato to Nietzsche* (Toronto: University of Toronto Press, 1979); Carol Gould and Marx Wartofsky, eds., *Woman and Philosophy: Toward a Theory of Liberation* (New York: Peligree Books, 1976); Ellen Kennedy and Susan Mendus, eds., *Women in Western Political Philosophy: Kant to Nietzsche* (Sussex: Wheatsheaf Books, 1987); Jean Elshtain, *Public Man, Private Woman: Women in Social*

and Political Thought (Princeton: Princeton University Press, 1981); Lloyd, *The Man of Reason*. Other philosophers also cited by some of the above works include Nietzsche, Marx, Spinoza, Sartre, Hume, Mill, Wollstonecraft, or Beauvoir.

10. Within the field that might be roughly termed "theology and feminism," a great deal of attention has been directed to these concerns. See, for example, Marina Warner, *Alone of All Her Sex: The Myth and the Cult of the Virgin Mary* (London: Weidenfeld and Nicolson, 1976); Marilyn Chapin Massey, *Feminine Soul: The Fate of an Ideal* (Boston: Beacon Press, 1985); Julia O'Faolain and Lauro Martines, eds., *Not in God's Image* (New York: Harper and Row, 1973); Rosemary Radford Ruether, "Sexism, Religion, and the Social and Spiritual Liberation of Women Today," and "Liberating Philosophy: An End to the Dichotomy of Matter and Spirit," both in Carol Gould, ed., *Beyond Domination: New Perspectives on Women and Philosophy* (Totowa, N.J.: Rowman and Allanheld, 1983); among many others. One might also refer to Raoul Mortley's *Womanhood: The Feminine in Ancient Hellenism, Gnosticism, Christianity, and Islam* (Sydney: Delacroix Press, 1981).

11. One feature of the kind of work identified as "new French feminism" is that the theorists concerned, notably Luce Irigaray, Julia Kristeva, Sarah Kofman (in particular her *Aberrations: Le devenir femme d'Auguste Compte* [Paris: Aubier-Flammarion, 1978]), and even Cixous's "Sorties" all seem to demonstrate a greater enthusiasm for considering the debt or interrelation between the representation of masculine and of divine identities. Perhaps it could also be said in passing that, again, this is not an area of their work much discussed by Anglophone commentators.

12. In fact, Nancy Jay in "Gender and Dichotomy," *Feminist Studies* 7, no. 1 (1981): 36–56, combines a discussion of man/woman as a contradictory (A/not-A) dichotomy, with a discussion of god/man as a contradictory (A/not-A) dichotomy. She points out that both woman and god occupy the position of the negative in relation to man, commenting that where god and woman are defined as the privation of man's qualities, the "infinition of the negative" is "used very differently" (45). She does draw attention to the perverse nature of such contradictory dichotomies. For example, she says, dualist religions seem to "put maleness in the infinite, not-A position: immortality, spirit, and transcendence are male in such religions. . . . Yet if we try to interpret men as not-woman . . . it is nowhere near that simple: dualist religions will not fit this formulation. In dualist religion, the *female* side is regularly phrased as Not-A, and therefore tends toward infinitation: impurity, irrationality, disorder, chaos, change, chance . . . error, and evil. . . . Those very Greeks, who seemed to . . . see men as not-women, offer the clearest expression of the reverse. . . . You might expect that this formulation would lead to a reversal of the nature of an infinite God approached by the *via negativa*, who perhaps would turn out to be female. Not at all, divinity and immortality are still safely male" (45–46).

Despite raising these questions, Jay does not enter into a discussion of how woman and man are to be reconciled as negatives of man, or of what the implications of this apparently shared position might be, or how we are to understand the reversing gender of the infinite.

13. Augustine, *The Confessions of Saint Augustine*, trans. and with introduction and notes by John K. Ryan (New York: Image Books, 1960). This work is henceforth referred to throughout the essay by section, followed, in brackets, by page number.

14. This point bears some relation to Jacques Derrida's discussion of Plato's account of the dichotomous relationship between speech and writing. Here, although Socrates attributes primacy to speech over writing, this is similarly not because of some "intrinsic" (internal to the opposition speech/writing) primacy, but because of an apparently external reference point, that of the Forms, which are here cast in an analogy with Thamus/Ammon, the sun king and father of the Gods—so that the power of speech and knowledge refers to this paternal (divine) origin. Derrida's reading of speech as itself a form of writing relates to the fact that speech is only held superior to writing because of its constant deferral to a theological/metaphysical reference. It is at the point of this deferral that Derrida finds the leverage position from which he begins to unravel the speech/writing opposition. See Jacques Derrida, *Dissemination*, trans. Barbara Johnson (Chicago: University of Chicago Press, 1981), 76–81, 88.

15. The term *man of reason* is now used to refer not only to Lloyd's book of the same name, but, as Susan Hekman, *Gender and Knowledge: Elements of a Postmodern Feminism* (Oxford: Polity Press, 1990), points out, more generally to the concept (variously diagnosed, but that "most contemporary feminists agree on") that, "since Plato, and most particularly since the Enlightenment, reason and rationality have been defined in exclusively masculine terms" (34).

16. Although this point could be complicated by the fact that sometimes the account of god as "not-man" is not put in terms of god's identity, but rather in terms of his identifiability. Here, his identity as "not-man" is considered to be not a point about god, so much as a point about man's insufficiency, his inability to comprehend god in any terms other than negative ones.

17. Again, the double move, or double identity, of god bears some relationship to Derrida's account of "undecidability" in a binary opposition. For example, returning to Derrida's *Dissemination* (97), there the hierarchy of the "speech/writing" opposition is found to be confounded by the paradoxical or undecidable description of writing as *pharmakon*, a term that in Plato's text is both poison and remedy (to speech, or live memory). Writing is dangerous, is poison, because it dulls memory, yet it dulls memory insofar as it supplants it or is a remedy for memory.

18. Augustine slips between referring to soul and to mind, but at the point at which he refers to the heavens of heavens, then the essence surviving man is no longer a slippage between mind and soul and is, rather, definitively soul.

19. At this point, since on my reading a definitive distinction between *man* and *woman*, *masculine* and *feminine*, breaks down, and materiality is a category encapsulating both, this could be interpreted as an argument that there is "really" no difference between men and women! (My thanks to Catriona Mackenzie for raising this point.) Instead, sexual difference is *excluded* by the "man/woman" dichotomy (again, see Irigaray's *Speculum*). Hypothetically, in an economy of radical sexual difference, the feminine or the bodily would *not* encompass man and woman such that masculine identity could recede, displacing its excess onto the feminized material. In other words, the deferrals and displacements I have discussed should be understood as further manifestations of the exclusion of sexual difference.

20. Again, I have in mind the discussion in Derrida's *Dissemination* about equivalences between the posited realms of truth, *logos*, form, sun, and God with regard to the speech/writing opposition.

21. A body of work that has become known as "philosophy of the body" counters the mobilization of the sex/gender distinction. The connection between that work and the kind of interrelation between the term *man* and *masculinity*, *woman* and *femininity*, that I have outlined here would be another question again, as would the operation of deferral in sex/gender theory proper.

To Aurelius Augustine from the Mother of His Son

Ann Conrad Lammers

You took Adeodatus to your baptism (I almost wrote:
your funeral). The boy came later
and told me how it was. I hardly listened.
I wanted only, then as now,
to meet you once on level ground
and hear from your mouth the sound of my name.

You could drown my name in silence
but not silence it in your mind.
I am in the pages of your writing:
Eve, Lilith, the daughters of men.
I am the slave on account of sin,
the flesh that weighs down wisdom,
the image that deceives, the vessel
that catches and holds captive. In me
you beat down your unruly flesh.

From a boy passionate with love and clarity
I watched you change into a driven man
who broke himself in two. Everything
for you is now split halves: Charity
is founded on rejection, sainthood on divorce.
Other men choose the downward path
away from the mother's heaven, toward
a holiness woven in the flesh. Those men grow up.
They face their opposites and know themselves,
and suffer what they cannot know.

I wish I had confronted you when I could,
as wives confront their husbands, but then

you never let me come so close. Philosophy
protected you, then your rank, and finally your mother.
Monica—the virgin mother and the heavenly city!

You turned to gaze with her into eternal space.
For you, holiness is Monica and her son, like the two
natures of Christ, united without showing how.

Since I am banished from that mystery
I will go elsewhere. You cannot unmake me by theology.
Aurelius, your mistress and the world are standing
outside closed church-doors excommunicate.
The story of our parting has two sides.
I wonder if Aurelius is still alive.

Select Bibliography

Primary Sources

Latin Editions of Augustine's Works

Corpus Christianorum. Series Latina. The Hague: Nijhoff, 1953–.
Corpus Scriptorum Ecclesiasticorum Latinorum. Vienna: Tempsky, 1887–1961ff.
Migne, J. P., ed. *Patrologiae Cursus Completus, Series Latina*. Vols. 32–47. Paris, 1841–64.

English Editions of Augustine's Works: Series, Collections, and Single Texts

Augustine. *The City of God*. Translated by Henry Bettenson and with an introduction by David Knowles. London: Penguin Classics, 1977.
———. *Confessions*. Edited by James J. O'Donnell. 3 vols. Oxford: Clarendon Press, 1992.
———. *Confessions*. Translated by Henry Chadwick. New York: Oxford University Press, 1991.
———. *Free Choice of the Will*. Translated by Anna S. Benjamin and L. H. Hackstaff. Indianapolis, Ind.: Bobbs-Merrill, 1964.
———. *Political Writings*. Translated by Michael Tkacz and Douglas Kries. Edited by Ernest Fortin and Douglas Kries. Indianapolis, Ind.: Hackett, 1966.
———. *Soliloquies: Augustine's Interior Dialogue*. Translated by Kim Paffenroth. Edited by John Rotelle. Hyde Park, N.Y.: New City Press, 2000.
———. *The Trinity*. Translated and with an introduction by Edmund Hill. In *The Works of Saint Augustine for the 21st Century*, edited by John E. Rotelle. Brooklyn, N.Y.: New City Press, 1991.
Deferrari, Roy et al., eds. *Fathers of the Church*. Washington, D.C.: Catholic University of America Press, 1948–.
Dods, Marcus, ed. *The Works of Aurelius Augustinus*. Edinburgh: T. and T. Clark, 1871–76.
Quasten, J. et al., eds. *Ancient Christian Writers*. Westminster, Md.: Newman Press, 1946–.
Rotelle, John E., ed. *Works of Saint Augustine: A Translation for the 21st Century*. Brooklyn, N.Y.: New City Press, 1990–.

Schaff, Philip, ed. *A Select Library of Nicene and Post-Nicene Fathers of the Church*. New York: Scribners, 1892.

Reference Works

Augustinus-Lexikon. Edited by Cornelius Mayer, Karl Heinz Chelius, Hans-Joachim Lange, Andreas E. J. Grote, et al. Basel: Schwabe, 1986–. www.augustinus.de.
Corpus Augustinianum Gissense. Edited by Cornelius Mayer, Karl Heinz Chelius, Hans-Joachim Lange, Andreas E. J. Grote, et al. www.augustinus.de. Electronic edition of Augustine's works.
Fitzgerald, Allan D., ed., *Augustine Through the Ages: An Encyclopedia*. Grand Rapids, Mich.: Eerdmans, 1999.
www.georgetown.edu/faculty/jod/augustine. This was the first and still is the best, most comprehensive, and most user-friendly Web site available on Augustine in English.

Bibliographies

Andresen, Carl. *Bibliographia Augustiniana*. Darmstadt, Germany: Wissenschaftliche Buchgesellschaft, 1973.
Fichier Augustinien. Boston: G. K. Hall, 1972–.
Revue des études augustiniennes. Paris, 1956–. Yearly survey of books and articles on Augustine.

Secondary Sources

Adams, Carol, and Marie M. Fortune, eds. *Violence Against Women and Children: A Christian Theological Sourcebook*. New York: Continuum, 1995.
Alexander, William M. "Sex and Philosophy in St. Augustine." *Augustinian Studies* 5 (1974): 197–208.
Arendt, Hannah. *Love and Saint Augustine*. Edited and with an interpretive essay by Joanna Vecchiarelli Scott and Judith Chelius Stark. Chicago: University of Chicago Press, 1996.
Asiedu, F.B.A. "The Song of Songs and the Ascent of the Soul: Ambrose, Augustine, and the Language of Mysticism." *Vigiliae Christianae* 55, no. 3 (2001): 299–317.
Atkinson, Clarissa W., Constance Buchanan, and Margaret Miles, eds. *Immaculate and Powerful: The Female in Sacred Image and Social Reality*. Boston: Beacon Press, 1985.

Bathory, Peter Dennis. *Political Theory as Public Confession: The Social and Political Thought of St. Augustine*. New Brunswick, N.J.: Transaction Books, 1981.

Benjamin, Jessica. *The Bonds of Love: Psychoanalysis, Feminism, and the Problem of Domination*. New York: Pantheon Books, 1988.

Bonner, Gerald. "Augustine's Attitudes Toward Women and 'Amicitia.'" In *Homo Spiritualis: Festgabe für Luc Verheijn*, edited by Cornelius Mayer and Karl E. Chelius. Würzburg, Germany: Augustinus Verlag, 1987.

———. "The Figure of Eve in Augustine's Theology." *Studia Patristica* 33 (1997): 22–34.

———. *St. Augustine of Hippo: Life and Controversies*. Norwich, U.K.: Canterbury Press, 1986.

Bordo, Susan. *Unbearable Weight: Feminism, Western Culture, and the Body*. Berkeley and Los Angeles: University of California Press, 1993.

Børresen, Kari Elisabeth. "In Defense of Augustine: How *Femina* Is *Homo*." In *Collectanea Augustiniana*. Louvain: Leuven University Press, 1990.

———. "Patristic Feminism: The Case of Augustine." *Augustinian Studies* 25 (1994): 139–52.

———. *Subordination and Equivalence: The Nature and Role of Women in Augustine and Thomas Aquinas*. Translated by Charles H. Talbot. Washington, D.C.: University Press of America, 1981.

Bowerstock, G. W., Peter Brown, and Oleg Grabar, eds. *Late Antiquity: A Guide to the Postclassical World*. Cambridge, Mass.: Harvard University Press, 1999.

Brock, Rita Nakashima. *Journeys by Heart: A Christology of Erotic Power*. New York: Crossroad, 1995.

Brown, Peter. *Augustine of Hippo: A Biography*. 2d ed. Berkeley and Los Angeles: University of California Press, 2000.

———. *The Body and Society: Men, Women, and Sexual Renunciation in Early Christianity*. New York: Columbia University Press, 1988.

———. *Religion and Society in the Age of St. Augustine*. New York: Harper and Row, 1972.

———. *The World of Late Antiquity*, A.D. 150–750. New York: Harcourt Brace Jovanovich, 1971.

Burke, Cormac. "St. Augustine and Conjugal Sexuality." *Communio* 17 (Winter 1990): 545–65.

Burrell, David. "Reading the *Confessions* of Augustine: The Case of Oedipal Analysis." In *The Hunger of the Heart: Reflections on the "Confessions" of Augustine*, edited by Donald Capps and James E. Dittes. West Lafayette, Ind.: Society for the Scientific Study of Religion, 1990.

Burrus, V. "An Immoderate Feast: Augustine Reads John's Apocalypse." *Augustinian Studies* 30, no. 2 (1999): 183–94.

Burt, Donald X. *Augustine's World: An Introduction*. Lanham: University Press of America, 1996.

Bynum, Caroline Walker. *The Resurrection of the Body in Western Christianity, 200–1336*. New York: Columbia University Press, 1995.

Cahill, Lisa Sowle. *Sex, Gender, and Christian Ethics*. New York: Cambridge University Press, 1996.

Capps, Donald, and James Dittes, eds. *The Hunger of the Heart: Reflections on the "Confessions" of Augustine*. West Lafayette, Ind.: Society for the Scientific Study of Religion, 1990.

Cavadini, John. "The Structure and Intention of Augustine's *De Trinitate.*" *Augustinian Studies* 23 (1992): 103–23.

Chadwick, Henry. *Augustine.* New York: Oxford University Press, 1991.

———. *The Early Church.* New York: Penguin Books, 1976.

Clark, Elizabeth. *Ascetic Piety and Women's Faith: Essays on Late Ancient Christianity.* Lewiston, N.Y.: Edwin Mellen Press, 1986.

———. "'Augustine's Only Companion': Augustine and the Early Christian Debate on Marriage." *Recherches Augustiniennes* 21 (1986): 139–62.

———. "Theory and Practice in Late Ancient Asceticism: Jerome, Chrysostom, and Augustine." *Journal of Feminist Studies in Religion* 5, no. 2 (1989): 25–46.

———. *Women in the Early Church.* Wilmington, Del.: Michael Glazier, 1983.

———, ed. *St. Augustine on Marriage and Sexuality.* Washington, D.C.: Catholic University of America Press, 1996.

Clifford, Anne. *Introducing Feminist Theology.* Maryknoll, N.Y.: Orbis Books, 2001.

Coakley, Sarah. "'Batter My Heart . . . ?' On Sexuality, Spirituality, and the Christian Doctrine of the Trinity." *Graven Images* 2 (1995). Reprinted from *Harvard Divinity Bulletin* 23, no. 3/4 (1994): 12–17.

Cooper, Kate. *The Virgin and the Bride: Idealized Womanhood in Late Antiquity.* Cambridge, Mass.: Harvard University Press, 1996.

Cunneen, Sally. *In Search of Mary: The Woman and the Symbol.* New York: Ballantine Books, 1996.

Daly, Mary. *Beyond God the Father: Toward a Philosophy of Women's Liberation.* Boston: Beacon Press, 1973.

———. *Pure Lust: Elemental Feminist Philosophy.* Boston: Beacon Press, 1984.

Derrida, Jacques. "Circumfession." In *Jacques Derrida,* edited by G. Bennington and J. Derrida. Chicago: University of Chicago Press, 1993.

Dittes, James E. "Augustine: Seach for a Fail-Safe God to Trust." In *The Hunger of the Heart: Reflections on the "Confessions" of Augustine,* edited by Donald Capps and James E. Dittes. West Lafayette, Ind.: Society for the Scientific Study of Religion, 1990.

Dixon, Sandra Lee. *Augustine: The Scattered and the Gathered Self.* St. Louis, Mo.: Chalice Press, 1999.

Dodaro, Robert. *Christ and the Just Society in the Thought of Augustine.* New York: Cambridge University Press, 2004.

Dodaro, Robert, and George Lawless, eds. *Augustine and his Critics: Essays in Honour of Gerald Bonner.* New York: Routledge, 2000.

Elm, Susanna. *Virgins of God: The Making of Asceticism in Late Antiquity.* Oxford: Clarendon, 1994.

Elshtain, Jean Bethke. *Augustine and the Limits of Politics.* Notre Dame: University of Notre Dame Press, 1995.

Evans, G. R. *Augustine on Evil.* New York: Cambridge University Press, 2000.

Ferrari, Leo. "The Dreams of Monica in Augustine's *Confessions.*" *Augustinian Studies* 8 (1979): 6–24.

Fox, Robin Lane. *Pagans and Christians.* New York: Alfred A. Knopf, 1987.

Frend, W. H. C. *The Donatist Church: A Movement of Protest in North Africa.* Oxford: Clarendon Press, 1952.

Gardner, Jane. *Women in Roman Law and Society.* Bloomington, Ind.: Indiana University Press, 1986.

Gilson, Etienne. *The Christian Philosophy of St. Augustine*. New York: Random House, 1960.

Griffiths, Paul J. *Lying: An Augustinian Theology of Duplicity*. Grand Rapids, Mich.: Brazos Press, 2004.

Hanby, Michael. *Augustine and Modernity*. New York: Routledge, 2003.

Harrison, Carol. *Augustine: Christian Truth and Fractured Humanity*. New York: Oxford University Press, 2000.

———. *Beauty and Revelation in the Thought of Saint Augustine*. Oxford: Clarendon Press, 1992.

Hefling, Charles, ed. *Our Selves, Our Souls, and Bodies: Sexuality and the Household of God*. Boston: Cowley, 1996.

Henry, Paul. *Path to Transcendence: From Philosophy to Mysticism in Saint Augustine*. Translated and with an introduction by Francis Burch. Pittsburgh, Pa.: Pickwick Press, 1981.

Heyward, Carter. *Touching Our Strength: The Erotic as Power and Love of God*. San Francisco: Harper and Row, 1989.

Hinsdale, Mary Ann, and Phyllis H. Kaminski, eds. *Women and Theology: Annual Publication of the College Theology Society*. Vol. 40. Maryknoll, N.Y.: Orbis Books, 1995.

Holler, Linda. *Erotic Morality: The Role of Touch in Moral Agency*. New Brunswick: Rutgers University Press, 2002.

Horowitz, Maryanne Cline. "The Image of God in Man: Is Woman Included?" *Harvard Theological Review* 72 (1979): 175–206.

Hunter, David G. "Augustinian Pessimism? A New Look at Augustine's Teaching on Sex, Marriage, and Celibacy." *Augustinian Studies* 25 (1994): 153–77.

Irigaray, Luce. *Speculum of the Other Woman*. Translated by G. C. Gill. Ithaca: Cornell University Press, 1985.

Jantzen, Grace. *Becoming Divine: Towards a Feminist Philosophy of Religion*. Bloomington, Ind.: Indiana University Press, 1999.

Jaspers, Karl. *Plato and Augustine*. Edited by Hannah Arendt. Translated by Ralph Manheim. New York: Harcourt, Brace and World, 1962.

Johnson, Elizabeth. *Women, Earth, and Creator Spirit*. New York: Paulist Press, 1993.

Keller, Catherine. *The Face of the Deep: A Theology of Becoming*. New York: Routledge, 2002.

Kirwan, Christopher. *Augustine*. New York: Routledge, 1991.

Kligerman, Charles. "A Psychoanalytic Study of the *Confessions* of St. Augustine." In *The Hunger of the Heart: Reflections on the "Confessions" of Augustine*, edited by Donald Capps and James E. Dittes. West Lafayette, Ind.: Society for the Scientific Study of Religion, 1990.

Knowles, Andrew, and Pachomios Penkett. *Augustine and His World*. Downers Grove, Ill.: Intervarsity Press, 2004.

Kraemer, Ross S. *Her Share of the Blessings: Women's Religions Among Pagans, Jews, and Christians in the Greco-Roman World*. New York: Oxford University Press, 1992.

———, ed. *Maenads, Martyrs, Matrons, Monastics: A Sourcebook on Women's Religions in the Greco-Roman World*. Philadelphia: Fortress Press, 1988.

Kraemer, Ross Shepard, and Mary Rose D'Angelo, eds. *Women and Christian Origins*. New York: Oxford University Press, 1999.

Kries, Douglas, and Catherine Brown, eds. *Nova Doctrina and Vetusque: Essays on Early*

Christianity in Honor of Frederic W. Schlatter, S.J. New York: Peter Lang, 1999, 169–85.

Kristeva, Julia. *"Stabat Mater."* Translated by León S. Roudiez. In *The Kristeva Reader*, edited by Toril Moi. Oxford: Basil Blackwell, 1986.

Kristo, J. G. *Looking for God in Time and Memory: Theology, Psychology, and Spirituality in Augustine's "Confessions."* New York: University Press of America, 1991.

Lacugna, Catherine. *God for Us: The Trinity and Christian Life.* San Francisco: HarperSan-Francisco, 1991.

Lawless, George. "Augustine and Human Embodiment." In *Collectanea Augustiniana.* Louvain: Leuven University Press, 1990.

Lionnet, Francoise. *Autobiographical Voices: Race, Gender, and Self-Portraiture.* Ithaca: Cornell University Press, 1989.

Livingstone, Elizabeth A. *Augustine and His Opponents: Jerome and Other Latin Fathers After Nicaea.* In *Studia Patristica* 33. Louvain: Peeters, 1997.

Lyotard, Jean-Francois. *The Confession of Augustine.* Translated by Richard Beardsworth. Stanford: Stanford University Press, 2000.

Macy, Gary, ed. *Theology and the New Histories.* Maryknoll, N.Y.: Orbis Press, 1999.

Markus, R. A., ed. *Augustine: A Collection of Critical Essays.* Garden City, N.Y.: Anchor Books, 1972.

———. *Conversion and Disenchantment in Augustine's Spiritual Career.* Villanova, Pa.: Villanova University Press, 1989.

———. *Saeculum: History and Society in the Theology of St. Augustine.* Cambridge, U.K.: Cambridge University Press, 1970.

Matter, E. Ann. "Christ, God, and Woman in the Thought of St. Augustine." In *Augustine and His Critics,* edited by Robert Dodaro and George Lawless. New York: Routledge, 2000.

Matthews, Gareth, ed. *Augustinian Tradition.* Berkeley and Los Angeles: University of California Press, 1999.

———. *Thought's Ego in Augustine and Descartes.* Ithaca: Cornell University Press, 1992.

Mayer, Cornelius, and Karl H. Chelius, eds. *Homo Spiritualis: Festgabe für Luc Verheijin.* Würtzburg, Germany: Augustinus Verlag, 1987.

McMahon, Robert. *Augustine's Prayerful Ascent.* Athens: University of Georgia Press, 1989.

Meagher, Robert. *Augustine: An Introduction.* New York: New York University Press, 1978.

Meconi, David Vincent, *"Grata Sacris Angelis:* Gender and the *Imago Dei* in Augustine's *De Trinitate* XII." *American Catholic Philosophical Quarterly* 74, no. 1 (2000): 48–62.

———. "St. Augustine on Marriage and Sexuality." *Review of Metaphysics* 51, no. 3 (1998): 667–69.

Miles, Margaret R. *Augustine on the Body.* Missoula, Mont.: Scholar's Press, 1979.

———. "The Body and Human Values in Augustine of Hippo." In *Grace, Politics, and Desire: Essays on Augustine,* edited by H. A. Meynell. Calgary, Alberta: University of Calgary Press, 1990.

———. *Carnal Knowing: Female Nakedness and Religious Meaning in the Christian West.* Boston: Beacon Press, 1992.

———. *Desire and Delight: A New Reading of Augustine's "Confessions."* New York: Crossroad Press, 1992.

———. "Roman North African Christian Spiritualities." In *African Spiritualities: Forms,*

Meanings, and Expressions, edited by Jacob K. Olupona. New York: Herder and Herder, 2001.

O'Connell, Robert J. "Sexuality in Saint Augustine." In *Augustine Today*, edited by Richard John Neuhaus. Grand Rapids, Mich.: Eerdmans, 1993.

———. *St. Augustine's "Confessions": The Odyssey of Soul*. Cambridge, Mass.: Harvard University Press, 1969.

———. *St. Augustine's Early Theory of Man*, A.D. 386–391. Cambridge, Mass.: Harvard University Press, 1968.

O'Donnell, James J. *Augustine*. Boston: Twayne, 1985.

———. *Augustine: A New Biography*. New York: Ecco-HarperCollins, 2005.

O'Donovan, Oliver. *The Problem of Self-Love in St. Augustine*. New Haven: Yale University Press, 1980.

Pagels, Elaine. *Adam, Eve, and the Serpent*. New York: Random House, 1988.

Patte, Daniel, and Eugene TeSelle, eds. *Engaging Augustine on Romans: Self, Context, and Theology in Interpretation*. Harrisburg, Pa.: Trinity Press International, 2002.

Pelikan, Jaroslav. *The Emergence of the Catholic Tradition: A History of the Development of Doctrine (100–600)*. Chicago: University of Chicago Press, 1971.

———. *Mary Through the Centuries: Her Place in the History of Culture*. New Haven: Yale University Press, 1996.

———. *Mystery of Continuity: Time and History, Memory and Eternity in the Thought of St. Augustine*. Charlottesville: University Press of Virginia, 1986.

Pellauer, Mary. "Augustine on Rape: One Chapter in the Theological Tradition." In *Violence Against Women and Children*, edited by Carol Adams and Marie Fortune. New York: Continuum, 1995.

Pomeroy, Sarah. *Goddesses, Whores, Wives, and Slaves: Women in Classical Antiquity*. New York: Schocken Books, 1975.

Power, Kim. *Veiled Desire: Augustine on Women*. New York: Continuum, 1996.

Prendiville, John. *Development of the Idea of Habit in the Thought of Saint Augustine*. New York: Fordham University Press, 1972.

Ramirez, J. Roland E. "Demythologizing Augustine as a Great Sinner." *Augustinian Studies* 12 (1981): 61–88.

Ramsey, Paul. *Ethics of Saint Augustine*. Atlanta: Scholars Press, 1991.

Ranke-Heinemann, Uta. *Eunuchs for the Kingdom: Women, Sexuality, and the Catholic Church*. Translated by Peter Heinegg. New York: Doubleday, 1990.

Rigby, P. "Paul Ricoeur, Freudianism, and Augustine's *Confessions*." *Journal of the American Academy of Religion* 53 (1985): 93–114.

Rist, John M. *Augustine: Ancient Thought Baptized*. New York: Cambridge University Press, 1995.

———. "Augustine on Free Will and Predestination." *Journal of Theological Studies* 20 (1969): 420–47.

Rogers, Eugene F. *Sexuality and the Christian Body: Their Way into the Triune God*. Malden, Mass: Blackwell, 1999.

Rogers, Katherine A. "Equal Before God: Augustine on the Nature and Role of Women." In *Nova Doctrina and Vetusque: Essays on Early Christianity in Honor of Frederic W. Schlatter, S.J.*, edited by Douglas Kries and Catherine Brown. New York: Peter Lang, 1999.

Rolston, Holmes, III. *Religious Inquiry: Participation and Detachment*. New York: Philosophical Library, 1985.

Rousselle, Aline. *Porneia: Desire and the Body in Antiquity*. Oxford: Basil Blackwell, 1988.

Ruether, Rosemary Radford. *Gaia and God: An Ecofeminist Theology of Earth Healing*. San Francisco: Harper and Row, 1992.

———, ed. *Gender, Ethnicity, and Religion: Views from the Other Side*. Minneapolis: Fortress Press, 2002.

———. *Mary: The Feminine Face of the Church*. Philadelphia: Westminster Press, 1977.

———. "Misogynism and Virginal Feminism in the Fathers of the Church." In *Religion and Sexism: Images of Women in the Jewish and Christian Traditions*, edited by Rosemary Radford Ruether. New York: Simon and Schuster, 1974.

———. *Sexism and God-Talk: Toward a Feminist Theology*. Boston: Beacon Press, 1983.

———. *Women and Redemption: A Theological History*. Minneapolis: Fortress Press, 1998.

———, ed. *Women and Sexism: Images of Women in the Jewish and Christian Traditions*. New York: Simon and Schuster, 1974.

Ruether, Rosemary Radford, and Eleanor McLaughlin, eds. *Women of Spirit: Female Leadership in the Jewish and Christian Traditions*. New York: Simon and Schuster, 1979.

Schlabach, Gerald W. *For the Joy Set Before Us: Augustine and Self-Denying Love*. Notre Dame: University of Notre Dame Press, 2001.

Schnaubelt, Joseph C., and Frederick Van Fleteren, eds. *Collectanea Augustiniana: Augustine, "Second Founder of the Faith."* New York: Peter Lang, 1990.

Schuld, J. Joyce. *Foucault and Augustine: Reconsidering Power and Love*. Notre Dame: University of Notre Dame Press, 2003.

Schussler Fiorenza, Elisabeth. *In Memory of Her: A Feminist Theological Reconstruction of Christian Origins*. New York: Crossroad, 1983.

———, ed. *Searching the Scriptures*. Vol. 2, *A Feminist Commentary*. New York: Crossroad, 1994.

Shanzer, D. "Latent Narrative Patterns, Allegorical Choices, and Literary Unity in Augustine's *Confessions*." *Vigiliae Christianae* 46, no.1 (1992): 51–71.

Shaw, Brent. "The Family in Late Antiquity." *Past and Present* 115 (1987): 33–36.

Shaw, Teresa M. *The Burden of the Flesh: Fasting and Sexuality in Early Christianity*. Minneapolis: Fortress Press, 1998.

Starnes, Colin. *Augustine's Conversion: A Guide to the Argument of Confessions I–IX*. Waterloo: Wilfred Laurier University Press, 1990.

Stock, Brian. *Augustine the Reader: Meditation, Self-Knowledge, and the Ethics of Interpretation*. Cambridge, Mass.: Belknap Press of Harvard University Press, 1996.

Stuart, Elizabeth, and Adrian Thatcher, eds. *Christian Perspectives on Sexuality and Gender*. Grand Rapids, Mich.: Eerdmans, 1996.

Stump, Eleonore, and Norman Kretzmann, eds. *Cambridge Companion to Augustine*. New York: Cambridge University Press, 2001.

Te Selle, Eugene. "Serpent, Eve, and Adam." In *Collectanea Augustinina: Augustine Presbyter Factus Sum*, edited by Joseph T. Lienhard et al. New York: Peter Lang, 1993.

Van Bavel, Tarsicius. "Augustine's View on Women." *Augustiniana* 39 (1989): 6–53.

———. "Woman as the Image of God in Augustine's *De Trinitate* XII," *Signum Pietatis: Festgabe für Cornelius Mayer, OSA*, edited by A. Zumkeller. Würzburg, Germany: Augustinus Verlag, 1989.

Van der Meer, F. *Augustine the Bishop*. Translated by Brian Battershaw and G. R. Lamb. New York: Sheed and Ward, 1961.

Vaught, Carl G. *Journey Toward God in Augustine's "Confessions": Books I–IV*. Albany: State University of New York Press, 2003.

Weaver, F. Ellen, and Jean Laporte. "Augustine and Women: Relationships and Teach-
    ings." *Augustinian Studies* 12 (1981): 115–32.
Williams, Jane. "The Doctrine of the Trinity: A Way for Feminists?" In *Women's Voices:*
    Essays in Contemporary Feminist Theology, edited by Teresa Elwes. London: Mar-
    shall Pickering (HarperCollins), 1992.
West, Rebecca. *St. Augustine*. London: P. Davies, 1933.
Williams, Rowan D. "Good for Nothing? Augustine on Creation." *Augustinian Studies* 25
    (1994): 9–24.
Wills, Garry. *Saint Augustine*. New York: Viking Penguin, 1999.
———. *Saint Augustine's Memory*. New York: Viking Press, 2002.
———. *Saint Augustine's Sin*. New York: Viking Press: 2003.
Ziolkowski, E. J. "St. Augustine: Aeneas' Antitype, Monica's Boy." *Literature and Theology*
    9, no.1 (1995): 1–23.

Contributors

ANNE-MARIE BOWERY is an associate professor of philosophy at Baylor University and director of graduate studies. She received her doctorate from the Pennsylvania State University. In addition to Augustine, she writes on Plato and philosophical pedagogy. She is completing a book, *A Philosophic Muse: Plato's Socrates as Narrator*.

VIRGINIA BURRUS is professor of early church history at Drew University. Her research interests in the field of late ancient Christianity center on issues of gender, sexuality, and the body; orthodoxy and heresy; and the literatures of martyrdom and hagiography. Her publications include *"Begotten, Not Made": Conceiving Manhood in Late Antiquity* (2000); *The Sex Lives of Saints: An Erotics of Ancient Hagiography* (2004); *Late Ancient Christianity* (2005; editor); and *Toward a Theology of Eros: Transfiguring Passion at the Limits of Discipline* (2006; coeditor). She is currently working on a book about ancient Christian views of shame.

PENELOPE DEUTSCHER is an associate professor in the Department of Philosophy, Northwestern University. She is the author of *Yielding Gender: Feminism, Deconstruction and the History of Philosophy* and of *A Politics of Impossible Difference: The Later Work of Luce Irigaray*. She coedited (with Kelly Oliver) *Enigmas: Essays on Sarah Kofman* and also coedited (with Francoise Collin) *Repenser le politique: L'apport du feminisme* and is now working on a project about Simone de Beauvoir, titled *Conversions of Ambiguity*.

CATHERINE KELLER is professor of constructive theology at Drew University. Her interests span a wide theopoetic/theopolitical spectrum, embracing feminist, ecological, process, and poststructuralist investigations. Her publications include *Apocalypse Now and Then: A Feminist Guide to the End of the World* (1996); *Process and Difference: Between Cosmological and Poststructuralist Postmodernisms* (2002; coeditor); *Face of the Deep: A Theology of Becoming* (2003); *God and Power: Counter-Apocalyptic Journeys* (2005); and *Toward a Theology of Eros: Transfiguring Passion at the Limits of Discipline* (2006; coeditor). She is currently working on a book for seminarians called *On the Mystery*, as well as a scholarly text titled *The Absolute and the Dissolute: Exercises in Truth*.

ANN CONRAD LAMMERS is a psychotherapist who had a private practice in Berkeley, California for many years. She is the author of *In God's Shadow: The Collaboration of*

Victor White and C. G. Jung (Paulist Press, 1994). She specializes in therapeutic treatments for trauma, stress, anxiety, and depression. Lammers currently practices in New England.

E. ANN MATTER is the William R. Kenan, Jr. Professor of Religious Studies and associate dean for Arts and Letters of the School of Arts and Sciences at the University of Pennsylvania. Her work has centered on the Bible in the Middle Ages and the role of women in Christian history. She is the author of *The Voice of My Beloved: The Song of Songs in Western Medieval Christianity* (2000).

FELECIA MCDUFFIE is T. Jack Lance Professor of Religion at Young Harris College in Young Harris, Georgia. She is the author of *To Our Bodies Turn We Then: The Body as Word and Sacrament in the Works of John Donne* (2005).

JOANNE ELIZABETH MCWILLIAM has taught at the University of Detroit, the University of Toronto, and the General Theological Seminary (New York City). She is professor emeritus at the University of Toronto and is the author of *The Theology of Grace of Theodore of Mopsuestia*; *Death and Resurrection in the Fathers*; and many articles. She also edited *Augustine: Rhetor to Theologian*. She is past president of the Canadian Society for Patristic Studies, the Canadian Theological Society, and the American Theological Society. She received an honorary D.D. from Queen's University in 2003.

MARGARET R. MILES is emerita professor of historical theology, the Graduate Theological Union, Berkeley, California. Her books include *A Complex Delight: The Secularization of the Breast, 1350–1750* (2007); *The Word Made Flesh: A History of Christian Thought* (2004); *Plotinus on Body and Beauty* (1999); *Seeing and Believing: Religion and Values in the Movies* (1996); and *Desire and Delight: A New Reading of Augustine's Confessions* (1992).

JULIE B. MILLER is associate professor of religious studies and chair of the Cultural Studies Program at the University of the Incarnate Word in San Antonio, Texas. She holds a doctorate in religion, gender, and culture from Harvard University. Her current research interests include the interactions between religion and sexual violence and environmental theology and ethics.

REBECCA MOORE is chair of the Department of Religious Studies at San Diego State University, where she teaches courses in the history of Christianity, religion in America, and new religious movements. She has written and published on medieval theologians and their biblical commentaries. Her most recent book is *Voices of Christianity: A Global Introduction* (2005).

ROSEMARY RADFORD RUETHER is the Carpenter Professor of Feminist Theology, emerita, at the Graduate Theological Union in Berkeley, California, as well as the Georgia Harkness Emerita Professor of Applied Theology at Garrett Evangelical Theological Seminary. She presently teaches at Claremont Graduate University in Claremont, California. Ruether has authored and edited more than forty books, including *Sexism and God-Talk*; *In Our Own Voices: Four Centuries of American Women's Religious Writing* (edited with Rosemary Skinner Keller); and *The Wrath of Jonah: The Crisis of Religious Nationalism in the Israeli-Palestinian Conflict*. Her most recent books include *Goddesses and the Divine Feminine: A Western Religious History* (2005) and *Integrating Ecofeminism, Globaliza-*

tion, and World Religions (2005). In March 2006, the multivolume *Encyclopedia of Women in American Religion* (with Rosemary Skinner Keller) was published, a project funded by the Lilly Endowment. Her most recent book, *America, Amerikkka: Elect Nation and Imperial Violence,* is due to be published in 2007.

JUDITH CHELIUS STARK is professor of philosophy at Seton Hall University in South Orange, New Jersey, where she teaches seminars on Augustine, feminist theories, and environmental ethics. She also team-teaches in the interdisciplinary University Honors Program, of which she is an associate director and former director. She publishes on Augustine, environmental issues, and human rights and is the coauthor (with Joanna Vechiarelli Scott) of *Hannah Arendt: Love and Saint Augustine* (1996).

Index

Acts of Paul and Thecla, 58

Adam and Eve, Augustine's discussion of, 52–57, 100–103, 188n.82, 204; grace and free will and, 239n.9; image of God and, 225–26; loss of self and, 251–54; punishment of soul through disobedience of, 254–55; woman's inferiority and, 104–10

addiction, Augustine's sexuality as, 245–46, 275nn.13–14

Adeodatus (son of Augustine), 26, 33, 49–51, 86, 131, 149, 167, 169, 181, 301

Admonition and Grace, 239n.9

adultery: Augustine on fidelity and, 178–79, 187n.61; Augustine's partnerships with women and, 170–72, 174, 184n.14, 185n.27; social arrangements for sexuality and, 177–82, 186n.47

Aeneid, 7, 148

African Christianity, 6–7, 159, 160–61, 176–77, 196–97

Against the Academicians, 157–58

Against the Manicheans, 180

Alaric, sack of Rome by, 20, 196

Albina, Augustine's letters to, 58, 189, 191–93, 206–7

Alypius (friend of Augustine), 4–5, 16, 75, 84, 89–90, 191–92, 200, 206–7; as bishop of Thagaste, 5, 191–93, 206–7

Ambrose (Bishop of Milan), 4, 20, 49, 60, 79; Augustine influenced by, 144n.32, 198, 218; Genesis text and, 224, 240n.16; masculinity of, 114–15; Monica and, 110, 159

Ambrosiaster, 54, 204–5, 214n.22

androcentrism, in Augustine's work, 53–56

androgyny, in Augustine's Scriptural interpretations, 229–30, 240n.18

antinomies of Greek-Roman thinking, Augustine's embodiment and, 24–29

Apocrypha, chastity stories in, 152

Apuleius, 123–25, 142nn.12, 15

Aquinas, Thomas, 5

Arendt, Hannah, 32, 138–39, 145nn.40, 42, 44; natality in Augustine, 138–39

Arian view of Trinity, 221, 226, 237–38

Aristotle: Christianity and, 5; feminist interpretations of, 21–22

Armentarius, 208

Armstrong, Hilary, 91n.7

Antony of Egypt, 176

asceticism: Augustine's discussion of, 27–29, 39–40, 45n.39, 49, 51, 204; contraception and, 180–82; exclusion of women from, 57–64; "women-of-worth" tales and, 152–56; women's status and, 175–77

Asiedu, F. B. A., 144n.32

Athanasius, 176

Atkinson, Clarissa, 73, 78

attachment theory, feminist versions of, 37

Augustine: baptism of, 4, 11–14, 49–50, 85–86, 121, with Adeodatus, 301–2; Catholic Church and, 159; concubines of, 15–18, 33–34, 48–49; conversion to Christianity, 3–4, 80–91, 111–12, 121–22, 141n.4; death of, 9; education of, 47–48, 82; family life of, 10–14; feminist interpretations of, 21–22, 30–33, 38–42; Pelagius's debate with, 8–9; spiritual and philosophical journey and, 2–4; women and, 9–14, 33–36

12, 157–58, 198–99, 205–6, 243–44, 249, 254–57, 260–62; as bridegroom, 115–16, 261, 277n.40; as father, 88–89, 285–86; feminine imagery, 77–78; language and distinctions in, 217–20, 286–91, 294–95; love of material as separation from, 107–10; as lover, in *Confessions*, 3, 16,112–16; moral dimensions of, 219–20; as mother, 88–89, 110–12; ontological dimensions of, 219; sex/gender identities and, 282–97, 299n.12; sexuality as barrier to, 245–46; Son of God, 261, 278n.41; women as lesser image of, 215–38

Golden Ass, The, 123–25, 142nn.12, 15
Good of Marriage, The, 181
grace, Augustine's discussion of, 8–9, 220, 239n.9
Grace of Christ, The, 207–8
Greek romances, chastity stories in, 152
Gregory of Nyssa, 126, 156–57, 160–61
grief, Augustine's discussion of, 131–33, 143n.25

happiness, Augustine's discussion of, 111–12, 197, 201n.6
Harré, Rom, 170–71
Heidegger, Martin, 138–39, 145nn.40
Hekman, Susan, 300n.15
Helvidius, 59, 66n.52
heresy, Augustine's discussion of, 209
heterology, defined, 163n.7
heterosexual bias, in Western Christianity, 270–71, 279n.57
Heyward, Carter, 245, 279n.60
hierarchy: in Augustine's *Confessions*, 98–117; Augustine's model of, 233–38; control of sexuality and, 28–29; of sexuality, Augustine's discussion of, 57–64, 272–74
Hill, Edmund, 221–22, 239n.12
Hippo, Augustine as bishop of, 5, 34–35, 191–93, 204–12
historicity: in *Dialogues*, 157, 165nn.56–57; as textual context, 1–2; women partners of Augustine and, 169–83
Holy Mother Church, Augustine's vision of, 18–21
homoeroticism, in Augustine's work, 136, 144n.31
Hortensius, 240n.16
human beings, Augustine's discussion of, 52–56; disarray in relations of, 255, 276n.28; ge-

neric model of humanity and, 77–78, 93n.36; as image of God, 219–20, 239n.8; original sin in, 245–46, 275n.12; trinity of memory, understand, and will in, 222–23, 239n.14
humility, Augustine's discussion of, 182, 187n.80
Hunter, David, 60, 66n.n.52, 67n.54, 204–5, 214n.22

image of God, 52–56, 150, 199, 205, 210, 212, 215–19, 248–51, 256, 259–61, 272; in contemporary theology, 235–38; man as and woman less so, 224–33; ontological and moral dimensions of, 219–20; women as or as not, 30, 54–57, 91 n.2, 204, 215–17, 218–37
Incarnation, 113, 237, 262, 271; gendered view of God, 78; Neoplatonists lack of 77, 84, 93 n.35
intellect, gendered status in Augustine's discussion of, 229–38
intentio, Augustine's concept of, 133–34
intersubjectivity, psychoanalytic theory and, 266–69
Irigaray, Luce, 135, 138, 299n.11, 300n.19
irrationality of woman, Augustine's portrayal of, 289–97
Italica, Augustine's correspondence with, 190–91, 206

Jantzen, Grace, 145n.40
Jay, Nancy, 299n.12
Jerome, 51, 59–60, 62, 126, 151; correspondence with women, 184n.6, 199; on marriage, 188n.75; sacrifice of family praised by, 152–53
Jerusalem, as symbolic "mother," 102–3
Jews in Augustine's time, marginalization of, 175–76, 186n.34
John Chrysostom, 147–48, 155–56, 184n.6
Johnson, Elizabeth, 41
Jovinian, 60–61, 66nn.50, 52, 180–81, 199–200
Juliana, Augustine's correspondence with, 200–201, 207–8
Julian of Eclanum, 52, 181, 257–58, 275n.8
Julian of Norwich, 91n.48
Justinian, 178

Keller, Catherine, 33, 119–40
Kligerman, Charles, 278n.47

Printed in the USA
CPSIA information can be obtained
at www.ICGtesting.com
JSHW020732101223
53334JS00001B/22

9 780271 032580